Dictionary of Texas Artists, 1800–1945

NUMBER THREE:
The West Texas A&M University Series
Gerald A. Craven, General Editor

Dictionary of Texas Artists,
1800–1945

Compiled by Paula L. Grauer and Michael R. Grauer

TEXAS A&M UNIVERSITY PRESS
College Station

Copyright © 1999 by the Panhandle-Plains Historical Society
Manufactured in the United States of America
First edition

The Panhandle-Plains Historical Society has been a pioneer in the collection, preservation, and interpretation of historic Texas art. In addition to the *Dictionary of Texas Artists, 1800–1945,* the museum's efforts have included a series of groundbreaking exhibitions and educational programs for both children and adults. Preservation of the artistic heritage of Texas is an important part of the mission of the Society, which was founded in 1921.

The paper used in this book meets the minimum requirements of the American National Standard for Permanenceof Paper for Printed Library Materials, z39.48-1984. Binding materials have been chosen for durability.

Library of Congress Cataloging-in-Publication Data

Grauer, Paula L.,   1958–
        Dictionary of Texas artists, 1800–1945 / compiled by Paula L.
    Grauer and Michael R. Grauer. — 1st ed.
            p.   cm. — (The West Texas A&M University series ; no. 3)
        Includes bibliographical references.
        ISBN 0-89096-861-6 (alk. paper)
        1. Artists—Texas—Biography—Dictionaries.   I. Grauer,
    Michael R.   II. Title.   III.   Series.
    N6530.T4G73   1999
    709'.2'2764—dc21
    [B]   98-51603
                                                                CIP

CONTENTS

ILLUSTRATIONS

TABLES

ACKNOWLEDGMENTS

The *Dictionary of Texas Artists, 1800–1945* was truly a team effort. While we were the compilers and editors for the biographical and exhibition information, we were supplied with much of that same information by two teams: a Scholars Council made up of some of the leading scholars in the field of historic Texas art and listed in the introduction; and an Advisors Council comprising collectors, gallery dealers, and foundation members, also listed there. Both of these groups supplied important historical and biographical information, without which the project would have gone nowhere. Because so many people contributed, we hope to acknowledge those who went the extra mile. And to those whom we inadvertently fail to acknowledge, we sincerely apologize; please know that any omission is due only to the scale of this project.

Any major project requires a champion, and ours was Bill Cheek. Beginning to collect historic Texas art in the 1980s, he planned to write a dictionary of Texas art. He compiled important biographical information on Texas artists in general, with an emphasis on the artists represented in his collection. However, he soon realized that in order to accomplish a biographical tool useful to Texas art collectors, he needed some help. Hence, the dictionary project was born. Bill Cheek has given generously, not only from his own pocketbook but also of a sometimes even more valuable resource—time. He wrote countless letters and placed innumerable telephone calls, FAXes, and e-mails, all to aid the dictionary. Furthermore, he organized the ever-changing Advisors Council of collectors and gallery owners and held their feet to the fire when lack of funding threatened the progress of the work. Moreover, Bill Cheek funded a color flyer about the project and hired historian and Edward G. Eisenlohr expert Diana Church to coordinate its design and mailing to all museums, libraries, and Texas art collectors in the state. Finally, he acted as initiator of the conversation between the Panhandle-Plains Historical Museum and the Summerlee Foundation, which provided the financial backing for the research and completion of the dictionary. Without Bill Cheek, there would not be a *Dictionary of Texas Artists.*

The Summerlee Foundation of Dallas provided three ten-thousand-dollar grants for the project. John Crain and the foundation's trustees were unwavering supporters of it from its inception and we feel that their influence aided in convincing other foundations to add their support.

Knowing of the importance of images to such a project, Texas art collectors Richard and Nona Barrett of Dallas came to the rescue at an important juncture with an extremely bountiful grant.

Given its backing of regional art in Dallas during the 1930s and 1940s, through purchase prize monies for the Dallas Allied Arts Exhibitions, and its own Texas art collection, the A. H. Belo Foundation Corporation was a natural supporter for the project. Consequently, this foundation gave generously. The William P. Clements Foundation, with its focus on Southwestern history—evidenced by its recent founding of the Institute for Southwestern Studies at Southern Methodist University—also gave generously. Finally, a grant from the Robert J. and Helen C. Kleberg Foundation helped push the project "over the hump." Others who gave generously include Charles Attal, Robert Brousseau, David Dike Fine Art, David Lackey, Rainone Galleries, Robert Rork, Charles Stevens, and Russell Tether.

Among the Advisors Council members who provided information on artists, the following were especially helpful: Jim Baker, Bill Blakeley, David Dike, and Kevin Vogel.

Perhaps the greatest thrill in compiling the information was when we were lucky enough to have some of the artists themselves to respond to our queries. Those artists with whom we corresponded included Herring Coe; J. B. Erwin; Sister M. Tharsilla; Marjorie Johnson (Lee); Tom Lea; Octavio Medellin; and Donald Vogel. Artists descendants' were extremely helpful when we could find them, but none was more helpful than Holly Cox, daughter and granddaughter, respectively, of El Paso artists Eugene Thurston and Fern Thurston. She scoured the pages of the El Paso Woman's Clubs scrapbook and pored over the files of the El Paso Public Library, her hard work yielding previously unpublished detail about a large number of El Paso artists.

Among other artists' descendants who provided important information previously unknown were Jonelle Foster Bandy (Cecile Foster), Sudan, Texas; Margaret Bell Good (Fannie Taber Camp and Frances Camp Bell), Brownwood; W. A. McQuiddy (Elizabeth Johnson), Austin; Marlys M. Roos (Mado M. Prideaux), Atlanta, Georgia; and Willetta Stellmacher (Alice Melinda Cobb), Dallas.

Those who responded to our queries and sent information on various artists are listed in the "Letters" section of the bibliography. Particularly helpful were those who either knew the artists intimately or had done their own research on various artists and were willing to share information throughout the project—Roger E. Saunders, New York; Richard Plumly, San Antonio; Samuel Shannon Blain Jr., Dallas; and A. C. Cook of Denton. As assistant to Jerry Bywaters on the Archives of American Art project in the 1970s, Samuel Blain came to know many of the artists in the Dallas area; he honed in on Olin Travis and has become *the* authority on Travis's work.

A. C. Cook's Hockshop Collection is the finest and most comprehensive Texas art collection anywhere. In addition to collecting art, Mr. Cook also collects archival material relating to Texas art. Although already committed to a similar Texas art reference project, he nevertheless provided us with meaningful biographical data. A. C. Cook and Bill Cheek have done more than anyone to promote Texas art.

We sent a statewide notice about our work and a request for information to all museums and libraries in Texas, a rather large number of institutions. While the response was not as successful as we had hoped it would be, we believe the lack of response from some institutions resulted from a lack of available material. However, several colleagues sent information readily. Among them were Lynn Castle, Art Museum of Southeast Texas; Eleanor Jones Harvey, Dallas Museum of Art; Ken Hopkins, Fort Worth Public Library; Lisa Rebori, Houston Museum of Natural Science; Jana Smith, Museums of Abilene; John Sigwald, Unger Memorial Library, Plainview; Bonnie Campbell, State Preservation Board; James Baker and Catherine Hastedt, Texas A&M University; David Baskin, Texas Bureau of Vital Statistics; Melissa Baldridge, Torch Energy; and Melissa McCann, Victoria Regional Museum Association.

At the Witte Museum, Rebecca Huffstutler spent countless hours photocopying the files germane to this project and held at the Witte. She also fielded numerous telephone calls and FAXes for clarification. Ms. Huffstutler did yeoman service on this project and deserves significant recognition for her contributions.

We would also like to thank Gaylon Polatti, assistant curator, Dallas Historical Society; Sally Baulch, Texas Memorial Museum; and Eve Fleishman, Harris County Heritage Society.

The staff members at Texas A&M University Press deserve a medal for their patience in dealing with the myriad eccentricities of both the authors and the project.

We wish to thank Dr. Russell Long, president, and Jerry Craven, professor of English, at West Texas A&M University, for their support of the project from its very inception.

At the Panhandle-Plains Historical Museum, we wish to thank the Panhandle-Plains Historical Society (the museum's support organization) for its backing and the director, Walter R. Davis II, for lending the time, the space, and his enthusiasm for the project. In the Panhandle-Plains Historical Museum Research Center, Betty Bustos, Cesa Espinoza, and Lisa Lambert provided references and support. Frances Kohout and Tammy Hefner helped in numerous clerical ways. And Diane Brake and Sidney Shaller always made sure we got the money we needed and spent it in the correct places.

Several museum volunteers played integral roles in the success of the project, as they spent long hours looking through microfilm of the Index of Texas Deaths. Betty Wallace began scouring the microfilm before illness prevented her from continuing. Fortunately, a rotating group of volunteers from the Church of Jesus Christ of Latter-Day Saints picked up where Mrs. Wallace left off, and they were elders Christopher Clements, Rob Harward, Andrew Mack Strong, James Thacker, and Matthew Woolley.

We would like to thank our parents, Paul and Carolyn Thornton, of Odessa, Texas, and Richard and Nancy Grauer, of Golden, Colorado, for their continued support of our efforts.

Finally, we would like to thank our children, Matthew, Hannah, and Sarah, for their patience in being dragged into a small office in the basement of the museum, often after school and on weekends, and left to entertain themselves while mom and dad pecked away on the computer. This study is for them and all young (and old) Texans.

Paula L. and Michael R. Grauer
JULY, 1998

In the days when the Indians ruled the land . . . an unknown artisan was yet carving on the great door to LaSalle's fort, Fort St. Louis, on Lavaca Bay, Texas, the Indians smote him down. Art is especially slow where scalping is in style.

—Esse Forrester-O'Brien, *Art and Artists of Texas*

INTRODUCTION

Texas was not a mecca for artists during the first three-quarters of the nineteenth century. In fact, Frances Battaile Fisk, writing in her 1928 *A History of Texas Artists and Sculptors*—one of the earliest biographical listings of Texas artists—placed the beginning of Texas' art history proper at 1888, when portraits of the presidents of the republic and of governors were underwritten by the legislature. Fisk felt that "Texans of earlier generations were too occupied with the development of material resources . . . to have any leisure for the enjoyment of beauty."

Furthermore, not until the Fort Worth Art Association formed in 1884 did interested parties—led by women—begin developing art leagues and art associations throughout the state. Initially these groups held exhibitions that included some Texas pieces. However, by the mid-1890s exhibitions specifically for Texas art were held occasionally. Then, in 1910, the Fort Worth Art Association held the first annual Texas artists exhibition. Finally, Texas art was recognized as a genre.

The art history of Texas paralleled that of the rest of the United States. As Texans became more settled in the relatively new state, people found more leisure time and undertook more concerted efforts at cultural pursuits. Noted Texas artist and writer Jerry Bywaters wrote in 1936: "As a result of the rough and vigourous energy of pioneering in Texas, wealth began to accumulate, and with it came cultural pretensions—pretensions parallel to those of the wealthy New England ship-builder and trader, the Colonial planter, the Southern plantation-owner, and the California silver king. This was the Roman pride which, wishing itself preserved for posterity, turned to art for portraits of the grandees and their ladies."

Following the artist-explorers and military survey artists came academically trained European artists, who settled in the German and French communities of Central Texas. Later, itinerant portrait painters arrived, centering their work around Austin, Houston, and San Antonio. By the 1870s, American artists trained in Europe and the eastern United States had relocated to Texas. It was not until around 1900 that native Texan artists began coming to the fore. By the 1930s, eastern U.S. and European styles applied to Texas subjects were being supplanted by the work of artists seeking to synthesize a truly Texas style.

As Texas art came into its own, the first attempts at recording the area's art history also began in earnest. The first effort at a biographical listing of Texas artists was Goldie Capers Smith's 1926 book, *The Creative Arts in Texas,* with brief biographical sketches of select Texas artists, writers, and playwrights. Smith's work was quickly followed by Fisk's 1928 *History of Texas Artists and Sculptors.* Although Fisk listed no sources for her information, obviously much of what she compiled came from the artists themselves. Her history has become one of two standard references on Texas art, the other being Esse Forrester-O'Brien's *Art and Artists of Texas,* published in 1935.

From her home at Waco, O'Brien corresponded directly with living artists, who varied in their willingness to divulge pertinent biographical information. Generally, most of O'Brien's female correspondents neglected to provide a birth year, but nearly all artists were forthcoming about their training and exhibition records. O'Brien also used the artist files at the Witte Memorial Museum in San Antonio, which have since grown to become one of the finest archival collections in the state on Texas artists.

More than thirty years passed before another historian picked up the Texas art baton—albeit with a limited scope: Pauline Pinckney published *Painting in Texas: The Nineteenth Century* (1967). Given the focus of her study, Pinckney limited her research to early portrait painters, military survey artists, and European artists who immigrated to Texas in the mid-1800s.

Monographs on selected Texas artists began to appear in the 1960s, often not written by art historians. Two books on Dallas artist Frank Reaugh, for example, surfaced during this time, one written by J. Evetts Haley and another by two Reaugh students. An autobiography of Pompeo Coppini appeared in the mid-1950s.

The European-trained artists held sway with many of the early biographers, though James Patrick MacGuire of San Antonio published excellent monographs on Julius Stockfleth and Hermann Lungkwitz, respectively, while Cecilia Steinfeldt of the Witte Museum wrote her seminal study of the Onderdonk clan. Biographers also examined the careers of Richard Petri and Theodore Gentilz, and the San Antonio Museum Association produced a study of Carl G. von Iwonski.

However, the 1986 Texas Sesquicentennial spawned a new interest in artists of the state. Exhibitions and accompanying catalogues at the Witte Museum, the Dallas Museum of Art, and the Museum of Fine Arts, Houston, helped light the fire that burns so intensely now.

In 1994, Dallas collector Bill Cheek approached the Panhandle-Plains Historical Museum about spearheading an effort to produce a biographical publication on Texas artists. Given the PPHM's own collection of Texas art and its recent exhibition history focusing on the subject, the project was a natural fit for this museum. Furthermore, its curator of art, Michael R. Grauer, had a track record of publications on and curation of exhibitions of historic Texas art. Paula L. Grauer (a native Texan who comes from a long line of Texans from North, East, and West Texas), brought to the project a knowledge of computer databases, organizational skills, and experience as a columnist for the *Canyon News*—which required an ability at succinctness—all essential to the handling of the tremendous volume of data the project generated. The museum applied to the Summerlee Foundation of Dallas to begin work on a biographical listing of Texas artists and was awarded a grant of ten thousand dollars.

Scholars from important geographical locations in the state were invited to participate based on their own publications and interest in historic Texas art. Members of this group became the Scholars Council for the *Dictionary of Texas Artists* and were assigned to oversee all decisions regarding the scope of the project as well as the inclusion of artists. These scholars are Michael R. Grauer, of Canyon; Alison de Lima Greene, Houston; Sam Ratcliffe, Dallas; Becky Duval Reese, El Paso; Cecilia Steinfeldt, San Antonio; and Ron Tyler, Austin; Lise Darst of Galveston was invited to join after it became clear that Galveston required its own representative.

The first meeting of the Scholars Council for the *Dictionary of Texas Artists* was held at PPHM in September, 1994. The scope of the project was determined to take in all artists who lived in Texas and whose work had been included in at least one professional exhibition in the state prior to or during 1945. Throughout the duration of the project, the council met periodically and consulted constantly by telephone, letter, and electronic mail. The scholars also made resources available from their institutional as well as personal files and offered suggestions about other places and people to consult.

In June, 1997, the council met to jury images for reproduction in the book. More than four hundred images in the form of thirty-five-millimeter slides, larger transparencies, and photographic prints of varying quality were discussed over six hours. Later, the council determined that it would serve the project best to locate and reproduce as many images by lesser-known artists as possible; hence the large number of color reproductions here.

Working simultaneously with the Scholars Council was a group made up primarily of collectors and gallery dealers, called the Advisors Council, whose task was to aid in securing funding for the dictionary project and to make available their own files on Texas art. Texas collectors are often the only source for works by lesser-known artists. Consequently, several members of the Advisors Council were tapped to supply images for reproduction. Some advisors provided monies from their own pockets as well as cultivating other potential donors. The Advisors Council was as integral to the success of the project as were the scholars.

More than one hundred collectors and all the museums in Texas were contacted with requests for any biographical information on artists. One of the significant conclusions of this project is that, generally speaking, Texas public institutions have done a poor job in preserving the records of Texas artists.

Moreover, as a tangential result of research on exhibitions, the authors have compiled the first indices to important pre-1945 Texas art exhibitions ever attempted. Unfortunately, much of the information on these exhibitions could not be located; hence the years and information missing from some of the entries in the exhibition lists (appendix B).

We remember the contributions of Stephen F. Austin and Sam Houston, Charles Goodnight and Quanah Parker, to the state of Texas, yet we are woefully ignorant of our own art history. In an effort to educate about historic Texas art, the Panhandle-Plains Historical Museum began this project to compile comprehensive biographical data on artists who exhibited in Texas prior to 1945.

It is our sincerest hope that this reference will not only help us learn to appreciate more fully the variety of artists consistent with the vastness of the Lone Star State but also—and perhaps more important—that this book will be used as a springboard for additional research on Texas art, particularly through the encouragement of theses and dissertations at Texas universities and colleges. For if this project taught us nothing else, it confirmed that there is an enormous amount of work yet to be done.

ABBREVIATIONS

AA	art association	Assoc.	association
AACFW	Allied Arts Club of Fort Worth	ATPE	Annual Texas Print Exhibitions, Dallas
AAPL	American Artists Professional League	Bywaters Coll.	Jerry Bywaters Collection of Art of the
AC	art club		Southwest, Southern Methodist
Acad.	academy		University, Dallas
AFA	American Federation of Artists	Bldg.	building
AG	art guild	BMFA	Boston Museum of Fine Arts
AHAE	Annual Houston Artists Exhibition	Broadmoor	Broadmoor Art Academy
AI	art institute	C	craftsperson
AIC	Art Institute of Chicago	Car.	cartoonist
AID	Art Institute of Dallas	Cer.	ceramicist
AJ	Académie Julian, Paris	Ch.	church
AL	art league	Cl.	club
AM	art museum	Coll.	collection(s)
Amer.	America(n)	Comm. A	commercial artist
AMST	Art Museum of South Texas, Corpus	Cr	critic
	Christi	Cotton Carn.	Cotton Carnival, Galveston
Arch.	architect(s)	Cotton Pal.	Cotton Palace, Waco
Arch. Lg.	architectural league	CSFAC	Colorado Springs Fine Arts Center
AS	art school	Ctr.	center Amer.
ASET	Artists of Southeast Texas Exhibitions,	D	draftsperson
	1937–39	DAA	Dallas Allied Arts Exhibition
ASL	Art Students League	DAL	Dallas Art League

DAS	Dictionary of American Sculptors	IPBR	Index to Probate Birth Records, Texas Bureau of Vital Statistics
Dec.	decorator	ITD	Index of Texas Death Records
Des.	designer	KCAI	Kansas City Art Institute
DMA	Dallas Museum of Art (formerly Dallas Museum of Fine Arts)	Lib.	library
		LOC	Library of Congress
DMFA	Dallas Museum of Fine Arts (now Dallas Museum of Art)	LPE	Louisiana Purchase Exposition
		LSP	Lone Star Printmakers
DRT	Daughters of the Republic of Texas	MA	museum of art
DWF	Dallas Woman's Forum Exhibition	MAMFW	Modern Art Museum of Fort Worth
École BA	L'École des Beaux Arts, Paris	Met.	Metropolitan Museum of Art, New York
EPAA	El Paso Artists Association	Met. SFA	Metropolitan Museum of Art, School of Fine Arts, New York
EPAG	El Paso Art Guild		
EPCC	El Paso Chamber of Commerce, 1922	MFA, Boston	Museum of Fine Arts, Boston
EPMA	El Paso Museum of Art	MFAH	Museum of Fine Arts, Houston
EPPL	El Paso Public Library	Min. P	miniature painter
EPSJ	El Paso San Jacinto Plaza Exhibition	MNM	Museum of New Mexico, Santa Fe
EPWC	El Paso Woman's Clubs	MoMA	Museum of Modern Art, New York
Exh.	exhibition	Mur. P	mural painter(s)
Exp.	exposition	Mus.	museum(s)
FA	fine art(s)	NAC	National Arts Club
Fed.	federation	NAD	National Academy of Design
Fontainebleau	École Americaine des Beaux Arts, Fontainebleau, France	Nat.	national
		NAWA	National Association of Women Artists
FRAC	Frank Reaugh Art Club	NAWPS	National Association of Women Painters and Sculptors
FSAA	Far Southwest Artists Association, El Paso		
FWAA	Fort Worth Art Association	NMAA Smithsonian	National Museum of American Art, (formerly National Collection of Fine Arts)
FWAM	Fort Worth Art Museum (now Modern Art Museum of Fort Worth)		
		NSS	National Sculpture Society
FWFCE	Fort Worth Frontier Centennial Exposition	"NTP"	Jerry Bywaters, "The New Texas Painters," *Southwest Review,* Spring 1936
FWPC	Fort Worth Painters Club		
FWPL	Fort Worth Public Library	NYSFAA	New York School of Fine and Applied Arts
FWSFA	Fort Worth School of Fine Arts		
Gall.	gallery (-ies)	OJAC	Old Jail Art Center, Albany, Texas
GGE	Golden Gate Exposition	OU	University of Oklahoma, Norman
GTPA	Greater Texas and Pan-American Exposition, Dallas, 1937	P	painter(s)
		PAFA	Pennsylvania Academy of the Fine Arts
HAG	Houston Artists Gallery	P&CC	Palette and Chisel Club
HAI	Herron Art Institute, Indianapolis	Ph.	posthumously
Hist.	historical	Photog.	photographer
HPAG	Highland Park Art Gallery	PL	public library
HPSA	Highland Park Society of Arts	Pm	printmaker(s)
HPSFA	Highland Park Society of Fine Arts	PMS	Plains Museum Society
HS	high school	Por. P	portrait painter
I	illustrator	Por. S	portrait sculptor
Inst.	institute/institution	PPHM	Panhandle-Plains Historical Museum
Int'l	international		

pr.	prize	TCapitol	Texas State Capitol
RL	Rosenberg Library, Galveston	TCE	Texas Centennial Exposition, Dallas, 1936
S	sculptor(s)	TCU	Texas Christian University
SAAG	San Antonio Art Guild	TFAA	Texas Fine Arts Association
SAAI	San Antonio Art Institute	TFWC	Texas Federation of Women's Clubs
SAAL	San Antonio Art League	TG	Texas General Exhibitions
SACE	San Antonio Competitive Exhibitions, 1927–29	TMM	Texas Memorial Museum
		TP	Texas Printmakers
SALA	San Antonio Local Artists Exhibitions	TPan	Texas Panorama Exhibition
SAMA	San Antonio Museum of Art	TPan m.	Texas Panorama monograph
Sartor	Sartor Galleries, Dallas	TSCW	Texas State College for Women (now Texas Woman's University)
Sch.	school		
SFA	school of fine arts	TSFA	Tri-State Fair, Amarillo
SFT	State Fair of Texas	TWF	Texas Woman's Forum
SIA	Society of Independent Artists	TWU	Texas Woman's University
SixTP	Six Texas Painters, Weyhe Gallery, New York, 1944	UCE	University Centennial Exposition
			1= June 28–July 15, 1936
			2= July 19–Aug. 2, 1936
SLSFA	St. Louis School of Fine Arts	USPO	U.S. post office
SMU	Southern Methodist University	UT	University of Texas at Austin
Soc.	society	UTEP	University of Texas at El Paso
SPCCE	South Plains Centennial Competitive Exhibition	W	writer
		WCC	Watercolor Club
SSAL	Southern States Art League	WCE	World Columbian Exposition, Chicago, 1893
T	teacher		
TAEN	Texas Artists Exhibition, Nashville, 1927	WCS	watercolor society
TAFW	Annual Exhibition by Texas Artists, Fort Worth Art Museum	WFNY	World's Fair, New York, 1939
		WTAE	West Texas Art Exhibitions
TAMC	Texas A&M College (now Texas A&M University)	WWWAA	*Who Was Who in American Art*
TAMU	Texas A&M University		

Dictionary of Texas Artists, 1800–1945

ABRAMS, Lucien [P] Dallas/San Antonio. Birthdate: 1870. Birthplace: Lawrence, Kans. Deathdate: 1941. Deathplace: New Haven, Conn. Studied: ASL; Benjamin-Constant; AJ; NAD; Princeton; France. Member: Lyme AA; Dallas AA; Société des Artistes Indépendants; San Antonio Art Acad.; AFA. Exhibited: TCE; SFT; DWF; Witte; TAFW; New Salon; Salon d'Automne; PAFA; NAD. Work: DMA. Sources: Church; Fielding; Fisk; Mallett; *New Handbook;* O'Brien; WWWAA.

ACEVES, Bartolo (Bert) [S; P] El Paso. Birthdate: 1893. Studied: Self-taught. Member: Del Norte Arts and Crafts Guild. Exhibited: EPWCE 1936. Work: El Paso Bowie HS; City of El Paso. Sources: *El Paso Herald; El Paso Times;* Price.

ACEVES, Jose [P; Mur. P; I] El Paso. Birthdate: 1909. Birthplace: Chihuahua, Mexico. Deathdate: 1968. Deathplace: El Paso. Studied: A. D. Nicols. Member: Paso del Norte AG. Exhibited: EPWCE. Work: Murals: USPOs, Borger and Mart, Tex. Sources: WWWAA; EPPL.

ACHNING, Estellyn Allday (Mrs. Walter J.) [P; Pm; I] San Antonio. Birthdate: 1909. Birthplace: Atlanta, Tex. Studied: CSFAC; UNM; A. Dasburg; Charles Rosen; Henry Lee McFee. Member: TFAA; SSAL; NAWA; SAAL; NAWPS. Exhibited: TFAA 1945; SSAL; NAWA 1941–46; DAM 1945; SALA; TG. Sources: TPan m; WWWAA.

ACOSTA, Manuel Gregorio [P; S; Mur. P; I] El Paso. Birthdate: 1921. Birthplace: Aldama, Chihuahua, Mexico. Deathdate: 1989. Deathplace: El Paso. Studied: P. Hurd; UTEP; Univ. Calif.; Chouinard Inst.; U. Soler. Exhibited: EPWCE 1940. Work: Texas Tech; MNM; EPMA; Nat. Portrait Gall., Washington, D.C.; Harmsen Coll., Denver; Time, Inc. Sources: DAS; Fielding; *New Handbook;* Samuels.

ADAIR, Lucie (Lucile) [P] San Antonio. Exhibited: SALA; TG 1944.

ADAMS, Carleton W. [P] San Antonio. Exhibited: SALA 1932.

ADAMS, Clarie [P] Houston. Exhibited: AHAE 1933.

ADAMS, Delia B. [P] Fort Worth. Exhibited: TFWC 1931.

ADAMS, Eleanor [P] Dallas. Studied: Reaugh. Member: FRAC. Exhibited: FRAC 1931; DAA 1929. Sources: PPHM files.

ADAMS, Margaret Boroughs (Mrs. Wayman) [P; Pm] Bryan/Austin/New York/Elizabethtown, N.Y. Birthplace: Austin. Deathdate: 1965. Studied: UT; Newcomb College; Tulane; Columbia; NYSFAA; Woodard; Chase. Member: SSAL; NAWA; Amer. WCS. Exhibited: SSAL; UT (solo) 1936; Corcoran. Sources: WWWAA.

ADAMSON, Alma Calista [P] Houston. Exhibited: AHAE; TG.

ADDIE, Gordon [P] San Antonio. Exhibited: SALA 1942; TG 1945; TFAA 1942. Sources: Witte files.

ADDIS, Elsinore M. [P; S] Dallas. Exhibited: DAA 1928.

ADDIS, William H. [P] Dallas. Exhibited: DAA 1928.

ADKINS, Alice [P] Dallas. Exhibited: DAA.

ADRIANCE, Ethel [P] Galveston. Exhibited: Cotton Carn. 1911.

AHRENBECK, Amelia [P] Navasota, Tex. Birthplace: Hempstead, Tex. Studied: Cincinnati Art Acad.; AJ. Exhibited: TFWC 1931. Sources: O'Brien.

AINSA, Marion [P] El Paso. Exhibited: EPWCE 1927.

AINSWORTH, Ford [P] Georgetown, Tex. Exhibited: TG 1941S.

AKIN, Elizabeth [P] Dallas. Exhibited: DAA.

AKIN, Horace [P] El Paso. Exhibited: EPWCE 1944.

ALBRIGHT, Frell [P] El Paso. Exhibited: EPWCE 1943.

ALBRIGHT, Lloyd L. [P; Interior Dec.; Des.; Pm] Dalhart, Tex. Birthdate: 1896. Birthplace: Cleburne, Tex. Deathdate: 1950. Deathplace: Rochester, Minn. Studied: Chicago Acad. FA; W. H. Dunton; E. Bisttram. Member: Amarillo Art Assoc.; TFAA. Exhibited: TCE; TSFA 1931; SFT 1939; TAFW; Dalhart 1929 (solo); TFWC; UCE 1. Work: PPHM; XIT Mus., Dalhart. Sources: Mallett; O'Brien; Samuels; WWWAA.

ALBRITTON, H. J. [P] Aransas Pass, Tex. Exhibited: ASET 1937.

ALDEN, Lowell Wavel [S; P; T; Pm; Cer.] Houston. Birthdate: 1911. Birthplace: Jonesboro, La. Studied: Louisiana Polytech. Inst. Member: Assoc. Art Houston; SSAL. Exhibited: AHAE; MFAH; DMFA; SSAL; TG. Sources: DAS; Fielding; WWWAA.

ALEXANDER, Martha Ray [P] Houston. Exhibited: AHAE 1945.

ALFEREZ, Enrique [S; T; I] El Paso/New Orleans. Birthdate: 1906. Birthplace: Zacatecas, Mexico. Studied: Taft Inst. Exhibited: EPWCE 1935; WFNY. Work: Chicago Tribune Bldg. Sources: *El Paso Herald-Post*; Price; WWWAA.

ALLEN, Alice [P] Fort Worth. Exhibited: TFWC 1931.

ALLEN, Charles [Pm] Dallas. Exhibited: TG; ATPE 1945.

ALLEN, Clarence [P] San Antonio. Exhibited: SACE 1927.

ALLEN, Dan Elbert [P] Fort Worth. Exhibited: TAFW 1925. Sources: FWPL.

ALLEN, Frances R. (Mrs. Nicholas D.) [P] New York. Birthdate: 1913. Birthplace: San Angelo. Studied: X. Gonzalez; R. Staffel. Member: SSAL. Exhibited: SSAL; San Antonio 1939. Sources: WWWAA.

ALLEN, George R. [Por. P] Huntsville/Galveston. Birthdate: 1830. Birthplace: Connecticut. Sources: *New Handbook*; Pinckney.

ALLEN, Mrs. F. W. [P] Fort Worth. Exhibited: TAFW. Sources: FWPL.

ALLEN, Mrs. George [P] San Angelo/Fort Worth. Exhibited: TAFW. Sources: FWPL.

ALLEN, Thomas [P] San Antonio/Boston. Birthdate: 1849. Birthplace: St. Louis, Mo. Deathdate: 1924. Deathplace: Boston, Mass. Studied: Washington Univ.; Paris; Royal Academy, Dusseldorf. Member: NAD; SAM; Boston Soc. Water Color Painters; Copley Soc. Exhibited: NAD, teens and early 1920s. Work: MFA, Boston; St. Louis Mus. FA; Witte. Sources: *New Handbook*; Samuels; Steinfeldt.

ALLEN, Troy (Mrs. Robert I. Lockard) [P; S; Des.] Lubbock. Birthplace: San Diego, Calif. Studied: TWU. Exhibited: WTAE 1940. Sources: Wilbanks.

ALLEN, Virginia [P] Houston. Exhibited: AHAE 1935.

ALLENSWORTH, Mrs. J. C. [P] Lubbock. Member: Lyme AA. Exhibited: PMS 1932; SPCCE; Lubbock AA 1933, 1935. Sources: Wilbanks.

ALSUP, Katherine [P] San Antonio. Exhibited: SALA 1940.

ALTHEIDE, C. Harvi [P] San Antonio. Exhibited: SACE 1928; SALA; SAAL 1924.

AMATEIS, Louis [S] Galveston/Washington, D.C. Birthdate: 1855. Birthplace: Turin, Italy. Deathdate: 1913. Deathplace: West Falls Church, Va. Studied: Royal Academy, Turin. Member: NSS. Exhibited: Royal Academy, Turin; Nat. Exp., Turin. Work: Texas Heroes Monument, Galveston; Rosenberg Monument, Galveston; RL Sources: DAS; Fielding; Fisk; *New Handbook*.

AMMON, M. [P] Galveston. Work: RL. Sources: RL.

ANDERSON, Ann [P] San Antonio. Exhibited: SALA 1944.

ANDERSON, Fern [P] Dallas. Deathdate: 1969. Deathplace: Dallas. Exhibited: DAA 1928. Sources: ITD.

ANDERSON, Florence Ann Mewhinney (Mrs. S. S.) [P] El Paso. Birthdate: 1874. Birthplace: Terre Haute, Ind. Studied: AIC; E. L. Boone; B. Emeree; L. Freeman. Member: TFAA; EPSJ 1934; EPWCE. Exhibited: TAFW; EPWCE; EPSJ 1934. Sources: WWWAA; Mallett.

ANDERSON, H. [P] Dallas. Exhibited: DAA 1928.

ANDERSON, Mrs. H. C. [P] Amarillo. Exhibited: WTAE 1942.

ANDERSON, Margaret [P] Cleburne/Fort Worth. Studied: Aunspaugh AS. Exhibited: DWF 1916; TAFW 1916, 1930; Cotton Carn. 1916. Sources: Fisk; Witte files.

ANDERSON, Mrs. Marvin C. [P] Fort Worth. Exhibited: TAFW. Sources: FWPL; WWWAA.

ANDERSON, Mrs. [P] Galveston. Exhibited: Texas Coast Fair 1895.

ANDRE, Joan [P] Houston. Exhibited: AHAE 1938; ASET 1937, 1938.

ANDRESS, Annie Lee [P] Dallas. Exhibited: TAFW 1930; DAA 1929. Sources: FWPL.

ANDREWS, Ambrose [Por. P; Min. P] Houston. Birthdate: 1805. Birthplace: West Stockbridge, Mass. Studied: NAD. Exhibited: Texas St. Cap., 1837; NAD 1849; PAFA 1848; Amer. Art Union, 1849; Royal Acad., London 1859. Work: NYHS. Sources: Fielding; Groce and Wallace; Pinckney.

ANDREWS, Golda (Mrs. Lloyd) [P; Por. P; Mur. P] Dallas. Birthplace: Timpson, Tex. Studied: SMU; DMFA w/ Dozier. Member: Dallas AA; Dallas Print and Drawing Soc. Exhibited: DAA 1943. Sources: Bywaters Coll., SMU.

ANDREWS, Mary Virginia [P] Houston. Exhibited: AHAE.

ANGELL, Mrs. C. Roy [P] San Antonio. Studied: P. L. Hohnstedt. Exhibited: SALA; Bright Shawl Gall. 1936 (solo). Sources: *San Antonio Light;* Witte files.

ANKENEY, John Sites [P; Mus. director; T; W] Dallas/ Columbia, Mo./Estes Park, Colo. Birthdate: 1870. Birthplace: Xenia, Ohio. Deathdate: 1946. Studied: Twachtman; Chase; St. Gaudens; Lefebvre; Aman-Jean. Member: NAC; AAPL; AFA; FRAC. Exhibited: FRAC; TAFW; GTPA; SF; DAA. Work: Univ, Mo.; Bethany Col.; Lindenwood Col., Mo. Sources: Fielding; O'Brien; WWWAA.

ANKROM, Francis [Mur. P; Arch.] San Antonio. Exhibited: SALA 1938. Work: USPO, Canyon, Tex. Sources: PPHM files; WWWAA.

ANTHONI, Lillian Prescott [P] San Antonio. Exhibited: SALA.

ANTON, Angelina (Mrs. F.?) [P] Dallas. Exhibited: DAA 1928.

ANTON, Mrs. F. [P] Dallas. Exhibited: TG 1944; DAA 1945.

ARMSTRONG, Amos Lee [P] Houston/Shreveport, La./ Many, La. Birthdate: 1899. Birthplace: Many, La. Studied: Bridgman; DuMond; Olinsky; T. H. Benton; M. Jacobs. Member: SSAL; Houston Sketch Cl.; Shreveport AC; AAPL; Natchitoches Art Colony. Exhibited: AHAE 1931; La. State Exh. 1938. Work: Shreveport Mus. Sources: WWWAA.

ARMSTRONG, Daniel L., Jr. [P] Houston. Exhibited: AHAE.

ARMSTRONG, Voyle Neville [P; I; W] Wichita Falls/ Bedford, Ind. Birthdate: 1891. Birthplace: Dobbin, W. Va. Studied: Cincinnati Art Acad., Duveneck. Member: Cincinnati AC; SSAL. Exhibited: TAFW; SSAL 1924. Work: Cincinnati AC. Sources: Fielding; FWPL; WWWAA.

ARNOLD, Elizabeth [P] Dallas? Exhibited: Crawford Gall. 1907.

ARNOLD, H. R. [P] San Antonio. Exhibited: Cotton Carn. 1910.

ARPA, Jose [P; Pm; Mur. P; T] San Antonio. Birthdate: 1860. Birthplace: Carmona, Spain. Deathdate: 1952. Deathplace: Seville, Spain. Studied: Acad. FA, Seville; E. Cano. Member: Brass Mug Cl. Exhibited: SFT 1901: Cotton Carn.; Galveston AL 1924 (solo); SAAG 1927; TAFW; SACE; SALA; TFWC 1931; SAAL; WCE. Work: PPHM; SAMA; Witte; SAAL; MFA, Boston. Sources: Fielding; Fisk; *New Handbook;* O'Brien; Samuels; Smith; Steinfeldt; Thieme-Becker; WWWAA.

ARRANTS, Edward B. [P] Houston. Exhibited: AHAE 1933.

ASHLEY, James F. [P] San Antonio. Exhibited: SALA.

ASHMORE, Rose [P] Fort Worth. Exhibited: TAFW 1937.

ASPGREN, Oscar [P] Amarillo. Exhibited: TSFA 1929. Sources: Amarillo newspapers.

ASTIN, John Heard [P] Bryan, Tex. Exhibited: ASET 1938; WFNY; SSAL 1940. Sources: WWWAA.

ATCHISON, Alice [P] Houston. Exhibited: AHAE 1930.

ATKINSON, Marion Koogler. See McNAY, Marion

AUDUBON, John James [P] Henderson, Ky. Birthdate: 1785. Birthplace: Haiti. Deathdate: 1851. Deathplace: New York, N.Y. Studied: David; Sully. Work: Witte. Sources: Fielding; *New Handbook;* Pinckney; Samuels.

AUDUBON, John Woodhouse [P] New York, N.Y. Birthdate: 1812. Birthplace: near Henderson, Ky. Deathdate: 1862. Deathplace: New York, N.Y. Studied: J. J. Audubon. Sources: *New Handbook;* Samuels.

AUGUR, Ruth Monro [P; T] El Paso. Studied: R. Henri; W. M. Chase. Member: EPAG; SSAL. Exhibited: EPWC 1927; EPCC; SSAL 1929. Sources: *El Paso Herald-Post; El Paso Times;* Price.

AUGUSTIN, Genevieve H. [P] Houston. Exhibited: AHAE 1930.

AUNSPAUGH, Vivian Louise [P; T] Dallas. Birthdate: 1869. Birthplace: Bedford City, Va. Deathdate: 1960. Deathplace: Dallas. Studied: Shorter College; Twachtman; A. Mucha; ASL; Italy;. Member: AFA—Richmond; DWF. Exhibited: SFT; DWF; Exp. Universelle, Paris, 1900. Work: PPHM. Sources: Church; Fielding; Fisk; Mallett; *New Handbook;* O'Brien; WWWAA.

AUSTIN, Belle [P] Fort Worth. Birthplace: Smith Co., Tex. Exhibited: TAFW; Dow Gallery 1940 (solo); Bandy's Gallery, Fort Worth, 1939 (solo). Sources: *Fort Worth Telegram;* O'Brien; Witte files.

AUSTIN, Dorothy [S] Dallas. Birthdate: 1911. Birthplace: Dallas. Living Dallas. Studied: ASL w/ A. Lee and W. Zorach. Exhibited: DAA; GTPA; SFT; TG 1940; PAFA; ASL; MoMA; Delphic Studios, New York; WFNY. Work: DMA; SMU; Hall of State, Dallas. Sources: O'Brien; Stewart; WWWAA.

AXLEY, Martha [P; Mur. P; T] San Antonio. Birthplace: Chattanooga, Tenn. Studied: Shorter College, Ga.; Itten Schule, Berlin. Member: ASL; Nat. Soc. of Mur. P; Mural Artists Guild. Exhibited: TG 1943; TFAA 1943; SALA 1944. Sources: *San Antonio Evening News; San Antonio Light;* Witte files.

AYARS, Beulah Schiller [P] Houston. Birthdate: 1869. Exhibited: AHAE; MFAH 1934 (solo); TCE; ASET 1937. Work: MFAH; PPHM.

AYERS, Atlee B. [P] San Antonio. Exhibited: SAAL 1924.

AYRES, Gwendolen Jane [P] Austin. Birthdate: 1900. Birthplace: Reading, England. Studied: Somerset w/ Knight; Portland AI; ASL w/ DuMond; Grand Central Gall. w/ W. Adams. Sources: O'Brien.

BABCOCK, Gertrude [P] Sonora. Exhibited: TG 1941S.

BACCANTE, Margaret Brisbine. See BRISBINE, Margaret

BACHMAN, Ruth [Pm] Denton. Exhibited: ATPE 1945.

BACHOFEN, Max Alben (Albin?) Castroville, Tex./Alliance, Ohio. Birthdate: 1903. Birthplace: Neubrunen, Switzerland. Studied: P. B. Travis. Exhibited: SACE 1929; SALA; Witte 1932 (solo); Cleveland. Work: City of Cleveland. Sources: *San Antonio Express; San Antonio Light;* Witte files; WWWAA.

BACKLOUPE, Emma (Mrs. O. L.) [P] Ennis, Tex. Exhibited: TFWC 1931.

BACKSTROM, Kathryn K. [P] Dallas. Member: FRAC. Exhibited: FRAC 1941. Sources: PPHM files.

BAEZNER, Andre Loti [P] Galveston. Birthdate: 1885. Birthplace: Geneva, Switzerland. Deathdate: 1940. Deathplace: Galveston. Exhibited: Cotton Carn. 1910. Sources: *Galveston Daily News;* RL.

BAGBY, Miss [P] Galveston? Exhibited: Texas Coast Fair 1895.

BAGNELL, E. W. [P] Houston. Exhibited: AHAE.

BAILEY, Beatrice S. [P] Fort Worth. Exhibited: TAFW; TFWC 1931. Sources: FWPL.

BAILEY, Ben P., Jr. [Pm; T; P; S] Dallas/Kingsville, Tex. Birthdate: 1902. Birthplace: Houston. Deathdate: 1981. Deathplace: Kingsville. Studied: Virginia Military Institute; UT, Gideon, Everett; X. Gonzalez; Columbia. Member: TFAA; Texas WCS; SSAL; South Texas AL, Corpus Christi. Exhibited: Ney Mus.; ASET 1937; TG 1940, 1941F. Work: AMST; Texas A&I; Alice, Tex. PL; Texas Mem. Mus. Sources: Bywaters Coll.; Fielding; Havlice; O'Brien.

BAILEY, Carden [P; T; Pm] Houston. Birthdate: 1911. Birthplace: Houston. Studied: PAFA; P. Lingan. Exhibited: SFT 1939; MFAH; AHAE; ASET; TG 1940; TFAA 1933. Sources: WWWAA.

BAILEY, Mrs. Charles [P] El Paso. Exhibited: EPWC 1936.

BAILEY, Mary Laws [P] El Paso. Exhibited: EPWC 1937.

BAILEY, Mynnye Moly [P; I] Dallas/Southbridge, Mass. Birthdate: 1890. Birthplace: Oberlin, Kans. Studied: Hawthorne; Connah; Pape. Exhibited: TAFW. Sources: Fielding; WWWAA.

BAILEY, Russell D. [P] Dallas. Studied: Hogue. Exhibited: DWF; Sartor Gall.; TAFW. Sources: Fisk; FWPL.

BAILEY, Willie Hamilton [P] El Paso. Exhibited: EPSJ 1934; EPWC 1927.

BAKER, Estes [P] Houston. Exhibited: AHAE; TG 1943.

BAKER, Ora Phelps [P; T] Fort Worth/Dallas. Birthdate: 1898. Birthplace: Stevens Point, Wis. Studied: Layton Sch. of Art, Milwaukee; AIC; ASL. Member: ASL of Chicago; AACFW. Exhibited: Int'l Watercolor Exh., Philadelphia; TAFW 1930–37. Sources: FWPL; Mallett; O'Brien; WWWAA.

BAKER, William Henry [P; Mur. P; I; T] Fort Worth/Dallas/Houston. Birthdate: 1899. Birthplace: Dallas. Studied: Reaugh; AIC. Member: AACFW. Exhibited: TAFW; AHAE 1936. Work: USPO, Fort Worth. Sources: Fisk; FWPL; O'Brien; Samuels; WWWAA.

BALL, Kate Krause (Mrs. Preston) [P; I; T] El Paso. Birthdate: 1892. Deathdate: 1973. Deathplace: El Paso. Studied: Federal Sch., Minn. (correspondence). Member: American Artists Group; TFAA; SSAL. Exhibited: EPWC; Sun Carnival, El Paso. Sources: Price.

BALTZEL, Marjorie [P; S; T] Denton. Birthdate: 1891. Studied: Syracuse; Columbia; Parsons Sch.; Member: TFAA. Exhibited: TFAA; TG; TCE; TAFW 1936; GTPA. Sources: O'Brien; TPan m.; WWWAA.

BARKER, Mrs. E. J. [P; T] Floydada, Tex. Studied: Mrs. C. L. Cowart; Mrs. L. C. Bennington; Mrs. F. C. Pressly. Exhibited: TFWC 1931. Sources: Wilbanks.

BARKER, H. A. [P] Dallas. Exhibited: DAA 1933.

BARNARD, John Herbert [P; Mur. P; Comm. A] San Antonio. Birthdate: 1880. Birthplace: Chicago. Deathdate: 1949. Deathplace: Houston. Studied: Self taught. Exhibited: SALA 1936. Sources: Artist's family through Dennis Baltuskonis. Lived in San Antonio, 1912–47; father was wood engraver; painted hotel murals; painted landscapes from 1932 until his death.

BARRETT, Robert D. [P; T] New York, N.Y./El Paso. Birthdate: 1903. Birthplace: Fulton, N.Y. Studied: Syracuse Univ. Exhibited: EPWC 1944; El Paso Mus., 1945; NAD; WFNY. Sources: WWWAA.

BARSE, Mrs. Robert [P] Fort Worth. Exhibited: TAFW 1911.

BARTEL, Arthur [P] San Antonio. Exhibited: SALA 1944.

BARTELS, Miss [P] Galveston. Exhibited: Texas Coast Fair 1895.

BARTHA, Maria [P] San Antonio. Exhibited: SALA 1944.

BARTLAM, Virginia Newson [P] Houston. Exhibited: AHAE.

BARTON, Martha [P] San Antonio/Kilgore. Exhibited: SALA 1940; TG 1941F.

BASSETT, Reveau Mott [P; T; Pm] Dallas. Birthdate: 1897. Birthplace: Dallas. Deathdate: 1981. Deathplace: Dallas. Studied: Reaugh; ASL; Leigh; Pennell; Robinson. Member: NAD; SSAL; Dallas AA; FRAC; LSP. Exhibited: DAA; TAFW; SFT; SSAL; LSP; TFWC 1931; Greenville 1924; FRAC; NAD. Work: Belo; DMA; PPHM; Stark; Hall of State, Dallas. Sources: Fisk; FWPL; Mallett; O'Brien; Samuels; Smith: WWWAA.

BATES, A. W. [P] Lubbock. Member: Lubbock AA. Exhibited: Lubbock AA 1933. Sources: Wilbanks.

BATSEL, Lawrence [Velvet P] Dallas. Exhibited: DAA 1931.

BAUGH, Worth [P] Cisco, Tex. Exhibited: WTAE 1942.

BAXTER, Henry [P] Houston. Exhibited: AHAE 1939.

BEACHMAN, Charles M. [D] San Antonio. Exhibited: SALA 1939.

BEADEL, Rosalie Muse [P] Brownwood, Tex. Exhibited: WTAE 1939.

BEADLES, Louise Hertford (Mrs. W. S.) [P] Galveston. Birthdate: 1869. Exhibited: Texas Coast Fair 1895. Sources: RL.

BEAN, Sallye [] Lubbock. Member: Lubbock AA. Exhibited: Lubbock AA 1933. Sources: Wilbanks.

BEARD, Evelyn Lucile [T; Pm; P] Dallas/Texarkana. Birthdate: 1909. Birthplace: Osawatomie, Kans. Living, Texarkana 1997. Studied: TSCW; Cleveland Soc. of Artists; NYU; UC; Berkeley; Calif. College Arts and Crafts; Haystack Mountain Sch.; Cincinnati Art Acad.; CSFAC. Member: TP; Dallas Art Education Assoc. Exhibited: TFAA; DAA; TFWC 1931; TG 1944. Sources: Harris.

BEARDEN, Edward Carpenter [P; T; Pm; Mus. director] Dallas. Birthdate: 1919. Birthplace: Dallas. Deathdate: 1980. Deathplace: Dallas. Studied: SMU; Colorado Springs FA Ctr. Member: Dallas–Fort Worth Men of Art Guild; Dallas Advertising Art Assoc.; Dallas–Forth Worth Art Directors Cl. Exhibited: TG; DAA; ATPE; SSAL. Work: DMA. Sources: Bywaters Coll.; Havlice; WWWAA.

BEAUBIEN, K. G. [P] El Paso. Exhibited: EPWC 1936; El Paso Centennial Mus. 1937. Sources: *El Paso Herald-Post.*

BECKER, Frederick W. [P] San Antonio/Palm Springs, Calif. Birthdate: 1888. Birthplace: Vermillion, S. Dak. Studied: Louisiana Sch. of Art and Design; Mackey Sch. of Art; PAFA; ASL of Los Angeles; Breckenridge; Garber; Reid; E. Carlsen. Member: Soc. Texas Artists; SSAL; Oklahoma AA. Exhibited: SALA. Work: OU; Oklahoma City AL. Sources: Fielding; WWWAA.

BECKMAN, John [Dr] San Antonio. Birthdate: 1847. Birthplace: San Antonio. Deathdate: 1912. Deathplace: San Antonio. Studied: German-English Sch.; German-English College, New York, N.Y. Exhibited: Yanaguana (ph.). Sources: O'Brien.

BECKSMITH, Louise Veach [P] Houston. Exhibited: AHAE 1937.

BEHREND, Ella Beall [P] Fort Worth. Exhibited: TAFW. Sources: FWPL.

BELL, Blanche Brown (Mrs. A. J.) [P; I; W; Pm] San Antonio. Birthdate: 1881. Birthplace: Helena, Tex. Deathdate: 1966. Deathplace: San Antonio. Studied: Arpa; Gonzales; De Young. Member: SAAL; SSAL; TFAA; San Antonio P&CC. Exhibited: SACE (all); SSAL 1929; SALA; SAAL 1924; TFWC 1931. Work: SAAL. Sources: Fisk; ITD; Steinfeldt; Witte files; WWWAA.

BELL, Corinne Elizabeth [P] Sour Lake/Smithville, Tex. Birthdate: 1905. Exhibited: TCE; TAFW.

BELL, Elizabeth [P] Houston. Exhibited: AHAE.

BELL, Frances Taber Camp [P; T] Brownwood, Tex. Birthdate: 1907. Birthplace: Brownwood. Deathdate: 1982.

Deathplace: Brownwood. Studied: F. Camp (her mother); Howard Payne College; Christoval w/ A. Bruent, W. Stevens; X. Gonzalez; J. Arpa; H. A. De Young; H. Roney; AIC. Member: TFAA; Brownwood Art League (founder). Work: Private Collections. Sources: Artist's daughter. Taught, Howard Payne College.

BELL, Gerald [P] Dallas. Exhibited: DAA 1929.

BELL, Mary Elizabeth [P] Houston. Exhibited: AHAE.

BELL, Nona [P] Houston. Exhibited: AHAE 1945.

BELSTERING, Mrs. Ed. [P; Des.] Dallas. Exhibited: DAA 1928.

BENEDICT, Clifford L. [P] San Antonio. Exhibited: SALA 1934.

BENJAMIN, Anne Cleveland [P] Houston. Exhibited: AHAE 1940.

BENNETT, Bertha Richardson [P; Pm] San Antonio. Birthdate: 1883. Birthplace: Eastland, Tex. Studied: San Antonio Sch. of Art w/ H. L. McFee; SAAI w/ Rosen, D. Bergamo. Member: SAAL; San Antonio Printmaker; TFA Acad. Exhibited: TFA Acad.; SALA; TG; ATPE 1945; SAAL 1933; SAAI 1943; Mill Race 1945; Denver Art Museum. Work: Marshall Field, Chicago. Sources: *San Antonio Evening News; San Antonio Express; San Antonio Light;* Witte files; WWWAA.

BENSON, Don [P] Lubbock. Exhibited: Lubbock AA 1937. Sources: Wilbanks.

BENSON, J. F. [P] Glen Rose. Exhibited: TFWC 1931.

BENSON, Olive [P] San Antonio. Deathdate: 1966. Deathplace: San Antonio. Studied: Self-taught. Exhibited: SALA 1933. Sources: O'Brien; *San Antonio Light;* Witte files.

BENTON, James G. [P] San Antonio. Birthdate: 1825. Deathdate: 1861. Studied: West Point. Sources: Pinckney; Samuels.

BENZAQUIN, Gold [D] San Antonio. Exhibited: SALA 1934.

BERGAMO, Dorothy Johnson (Mrs. Ralph) [P; Pm; T] San Antonio/New Hope, Pa. Birthdate: 1912. Birthplace:

Chicago. Studied: Univ. Chicago; AIC; Northwestern. Exhibited: SALA; TFAA; TG 1945; Witte 1945 (solo); AIC 1943; Calif. Art Exh. Work: Witte; SAAI. Sources: Falk AIC; *San Antonio Express; San Antonio Light;* WWWAA; Witte files.

BERGE, Edward [S] Baltimore, Md. Birthdate: 1876. Birthplace: Baltimore. Deathdate: 1924. Deathplace: Baltimore. Studied: Maryland Inst.; Rinehart Sch.; AJ; Verlet; Rodin. Member: Charcoal Cl.; NSS; NAC. Exhibited: Pan-American Exp., Buffalo, N.Y.; LPE; Panama-Pacific Exposition. Work: RL; Baltimore (monuments); Honolulu. Sources: RL; Fielding; DAS; WWWAA.

BERGQUIST, Carl O. [P] Georgetown. Exhibited: TG 1940, 1941S.

BERKOWITZ, Rosalie D. (Mrs. Sidney) [P; Pm] San Antonio. Birthdate: 1906. Birthplace: Memphis, Tenn. Deathdate: 1990. Deathplace: New York, N.Y. Studied: NAD; Hawthorne; Olinsky; Luks. Member: AFA. Exhibited: TCE; TG; Witte; SSAL; PAFA; SALA; ASET 1937; ATPE 1942, 1944; Albany Inst., N.Y. Sources: Mallett; O'Brien; *San Antonio Evening News; San Antonio Express-News; SA Light;* Witte files.

BERLON, Charles [P] El Paso. Exhibited: EPWC 1945.

BERNSON, Maurice Henry [P; Por.P; Mur. P; S; Cer; Pm; Comm.A; T] Canadian, Texas. Birthdate: 1920. Birthplace: Canadian. Deathdate: 1998. Deathplace: Canadian. Studied: WTSC w/ I. Robinson; Cranbrook; J. Farnsworth; H. Leach. Exhibited: TSFA 1941; Canadian 1948 (solo). Work: Canadian PL; PPHM. Sources: Artist's family; *Amarillo Daily News.* Crew chief on B-26 for U.S. Army Air Corps in WWII.

BESS, Forrest Clemenger [P; Pm] Bay City, Tex. Birthdate: 1911. Birthplace: Bay City. Deathdate: 1977. Deathplace: Bay City. Studied: TAMC; UT; Acad. de San Carlos, Mexico City. Member: Artists Equity. Exhibited: MFAH; ASET 1938; AHAE 1939; TG 1940; Witte 1940 (solo); Corcoran 1939. Work: MFAH; Menil Coll.; Witte. Sources: Bywaters Coll.; Havlice; Mallett; *New Handbook;* WWWAA.

BESSELL, Evelyne Byers [P; T] Houston. Birthdate: 1900. Birthplace: Houston. Deathdate: 1990. Deathplace: Houston. Studied: Rice w/ J. Tidden; PAFA; Garber; Carles; AIC. Member: Houston AL? Exhibited: AHAE; TCE; ASET; SFT 1938; TG 1940; TAEN; SAAL; TFAA; SSAL.

Work: MFAH. Sources: Fisk; Kalil and Rose; Mallett; O'Brien; Smith; WWWAA; Witte files.

BESSER, William V. [P; Por. P] Dallas. Exhibited: Crawford Gall., Dallas. 1907.

BEST, Margaret Callahan [P; Min. P; Pm; T] Houston. Birthdate: 1895. Birthplace: Arima, Japan. Studied: Arkansas Univ; B. Hellman; J. Muench. Member: SSAL; MFAH. Exhibited: AHAE. Sources: WWWAA.

BETHEL, Julia [P] Dallas. Member: FRAC. Exhibited: DAA; FRAC.

BETTER, Gladys B. [P] San Antonio. Exhibited: SALA 1932.

BETTS, Virginia Battaile [P; I; Mur. P] Waco/Dallas. Birthplace: Yazoo City, Miss. Studied: W. M. Chase. Member: FRAC. Exhibited: FRAC. Work: Formerly Adolphus Hotel, Dallas. Sources: Fisk; O'Brien.

BEVAN, Haddie Fulton [P] Houston. Exhibited: AHAE 1945.

BEVERLY (BEVERLEY), E. N. [P] Dallas. Exhibited: DAA; SFT 1939.

BEWLEY, Murray Percival [P; Por. P] Fort Worth/Paris, France/Beverly Hills, Calif./Lyons, France. Birthdate: 1884. Birthplace: Fort Worth. Deathdate: 1964. Deathplace: Lyons. Studied: AIC; PAFA; Chase; Henri; C. Beaux. Member: Mystic AC; Salmagundi Club; Allied Artists of Amer.; Salmagundi. Exhibited: TAFW; Paris salon; PAFA; NAD; AIC; SFT; Salmagundi; Cotton Carn. 1912. Work: MAMFW; PAFA; DMA; MFAH. Sources: Bywaters Coll.; Fisk; Havlice; *New Handbook;* O'Brien; Smith; WWWAA.

BIDDLE, George [P; S; Pm; W; T] San Antonio/Croton-on-Hudson, N.Y. Birthdate: 1885. Birthplace: Philadelphia, Pa. Deathdate: 1973. Deathplace: New York. Studied: Harvard; PAFA; Paris; Munich. Member: Amer. Soc. Painters, Sculptors and Gravers; Soc. of Mural Painters. Exhibited: Met; Whitney Mus. American Art; PAFA; MFA, Boston; San Francisco MA; LA County Mus. of Art; New York PL; Philadelphia Mus. of Art; San Antonio. Work: MoMA; Whitney Mus. American Art; Met; PAFA; Philadelphia Mus. of Art; MFA, Boston; DMA. Sources: "An American Artist's Story"; Fielding; Havlice; Samuels; WWWAA.

BIERSCHWALE, Edna Helen [P] San Antonio. Birthdate: 1907. Birthplace: Comfort. Deathdate: 1975. Deathplace: Fredericksburg. Studied: Newcomb College; J. Arpa; X. Gonzalez; E. Ret; D. Faucett. Exhibited: SALA 1930–34; Artists of Southeast Texas 1938. Sources: Maguire.

BIGGERS, Mrs. N. L. [P] Fort Worth/El Paso. Exhibited: TAFW; EPWC 1938.

BIGGS, Electra Waggoner [S] Vernon, Tex.. Birthdate: 1912. Birthplace: Vernon. Deathplace: Living Vernon, 1997. Studied: Self-taught. Exhibited: Seligmann Galleries, N.Y., 1938. Work: Amarillo Art Ctr.; USPO, Electra. Sources: Hendricks and Reese.

BILLFALDT, Jeanne [P] Houston. Exhibited: AHAE 1945.

BILLFALDT, Patye [P] Houston. Exhibited: AHAE 1944; TG 1944.

BILLINGSLEY, Alys [P] Fort Worth. Exhibited: TAFW 1926–28.

BILLINGTON, Estelle Allen (Mrs. J. T.) [P] Stratford, Tex. Deathdate: 1988. Deathplace: Oklahoma City? Exhibited: TFWC 1931. Sources: Artist's family.

BINKLEY, Betty [P] El Paso. Birthdate: 1915. Studied: Radford; UNM; Newcomb College; F. Ellis. Exhibited: EPWC 1935, 1941. Sources: Price.

BIRD, Laura Lee [D] Brenham, Tex. Exhibited: ASET 1939.

BISHOP, Dr. Ida [P] El Paso. Exhibited: EPWC 1927. Sources: El Paso Herald.

BISHOP, J. W. [P] El Paso. Exhibited: EPWC 1936.

BISHOP, Travis [P] Dallas. Exhibited: DAA 1928.

BITTER, Marion M. (Mrs. F. W.) [P] San Antonio. Exhibited: SALA.

BLACK, Alma (Mrs. J. H.). [P] Kingsville. Exhibited: TFWC 1931.

BLACK, Harding [S; Cer.] San Antonio. Birthdate: 1912. Birthplace: Aransas Pass, Tex. Deathplace: Living San Antonio, 1997. Studied: San Antonio College; R. Staffel. Member: SAAL. Exhibited: SALA; TG; SAAL 1945. Work: SAMA; San Angelo MFA; New Orleans MA; Witte. Sources: Steinfeldt; Witte files.

BLACK, Mary Roberta Nichols. See GORMAN, Mary Nichols

BLACK, Nell [P] Houston. Exhibited: AHAE 1937.

BLACKMON, Thomas Lawson [P; Pm] San Antonio/ Corpus Christi. Birthdate: 1901. Birthplace: Ennis, Tex. Studied: AIC; AJ. Exhibited: SACE; TAEN; SALA 1939; TG 1940. Sources: Fisk; WWWAA.

BLACKSHEAR, Kathleen [P; Pm; T; Cer.; S] Navasota, Tex. Birthdate: 1897. Birthplace: Navasota. Deathdate: 1988. Deathplace: Navasota. Studied: Baylor; ASL w/ Borglum; DuMond; Bridgman; AIC w/ Norton, Kelly, Owen; Ahrenbeck. Member: ASL of Chicago; Chicago Soc. Artists. Exhibited: AHAE; TAFW; TFWC 1931; TCE; SFT 1938–39; GTPA; ASET 1937, 1939; Witte 1941 (solo); ASL. Work: MAMFW; MFAH; PPHM. Sources: Mallett; New Handbook; O'Brien; WWWAA; Witte files.

BLAIR, Catherine Stone [P] Houston/St. Louis, Mo. Exhibited: ASET 1937.

BLAKE, Beth MacLafferty (Mrs. Frank O.) [P; Pm; S] El Paso/Berkeley, Calif. Birthdate: 1901. Studied: P. Nahl; R. Boynton; Hofmann; C. Obata; E. Neuhaus; Sheets; Univ. Calif. Member: NAWPS; Phoenix FA Assoc.; Arizona Soc. of Painters and Sculptors. Exhibited: EPWC; Phoenix FA Assoc.; Mus. Northern Arizona. Work: El Paso Public Works of Art Project. Sources: El Paso Times; EPWC scrapbook; Price; WWWAA.

BLAKE, Viola [S] San Antonio. Exhibited: SALA 1934.

BLANC, Flora [P] Fort Worth. Birthdate: 1917. Birthplace: New York, N.Y. Deathdate: 1995. Deathplace: Fort Worth. Studied: ASL; Grosz-Stern Sch., N.Y.; Paris. Exhibited: TG; SixTP; Corcoran; Contemporary Arts Mus., N.Y. Work: FWAM; DMA; OJAC. Sources: Gillespie and Nail.

BLANTON, Daisy [P] Galveston. Exhibited: Cotton Carn. 1912.

BLANTON, Hart B. [P] Fort Stockton. Exhibited: TFWC 1931.

BLEIBLER, Helen [P] Dallas. Member: FRAC. Exhibited: FRAC 1934. Sources: PPHM files.

BLINEBERRY, Frances [P] El Paso. Exhibited: EPWC 1943. Sources: *El Paso Times;* EPPL.

BLOOMFIELD, James [P] Dallas. Exhibited: TAFW 1918.

BLOYS, J. D. [P] Galveston? Exhibited: Texas Coast Fair 1895.

BLUDWORTH, Ella Mae Connor (Mrs. G. T.) [P] Austin. Exhibited: TFWC 1931.

BLUM, Andre [D] Galveston? Exhibited: Texas Coast Fair 1895.

BLUMBERG, Ron [P] . Birthdate: 1908. Exhibited: TCE.

BOATRIGHT, Elizabeth E. Keefer [Pm; T; P] Austin/Alpine. Birthdate: 1899. Birthplace: Houston. Deathdate: 1989. Deathplace: Corpus Christi. Studied: AIC; Pennell; ASL. Member: ASL of Chicago; ASL. Exhibited: WTAE 1939–40; TAEN; TCE; TAFW; GTPA; SFT 1938; AHAE 1925; ASET; UCE 1; AIC; EPSJ 1934. Work: PPHM; MNM; Southwest Mus., La. Sources: Fielding; Fisk; *New Handbook;* O'Brien; WWWAA.

BOCK, Charles Peter [P] Dallas/Manvel/Houston. Birthdate: 1872. Birthplace: Fleusberg, Germany. Studied: AIC; Paris. Member: Dallas Painters. Exhibited: SFT 1908; AIC. Work: Dallas PL. Sources: PPHM files; WWWAA.

BODE, Ruth Simon [P; T] San Antonio/Junction, Tex. Birthdate: 1901. Birthplace: Mason Co., Tex. Deathdate: 1979. Deathplace: Kerrville. Studied: H. Payne Acad.; Trinity Univ.; L. Patterson; A. Brunet; R. Bassett; P. Hohnstedt; Christoval Colony. Member: SAAL; San Antonio River Art Group; Sonora AC (founder). Exhibited: SALA; TFAA 1942. Sources: Artist's scrapbook.

BODET, Marjorie Lockman [P] Houston. Exhibited: AHAE 1931.

BOHN, Mildred Knight [P] Houston. Exhibited: ASET 1938.

BOLDING, Nola [P] Dallas. Exhibited: TAFW 1925.

BOLTON, Grant [S] San Antonio. Exhibited: SALA 1943.

BOLTON, Hale William [P] Dallas/Los Angeles. Birthdate: 1879. Birthplace: Fredericksburg, Iowa. Deathdate: 1920. Deathplace: Rusk, Tex. Studied: SLSFA; Reaugh; France; Holland. Exhibited: TAFW; DWF; Galveston; SFT 1920; Greenville, Tex. 1924; TWF 1917. Sources: Church; Fisk; *New Handbook;* O'Brien; Samuels; WWWAA.

BOMAR, Bill [P; Pm] Fort Worth/Taos, N.M. Birthdate: 1919. Birthplace: Fort Worth. Deathdate: 1991. Deathplace: Taos. Studied: Cranbrook Acad., Mich.; J. Bakos; J. Sloan; H. Hofmann, A. Ozenfant. Member: Taos AA? Exhibited: TG; SixTP; Harwood Foundation, N.M.; Whitney; SSAL. Work: MAMFW; MFAH; OJAC; Gugenheim Mus.; Brooklyn Mus.; MAMFW; Harwood Mus. Sources: Bywaters Coll.; Fielding; Fort Worth Circle; Gillespie and Nail; Witte files.

BONNER, B. [P] Dallas. Birthdate: Member: FRAC. Exhibited: FRAC 1935. Sources: PPHM files.

BONNER, Julia M. [P] Dallas. Exhibited: DAA 1928.

BONNER, Mary Anita [Pm: P] San Antonio. Birthdate: 1887. Birthplace: near Bastrop, La. Deathdate: 1935. Deathplace: San Antonio. Studied: R. J. Onderdonk; R. Miller; B. Brown; E. Leon; UT. Member: SSAL. Exhibited: TAFW 1933; SFT 1926, 1938; SALA; TFWC 1931; Paris Salon 1926, 1931. Work: MAMFW; MFAH; SAMA; Stark; Witte. Sources: Fisk; Mallett; *New Handbook;* O'Brien; Samuels; Steinfeldt; WWWAA.

BONNER, Mrs. M. (Julia M. ?) [P] Dallas. Member: FRAC. Exhibited: FRAC 1929–34, 1941; DAA 1933; TAFW 1928, 1929. Sources: PPHM files.

BOONE, Elmer L. [P] El Paso. Birthdate: 1881. Birthplace: New Cambria, Mo. Deathdate: 1952. Deathplace: El Paso. Studied: Smith Sch., Chicago; AIC. Member: El Paso AA; FSAA. Exhibited: Sun Carnival; EPWC 1935–38, 1940–45. Work: EPMA; PPHM; UTEP Lib. Sources: PPHM files; Price.

BOONE, G. [D] Houston. Exhibited: AHAE 1934.

BOOTH, Nell. [S] Dallas. Exhibited: DAA 1938.

BOREN, Esther A. Jones [P] Dallas/Grand Prairie. Birthdate: 1896. Birthplace: Memphis, Tenn. or Texas. Studied: Aunspaugh AS. Member: Dallas ASL. Exhibited: TAFW 1922, 1923. Sources: WWWAA.

BORGLUM, John Gutzon de la Mothe [P; S] San Antonio. Birthdate: 1867. Birthplace: Bear Lake, Idaho. Deathdate: 1941. Deathplace: Chicago. Studied: San Francisco Art Acad.; AJ. Member: Soc. Nat. Beaux Arts. Exhibited: Louisiana Purchase Exp. Work: SAMA; Witte; U.S. Capitol; Met. Sources: DAS; Fielding; Fisk; *New Handbook;* O'Brien; Samuels; Steinfeldt; WWWAA.

BORN, Annette [P] Dallas. Exhibited: DAA.

BOSSY, Mrs. H. G. (or Mrs. H. C.) [P] Uvalde. Exhibited: TFWC 1931; TFAA 1943.

BOUCHARD, Thomas [P] Fort Worth. Exhibited: TAFW 1920.

BOULTON, Joseph Lorkowski [S] Fort Worth/New York. Birthdate: 1896. Birthplace: Fort Worth. Studied: NAD; Beaux Arts Inst. of Design, N.Y.; Herman McNeil. Exhibited: TAFW 1932, 1933. Work: Marine Barracks, Washington. Sources: DAS; Fisk; Mallett; O'Brien; Smith; WWWAA.

BOURLAND, Ethel [P] Childress. Member: Lubbock AA. Exhibited: Lubbock AA 1937. Sources: Wilbanks.

BOWLES, Minnie [P] Grand Prairie. Member: FRAC. Exhibited: DAA; FRAC.

BOWLES, Ray Earnest, Jr. [P] Houston. Exhibited: AHAE.

BOWLING, Charles Taylor [P; Pm] Dallas. Birthdate: 1891. Birthplace: Quitman, Tex. Deathdate: 1985. Deathplace: Dallas. Studied: AID; Travis; F. Klepper; Hogue. Member: LSP; Dallas AA; FRAC; Klepper AC; SSAL. Exhibited: FRAC; DAA; TAFW; TCE; GTPA; TG; TPan; SFT; LSP (all); ATPE 1941–45; SSAL; WFNY; Carnegie 1941; NAD 1942; PAFA 1942. Work: DMA; SMU; Abilene Mus. FA; UT; Witte. Sources: Havlice; *New Handbook;* O'Brien; Stewart; WWWAA.

BOWLING, Jack (Frank) [Pm; I] Dallas/Washington, D.C. Birthdate: 1903. Birthplace: Bonham, Tex. Studied: U.S. Naval Acad. Member: Honolulu Pm. Exhibited: ATPE 1942; Honolulu Pm; SAE; Southern Calif. Pm; Southern Pm. Work: LOC; Honolulu Acad. Art. Sources: WWWAA.

BOYD, Lydie Karbach [P] Lubbock. Exhibited: TFWC 1931. Sources: Wilbanks.

BOYER, Josephine [P] Dallas. Exhibited: DAA 1929.

BOYLES, Allan K. [S] San Antonio. Exhibited: SALA 1938.

BRACK, Olive (Mrs. D. F. Strickland) [P] San Antonio/Mission. Birthdate: 1890. Birthplace: San Antonio. Deathdate: 1957. Deathplace: Mission. Work: Private coll.; PPHM. Sources: David Lackey Antiques, Houston.

BRADFORD, Dewey [P] Austin. Exhibited: TFWC 1931.

BRADFORD, G. R. [P] Fort Worth. Exhibited: TAFW 1918.

BRADFORD, Mary Katharine Hudson [T; Pm] Dallas. Birthdate: 1884. Birthplace: Boliver, Tenn. Deathdate: 1963. Deathplace: Dallas. Studied: TWU; Colorado Univ.; Columbia; UT. Member: Texas Pm; Dallas Print Soc. Exhibited: DAA 1931. Work: DMA. Sources: Harris.

BRADSHAW, J. Reily [P] San Antonio. Exhibited: SAAG 1927.

BRADY, Marie [D] Dallas. Exhibited: DAA 1928.

BRAKE, Dorothy Hawkins [P] Dallas. Exhibited: DAA 1942, 1943.

BRAND, Frances Christian. [P; Por. P; Mur. P] San Antonio. Birthdate: 1901. Deathdate: 1990. Deathplace: Charlottesville, Va. Studied: Goucher College; Mexico City College. Exhibited: SALA; TG 1941S; ASET 1938; SSAL 1940, 1941. Sources: Michelle Branigan (artist's biographer).

BRANNIN, Mrs. E. B. [P] Dallas. Exhibited: DAA 1931.

BRASHER, Grace (Mrs. Edgar) [P] Dallas. Member: FRAC. Exhibited: FRAC 1930, 1932. Sources: PPHM files.

BRECKENRIDGE, Dorothy [Por. P] Houston/Gloucester, Mass. Birthplace: Tampa, Fla. Studied: PAFA; NYSFAA. Exhibited: DAA 1945. Sources: WWWAA.

BRENDLEY, Eleanor [P] El Paso. Exhibited: EPWC 1938.

BRENNAN, Joe, Jr. [P] Austin. Exhibited: TG 1941F.

BRENT, Adalie Margules [P; T; Pm] Dallas/Baton Rouge, La. Birthdate: 1920. Birthplace: Dallas. Studied: UT;

UCLA; Hogue. Exhibited: GTPA; SFT 1938; DMFA 1943; TG; Houston Associated Artists 1944; Witte; DAA; TFAA 1943. Sources: WWWAA.

BRETZ, Mrs. L. N. [P] El Paso. Exhibited: EPWC 1944.

BREWER, Adrian Louis [P; Por. P; Pm; T; Comm. A] San Antonio/Little Rock, Ark. Birthdate: 1891. Birthplace: St. Paul, Minn. Deathdate: 1956. Deathplace: Little Rock. Studied: N. R. Brewer (his father); AI of St. Paul; Univ. Minn.; E. Blashfield; C. Hawthorne; I. Wiles. Member: SSAL; Chicago Soc. Artists; Chicago P&CC. Exhibited: Witte 1927; SACE (all); San Antonio Women's Cl. 1928 (solo); Victoria AL 1928 (solo); Dallas AA. 1929; Cotton Pal. 1929; San Angelo Fair. Work: SAAL; Witte; NMAA; Arkansas State Capitol. Sources: Fielding; Halinksi thesis; Havlice; WWWAA.

BREWER, Mrs. B. [P] Canyon, Tex. Exhibited: TFWC 1931.

BREWSTER, J. L. [P] Plainview, Tex. Exhibited: TFWC 1931.

BREWSTER, Stanley H. [P] Dallas. Exhibited: DAA 1930.

BRICE, Louise [P] El Paso. Exhibited: EPWC 1941.

BRIGGS, Mae [P] San Antonio. Exhibited: SALA. Sources: Witte files.

BRILES, Worthie Harwood [P] Fort Worth. Exhibited: TAFW 1937.

BRISAC, Edith Mae [P; Pm; T] Denton. Birthdate: 1894. Birthplace: Walton, N.Y. Deathdate: 1974. Deathplace: La Jolla, Calif. Studied: Columbia; Pratt Inst.; Fontainebleau; Cranbrook. Member: TFAA; SSAL; NAWPS; Dallas Print Soc.; Texas WCS. Exhibited: Sartor; TCE; GTPA; TAFW; TPan; GTPA; TG; SFT; WTAE; Coronado Cuarto Centennial Exp., Albuquerque, 1941; ATPE; TFAA 1943; SSAL 1940, 1944. Work: DMA; TWU. Sources: Bywaters Coll.; Fielding; Havlice; Mallett; O'Brien; WWWAA.

BRISBINE, Margaret (Mrs. Euzo Baccante) [P] Houston. Birthdate: 1901. Studied: Rice; PAFA. Exhibited: TCE; AHAE 1925–32, 1934–37; MFAH 1926 (solo); TAFW; ASET 1937; SAAL 1924; TFAA 1928, 1929. Sources: Fisk; Mallett; Smith.

BROAD, Thomas D. [P; Arch.] Dallas. Birthdate: 1893. Birthplace: Paris, Tex. Studied: UT; Harvard. Exhibited: DMFA; DAA. Sources: O'Brien; Bywaters Coll.

BROBECK, Charles Irving [P; Pm] San Antonio. Birthdate: 1888. Birthplace: Columbus, Ohio. Studied: Columbus AS; Detroit SFA. Member: Independent A Amer.; Columbus Pen and Pencil Cl. Exhibited: TAFW 1931; SALA; Witte 1931 (solo). Sources: WWWAA; Witte files.

BROCK, Gene H. [P; Pm; T] Houston/College Station. Exhibited: TFWC 1931; ASET 1938; ATPE 1945.

BROCKMAN, Marie [P] Mason, Tex. Birthdate: . Exhibited: SACE 1927.

BRODNAX, Ethel May [P] Dallas. Birthdate: 1904. Birthplace: Dallas. Studied: SMU; AID. Member: Dallas AA; New Orleans AA; TFAA; Dallas Print and Drawing Soc. Exhibited: DAA; TG 1943; TFAA 1945. Work: DMA. Sources: Bywaters Coll.

BROOKS, F. S. [P] El Paso. Exhibited: EPWC 1937.

BROOKS, Helen [P] Dallas. Birthdate: 1915. Exhibited: TCE; TAFW 1935; DAA 1935. Work: DMA. Sources: Mallett.

BROOKS, James [P; Mur. P;] Dallas/New York. Birthdate: 1906. Birthplace: St. Louis, Mo. Deathdate: 1992. Deathplace: Brookhaven, N.Y. Studied: SMU; DIA; ASL. Member: Amer. Inst. of Arts and Letters; Century Assoc. Exhibited: DAA 1933; TCE; GTPA; DMA; Whitney; Portland MA. Work: DMA; AIC; Carnegie; Corcoran; DMA; Meadows; Guggenheim; Hirschhorn; Met.; Whitney. Sources: Fisk; Mallett; New Handbook; O'Brien; WWWAA.

BROOKS, Lydia Price [P] El Paso. Exhibited: EPCC.

BROOKS, Mabel H. [P; Comm. A] Austin. Birthplace: Greenville, Ala. Deathdate: 1929. Deathplace: Bexar Co., Tex. Studied: UT; NAD; ASL; Woodstock; AIC; Chase in Italy. Member: Three Arts Cl., N.Y.; ASL. Exhibited: TAFW; ASL; MacBeth. Sources: Fisk; O'Brien; Smith; WWWAA.

BROOKS, Mary Nell [P; Por. P] Dallas. Birthdate: 1912. Exhibited: TCE; DAA. Sources: Mallett.

BROOKS, Shelby [P] El Paso. Exhibited: EPWC 1936.

BROSSIUS, H. [D; Pm] . Sources: Pinckney.

BROTCHER, Mrs. A. G. [P] Thalia, Tex. Exhibited: TFWC 1931.

BROUGH, Richard [Pm] San Antonio. Exhibited: ATPE 1945.

BROUGHTON, Willie Riddle [P] San Antonio. Exhibited: SALA 1936.

BROUSSARD, Laura [P; Music T] Galveston. Exhibited: Texas Coast Fair 1895. Sources: RL.

BROWN, Mrs. C. A. [P] Brownsville, Tex. Exhibited: TFWC 1931.

BROWN, Donnell Adair "Don" [P; Pm; T] Marshall/ Shreveport/Cleveland, Ohio. Birthdate: 1899. Birthplace: Taylor, Tex. Deathdate: 1958. Deathplace: Shreveport, La. Studied: AIC; ASL w/ Robinson, Benton, Miller, Sloan; Acad. Chaumière w/ Lhote. Member: LSP; SSAL. Exhibited: TAFW 1916, 1936; TCE; GTPA; LSP 1940–41; SSAL 1939, 1941; WFNY. Work: DMA; Mus. of Mississippi River, St. Louis; Witte. Sources: Havlice; O'Brien; Samuels; Stewart; WWWAA.

BROWN, Elbert. [P] Dallas. Exhibited: DAA 1937.

BROWN, Genevieve S. [P] San Antonio. Exhibited: TFWC 1931.

BROWN, George C. [S] San Antonio. Exhibited: SALA 1935.

BROWN, G. Turner [P] San Antonio. Exhibited: TG 1941F.

BROWN, Hamilton [P] Houston. Exhibited: AHAE 1934.

BROWN, John H. [P] Houston. Exhibited: AHAE.

BROWN, Kenneth [P] Dallas. Exhibited: DAA 1937.

BROWN, Marion Taylor [P] Dallas. Birthdate: 1857. Deathdate: 1939. Deathplace: Dallas. Studied: J. Onderdonk. Exhibited: SFT. Work: UT Archives. Sources: *Marion T. Brown: Letters from Fort Sill.*

BROWN, Mary Johnston (Mrs. DeWitt, Jr.) [P] San Antonio/New Augusta, Ind. Birthdate: 1918. Birthplace: Indianapolis. Studied: HAI; Butler Univ.; Indiana Univ. Exhibited: SALA 1944; HAI; AIC. Sources: WWWAA.

BROWN, Olivia (MORRISON, Olivia Brown) [P] Houston/Lake Charles, La. Exhibited: TAFW; AHAE; TFWC 1931; TFAA 1932.

BROWN, Rose [P] Fort Worth. Exhibited: TAFW 1937.

BROWN, Susan [P] Houston. Exhibited: AHAE 1930.

BROWN, Tom Linn [P] San Antonio. Birthdate: 1857. Birthplace: Providence, R.I. Deathdate: 1917. Deathplace: San Antonio. Studied: Self-taught. Member: Brass Mug Cl.; SAAL. Exhibited: TAFW; SFT 1907; TCE; Early Texas Paintings, Witte, 1936; SAAL 1912. Work: SAAL. Sources: Steinfeldt; WWWAA; Witte files.

BROWNE, Amelie N. [P] Houston. Exhibited: AHAE 1934.

BROWNE, Frederic W. [P] Houston. Birthdate: 1877. Birthplace: Belfast, Ireland. Deathdate: 1966. Deathplace: Houston. Studied: PAFA; Acad. Chaumière; Acad. Colarossi; AJ. Exhibited: TCE; GTPA; AHAE. Work: MFAH. Sources: Fisk; Mallett; O'Brien; WWWAA; taught at Rice Institute.

BROWNE, Jean Calerdine [P] Dallas. Exhibited: DAA 1945.

BROWNING, John Gaitha [P; S; T] Brownwood, Tex. Birthdate: 1912. Birthplace: Oxford, Miss. Deathdate: 1992. Deathplace: Brownwood. Studied: H. A. De Young; J. H. Sharp; X. Gonzalez; F. Taubes; E. Dickinson; G. Prestopino; I. Soyer. Member: Brownwood AL. Exhibited: WTAE 1940, 1942. Work: Brownwood Coliseum; PPHM. Sources: Brown County Mus.; "New Mexico Magazine." U.S. Army vet.; taught D. Baker College, Brownwood, 1942–82.

BRUBAKER, Harley [D] Houston. Exhibited: AHAE.

BRUCE, Florence. [P] San Antonio. Exhibited: TFWC 1931.

BRUCE, Granville [P; I] San Antonio/Dallas/Irving. Birthdate: 1906. Birthplace: Grand Island, Nebr. Studied: Layton Sch. of Art; AIC; Pohl. Exhibited: SACE 1929;

SFT; DAA; Witte (solo). Work: DMA; DMNH; Reagan Bldg., Austin. Sources: O'Brien.

BRUNET, Adele Laure [P; T] Dallas. Birthdate: 1879. Birthplace: Austin. Deathdate: 1965. Deathplace: Dallas. Studied: UT; ASL; AIC; Bridgman; M. Young. Member: NAWPS; SSAL; TFAA; Boston AC; FRAC. Exhibited: FRAC; TFAA; TAFW; DAA; SFT; UCE 1; DMFA; SSAL; MNM. Sources: Bywaters Coll.; Mallett; O'Brien; WWWAA.

BRUSH, Maurine [P] Dallas. Exhibited: SFT 1939. Sources: Dallas Hist. Soc. files.

BRYAN, Dorothy (Mrs. H. Bruce). [P; T; Mosaic; Cr] Lubbock. Studied: TWU; Aunspaugh AS; Redin; Dozier; Utter; J. Meigs; W. Harrison. Member: Lubbock AA; TFAA. Exhibited: Lubbock AA 1933. Sources: Wilbanks.

BRYAN, Katharine McGown [D] Houston. Exhibited: AHAE.

BRYAN, Mary Alice [D] Houston. Exhibited: AHAE 1930.

BRYAN, Ralph [P] Dallas. Exhibited: DAA.

BRYAN, William Edward [P; I; T; Por. P] Dublin, Tex. Birthdate: 1876. Birthplace: Iredell or Whitney, Tex. Deathdate: 1951. Deathplace: Dublin, Tex. Studied: Baylor; Cincinnati AA; AJ; Acad. Colarossi. Member: Soc. Western Artists. Exhibited: Louvre 1907; TAFW; SACE 1927, 1928. Work: FWAM; Dublin PL; San Jacinto Mus. Sources: O'Brien; Fisk; Samuels; Smith; WWWAA.

BRYANT, William H. [P; Mur. P] Dallas. Birthdate: 1891. Birthplace: Florence, Ala. Studied: Self-taught. Exhibited: DAA; TG 1944. Sources: Bywaters Coll.

BUCHANAN, Laura [P; I; Des.] Dallas/Amarillo. Birthplace: Waxahachie, Tex. Studied: Reaugh; J. Knott. Member: TFAA; Dallas AA; SSAL; FRAC. Exhibited: TAFW; DAA; FRAC; TFWC 1931; SFT; TCE; UCE 2; GTPA; TFAA 1932, 1933; TG 1940, 1941S; SSAL 1930. Sources: Mallett; O'Brien; WWWAA.

BUCHANAN, Louise [P] Fort Worth. Exhibited: TAFW 1934.

BUCK, William Quinn [P] Crosbyton/Fort Worth. Exhibited: TAFW 1928, 1929, 1931, 1934.

BUCKANOU, Ella [P] El Paso. Exhibited: EPWC 1936.

BUCKLEY, Eleanor Ann [P] San Antonio. Exhibited: SALA 1936.

BUENZ, J. Fred [P; Arch.] San Antonio. Birthdate: 1903. Birthplace: Laredo. Deathdate: 1991. Deathplace: San Antonio. Studied: MIT. Member: Amer. Inst. of Arch. Exhibited: SALA 1931; Witte 1933, 1941. Work: Witte. Sources: Witte files.

BUFFINGTON, Ralph Meldrin [P; Des.; Arch.] Houston. Birthdate: 1907. Birthplace: White Sulphur, Ga. Studied: Georgia Tech; M. Guy-Loe, Paris. Member: SSAL; Assoc. Georgia Artists. Exhibited: AHAE 1937. Work: Indian Springs State Park, Ga.; Gastonia, N.C. Sources: WWWAA.

BUGBEE, Harold Dow [P; Mur. P.; S; Pm; I; W; Curator; T] Clarendon, Tex. Birthdate: 1900. Birthplace: Lexington, Mass. Deathdate: 1963. Deathplace: Clarendon. Studied: TAMC; Cumming Sch. of Art. Member: Panhandle-Plains Hist. Soc.; Amarillo AA. Exhibited: PPHM 1933; UCE 1; FWFCE; TAFW 1937; TSFA; SFT 1937; WTAE 1939–40; TFWC 1931. Work: PPHM; Cattleman's Mus.; Amer. Quarter Horse Heritage Ctr., Amarillo; TAMU; Mus. of the Southwest, Midland; Haley Lib.; Dallas Hist. Soc. Sources: Bywaters Coll.; Fisk; Mallett; *New Handbook*; O'Brien; PPHM files; Panhandle-Plains Historical Review; Samuels; WWWAA.

BUIE, Helen Spencer [P] Fort Worth. Exhibited: TAFW 1930.

BULLINGTON, Maida P. [P] Houston. Exhibited: AHAE 1935.

BULLOCK, Mrs. L. W. [P] Lubbock. Member: Lubbock AA. Exhibited: Lubbock AA 1933. Sources: Wilbanks.

BULLOCK, Mary Jane McLean (Mrs. Kenneth R.) [P; C; T] Fort Worth. Birthdate: 1898. Birthplace: Fort Worth. Studied: TWC; TCU; AIC; Fleck; F. Klepper. Member: AAPL; SSAL; TFAA; FWAA. Exhibited: SSAL 1939; TFAA; TAFW 1927–37; UCE 2. Work: PPHM. Sources: Mallett; O'Brien; WWWAA.

BUNJES, Emil [D; I; P] Galveston/Houston. Birthdate: 1902. Birthplace: Schulenburg, Tex. Deathdate: 1974. Deathplace: Houston. Studied: Self-taught. Member:

Coppini Acad.; Conservative Arts of Houston. Exhibited: AHAE. Work: RL Sources: *Galveston Daily News.*

BUNTYN, Edrie [Min. P] Fort Worth. Exhibited: TAFW 1933.

BURGE, Arthur Lee. [D] Houston. Deathdate: 1969. Deathplace: Houston. Exhibited: AHAE 1936. Sources: ITD.

BURK, Robert [P; Mur. P] El Paso. Exhibited: EPWC 1927.

BURKS, Ida Mae [P] Marathon, Tex. Exhibited: TFWC 1931.

BURLINGHAM, Hilda Shepard (Mrs. Lloyd) [P] El Paso. Deathdate: 1976. Deathplace: El Paso. Studied: ASL. Member: El Paso AA. Exhibited: EPWC 1941, 1943. Sources: El Paso Artists Assoc.; *El Paso Herald-Post; El Paso Times.*

BURNETT, Elinor [P] San Antonio. Exhibited: TG 1942.

BURNSIDE, Erial [P] San Antonio. Exhibited: SALA 1937.

BURR, Mae A. [P] Corsicana, Tex. Member: FRAC. Exhibited: FRAC 1930. Sources: PPHM files.

BURRIS, Burmah [Pm] Austin. Exhibited: TG 1940.

BURTON, Caroline (Mrs. Clayton B. Claasson) [S] Galveston/Montgomery, Ala. Birthdate: 1908. Birthplace: Galveston. Living Galveston, 1997. Studied: Schumann; ASL w/ E. McCartan; W. Reiss; H. Rhusse. Member: ASL; Galveston AL; Houston AL. Exhibited: AHAE 1934; Witte 1932; GTPA; MNM. Sources: Artist; Fisk; O'Brien; RL; Witte files.

BURTON, Lura Mae [P; T] Denton. Birthdate: 1910. Exhibited: Sartor 1935; GTPA. Sources: O'Brien; WWWAA.

BUSH, Maurine Bass [P] Amarillo. Exhibited: WTAE 1939, 1942. Sources: Amarillo PL.

BUSKS, Mrs. A. H. [P] Abernathy, Tex. Exhibited: TFWC 1931.

BUSTER, Mrs. C. [P] Dallas. Exhibited: DAA 1928.

BUTLER, Mrs. L. [P] San Antonio. Exhibited: TFWC 1931.

BUTLER, Robert Alcius [P; T] McAdoo, Tex. Birthdate: 1887. Birthplace: Dallas. Deathdate: 1959. Deathplace: Dallas. Studied: Trinity Univ., Waxahachie; Univ. Munich. Member: Lubbock AA. Exhibited: PMS; Lubbock AA; Century of Progress, Chicago. Sources: Wilbanks.

BUVENS, Ethel [S] Dallas. Exhibited: DAA.

BYERS, Evelyne. See BESSELL, Evelyne Byers

BYNUM, Bertha Kate Nunn (Mrs. B. C. D.) [P; T] Amarillo. Birthdate: 1886. Birthplace: Crockett, Tex. Deathdate: 1963. Deathplace: Amarillo. Studied: Cottey College; Chicago and Chatauqua, N.Y., w/ F. Lancken. Exhibited: TSFA. Sources: Artist's daughter-in-law.

BYRNES, Olive Audrey [P] Houston. Exhibited: AHAE 1940.

BYWATERS, Llewellyn [P] Dallas. Exhibited: TAFW 1923. Sources: WWWAA.

BYWATERS, Williamson Gerald "Jerry" [P; Pm; T; W; Mus. director; Cr; Mur. P] Dallas. Birthdate: 1906. Birthplace: Paris, Tex. Deathdate: 1989. Deathplace: Dallas. Studied: SMU; AID; ASL. Member: LSP. Exhibited: DAA; TCE; SFT; TAFW; GTPA; TG; TPan; LSP (all); ATPE; WFNY; SSAL. Work: Bywaters Coll.; DMA; SMU, Univ. Art Coll.; MFAH; PPHM; AMST; TAMU; TWU. Murals: USPOs, Houston, Farmersville, Trinity, and Quanah, Tex. Sources: Carraro bio.; Fisk; *New Handbook;* O'Brien; Samuels; Stewart; WWWAA.

CAHERO, Emilio Garcia [P; Pm; T] El Paso. Birthdate: 1897. Birthplace: Vera Cruz, Mexico. Studied: France; Spain; Italy; D. Rivera. Member: Artist Painters Syndicate. Exhibited: EPWC 1935; Madrid; Mexico. Murals: Holliday Hall, UTEP. Sources: O'Brien; Price.

CAHOON, Guy E. [Pm] Dallas. Exhibited: DAA. Sources: O'Brien.

CAIFASSI, M. [S] Austin. Work: Texas State Cemetery. Sources: Hendricks and Reese.

CALDER, Frank Hill [P] Dallas. Exhibited: TAFW 1922, 1923. Work: PPHM. Sources: WWWAA.

CALDWELL, Esther [S] Houston. Exhibited: AHAE 1943.

CALDWELL, Marjorie [P] San Antonio. Exhibited: SALA; TG 1942. Work: TCapitol.

CALHOUN, Harold [P] Houston. Exhibited: AHAE 1939.

CALHOUN, Mrs. M. [P] San Antonio. Exhibited: SALA. Sources: Witte files.

CALLCOTT, Frank [P; T; Pm] San Marcos/New York. Birthdate: 1891. Birthplace: San Marcos, Tex. Studied: Southwestern Univ.; Columbia; Bridgman; Nicolaides; ASL. Member: SSAL; Chicago Acad. FA; Southern Pm.; Southwestern AG; AAPL. Exhibited: TCE; TAFW 1937; SSAL; Witte. Work: DMFA; Southwestern Univ.; Texas Tech; Columbia; Met. Sources: Havlice; Mallett; WWWAA; Witte files.

CAMMOCK (CAMMACK?), John F. [P] Fort Worth. Exhibited: TAFW 1925, 1926.

CAMP, Frances Taber. See BELL, Frances Taber Camp

CAMP, Sarah Frances (Fannie) Taber [P; T] Brownwood, Tex. Birthdate: 1871. Birthplace: Holly Springs, Miss. Deathdate: 1959. Deathplace: Brownwood. Studied: Coggin Acad.; Lester Seminary; Waco Female College; Christoval w/ W. Stevens, X. Gonzalez, A. Brunet. Member: TFAA; AAPL; Brownwood AL (founder and 1st pres.). Exhibited: WTAE 1940; TFWC 1931; TFAA 1931. Work: Brown County Mus., Brownwood. Sources: Artist's granddaughter.

CAMPBELL, Dorothy J. [P] Pharr, Tex. Exhibited: UCE 2.

CAMPBELL, Earl [P] Denison. Exhibited: TAFW 1928.

CAMPBELL, James I. [D] Houston. Exhibited: AHAE 1934.

CAMPBELL, Orville A. [P] San Antonio. Exhibited: SALA 1930.

CAMPBELL, W. Edward [P] Dallas. Exhibited: DAA.

CAMPOS, Ruben Lara [P; Mur. P] El Paso. Exhibited: EPWC 1940, 1941; EPWC 1940 (solo). Sources: *El Paso Herald-Post;* EPWC scrapbooks.

CANADAY, John Edwin [P; Pm; T; W; Des.] Dallas/San Antonio. Birthdate: 1907. Birthplace: Fort Scott, Kans. Deathdate: 1985. Deathplace: New York, N.Y. Studied: UT; Yale. Member: SSAL; FRAC. Exhibited: FRAC 1930; TAFW 1936; Witte; TCE; GTPA; SALA; Yale; Grand Central Gall.; Prix de Rome. Work: PPHM. Sources: *New Handbook;* O'Brien; Steinfeldt; WWWAA.

CANTEY, Maurine Martin (Mrs. Craig C.) [P; Pm.; Dec.] Dallas/South Pasadena, Calif. Birthdate: 1901. Birthplace: Fort Worth. Studied: G. Luks; AID. Member: SSAL. Exhibited: SSAL 1932; DAA 1933 (pr.), 1949, 1950; TAFW; TCE. Work: DMA. Sources: Mallett; O'Brien; WWWAA.

CANTRELL, Vivian (Mrs. Steve) [P] El Paso. Exhibited: EPWC 1942, 1944.

CARD, Lottie Holman [P] Comanche/Dallas. Exhibited: TAFW 1925, 1930, 1935.

CARDENAS, Edward [P] San Antonio. Exhibited: SALA.

CARLSON, Nione [P] Houston. Exhibited: AHAE.

CARLSON, Robert [P] El Paso. Exhibited: EPWC 1945.

CARNOHAN, Harry Peyton [P; W; T] Dallas/Colorado Springs. Birthdate: 1904. Birthplace: Milford, Tex. Deathdate: 1969. Deathplace: San Diego, Calif. Studied: Aunspaugh AS; Reaugh; AIC; Lhote. Member: LSP; DAL. Exhibited: SFT 1934; TCE; TAFW 1937; LSP 1938; Whitney 1934; GGE 1939; Paris Salon 1927; AIC; Columbia 1940 (solo). Work: DMA; PPHM. Sources: Fisk; *New Handbook;* O'Brien; Stewart; WWWAA; Witte files.

CAROW, Thomas H. [P] San Antonio. Exhibited: SAAG 1927.

CARPENTER, A. M. (Miss) [P; Pm; Comm. A; Des.; Interior Des.; T] Abilene. Birthdate: 1887. Birthplace: Prairie Home, Mo. Studied: Hardin College, Mo.; D. C. Smith; C. A. Harbert; E. E. Cherry; AIC. Member: College Art Assoc.; TFAA; AAPL; AFA. Exhibited: TFWC 1931; TAFW 1935; TFAA; West Texas Fair. Work: Abilene high schools. Sources: Fielding; Fisk; O'Brien; WWWAA.

CARR, Bess Mae [P] Dallas. Birthdate: 1890. Deathdate: 1966. Deathplace: Dallas. Exhibited: TAFW; TCE; GTPA; SFT 1939; DAA; TG 1941S. Sources: ITD.

CARR, Georgia (Georgie) [P] San Antonio. Birthdate: 1903. Birthplace: Navasota, Tex. Deathplace: Living San Antonio, 1997. Studied: Baylor; UT; New York. Member: TFAA. Exhibited: SALA; TG 1940–44; SSAL 1941. Sources: Mary Rhodes Gibson, owner of Carr's work; Witte files.

CARR, J. R. [P] Waco. Birthplace: New York. Studied: École BA; Rome w/ Califano. Member: Waco AA. Sources: Fisk; O'Brien.

CARRILLO-GONZALEZ, Pedro [P; S; Comm. A.; Mur. P.; T] El Paso. Birthplace: Guadalajara, Mexico. Studied: Nat. SFA, Mexico City; Nat. SFA, Paris; Royal Acad., Spain; D. Rivera. Member: EPAG; Del Norte Arts and Crafts Guild. Exhibited: EPWC. Sources: *El Paso Herald-Post; El Paso Times;* Price.

CARRINGTON, Joi Harrell [P] San Antonio. Exhibited: SALA.

CARROL, Edwin W. [P] El Paso. Exhibited: EPWC.

CARRON, Maudee Lilyan [P] Houston/Port Arthur. Exhibited: AHAE; ASET 1937; TG 1944. Sources: WWWAA.

CARRUTH, Margaret Ann Scruggs [Pm; T] Dallas. Birthdate: 1892. Birthplace: Dallas. Deathdate: 1988. Deathplace: Dallas. Studied: Bryn Mawr; SMU; Reaugh. Member: TFAA; Dallas AA; SSAL; AFA; Prairie Pm; FRAC; Dallas Print Soc.; HPAG. Exhibited: TAFW 1934, 1937; DAA; SFT 1934; GTPA; TCE; TFAA 1932; WFNY. Work: PPHM; Ney Mus.; Corcoran. Sources: Bywaters Coll.; Fisk; Mallett; O'Brien; Smith; WWWAA.

CARSEN, Gladys Minter [P] El Paso. Exhibited: EPCC.

CARSON, Lissa Bell [P] Dallas. Exhibited: TAFW 1922.

CARSON, M. (Miss) [P] San Antonio. Exhibited: SALA 1931.

CARTER, Mrs. J. Oran [P] Ennis, Tex. Exhibited: TFWC 1931.

CARTTER, M. Gillett [P] San Antonio. Exhibited: SALA 1944; TG 1940, 1941S; SSAL 1944.

CARTTER, Myrtle [P] San Antonio. Exhibited: SALA 1934.

CARTWRIGHT, Isabel Branson [P; Por. P] Philadelphia, Pa./Terrell, Tex. Birthdate: 1885. Birthplace: Coatesville, Pa. Deathdate: 1966. Deathplace: Carmel, Calif. Studied: Philadelphia Sch. Design, Women; Brangwyn; Daingerfield; H. B. Snell. Member: "The Philadelphia Ten"; NAWPS; Philadelphia Art Alliance; AFA; Carmel AA, Calif. Exhibited: SACE; TFWC 1931; SFT 1934; Sartor 1934 (solo), 1940 (solo); Abilene Mus. FA 1940 (solo); FWAA 1941 (solo); PAFA; NAD; AIC; Corcoran. Work: Moore Inst. Art, Philadelphia; SAAL. Sources: Fielding; Havlice; Talbott; WWWAA.

CASE, Mrs. M. R. [P] San Antonio. Exhibited: SALA 1935.

CASEY, William [P] Dallas. Exhibited: DAA 1938.

CASHMAN, John [S] Houston. Exhibited: AHAE 1937.

CASKEY, Lucile Orr (Mrs. Lee Roy) [P] San Antonio. Studied: C. Rosen. Exhibited: SALA; TG 1940, 1941S. Sources: Witte files.

CASTLE, Mrs. A. M. [P] Beaumont. Exhibited: TFWC 1931.

CATHART, Mary [P] Dallas. Exhibited: DAA 1928.

CATLIN, George [P; Min. P] St. Louis, Mo. Birthdate: 1796. Birthplace: Wilkes Barre, Pa. Deathdate: 1872. Deathplace: Jersey City, N.J. Studied: Self-taught. Member: PAFA. Exhibited: Pennsylvania Acad. FA. Work: NMAA; Gilcrease; PPHM. Sources: Fielding; Goetzmann and Reese; *New Handbook;* Samuels; Truettner.

CAVAZOS, Humberto [P] Penitas, Tex. Exhibited: ASET 1938.

CAVE, Bertha [P; Pm] Dallas. Exhibited: DAA.

CAVITT, Mary [P] Houston. Exhibited: AHAE 1937.

CAYLOR, Harvey Wallace [P] Big Spring, Tex. Birthdate: 1867. Birthplace: Noblesville, Ind. Deathdate: 1932. Deathplace: Big Spring. Studied: Jacob Cox, Indianapolis. Exhibited: TFWC 1931. Work: Heritage Mus., Big Spring; Nat. Cowboy Hall of Fame, Oklahoma, City; Old Trail Drivers Mus. Sources: Fisk; *New Handbook;* Pickles bio; Samuels; WWWAA.

CERRACHIO, Enrico Filberto [S; Por. S] Houston/New York. Birthdate: 1880. Birthplace: Italy. Deathdate: 1956.

Deathplace: New York, N.Y. Studied: Inst. Avellina, Italy; Rafael Belliazzi. Work: TCapitol; Tex. State Cemetery; Hermann Park, Houston. Sources: DAS; Fielding; Fisk; Hendricks and Reese; *New Handbook;* Smith.

CHABOT, Mary Van Derlip [P] San Antonio. Birthdate: 1842. Birthplace: Gonzales, Tex. Deathdate: 1929. Deathplace: San Antonio. Studied: R. J. Onderdonk. Member: Texas Press Assoc. AL; Van Dyke AC. Exhibited: Yanaguana (ph.). Work: Witte. Sources: Pinckney; O'Brien; Steinfeldt.

CHAFFIN, Lina Evetts [P; T] Temple. Birthdate: 1882. Birthplace: Moffat, Tex. Deathdate: 1942. Deathplace: Temple. Studied: Baylor Female College. Exhibited: TFWC 1931; Temple; Belton. Work: Private coll. Sources: Railroad and Pioneer Mus., Temple.

CHAFFIN, Margaret Ann (Mrs. W. S. Baird) [P] Temple. Birthdate: 1909. Birthplace: Temple. Deathdate: 1988. Deathplace: Little River, Tex. Studied: Baylor Female College; L. Chaffin. Exhibited: TFWC 1931; Temple; Belton; Salado. Work: Private coll. Sources: Railroad and Pioneer Mus., Temple.

CHAFFIN, Mary Rebecca (Mrs. L. F. Palmer) [P] Temple. Birthdate: 1916. Birthplace: Temple. Living Wichita Falls, 1997. Studied: UT; L. Chaffin. Member: Wichita Falls Porcelain AC (founder). Exhibited: TFWC 1931; Temple; Belton; Wichita Falls. Work: Private coll. Sources: Railroad and Pioneer Mus., Temple.

CHAFFIN, Sudie Puett [P] Temple/Jacksonville, Fla. Birthdate: 1914. Birthplace: Temple. Deathplace: Living Jacksonville, Fla., 1997. Studied: UT; L. Chaffin. Exhibited: TFWC 1931; Temple; Belton. Work: Private coll. Sources: Railroad and Pioneer Mus., Temple.

CHAMBERLAIN, Johnnie [P] Dallas. Exhibited: DAA 1938.

CHAMBODUT, Marie H. [P; Por. P] San Antonio. Exhibited: Cotton Carn. 1911. Work: Witte. Sources: Steinfeldt; Witte files.

CHANDLER, Clyde Giltner (Miss) [S; T] Dallas/Chicago/Santa Monica, Calif. Birthdate: 1879. Birthplace: Evansville, Ind. Deathdate: 1961. Deathplace: Santa Monica. Studied: R. J. Onderdonk; Ney Mus.; Mass. Normal AS; AIC w/ Taft; St. Mary's College, Dallas. Exhibited: Crawford Gall. 1907; SFT; AIC 1907–1909. Work:

Smith Fountain, Fair Park, Dallas. Sources: Bywaters Coll.; Church; DAS; Fisk; Fielding; Mallett; *New Handbook;* O'Brien; WWWAA.

CHANDLER, Helen [P] Galveston. Exhibited: Texas Coast Fair 1895.

CHANDOR, Douglas Granvil [P; Por. P] Weatherford, Tex. Birthdate: 1897. Birthplace: Surrey, England. Deathdate: 1953. Deathplace: New York, N.Y. Studied: Slade Sch., London. Exhibited: Andrews Gallery, N.Y., 1927. Work: FRAC. Sources: Bywaters Coll.; *New Handbook.*

CHAPMAN, Joseph P. [P] San Antonio. Exhibited: SALA 1935.

CHARLESTON, F. [P] Galveston. Exhibited: Cotton Carn. 1912.

CHARLTON, A. R. [P] Houston. Exhibited: AHAE 1945.

CHARLTON, Frances [P] Houston. Exhibited: AHAE.

CHARLTON, Gene [P; Pm] Houston. Birthdate: 1909. Birthplace: Cairo, Ill. Studied: M. Davidson. Exhibited: GTPA; SFT 1939; MFAH 1938; AHAE; ASET 1938; TG; SSAL 1941; Corcoran 1939. Work: MFAH. Sources: WWWAA.

CHASE, Carrie A. [P] Galveston. Birthdate: 1863. Birthplace: South Orrington, Me. Deathdate: 1934. Deathplace: South Orrington. Exhibited: Cotton Carn. 1910. Sources: *Galveston Daily News.*

CHASE, Susan B. [P] San Antonio. Exhibited: SALA 1938.

CHATTIN, Lou Ellen (Mrs. Showe) [P] Temple/Towson, Md./Chautauqua, N.Y. Birthdate: 1891. Birthplace: Temple. Deathdate: 1937. Studied: J. Carlson; F. DuMond; Bridgman; O. Linde; K. Cherry; H. Brockinridge. Sources: Fielding; WWWAA.

CHENEY, F. Michael [P] Dallas. Birthdate: 1914. Birthplace: Corsicana, Tex. Studied: AID; Art Ctr. Sch., Los Angeles. Member: Dallas AA. Exhibited: DAA; TG 1941F. Sources: Bywaters Coll.

CHERRY, Emma Richardson [P; Por. P; T; Pm] Houston. Birthdate: 1859. Birthplace: Aurora, Ill. Deathdate: 1954. Deathplace: Houston. Studied: ASL; Chase; AJ;

Lhote; AIC. Member: Soc. Western Artists; ASL; Houston AL; SAAL. Exhibited: Texas Coast Fair 1895; AHAE; SALA; TAFW; MFAH 1925 (solo); SACE; TFWC 1931; TCE; UCE 1; SFT 1939; GTPA; NAD; AIC; St. Louis Mus. FA; Salon; SSAL. Work: Witte; Ney Mus.; SAAL; MFAH; Houston PL. Sources: Bywaters Coll.; Fielding; Fisk; Mallett; *New Handbook;* O'Brien; Samuels; Smith; Steinfeldt; WWWAA.

CHERRY, Eunice L. [P] Dallas. Exhibited: DAA 1930, 1932.

CHERRY, Phyllis [P] El Paso. Exhibited: EPWC 1938.

CHILDRESS, Doris [P; S] Houston. Birthdate: 1909. Birthplace: Salina, Kans. Deathplace: Living Houston, 1997. Studied: Aunspaugh AS; Newcomb College; College of Industrial Arts (now TWU); AIC; V. George Sch. of Art, Boston. Member: Houston AL. Exhibited: AHAE; ASET 1938; TG 1941S. Sources: Mus. of East Texas, Lufkin.

CHILLMAN, James, Jr. [P; Mus. director; Arch.; Pm; T; W] Houston. Birthdate: 1891. Birthplace: Philadelphia. Deathdate: 1972. Deathplace: Houston. Studied: Penn; PAFA; Amer. Acad., Rome. Member: Amer. Inst. of Arch.; Amer. Assoc. of Univ. Professors; Amer. Assoc. of Mus.; SSAL; TFAA. Exhibited: TAFW 1925, 1926; AHAE; TWF 1917; SSAL; TAEN; Amer. Acad., Rome. Work: MFAH. Sources: Fielding; Fisk; O'Brien; Smith; WWWAA.

CHILTON, Alice [P] San Antonio. Exhibited: SALA 1930.

CHIPLEY, Mrs. L. P. [P] Dallas. Exhibited: DAA 1932.

CHRISTENSEN, Andrew [P; Pm] San Antonio. Birthdate: 1917. Birthplace: San Antonio. Studied: Witte w/ J. Griffith, R. Staffel; Schaeffer Sch., San Francisco. Exhibited: TAFW 1934, 1936; SALA. Work: Witte. Sources: Witte files.

CHRISTIANSON, Carl [P] Austin. Exhibited: TAFW 1926–29, 1932; SACE 1928.

CHRISTIANSON, Stanley H. [D] Houston. Exhibited: AHAE.

CHURCHILL, J. E. [Por. P] Washington/Matagorda. Sources: Pinckney.

CIAMPA, Anthony [P; Pm] San Antonio. Exhibited: SALA 1944; ATPE 1945.

CIMAREC, G. W. [S] Houston. Exhibited: AHAE 1943.

CISNEROS, José [P; D; I] El Paso. Birthdate: 1910. Birthplace: Villa Campo, Durango, Mexico. Deathplace: Living El Paso, 1997. Studied: Self-taught. Exhibited: EPWC 1938, 1940–42; EPPL 1938 (solo). Work: UTEP Lib.; TAMU. Sources: Price; Samuels.

CLACK, Clyde Clifton [P; Pm; T; W] Dallas. Birthdate: 1896. Birthplace: Bonham, Tex. Deathdate: 1955. Deathplace: Dallas. Studied: OU w/ O. Jacobson; Southeastern (Okla.) State. Member: Western AA; Eastern AA; SSAL; Dallas AA. Exhibited: DAA; MFAH; DMFA; ATPE; TG 1941F, 1942; SSAL. Sources: Bywaters Coll.; ITD; O'Brien; WWWAA.

CLAIBORNE, Madge Louise [P] Galveston. Birthdate: 1885. Birthplace: New Orleans. Deathdate: 1970. Deathplace: Galveston. Exhibited: Cotton Carn. 1911. Sources: Galveston City Directory; *Galveston Daily News;* RL.

CLANCY, Eliza R. (Mrs. Charles Edwin) [P] Fort Worth. Exhibited: TAFW 1919. Sources: WWWAA.

CLARK, Clyde S. [Pm] Dallas. Exhibited: ATPE 1945.

CLARK, Lorena [P] San Antonio. Studied: Witte w/ C. Rosen. Exhibited: SALA; TG 1940; SSAL 1941. Sources: Witte files.

CLARK, Mary Lee (Minnie) [P] San Antonio/Corpus Christi. Deathdate: 1966. Deathplace: Nueces County, Tex. Exhibited: SALA; ASET 1938; TG 1940; TFAA 1941; SSAL 1939, 1940. Sources: ITD.

CLARK, Sydney George [Pm] Houston. Exhibited: AHAE 1945.

CLARKE, Lucy Milby [S] Houston. Deathdate: 1969. Deathplace: Houston. Exhibited: AHAE. Sources: ITD.

CLARKSON, Charles W. [P] Fort Worth. Exhibited: TAFW 1934.

CLARKSON, Florence [P] Dallas. Exhibited: DAA 1928.

CLAUSEN, Alfred Bruno Leopold [P] Fort Worth. Birthdate: 1883. Birthplace: Hamburg, Germany. Studied: Hamburg Art Acad.; Genoa; Cooper-Union. Exhibited: TFWC 1931; Century of Progress, Chicago; LPE.

Work: Masonic Temple, Fort Worth; Methodist Ch., Fort Worth. Sources: O'Brien; WWWAA.

CLAXTON, Virginia (Virgie) [P] Houston. Birthdate: 1884. Birthplace: Gatesville, Tex. Deathdate: 1954. Deathplace: Houston. Studied: Bisttram; Lhote; G. Wood; Arpa. Member: MFAH; SSAL; TFAA; San Antonio P&CC; HAG. Exhibited: TFWC 1931; TAFW; AHAE; ASET; TG 1940; SSAL. Work: PPHM. Sources: Mallett; Who's Who of Amer. Women Painters (1935); WWWAA.

CLAY, Sybil [P] Graham. Exhibited: TFWC 1931.

CLEARY, W. P. [P] Houston. Exhibited: AHAE 1933.

CLEAVELAND, James [P] El Paso. Exhibited: EPWC.

CLEMMER, Thelma [P] San Antonio. Exhibited: SALA 1943.

CLEMONS, Callie [P] Houston. Exhibited: AHAE 1930.

CLEVELAND, Mary (Mrs. Alexander D.) [P] Galveston. Exhibited: Texas Coast Fair 1895.

CLEVELAND, Sarah D. [P] Amarillo. Exhibited: TFWC 1931. Sources: Amarillo City Directory 1939–40.

CLICK, O'Bera [P] El Paso. Exhibited: EPWC 1938.

CLOONAN, Frank A. [P] San Antonio. Birthdate: 1864. Deathplace: San Antonio. Member: River Art Group. Exhibited: SALA; SAAL 1926; SAAG 1927. Work: San Antonio Elks Cl.; San Antonio Women's Cl. Sources: Witte files.

COBB, Alice Melinda [P] Lewisville. Birthdate: 1870. Birthplace: Rae Springs, Tenn. Deathdate: 1900. Deathplace: Lewisville. Studied: Self-taught. Exhibited: Cobb Dry Goods Store, Lewisville; United Methodist Ch., Lewisville. Work: Private coll. Sources: Willetta Stellmacher, niece of artist.

COCHRAN, Adelaide [P] Houston. Exhibited: AHAE 1943.

COCHRAN, Billy [P] Houston. Exhibited: AHAE 1938.

COCKE, Bessie H. (Mrs. Emmett) [P] San Antonio. Studied: Arpa; H. A. De Young; A. Chilton. Exhibited: SALA.

COCKRELL, Dura Brokaw (Mrs. E. R.) [P; W; T] Dallas/Fort Worth. Birthdate: 1877. Birthplace: Lipscomb, Iowa. Deathplace: Winslow Heights, Ark.? Studied: Drake Univ.; TCU; AIC; ASL; K. H. Miller; F. Mora; Henri; Chase. Member: TFAA (president); FWPC. Exhibited: DWF 1919 (pr.); DMFA 1926; TAFW. Sources: Fisk; Mallet; O'Brien; Smith; Witte files.

COCKRELL, Marie [P] Houston. Exhibited: AHAE; ASET 1937.

COE, Matchett Herring [S] Beaumont, Tex. Birthdate: 1907. Birthplace: Loeb, Tex. Studied: Lamar College; Cranbrook. Work: Beaumont; Herman Park, Houston; Sabine Pass. Sources: Bywaters Coll.; DAS; Fielding; WWWAA.

COINDREAU, J. M. [P] San Antonio. Exhibited: SAAG 1927.

COLE, Elsie W. [D] Houston. Exhibited: AHAE 1936.

COLE, M. B. "Max" [P] Marshall. Birthdate: 1901. Birthplace: Lansing, Mich. Deathdate: 1987. Deathplace: Marshall. Studied: Self-taught. Work: PPHM. Sources: Harrison County Historical Soc.

COLE, Ross [P] Houston. Exhibited: AHAE 1938.

COLE, William [P] Dallas. Exhibited: DAA 1931.

COLEMAN, Ammie E. [P] San Antonio. Deathdate: 1966. Deathplace: Fort Bend County, Tex. Exhibited: SAAG 1927. Sources: ITD.

COLEMAN, Florence [P] San Antonio. Studied: Arpa. Exhibited: SALA; Arpa Students, Witte 1928; TFWC 1931; TG 1942. Work: Witte. Sources: Witte files.

COLEMAN, Harvey Fisk (B.?) [P] Fort Worth/Los Angeles. Studied: Self-taught. Exhibited: TAFW 1926–28. Sources: Fisk.

COLEMAN, Mary Sue Darter [P; T] Fort Worth/Los Angeles. Birthdate: 1894. Birthplace: Fort Worth. Studied: TCU w/ Cockrell; ASL w/ Bridgman, Mora; Woodstock w/ Carlson; E. Payne; A. Hansen. Member: FWPC; Glendale AA, Calif. Exhibited: TAFW; Los Angeles Athletic Cl.; Soc. FA of Arizona. Sources: Fisk; O'Brien; Samuels; WWWAA.

COLEMAN, Roi Clarkson [P] Waco/Laguna Beach, Calif. Birthdate: 1884. Birthplace: Elgin, Ill. Deathdate: 1945. Deathplace: Laguna Beach? Studied: AJ; Laurens in Paris; Chicago. Member: Calif. AC; San Diego AG; Laguna Beach AA; Illinois Acad. FA. Exhibited: Cotton Pal. 1910; Cotton Carn. 1912; Riverside Fair, Calif. 1917; Laguna Beach AA; Calif. State Fair. Work: Waco PL; Ajo PL, Ariz.; Santa Monica Women's Cl.; La Jolla Yacht Cl.; Liggett Coll., Tulsa. Sources: Fielding; WWWAA.

COLEMAN, Mrs. W. P. [P] San Antonio. Exhibited: SACE 1927; TAFW 1927; SALA 1930.

COLEY, Elizabeth Thomson [P] Houston. Exhibited: AHAE.

COLLIER, Jack Atherton [Min. P] Fort Worth. Exhibited: TAFW 1926–33; SFT 1930. Sources: Fisk.

COLLIER, M. Frances [P] Wichita Falls. Exhibited: WTAE 1939.

COLLINS, Edna Gertrude [P; Port. P] Austin/San Antonio/Dallas. Birthdate: 1885. Birthplace: Toronto, Canada. Studied: R. Jerome Hill; Newcomb College; ASL. Member: TFAA. Exhibited: SFT 1924 (pr.); TAFW; SACE 1928; FWAM; UCE 1. Sources: Fisk; O'Brien; Smith; Witte files.

COLLINS, Hattie McGee (Mrs. C. O.) [P] Fort Worth. Exhibited: TAFW 1931.

COLLINS, Pearle D. [P] Wichita Falls. Exhibited: WTAE 1940.

COLMAN, Roi Clarkson [P] Waco. Birthdate: 1884. Birthplace: Elgin, Ill. Deathdate: 1945. Deathplace: Laguna Beach, Calif.? Studied: AJ; Laurens in Paris; Chicago. Member: Calif. AC; San Diego AG; Laguna Beach AA; Ill. Acad. FA. Exhibited: Cotton Pal. 1910; Cotton Carn. 1912; Riverside Fair, Calif., 1917; Laguna Beach AA; Calif. State Fair 1920;. Work: Waco PL; Ajo PL, Ariz.; Santa Monica Women's Cl; La Jolla Yacht Cl.; Liggett Coll., Tulsa. Sources: Fielding; WWWAA.

COLYER, Vincent [P; Por. P; Pm] New York/Connecticut. Birthdate: 1825. Birthplace: Bloomingdale, N.Y. Deathdate: 1888. Deathplace: Darien, Conn. Studied: J. R. Smith; NAD. Member: NAD. Exhibited: NAD; PAFA; Boston Athenaeum; American Art-Union. Work: MFAH; Gilcrease; NAD. Sources: Falk PAFA; Fielding; MFAH files; Samuels.

COMBE (COMBS?), Mary Postell [P] Fort Worth. Exhibited: TAFW 1922, 1930. Sources: WWWAA.

COMBS, Arthur (W. A.?) [P] Houston. Exhibited: AHAE 1943.

COMBS, W. A. (Arthur?) [P] Houston. Exhibited: AHAE 1944.

COMITO, Nicholas U. [P; Pm] San Antonio/Brooklyn. Birthdate: 1906. Birthplace: New York, N.Y. Studied: NYU; NAD; Italy. Member: Brooklyn Soc. Art. Exhibited: SALA 1944; NAD; Carnegie; Philadelphia WCC; Washington WCC. Sources: WWWAA.

COMPTON, Carl Benton [P; T; Pm; W; S] Denton/Georgetown, Tex. Birthdate: 1905. Birthplace: Esterville, Iowa. Deathdate: 1981. Deathplace: Denton. Studied: Notre Dame; AIC; Acad. Chaumière; Colarossi; Escuela Universitaria de Bellas Artes, San Miguel, Mexico. Member: Texas Sculpture Group; Austin AL; AAPL; Tex. Fed. A. Exhibited: ASET 1938; TG; ATPE 1945; DMFA; Texas Tech; Abilene Christian Univ.; Philbrook; MFAH; DMA; AIC. Work: Texas Tech; TFWC; Texas State Gall., Austin; Seattle AM. Sources: Bywaters Coll.; Falk AIC; WWWAA.

COMPTON, Mildred Norris [P; T] Denton/Georgetown. Birthdate: 1912. Birthplace: Vernon, Ill. Deathdate: 1976. Deathplace: Denton. Studied: AIC w/ B. Anisfield; Milliken Univ.; North Texas State College. Exhibited: ASET 1937; TG 1941S, 1941F, 1942, 1945. Sources: Artist's daughter-in-law.

COMPTON, Wolford [P] San Antonio. Exhibited: TG 1945.

CONDIT, Cora L. (Mrs. Charles L.) [P; Cer.; T] Austin. Birthdate: 1863. Birthplace: Perrysburg, Ohio. Studied: UT w/ R. Everett, S. Gideon, W. Rolfe. Member: Austin AL; TFAA. Sources: Fielding; O'Brien; WWWAA.

CONERLY, Ruth (Mrs. Theo. H. Smith) [S; P; Por. P; I; Des.] Marshall/Dallas/New York. Birthdate: 1908. Birthplace: Marshall. Deathdate: 1994. Deathplace: Curridabat, Costa Rica. Studied: Sullins College, Va.; Strahalm. Exhibited: DWF 1928; DAA. Work: Alamo; Harrison County Mus.; Marshall PL. Sources: *Holland's Magazine;* Fisk; Harrison County Mus.; *Marshall News Messenger;* O'Brien.

CONGDON, Mrs. W. L. [P] El Paso. Exhibited: EPWC 1935, 1936, 1941.

CONKLIN, Orville W. [P] Houston. Exhibited: AHAE 1942.

CONN, Mrs. Leonard [P] Bartlett. Exhibited: TFWC 1931.

CONNER, Mrs. [P] Dallas. Exhibited: TAFW 1916; Cotton Carn. 1916. Sources: Witte files.

CONNOR, Barbara [P] Houston. Exhibited: AHAE.

CONNOR, Ed. C. [P; Por. P] Dallas. Exhibited: Crawford Gall. 1907.

CONNOR, Roma Reagan (Mrs. Edgar F.) [P; Pm; T] Dallas/Abilene. Studied: Aunspaugh AS; F. Klepper; Simkins; ASL; Chicago Acad. FA; Columbia; Woodstock. Member: Creative Sketch Cl.; Abilene AL; Klepper AC; FRAC. Exhibited: FRAC 1930; UCE 2; TAFW; TFAA; TFWC 1931; WTAE; TG 1941F; ATPE 1942; AFA. Sources: Fisk; O'Brien.

CONTOIS, Isabel [.D] San Antonio. Exhibited: SALA 1943.

CONTRERAS, Jose [P] El Paso. Deathdate: 1966. Deathplace: El Paso. Exhibited: EPWC 1940. Sources: ITD.

CONTRERAS, Theones [P] Houston. Exhibited: AHAE.

COOK, Margot [P] Houston. Birthdate: 1915. Exhibited: GTPA.

COOK, Mary [P] Dallas/Rosebud. Member: FRAC. Exhibited: DAA 1929; FRAC 1930; TFWC 1931.

COOK, Paul Rodda. [P] San Antonio/Houston. Birthdate: 1897. Birthplace: Uvalde, Tex. Deathdate: 1972. Deathplace: Mexico City. Studied: Pohl; Ufer; Gaspard; H. D. Murphy; Woodstock. Member: SSAL; SAAL; AAPL; New York WCS. Exhibited: SACE (all); TAFW; San Angelo; Witte 1935; ASET 1937; SALA; Cotton Pal.; TCE; SFT 1939; SSAL; TFWC 1931; TG 1940, 1941S. Work: Witte; San Antonio Carnegie Lib.; San Antonio San Pedro Lib.; Stark; Vanderpoel. Sources: Fielding; Fisk; O'Brien; Steinfeldt; WWWAA.

COOK, Sterling [P] Denton. Studied: NTSTC. Exhibited: TG 1940; Witte 1939 (solo). Sources: *San Antonio Light;* Witte files.

COOKE, Regina Tatum [P; W] Dalhart/Taos. Birthdate: 1902. Birthplace: Corsicana, Tex. Deathdate: 1988. Deathplace: Santa Fe. Studied: Sandzen; Broadmoor; Ufer. Member: Taos AA. Exhibited: TSFA 1931–32; TCE; TFWC 1931. Work: Dalhart Courthouse; Raton Courthouse, N.M. Sources: *New Handbook;* WWWAA.

COONEY, Mary Wheeler [P] San Antonio. Birthdate: 1869. Birthplace: Selma, Tex. Studied: Columbia Female Inst., Tenn.; Ward's Seminary; R. Everett; J. Arpa. Member: SAAL; Coppini Acad. Exhibited: UCE 1; SALA; TFWC 1931; SAAG 1927. Work: Witte. Sources: O'Brien; *San Antonio Light;* Steinfeldt; Witte files.

COOPER, H. R. [I] Dallas. Exhibited: DAA 1933.

COOPER, Mrs. J. R. B. [P] Lubbock. Studied: Reaugh. Member: Lubbock AA. Exhibited: Lubbock AA 1933. Sources: Wilbanks.

COPPINI, Pompeo Luigi [S; T] San Antonio. Birthdate: 1870. Birthplace: Moglia, Italy. Deathdate: 1957. Deathplace: San Antonio. Studied: Academia di Belle Arti, Florence. Member: NAC. Exhibited: NAD; NAC. Work: PPHM; TAMU; TCapitol; Texas State Cemetery; UT; Coppini-Tauch Studio; Witte. Sources: DAS; Fielding; Fisk; Hendricks and Reese; *New Handbook;* O'Brien; Smith; WWWAA.

CORBETT, Nancy D. [P] Bay City, Tex. Exhibited: TG 1940; ASET 1937, 1938.

CORDER, Flora [D; I] Dallas. Exhibited: DAA.

CORDER, Ruth [P] San Antonio. Exhibited: SALA 1931.

CORLEY, Viola [P] Del Rio. Exhibited: TFWC 1931; WTAE 1942.

CORNELL, Wellington [P] Dallas. Exhibited: DAA 1929.

COSGROVE, Suzanna (Mrs. James A.) [P; T] San Antonio. Member: SSAL. Exhibited: SACE 1929; TAFW 1929; SALA; TFWC 1931; SSAL 1929.

COSTELLO, E. J. [P] Houston. Exhibited: AHAE.

COTTON, Robert Leo [P; Por. P] San Antonio/Fort Worth/Los Angeles. Birthdate: 1880. Birthplace: San Antonio. Studied: R. J. Onderdonk; Holmes Sch., St. Louis, Mo. Member: Brass Mug Cl.; FWPC; FWAA; SSAL; Christoval Camp. Exhibited: Dallas AA 1920; TAFW 1922, 1923; West Texas Fair, San Angelo. Sources: Fisk; Steinfeldt; WWWAA.

COUSE, Lucile [P] Dallas. Exhibited: DAA 1929.

COVERT, Lucille [P; Des.] San Antonio. Birthdate: 1922. Studied: Witte Mus. Sch. of Art w/ Neuheisel. Exhibited: SALA; Coronado Cuarto Centennial Exp., Albuquerque; Witte 1940. Sources: *San Antonio Express; San Antonio Light;* Witte files.

COWART, Lottie Mae [P; T] Lubbock. Member: Lubbock AA. Exhibited: Lubbock AA 1933. Sources: Wilbanks.

COWDEN, Mary S. [P] San Antonio. Exhibited: SALA 1935.

COWEN, Lawrence L. [Por. P; Photog.] Houston. Sources: Pinckney.

COX, Abbie (or Abbe) Rose [P; Des.; T] Port Arthur. Birthdate: 1906. Birthplace: Houston. Studied: Texas State College; AIC; Chicago Acad. FA. Member: SSAL. Exhibited: ASET 1937; SSAL 1929, 1941. Work: Texas Oil Company, N.Y. Sources: WWWAA.

COX, Carroll (Miss) [P] Stephenville. Exhibited: TFWC 1931.

COX, Charles Hudson [P; I; T] Waco. Birthdate: 1829. Birthplace: Liverpool, England. Deathdate: 1901. Deathplace: Boulder, Colo. Studied: Kensington Sch., London. Member: Waco AL; Liverpool WCS; RWS. Exhibited: WCE; Texas Coast Fair 1895 (?); Crawford Gall. 1907. Work: Norwich Mus., England. Sources: *New Handbook;* O'Brien; Samuels; WWWAA.

COX, Clark [P] Dallas. Birthdate: 1850. Exhibited: Texas Coast Fair 1895 (?); DAA. Sources: Fisk; Houston City Directory 1919; Samuels; WWWAA.

COX, Thelma [S] Dallas. Exhibited: DAA 1937.

CRABB, Robert James (Bob) [P] Houston. Birthdate: 1888. Birthplace: Livermore, Ky. Member: SSAL; Hous-

ton AG; ASET. Exhibited: TAFW; TCE; GTPA; SFT 1938; MFAH 1935; AHAE; TG 1940. Sources: WWWAA.

CRAIG, Camille Kibler [P; Mur. P; Set Des.] El Paso. Birthdate: 1898. Birthplace: Waco. Deathdate: 1982. Deathplace: El Paso. Studied: Otis AI; C. Kay-Scott. Member: Nat. Soc. Arts and Letters. Exhibited: EPWC. Work: El Paso Little Theater; Fort Bliss. Sources: *El Paso Times;* Price.

CRAIG, Mrs. R. C. [P] El Paso. Exhibited: EPWC 1936.

CRATE, Herbert L. [P] Houston. Exhibited: AHAE 1943.

CRAVENS, Leila Groce [P] Houston. Exhibited: AHAE 1930.

CRAWFORD, Dorsey Gibbs [P] Dallas. Exhibited: TAFW 1919. Sources: WWWAA.

CRAWFORD, Katherine Lester (Mrs. W. L.) [P; T] Dallas. Birthdate: 1864. Birthplace: Oxford, Miss. Deathdate: 1947. Deathplace: Dallas. Studied: AJ. Member: Texas AL (first president). Exhibited: Crawford Gall. 1907. Sources: Church; Fisk; *New Handbook.*

CRENSHAW, Mrs. James [P; Por. P] Dallas. Exhibited: DAA 1928.

CREW, C. C. [S] Houston. Exhibited: AHAE 1936.

CREW, Grace [P; S] Houston. Exhibited: AHAE.

CREWS, Seth Floyd [P; I; Des.] El Paso. Birthdate: 1885. Birthplace: Mt. Vernon, Ill. Deathdate: 1958. Deathplace: El Paso. Studied: AIC. Member: FSAA; EPAG. Exhibited: SACE (all); TAFW; TFWC 1931; EPWC; NAD 1921. Work: YMCA, El Paso; Hotel St. Regis, El Paso; Trinity Methodist Ch., El Paso. Sources: *El Paso Herald-Post;* EPPL; *El Paso Times;* Falk NAD; O'Brien; Price; Samuels; WWWAA.

CRISWELL, Howard B. [P] Dallas. Studied: Reaugh. Member: FRAC. Exhibited: FRAC 1929. Work: PPHM. Sources: PPHM files.

CRITTENDEN, Ethel Stuart [P] Houston. Birthdate: 1894. Birthplace: Cincinnati, Ohio. Studied: Cincinnati Art Acad.; Univ. Cincinnati; W. Adams. Member: SSAL. Exhibited: SSAL; TCE; TAFW; AHAE 1934–36, 1942; ASET. Sources: Mallett; WWWAA.

CROCKER, Edna Earl [P] San Antonio/Dallas. Exhibited: SACE 1927, 1928. Sources: Fisk.

CROCKER, J. C. [P] Galveston? Exhibited: Texas Coast Fair 1895.

CROCKETT, Grace A. [Pm] Dallas. Birthdate: 1923. Birthplace: Denton. Deathplace: Living in Dallas, 1997. Studied: SMU; DMFA. Member: Texas Pm. Exhibited: DAA; DMFA 1944 (solo); TG 1943–44; ATPE 1945; SSAL. Work: DMA. Sources: Harris.

CRONIN, Marie [P; Por. P] Palestine/Bartlett, Tex. Birthdate: . Birthplace: Palestine. Deathdate: 1951. Deathplace: Bell Co. Studied: AGC; L. Simon; C. Castelucho. Member: TFAA; SSAL. Exhibited: Cotton Carn. 1910; SFT 1913; TAFW; SAAL 1926; SACE 1929; TFWC 1931; TCE; ASET 1938; TAEN. Work: TCapitol; SA Cl. Sources: Fisk; ITD; O'Brien; WWWAA; Witte files.

CROSBY, Kathryn Oram [P] Dallas. Deathdate: 1966. Deathplace: Dallas. Exhibited: DAA 1928. Sources: ITD.

CROSS, Verna M. [P] Fort Worth. Exhibited: TAFW 1923–24, 1926–27. Sources: WWWAA.

CROUCH, Penelope Thomas [Por. P] . Sources: O'Brien.

CROWELL, Reid Kendrick [P; Pm; I] Dallas. Birthdate: 1911. Birthplace: Alta, Iowa. Deathplace: Dallas. Studied: AID w/ Travis, Stone, Gasslander, McCann. Exhibited: TCE; GTPA; SFT; DAA; AID; Galveston AL 1941. Sources: Bywaters Coll.; O'Brien.

CROWTHER, Mollie L. (Mrs. Sam) [P] San Angelo. Birthdate: 1867. Birthplace: Baton Rouge, La. Deathdate: 1927. Deathplace: San Angelo? Studied: AIC; Reaugh; O. H. Travis; K. H. Travis; Arpa; Taylor; Gonzales; Brunet. Member: SSAL; AFA; FRAC. Exhibited: TAFW 1923, 1924; SACE 1927; Cotton Pal.; FWAM; West Texas Fair (memorial). Sources: Fisk; O'Brien; WWWAA.

CRUM, Dorothy Rea [P] Houston/Dallas. Member: FRAC. Exhibited: AHAE; DAA; FRAC 1930; TFWC 1931.

CUILTY, Lia [Pm] Fort Worth. Birthdate: 1920. Birthplace: Chihuahua, Mexico. Deathdate: 1965. Studied: AID; FWSFA w/ McVeigh. Member: Texas Pm. Exhibited: TG 1944; Knoedler Gall., N.Y.; FWAA. Work: OJAC. Sources: Gillespie and Nail; Harris.

CULMER, Lessi Wooldridge. See WOOLDRIDGE, Lessi Ellen

CULPS, Lucille P. (Mrs. A. C.). [P] Fort Worth. Exhibited: TAFW 1933–34, 1937.

CULWELL, Ben Lee [P] Dallas/Temple. Birthdate: 1918. Birthplace: San Antonio. Deathdate: 1992. Deathplace: Temple. Studied: SMU; Columbia; Colgate Inst.; Cornell. Exhibited: DMFA 1945 (solo); SFT 1939; DAA 1938. Work: DMA; MAMFW; MFAH. Sources: Bywaters Coll.; WWWAA.

CULWELL, Billie [P] Lubbock. Exhibited: Plains Mus. Soc. 1932. Sources: Wilbanks.

CUMMINGS, Ben H. [P] Houston. Exhibited: AHAE 1945.

CUMMINS, Sascha M. [P] Houston. Exhibited: AHAE; ASET 1938.

CUNNINGHAM, Dr. A. B. [P] Lubbock. Member: Lubbock AA. Exhibited: Lubbock AA 1933. Sources: Wilbanks.

CUNNINGHAM, Nickey (Mrs. E. N.) [P; T] El Paso. Birthdate: 1889. Birthplace: Toledo, Ill. Deathdate: 1983. Studied: Goodwell Agricultural College, Okla. Exhibited: EPWC; EPWC 1938 (four-person). Sources: UTEP Oral History.

CUNNINGHAM, Theodore Saint-Amant [P] Ennis, Tex./Clarksboro, N.J. Birthdate: 1899. Birthplace: Ennis. Studied: Aunspaugh AS; Eisenlohr; AIC; NAD; B. Harrison; G. Bellows. Member: ASL; Chicago P&CC; AAPL. Exhibited: SFT; Cotton Pal.; NAD. Sources: Falk NAD; O'Brien; WWWAA.

CUNY, Lillian Merry Wiley [P] Hempstead? Birthdate: 1866. Deathdate: 1900.

CUPRIEN, Frank W. [P; Marine P] Fort Worth/Laguna Beach, Calif. Birthdate: 1871. Birthplace: Brooklyn, N.Y. Deathdate: 1948. Deathplace: Laguna Beach? Studied: Munich; Dresden; Paris; ASL. Member: Dallas AA; Long Beach AA; Denver AA. Exhibited: SFT; TAFW 1911; Galveston 1913; Cotton Carn. 1910–11; Witte 1929. Work: HAI; Chamber of Commerce, Laguna Beach. Sources: Fielding; Samuels; WWWAA.

CURRIE, D. K. [P] Galveston. Exhibited: Cotton Carn. 1910.

CURTIN, Alice M. [P] Galveston? Exhibited: Texas Coast Fair 1895.

CURTIS, Ben R. [P] San Antonio. Exhibited: SAAG 1927.

CURTIS, Frances [P] Houston. Exhibited: AHAE 1945; TG 1945.

CUSACK, Charles [P] Dallas. Exhibited: TAFW 1925–26; DAA 1928. Sources: Fisk.

DAGGETT, Vivian Sloan. See YARBROUGH, Vivian Sloan Daggett

DAHL, George [Arch.; Pm; P] Dallas. Exhibited: DAA 1928.

DAILEY, Modena Stroud [P] Dallas. Birthdate: 1896. Birthplace: Kaufman Co., Tex. Deathdate: 1990. Deathplace: Belmont, Calif. Studied: UT; Univ. Mexico; D. Rivera; Reaugh. Member: FRAC. Exhibited: FRAC; DAA 1945; Mexico; NYC; SSAL. Sources: *Dallas Morning News.*

DALSEIMER (DELSEMER), Rosalie [P] San Antonio. Exhibited: SALA 1930, 1931; TAFW 1931.

DANNA, J. B. [P] Dallas. Exhibited: DAA 1932.

DARGAN, Margaret [P] Dallas. Exhibited: DAA.

DARGE, Fred [P; S] Dallas. Birthdate: 1900. Birthplace: Hamburg, Germany. Deathdate: 1978. Deathplace: Dallas. Studied: AIC. Member: DAL. Exhibited: Witte; DAA; SALA 1934; TCE; GTPA; TG; SFT 1939, 1941 (solo); TAFW 1937; AIC. Work: PPHM; Boys Ranch, Tex.; Texas Tech. Sources: Bywaters Coll.; Falk AIC; PPHM files; Samuels; WWWAA.

DARTER, Dick [P] Fort Worth. Exhibited: TAFW 1924.

DARTER, Mary. See COLEMAN, Mary Sue Darter

DARVER, Capt. A. [P] Dallas. Exhibited: DAA 1943.

DAUGHERTY, Bob [P] Dallas. Exhibited: DAA 1945.

DAUGHERTY, Louise [P] Abilene. Exhibited: WTAE 1939.

DAVENPORT, Jack. [Pm] San Antonio. Exhibited: SALA 1935.

DAVID, Lorene [P; Pm; T] Beaumont. Birthdate: 1897. Birthplace: Independence, Mo. Deathdate: 1987. Deathplace: Beaumont. Studied: Central Missouri State College; Columbia; C. Martin; A. Young; ASL w/ Laurent; KCAI. Member: NAWA; SSAL; New Orleans AA; TFAA; Texas Pm. Exhibited: GTPA; ATPE; ASET; TG 1940; ATPE 1941–42, 1944–45; SSAL. Work: Art Mus. of Southeast Texas, Beaumont; DMA; MNM; SMU; Texas Tech. Sources: Art Mus. of Southeast Texas, Beaumont, files; Harris; WWWAA.

DAVID, Selim A. [P] Fort Worth. Exhibited: TAFW 1910.

DAVIDSON, Nathalee [P] Bellevue, Tex. Exhibited: WTAE 1942.

DAVIDSON, Ola McNeill [P; T] Houston. Birthdate: 1884. Birthplace: Brazoria Co., Tex. Deathplace: Houston? Studied: E. Fowler; E. R. Cherry. Member: SSAL; MFAH; DWF. Exhibited: TAFW; AHAE; SACE; GTPA; ASET; TFWC 1931; TG 1941S; SSAL 1930. Sources: Fisk; Mallett; Rose and Kalil; TPan m.; WWWAA.

DAVIS, Helen Cruikshank (Mrs. William B.) [P; Min. P] Houston. Birthplace: Elizabeth, N.J. Studied: ASL w/ Chase, DuMond; LaFarge; Acad. Colarossi; Paris w/ Menard, L. Simon; Parsons Sch. Member: Amer. Soc. of Min. P; SSAL. Exhibited: Witte 1931; TAFW 1934; TCE; AHAE 1925–39; TG 1943; SSAL 1933; NAD 1915–18. Sources: Falk NAD; Fisk; Mallett; O'Brien; Smith; WWWAA.

DAVIS, Jessie Freemont Snow (Mrs. Clifford J.) [P; S; T] Dallas. Birthdate: 1887. Birthplace: Williamson Co., Tex. Deathdate: 1962. Deathplace: Jefferson Co., Tex. Studied: Reaugh; Simkins; ASL; Bridgman. Member: SSAL; NAWA; Dallas AA; FRAC. Exhibited: FRAC; TFWC 1931; TAFW; DAA; SFT; GTPA; SSAL; UCE 2; TG; Sartor. Work: DMFA; San Angelo PL. Sources: DAS; Fielding; Fisk; ITD; O'Brien; Samuels; WWWAA.

DAVIS, Mrs. Lynn B. [P] El Paso. Exhibited: EPWC 1936.

DAVIS, Margaret Tolar [P] Houston. Exhibited: Cotton Carn. 1910, 1912.

DAVIS, Martha [P] San Antonio. Exhibited: SALA 1930.

DAVIS, Maude Frances. [D] Houston. Exhibited: AHAE.

DAVIS, Ralph [P] Houston. Exhibited: AHAE 1936.

DAVIS, Redwood [D] Houston. Exhibited: AHAE 1935.

DAVIS, Russel F. [P] Houston. Exhibited: ASET 1938; AHAE 1939.

DAVIS, Velma (Mrs. Otis Dozier) [P; Des.; Jewelry Des.] Dallas. Birthdate: 1901. Birthplace: Waco. Deathdate: 1988. Deathplace: Dallas. Studied: Aunspaugh AS; SMU; Univ. Chicago; TSCW; Columbia. Exhibited: TCE; DAA; TG 1940. Work: DMA. Sources: Bywaters Coll.; *New Handbook;* O'Brien.

DAVIS, Zoe [P] Fort Worth. Sources: O'Brien.

DAVITTE, Lola. [P] Fort Worth. Exhibited: TAFW 1936.

DAWSON, Mrs. J. T. [P] Sinton. Exhibited: TFWC 1931.

DAWSON-WATSON, Dawson [P; Pm; T] San Antonio/ Houston. Birthdate: 1864. Birthplace: London, England. Deathdate: 1939. Deathplace: San Antonio. Studied: Fisher; Carolus-Duran; Glaize; Olivier-Merson; Collin. Member: SAAL; TFAA. Exhibited: TAFW; SACE; SSAL; Royal Acad., London; Salon 1888; Exp. Universelle, Paris, 1889; Lewis and Clark Exp.; Witte (solo); SFT 1934. Work: RL; Stark; TAMU; UT; Witte; St. Louis Art Mus.; Vanderpoel; Lotus. Sources: Fielding; *New Handbook;* O'Brien; Samuels; Steinfeldt; WWWAA.

DAWSON-WATSON, Edward [P] San Antonio. Member: SSAL. Exhibited: SACE 1929; SALA; SAAL; SSAL 1933. Work: Stark. Mural: UT. Witte. Sources: O'Brien.

DAY, Agnes Nelson [P] Houston. Exhibited: AHAE; TG 1941S.

DAY, Hallie [P] San Antonio/Findlay, Ohio. Studied: Witte Mus. Sch. of Art; SAAI. Member: Cincinnati Women's AC. Exhibited: SALA; Witte 1940. Sources: *San Antonio Express; San Antonio Light;* Witte files; WWWAA.

DEAL, Homer T. [P] San Antonio. Exhibited: SALA 1944.

DEAL, L. Kate [D] Dallas. Exhibited: DAA 1932.

DEAN, Douglas. [P] El Paso. Exhibited: EPWC 1938.

DEANE, Granville M. [P] Dallas. Birthdate: 1857. Exhibited: TAFW 1935.

DeBORD, Marjorie Evelyn [P] Tyler. Exhibited: SFT 1938, 1939; TG 1941F. Sources: Dallas Hist. Soc. files.

DE BRECEDA, A. R. [P] San Antonio. Exhibited: SALA 1930.

DE BROUILETTE, Francois [P] San Antonio. Exhibited: SALA; TG 1940. Sources: Witte files.

DE BROUILETTE, M. Henard [P] San Antonio. Exhibited: SALA 1940. Sources: Witte files.

DECKERT, Verna [P] San Marcos. Exhibited: SALA 1938; ASET 1937, 1938.

DEEGAN, Jim [Pm] San Antonio. Exhibited: ATPE 1944.

DE GRUMMOND, Mary Louise [P] Temple. Exhibited: UCE 2; Arno Art Group. Sources: O'Brien.

DE LANEY, Ellen Nora [P] San Antonio. Exhibited: TFWC 1931.

DELLENEY, Marie Isle. [P, Pm; T] Denton. Birthdate: 1902. Studied: TWU; Columbia. Member: TFAA. Exhibited: TCE; TAFW; GTPA; SFT 1938; TFAA; WTAE 1939, 1940; ATPE 1942, 1945; WFNY. Work: MFAH. Sources: Havlice; Mallett; O'Brien; WWWAA.

DELLSCHAU, C. A. A. [D; Des.] San Antonio. Birthdate: 1830. Birthplace: Germany. Deathdate: 1923. Deathplace: Houston? Work: Witte; Menil Coll.; SAMA. Sources: *New Handbook;* Steinfeldt.

DELSEMER, Rosalie. See DALSEIMER, Rosalie

del SOCORRO, Sister Maria [P; Por. P; T] Amarillo/San Antonio. Birthdate: 1893. Birthplace: Chihuahua, Mexico. Deathdate: 1956. Deathplace: San Antonio. Studied: Peabody College; Reaugh; Incarnate Word College, San Antonio; AIC. Member: SAAL; Amer. WCS; River Art Group; Nat. Assoc. of Educators of Art. Exhibited: TAFW 1937; TSFA 1931; Amarillo AA 1933. Work: Incarnate Word College. Sources: Incarnate Word Univ.; PPHM files; *San Antonio Express;* Witte.

DENE, Pierre [D] Galveston. Exhibited: ASET 1938; TG 1944.

DENTON, Lois C. [P; T] El Paso. Studied: C. Kay-Scott; X. Gonzales; Otis AI. Member: AC of El Paso; TFAA; SSAL. Exhibited: TFAA; TAFW 1931, 1932; TFWC 1931; Paso del Norte AG 1937; EPWC 1935–38; 1940–41; El Paso Community Theatre 1940 (solo). Work: UTEP Lib. Sources: *El Paso Herald-Post; El Paso Times;* O'Brien; Price.

DeRIBCOWSKY, Dey [Marine P] El Paso. Birthdate: 1880. Birthplace: Rustchuk, Bulgaria. Deathdate: 1936. Deathplace: El Paso. Studied: Paris; Florence; Petrograd; AJ. Member: Newport AA; Buenos Aires Soc. FA; AFA. Exhibited: El Paso; Greenville 1924; Southwestern Int'l Fair, El Paso, 1924; Petrograd 1902; Uruguay 1908; Rio de Janeiro 1909; Moscow 1910. Work: Petrograd; Buenos Aires; Barbados; Manchester, N.H. Sources: Fielding; Price; WWWAA.

DESHA (TAKSA, Desha Milcinovic) [P; S; Pm; Des.; T; I] San Antonio/New York, N.Y. Birthdate: 1914. Birthplace: Zagreb, Yugoslavia. Studied: Europe w/ Ivan Mestrovic. Member: AAPL; Greenwich Soc. Art. Exhibited: ATPE 1944; AAPL 1940–42; Witte 1944 (solo). Work: Witte; Greenwich Lib. Sources: Fielding; WWWAA.

DEUSSEN, Frank H. [P] San Antonio. Exhibited: SAAG 1927.

DE VAUDRICOURT, A. [D; Pm] Sources: Pinckney; Samuels.

DEVEREUX, Joy [P] Dallas. Exhibited: DAA 1928.

DEWITT, Minnie A. [P] Dallas. Exhibited: DAA 1933.

DEXTER, Henr. [S] Boston. Birthdate: 1806. Birthplace: Nelson, N.Y. Deathdate: 1876. Deathplace: Cambridge, Mass. Studied: Self-taught. Exhibited: Boston Athenaeum 1834. Work: TCapitol. Sources: DAS; Fielding; Hendricks and Reese.

DE YOUNG, Harry Anthony [P; T] San Antonio. Birthdate: 1893. Birthplace: Chicago. Deathdate: 1956. Deathplace: San Antonio. Studied: Illinois; AIC. Member: Chicago Painters and Sculptors Assoc.; All-Illinois SA; San Antonio AA; Tex. Fed. A. Exhibited: SACE 1929; TAFW; Witte 1934 (solo); AIC; UCE 1; SALA 1933–35. Work: Witte; Chicago Public Schools; Ft. Davis HS, Tex.; Brackenridge HS, San Antonio. Sources: *New Handbook;* O'Brien; Samuels; Steinfeldt; WWWAA.

DIAL, Dan [P] Dallas. Exhibited: SFT 1938; DAA. Work: DMA.

DIAZ, Emilio G. [P] San Antonio. Exhibited: SACE 1928.

DIAZ, Ricard. [P; T] El Paso. Birthdate: 1913. Studied: Emilio Cahero. Exhibited: EPWC 1936.

DICKARD, Bess Gray [P] Austin. Exhibited: TFWC 1931.

DICKSON, Lillian Ruth (Mrs. Henry Mockhaney) [P] Fort Worth. Birthplace: Atlanta, Ga. Studied: SLSFA; Washington Univ.; Dawson-Watson. Exhibited: TAFW 1927–37. Sources: O'Brien.

DICKSON, Melvin [P] Houston. Exhibited: AHAE 1933.

DIEDRICH, B. H. [P] San Antonio. Exhibited: SALA 1933.

DIEMAN, Clare Sorenson [S, T] Houston/New York, N.Y. Birthplace: Indianapolis, Ind. Studied: AIC; Columbia; Ozenfaut; Zadleine; Archipenko. Member: NAWA; Santa Fe P and S; Philadelphia Art Alliance; Philadelphia Print Club. Exhibited: AHAE; AIC; PAFA; NAWA; Philadelphia Art Alliance; Santa Fe P and S. Work: Gulf Bldg., Houston; Ind.; Colo.; Iowa. Sources: DAS; Fielding; Fisk; WWWAA.

DIGGINS (DIGINS/DIGINGS?), Loraine [P] Dallas. Member: FRAC. Exhibited: DAA; FRAC. Sources: PPHM files.

DILL, Frank C. [D] Houston. Exhibited: ASET 1937.

DILLARD, Emma D. [P] Dallas. Member: FRAC. Exhibited: TAFW 1930; FRAC.

DILLARD, Mrs. W. D. (Emma?) [P] Dallas. Exhibited: DAA.

DIXON, Ethel [P] Waco. Birthplace: North Dakota. Deathdate: 1916. Deathplace: India. Studied: Baylor w/ E. Wragg, C. H. Cox. Work: AIC. Sources: O'Brien; Waco PL.

DIXON, Mildred Wood [P] Houston. Exhibited: ASET 1937.

DIXON, Tola [D] San Antonio. Exhibited: SALA.

DODSON, Helen M. [P] Dallas. Exhibited: DAA 1935.

DOKE, Sallie George (Mrs. Fred) [P] Corsicana/ Lampasas/Shreveport. Birthplace: Keachie, La. Studied: Cincinnati Art Acad.; Chicago Acad. FA. Member: Soc. of Independent Artists. Exhibited: TAFW 1915–17, 1920, 1922–25, 1927–29. Sources: Fielding; WWWAA.

DOLEJSKA, Frank [P] Houston. Birthdate: 1921. Birthplace: Houston. Studied: O. M. Davidson. Exhibited: SFT 1938, 1939; AHAE; ASET; TG 1940. Sources: Bywaters Coll.; WWWAA.

DONALDSON, Olive [P; T; C; Cer.] Dallas. Birthplace: Ohio. Studied: Univ. Chicago; Univ. Heidelberg; AIC. Member: Dallas AC. Sources: Fisk; O'Brien.

DONNELL, Mrs. E. R. [P] Dallas. Studied: Reaugh. Member: FRAC. Exhibited: FRAC 1931. Sources: PPHM files.

DONNELL, L. A. [P] Dallas. Member: FRAC. Exhibited: FRAC 1941. Sources: PPHM files.

DONNELL, Lucretia (Mrs. Jack Coke) [P; T] Dallas. Birthdate: 1917. Birthplace: Temple. Living Austin, 1997. Studied: F. Reaugh; R. Bassett; L. Goff; J. Davis; SMU; New York Art Inst. Member: FRAC; Austin Palette Cl.; Capitol Art Soc.; Pastel Soc. of the Southwest. Exhibited: DAA 1937; Manhasset, N.Y. 1943 (solo). Sources: Artist; PPHM files.

DONNELLAN, Thurston John [Por. P] Houston. Birthdate: 1840. Birthplace: Houston. Deathdate: 1908. Deathplace: Houston. Studied: Chicago; New Orleans w/ O. Wilson. Work: Rice. Sources: *New Handbook;* Witte files.

DONOHUE, Margaret [P] Dallas. Exhibited: DAA 1932.

DONOP, Edna Bierschwale. See BIERSCHWALE, Edna

DOOLEY, Mrs. C. C. [P] Throckmorton, Tex. Exhibited: TFWC 1931.

DOOLEY, Maxine [P] Throckmorton, Tex. Exhibited: TFWC 1931.

DOOLITTLE, Leda Stinson [P] Dallas. Deathdate: 1966. Deathplace: Dallas. Exhibited: DAA 1937, 1938. Sources: ITD.

DORAN, Robert C. [P; Pm; Dec.] Dallas/New York. Birthdate: 1889. Birthplace: Dallas. Studied: K. H. Miller. Exhibited: TAFW 1918. Sources: Fielding; WWWAA.

DORSETT, Modesta [Des.] Dallas. Exhibited: DAA 1929.

DOUGLAS, Lucile [P] San Angelo. Exhibited: TAFW 1913.

DOUGLAS, Richard [P] El Paso. Exhibited: EPWC 1944.

DOUGLASS, Miss [P] Galveston? Exhibited: Texas Coast Fair 1895.

DOUGLASS, John Edwin [P; Pm; Cr] Dallas. Birthdate: 1905. Birthplace: Bennington, Okla. Deathdate: 1969. Deathplace: Dallas. Studied: Reaugh; ASL w/ Benton, Robinson. Member: FRAC; LSP. Exhibited: TAFW 1927–33; FRAC; SFT 1934; TCE; DAA; LSP (all); ATPE 1944. Work: DMA. Sources: Fisk; O'Brien.

DOW, Nell Pierce [P] Fort Worth. Exhibited: TAFW 1924, 1926, 1928, 1936.

DOWNIE, Janet [P; Pm] Austin. Birthplace: Detroit, Mich. Studied: S. Kensington Sch; PAFA; AIC; Broadmoor w/ Sandzen. Member: TFAA; SAAL; SSAL. Exhibited: TAFW 1925–33, 1935; UCE 2. Work: UT; MAMFW. Sources: Fisk; O'Brien.

DOYLE, Mary Frances [Pm; T] Dallas/Brownwood, Tex. Birthdate: 1904. Birthplace: Stephenville, Tex. Deathplace: Living, Dallas. Studied: SW Texas State Teachers College, San Marcos; TWU. Member: Texas Pm. Exhibited: WTAE 1939–40; DAA. Work: DMA; KSU; Longview AM; New Mexico Highlands Univ.; TWU. Sources: Harris.

DOZIER, Otis Marion [P; Pm; T; S; Mur. P] Dallas. Birthdate: 1904. Birthplace: Forney, Tex. Deathdate: 1987. Deathplace: Dallas. Studied: Aunspaugh AS; CSFAC. Member: Dallas AA; LSP; FRAC. Exhibited: TAFW 1927; FRAC; SFT; DAA; TCE; GTPA; TPan; DMFA 1944 (solo); TG; LSP (all); Rockefeller 1936; WFNY; MoMA; SSAL. Work: DMA; Longview AM; MAMFW; MFAH; PPHM; SMU; TAMU; Witte; USPOs, Giddings, Arlington, and Fredericksburg, Tex; Amarillo Mus. of Art; MAMFW. Sources: Carraro thesis; *New Handbook;* O'Brien; Samuels; WWWAA.

DOZIER, Velma Davis. See DAVIS, Velma

DREYER, Margaret Webb [P; Gallery owner] Houston. Birthdate: 1911. Birthplace: East St. Louis, Ill. Deathdate: 1976. Deathplace: Houston. Studied: Westmoreland College; UT; MFAH; Inst. Allende, Mexico. Member: Texas WCS. Exhibited: AHAE; Texas WCS; TG 1943, 1944. Work: Witte; Inst. Int'l Education, N.Y. Sources: Fielding; *New Handbook*.

DREYER, Martin [P] Houston. Exhibited: AHAE; TG 1943, 1945.

DRIVER, Beulah [P] Dallas. Exhibited: TAFW 1924.

DRIVER, Rose Buford (Mrs. Sim) [P] Dallas. Birthdate: 1900. Member: SSAL; FRAC. Exhibited: TFWC 1931; FRAC 1931; DAA; TAFW 1936; TCE; SFT 1939; TG 1941F; SSAL 1941. Sources: Mallett.

DROUET, Rosalind M. [P] San Antonio. Exhibited: SALA 1940.

DROUGHT, Frederick Gerald [P] San Antonio. Exhibited: TAFW 1933.

DU BOIS, Donald E. [D] Dallas/Ft. Sam Houston. Exhibited: DAA 1943; TG 1944.

DUDLEY, Wilburine [P] Dallas. Exhibited: DAA 1929.

DUER, Clare Mae [P; Pm; T] San Antonio/Dallas/Texarkana. Member: San Antonio Pm. Exhibited: TAFW 1928, 1929, 1933; SALA 1942; ATPE 1942. Work: Witte. Sources: Witte files.

DUFFY, Rebecca [S] Houston. Exhibited: AHAE 1945.

DUGGER, Ruth [P] Dallas. Exhibited: DAA 1929.

DUGOSH, Ruby Evelyn [P; Des. T] San Antonio. Birthdate: 1907. Birthplace: San Antonio. Deathdate: 1997. Deathplace: San Antonio. Studied: College of Industrial Arts (now TWU); Columbia; ASL; C. Martin; S. Davis; H. Hoffmann. Member: SSAL; SAAL; TFAA. Exhibited: TCE; TAFW 1936; MFAH 1938, 1939; SFT 1939; Witte; ASET; SALA; TG; Bright Shawl Gall. 1936 (solo). Work: PPHM. Sources: Mallett; O'Brien; WWWAA; Witte files.

DUHIG, Camilla F. [P] Houston. Exhibited: AHAE 1936.

DUHIG, W. G. [P, S] Houston. Exhibited: AHAE.

DUMONT, Arrie Ella Elgar [S] Paducah. Birthdate: 1861. Birthplace: Lee Co., Miss. Deathdate: 1943. Deathplace: Paducah. Studied: Self-taught. Work: Tombstone, Quanah, Tex. Sources: *New Handbook*.

DUMUTH, Werner [P] San Antonio. Exhibited: SALA 1944. Sources: Witte files.

DUNAHOO, Mildred F. [P] Mercedes, Tex. Exhibited: TG 1941F.

DUNLAP, Ellen L. [P] Dallas/El Paso/Chicago. Studied: Aunspaugh AS. Exhibited: TAFW 1912–14; Cotton Carn. 1912. Sources: Fisk; Price.

DUNLAP, Minnie [P] Dallas. Member: FRAC. Exhibited: FRAC 1930, 1933, 1935. Sources: PPHM files.

DUNN, Bert [P] Aransas Pass. Exhibited: TFWC 1931.

DURAN, Santa Maria de los Reyes Mombelli [P] San Antonio. Birthdate: 1909. Birthplace: Mexico City, Mexico. Living San Antonio, 1997. Studied: Arpa; X. Gonzalez; H. A. De Young; H. Roney; R. Taylor; Earl. Member: Coppini Acad.; SAAL. Exhibited: SALA; Arpa Student Exh., Witte, 1928. Sources: The artist; Witte files; SAAL files. Lived in San Antonio since 1917; daughter of Italian sculptor Victorio Mombelli.

DURRETT, Nell M. [P] Fort Worth. Exhibited: TAFW 1930.

DURST, Frances [P; D] San Antonio. Exhibited: SALA 1939; ASET 1939. Sources: Witte files.

DUVAL, Ella Moss (Mrs. G. B.) [P; Por. P] San Antonio. Birthdate: 1843. Birthplace: Pass Christian, Miss. Deathdate: 1911. Deathplace: St. Louis, Mo. Studied: Dusseldorf w/ A. W. Sohn. Exhibited: NAD 1877. Work: No public coll. Sources: Pinckney; *New Handbook*.

DuVALL, Jo [P] Fort Worth. Exhibited: TAFW 1927.

DYER, Laura [P] Houston. Exhibited: AHAE.

EARNEST, Billy [D] San Antonio. Exhibited: SALA. Sources: Witte files.

EAST, Pattie Richardson [P; Pm; T] Fort Worth. Birthdate: 1894. Birthplace: Hardesty, Okla. Studied: AIC; Broadmoor; Sandzen; Fleck; Arpa; H. A. De Young.

Member: SSAL; TFAA; FWAA. Exhibited: TFAA; MFAH; TAFW 1924–37; UCE 2; GTPA; TG; SSAL. Work: MAMFW; PPHM. Sources: Mallett; O'Brien; Samuels; WWWAA.

EASTMAN, Seth [P; T] San Antonio/near Fredericksburg. Birthdate: 1808. Birthplace: Brunswick, Me. Deathdate: 1875. Deathplace: Washington, D.C. Studied: West Point. Member: NAD. Exhibited: None in Texas. Work: RL; Witte; McNay; Peabody; J. J. Hill Lib., St. Paul, Minn.; U.S. Capitol. Sources: Fielding; *New Handbook;* Pinckney; Samuels; Steinfeldt.

EASTON, Mary C. F. (Mrs. Alexander) [P] Galveston. Exhibited: Cotton Carn. 1910. Sources: Galveston City Directory.

EBERHARDT, Eugenia McCorkle (Mrs. H. C.) [P] Fort Worth. Birthplace: Alabama. Studied: Texas State Dental College; Aunspaugh AS; AIC; TCU w/ Ziegler. Member: FWAA; TFAA. Exhibited: TAFW 1923, 1927–37; TFWC; DWF; TFAA; UCE 2. Sources: O'Brien; WWWAA.

ECKFORD, Jessiejo [P; Pm] Dallas. Birthdate: 1895. Studied: Reaugh; Bolton; Aunspaugh AS; Christoval Colony. Member: SAAL; FRAC. Exhibited: DWF 1915–17; TAFW 1916–20, 1922–37; Greenville 1924; FRAC; SACE 1929; TCE; DAA; SFT; GTPA. Work: Ney Mus.; PPHM; UT Arlington; Witte. Sources: Fielding; Fisk; Mallett; O'Brien; Samuels; Smith; WWWAA.

EDGE, Altha [P] Waco. Exhibited: WTAE 1939–42.

EDGE (EDE?), Marian [P; Pm] Dallas. Exhibited: DAA.

EDMENSON, Fannie Mae [P] San Antonio. Exhibited: SALA 1944.

EDWARDS, Emily (Mrs. Librado Cantabrana) [P; Pm; T; W] San Antonio. Birthdate: 1888. Birthplace: Bexar Co., Tex. Deathdate: 1980. Deathplace: San Antonio. Studied: P. Coppini; Vanderpoel; AIC w/ Walcott; D. Rivera. Member: Provincetown Woodblock Printers. Exhibited: TAFW 1922; SACE 1929; SALA 1935. Work: Witte. Sources: Fisk; Mallett; *New Handbook;* O'Brien; Steinfeldt; WWWAA.

EDWARDS, Ethel [P] Alpine. Exhibited: WTAE 1939. Work: OJAC.

EDWARDS, Frank Mudge [P; Mur. P] San Antonio. Birthdate: 1855. Birthplace: San Antonio. Deathdate: 1956. Deathplace: San Antonio. Studied: Self-taught. Exhibited: Witte 1946; SALA 1935. Work: Witte. Sources: Steinfeldt.

EDWARDS, Mrs. K. J. [P] Galveston. Exhibited: Cotton Carn. 1910.

EDWARDS, Marie (Mrs. Jack) [P] Amarillo. Exhibited: TSFA. Work: Panhandle Children's Home; PPHM.

EDWARDS, Mrs. N. Z. [P; Interior Des.] Sherman. Studied: E. Fowler; F. Klepper. Member: Klepper AC. Exhibited: Klepper AC. Sources: O'Brien.

EDWARDS, Mrs. O. D. [P] San Antonio. Exhibited: SALA 1930.

EDWARDS, Mrs. Wiley M. [P] El Paso. Exhibited: EPWC 1935–37, 1941.

EGLIN, Mrs. F. I. [P; Por. P] San Antonio. Exhibited: SAAG 1927.

EIGNUS, Everett [P] San Antonio. Exhibited: SALA 1932.

EINFELDT, George [P] Houston. Birthplace: Germany. Exhibited: AHAE 1934–38; Artists of Southeast Texas 1937, 1938. Sources: Houston PL; Witte files.

EISENLOHR, Edward Gustav [P; Pm; T] Dallas. Birthdate: 1872. Birthplace: Cincinnati, Ohio. Deathdate: 1961. Deathplace: Dallas. Studied: Reaugh; R. J. Onderdonk; Woodstock; Acad. Karlsruhe, Germany. Member: Salmagundi Cl.; Dallas AA; TFAA; SSAL; LSP. Exhibited: SFT; TAFW; Greenville 1924; TWF 1917; TCE; FWFCE; GTPA; DAA; SACE (pr.); TFWC; TPan; LSP; ATPE 1945; SSAL; NAD; Corcoran; WFNY. Work: DMA; PPHM; Grace Cultural Ctr., Abilene; Abilene Mus. FA; MFAH; Stark; Witte; Ney Mus.; Dallas Hist. Soc. Sources: Church; Fisk; *New Handbook;* O'Brien; Samuels; Smith; WWWAA.

ELDER, Inez Staub [P; Por. P] Dallas. Birthdate: 1894. Birthplace: Kosuth, Ohio. Studied: Otterbein College; Cincinnati Art Acad.; New Sch., Boston; ASL; Bridgman; DuMond. Member: SSAL; TFAA; FRAC; Klepper AC. Exhibited: DAA; FRAC; SFT; TAFW; TCE; UCE 2; GTPA; Sartor 1935 (solo); MFAH; DMFA 1943 (solo). Work: DWF; Oak Cliff YMCA. Sources: Bywaters Coll.; Mallett; O'Brien; WWWAA.

ELFENBEIN, Julian [Pm] Dallas. Studied: ASL w/ J. Pennell. Sources: O'Brien; Dallas Morning News.

ELKINS, Mrs. G. R. [P] Spur, Tex. Exhibited: TFWC 1931.

ELLEDG, Pearl [P] Houston. Exhibited: AHAE 1937.

ELLET, Lois [] San Antonio. Exhibited: SALA 1935.

ELLIOTT, Jouett Fall [P] El Paso. Deathdate: 1956. Exhibited: EPWC 1927.

ELLIOTT, Kathryn [P] Dallas. Exhibited: DAA 1929.

ELLIOTT, Minnie C. [P] Tahoka, Tex. Exhibited: TFWC 1931.

ELLIOTT, William C. [P; Pm.; Comm. A] Dallas. Birthdate: 1909. Birthplace: Sedalia, Mo. Deathplace: Living Dallas, 1997. Studied: Tarleton State; AID w/ Travis and Stone. Member: LSP. Exhibited: TAFW 1933; SFT 1934; Sartor; DAA; LSP 1940–41. Work: PPHM. Sources: O'Brien.

ELLIS, Fremont F. [P; T; Pm; Por. P] El Paso/Santa Fe. Birthdate: 1897. Birthplace: Virginia City, Mont. Deathdate: 1985. Deathplace: Santa Fe. Studied: ASL. Member: Santa Fe P and S; Los Cinco Pintores (founder); Calif. AC. Exhibited: EPWC 1935; Los Angeles MA 1924. Work: EPMA; MAMFW; PPHM; Mus. FA, Santa Fe. Sources: Fielding; Price; Samuels; WWWAA.

ELLIS, John Bryant [P] Dallas. Exhibited: DAA 1942.

ELLISON, Gussie [P] San Antonio. Exhibited: SALA 1930.

ELMENDORF, Stella. See TYLOR, Stella Elmendorf

ELMORE, Kate L. (LaGOW, Kate Elmore) [P; Pm] Dallas. Exhibited: DAA 1928; ATPE 1944.

EMEREE, Berla Iyone (Mrs. William Henry) [P; T; C] El Paso/San Antonio. Birthdate: 1899. Birthplace: Wichita, Kans. Deathdate: 1948. Deathplace: El Paso. Studied: San Antonio Art Acad.; Arpa; X. Gonzales; R. Taylor. Member: EPAG; SSAL. Exhibited: TAFW; TFAA; TWCE; SACE 1928; TCE; TFWC 1931; EPWC; EPSJ 1934. Work: MNM; FWPL; UTEP; EPWC. Sources: El Paso Herald-Post; El Paso Times; EPPL; Fielding; Mallett; O'Brien; Samuels; WWWAA.

EMERY, Nellie Augusta [P; T] Dallas. Birthplace: Hartford, Me. Deathdate: 1931. Deathplace: Brazoria Co., Tex. Studied: Enneking; DuMond; W. M. Chase; Rolshoven; Whistler; École BA w/ L. Merson and R. Collin. Member: SSAL. Exhibited: TAFW 1922–28. Work: St. Paul AG, Minn. Sources: Fisk; ITD; O'Brien; Smith; WWWAA.

EMIG, Adolph P. [P] Houston. Exhibited: AHAE; ASET; TG 1940, 1945. Sources: WWWAA.

ENGELKING, Robert Sigismund [P] San Antonio/ Comfort. Birthdate: 1915. Birthplace: San Antonio. Studied: UT. Exhibited: SALA 1939; TG 1940; Mexico City 1942 (solo). Sources: Witte files.

ENGELMEYER, Louis [P] Galveston. Exhibited: Cotton Carn. 1910–12. Sources: Galveston City Directory 1903–14.

ENSER, John F. [P; I; Pm; T] San Antonio/Lexington, Mass. Birthdate: 1898. Birthplace: Ennis, Tex. Studied: AIC; Chicago Acad. FA; Arpa. Member: SSAL; SAAL; San Antonio P&CC; TFAA. Exhibited: SAAL 1926, 1941 (solo); SACE 1927; SALA; SFT 1934; TAFW; UCE 1; GTPA; SSAL; Boston AC; Dayton AI. Work: USPO, Boston. Sources: WWWAA; O'Brien; Witte files.

ENSOR, Rettie Kelly [P] Dallas. Exhibited: DAA 1929.

EPHRAIM, Eleanor [D] Houston. Exhibited: AHAE.

ERLICH, Jake [P] El Paso. Studied: H. Kidd. Exhibited: EPWC; Desert Art Shop, El Paso 1936 (solo). Sources: El Paso Herald-Post; EPWC scrapbook.

ERWIN, John Bruce "Jack" (J. B.). [P; Arch.; Violin maker] Dallas. Birthdate: 1920. Birthplace: Jacksboro, Tex. Living Dallas, 1997. Studied: UT; S. Gideon. Exhibited: TG 1941F; California WCS. 1945. Work: PPHM. Sources: PPHM files; the artist.

ERWIN, Margaret D. [P] McKinney. Studied: Peace Inst., Raleigh, N.C.; ASL w/ Twachtman, DuMond; Chase at Southampton. Sources: O'Brien.

ESCHER, Erwin [P] Houston. Exhibited: AHAE 1925.

ESTILL, Nell Gene [Pm] Fort Worth. Exhibited: TAFW 1934, 1936, 1937.

EUBANK, Lydia [P] Dallas. Exhibited: DAA; TG 1942.

EVANS, Ada Smith (EVANS, Mrs. Henry A. ?) [P] Dallas. Member: FRAC. Exhibited: FRAC 1933, 1934. Sources: PPHM files.

EVANS, Mrs. Henry A. (EVANS, Ada Smith?) [P] Dallas. Member: FRAC. Exhibited: FRAC 1930. Sources: PPHM files.

EVANS, Margaret [P] Fort Worth. Exhibited: TAFW 1926.

EVERETT, Edward [P; D] San Antonio/Boston. Birthdate: 1818. Birthplace: London, England. Deathdate: 1903. Deathplace: Boston, Mass. Studied: Self-taught. Work: Amon Carter. Sources: *New Handbook.*

EVERETT, Raymond [P; S; L; T] Austin. Birthdate: 1885. Birthplace: Englishtown, N.J. Deathdate: 1948. Deathplace: Austin. Studied: Drexel; Harvard; Pyle; AJ; D. Ross; J. Smith. Member: TFAA; SSAL; Amer. Inst. of Arch.; Pen and Brush, Boston; Amer. Bookplate Soc. Exhibited: TAFW; SSAL 1929; SACE 1927; HPSA 1927 (three-person); UCE 1; TSFA 1929; ASET 1937. Work: PPHM; Stark; Detroit PL; Ney Mus.; Colorado Univ. Mus; Witte. Sources: *Austin American-Statesman;* Claycomb; Dawdy; Fielding; Fisk; Havlice; O'Brien; Samuels; Smith; WWWAA.

EYTH, Louis [P; Por. P; I] Galveston. Birthdate: 1838. Deathdate: 1889. Studied: Blessing and Company (daguerreotypists), Galveston. Work: TCapitol. Sources: *New Handbook;* O'Brien; Pinckney; Ratcliffe; Samuels.

FAHRENBERG, Albert, Sr. [Por. P.; Ph] San Antonio. Birthdate: 1828. Birthplace: Cologne, Germany. Exhibited: San Antonio 1876. Work: Witte. Sources: Groce and Wallace; Steinfeldt.

FAIN, Hazel Barr [P] Houston. Exhibited: AHAE 1931.

FAIRCHILD, Everett D. [Mur. P] Lubbock. Birthdate: 1909. Birthplace: Troy, Okla. Studied: Texas Tech w/ F. Kleinschmidt. Mural: Texas Tech Engineering Bldg. Sources: O'Brien; Wilbanks.

FALL, Mrs. C. G. [P] Dallas. Exhibited: DAA 1928.

FALL, Frieda Kay [P] Dallas/Houston. Exhibited: AHAE 1938; SFT 1939; DAA; TG 1941S, 1943; ATPE 1942; NAWPS 1938. Sources: WWWAA.

FALL, Willie Kay [P] Dallas. Exhibited: TAFW 1928–30, 1932–34.

FARIS, Polly [D] San Antonio. Exhibited: SALA 1934.

FARMER, Evangeline [P] Fort Worth. Exhibited: TAFW 1925.

FARNSWORTH, Otis [P] San Antonio. Exhibited: SALA 1938–40; TG 1940, 1942, 1945; ASET 1939; SSAL 1940. Sources: Witte files.

FARQUHARSON, Thelma A. [P] Houston. Exhibited: AHAE 1935.

FAULKNER, Margaret Y. [P] San Antonio. Exhibited: TFWC 1931.

FAUSETT, William Dean [P; Mur. P; Pm] San Antonio/ Dorset, Vt. Birthdate: 1913. Birthplace: Price, Utah. Studied: BYU; ASL; Beaux Arts Inst. of Design, N.Y.; CSFAC; K. Miller; B. Robinson; C. Locke; Nicolaides. Member: ASL; Nat. Soc. of Mur. P; Southern Vt. AA. Exhibited: SALA; NAD; AIC; Carnegie; Corcoran; Met.; HAI; Toledo MA. Work: Witte; Met.; MoMA; Toledo Mus. of Art (Ohio); AIC; Univ. Nebraska; Univ. Arizona. Sources: WWWAA.

FEARING, Kelly [P; W; T; Pm] Fort Worth. Birthdate: 1918. Birthplace: Fordyce, Ark. Living Austin, 1996. Studied: Louisiana Tech. Univ.; Columbia. Member: FWAA; Dallas AA. Exhibited: FWAA 1944, 1945; Dallas Print Soc. 1945; SAAL 1945; MFAH 1944, 1945; TG 1944, 1945; Carnegie; San Francisco MA; SSAL. Work: Longview AM; MAMFW; OJAC; SAMA; TAMU; Louisiana Tech; Milwaukee AM; Inst. of Contemporary Art, Boston. Sources: Bywaters Coll.; Gillespie and Nail; WWWAA.

FEATHER, Henrietta Gibson [D] San Antonio. Exhibited: SALA 1938.

FEIGERLE, Franz [S] San Antonio. Exhibited: SALA 1944.

FENLEY, Mary Hornley [P] San Antonio. Exhibited: SAAL 1924.

FERGUSON, W. B., III. [P] Houston. Exhibited: AHAE 1940.

FERNEAU, J. [P] Dallas. Exhibited: DAA 1945.

FICKESSEN, Dot [P] San Antonio. Exhibited: SALA 1937.

FICKLIN, Jack [S] Dallas. Exhibited: DAA 1929.

FILIPPONE, John C. (Ginanni Battista) [P; Pm; I; Mur. P] San Antonio. Birthdate: 1882. Birthplace: Brackettville, Tex. Studied: Arpa; St. Louis w/ C. Swanson. Member: Villita Artists; SAAG. Exhibited: Witte; TCE; TAFW; SALA; TFWC 1931. Work: Witte. Sources: O'Brien; Steinfeldt.

FILLEAU, E. A. [P, T] Houston. Exhibited: AHAE 1926, 1930. Sources: Fisk; Houston City Directory 1918–24; Witte files.

FILSON, Genevieve Winnifred [P] Houston/Laporte. Birthdate: 1913. Studied: Newcomb College; MFAH. Member: SSAL. Exhibited: TCE; AHAE; ASET; SSAL. Work: MFAH. Sources: WWWAA.

FINDLEY, Mrs. H. F. [P] El Paso. Exhibited: EPWC 1936.

FINNEY, C. J. [P] College Station. Exhibited: ASET.

FIRMIN, Albert Edwin [S; Por. S] Dallas. Birthdate: 1890. Birthplace: Mexia, Tex. Studied: Aunspaugh AS; Chicago Acad. FA. Exhibited: DAA 1933. Sources: DAS; Fisk; WWWAA.

FISCHER, Florence [P] Houston. Exhibited: AHAE 1925.

FISH, Margaret. [P] Palestine, Tex. Exhibited: TAFW 1928–30, 1932–35; DWF 1928; TAEN. Sources: Fisk.

FISHER, Mrs. E. D. [P] Goose Creek, Tex. Exhibited: TFWC 1931.

FISHER, Ella Scott [P] Galveston. Exhibited: Texas Coast Fair 1895. Sources: Galveston City Directory 1898; RL.

FISHER, Frank Preston, Jr. [P] Fort Worth. Birthdate: 1907. Birthplace: Dallas. Deathdate: 1959. Deathplace: Fort Worth. Studied: S. Ziegler; S. Gillespie; W. Jolly. Member: Fort Worth Allied Artists (pres.). Exhibited: TAFW 1932–36; Collins Art Co., Fort Worth 1934 (solo); TCE; SFT 1939; FWAL 1939–41; TG 1941S. Sources: O'Brien; United Pawn. Withdrew from public in 1941; early abstract painter in Fort Worth.

FISHER, John V. [P] Dallas. Exhibited: DAA.

FISHER, May [P] Houston. Exhibited: AHAE 1929.

FISHER, Oriole [P] Amarillo. Exhibited: TFWC 1931.

FITZGERALD, Elsie Luthy [S] San Antonio. Exhibited: SALA 1940.

FLACK, Jack [P] Houston. Exhibited: AHAE 1943.

FLANAGAN, Jack Key [P] Houston. Exhibited: AHAE; TG 1942, 1943, 1945. Work: MFAH.

FLANARY, Lolah A. (Mrs. A. B.) [P] Dallas. Member: FRAC. Exhibited: FRAC 1930. Sources: PPHM files.

FLANARY, Suzanne [P] Ralls, Tex. Exhibited: TFWC 1931.

FLEMING, Margaret [P] Dallas. Exhibited: DAA 1935.

FLEMING, Sally K. [P] Channing, Tex. Exhibited: TFWC 1931.

FLETCHER, Valentine Bertha (Vallie) [P] Beaumont. Birthdate: 1874. Birthplace: Beaumont. Deathdate: 1959. Deathplace: Beaumont. Studied: Mary Hardin-Baylor College; Cooper Union, N.Y.; R. Graham. Exhibited: TAFW; SACE 1927; TFWC 1931; SALA 1933; UCE 1, 2. Sources: *Beaumont Sunday Enterprise;* Witte files. Born on Valentine's Day and named for it; painted first landscapes in Colorado in 1917.

FLINTOFF, Thomas [Por. P] Galveston/Austin/Corpus Christi/ Matagorda. Birthdate: 1809. Birthplace: Newcastle-upon-Tyne, England. Deathdate: 1891. Deathplace: Melbourne, Australia. Studied: Self-taught. Exhibited: Houston. Work: MFAH; TCapitol; UT; Austin College; Texas State Archives; Hogg Coll. Sources: Benezit; *New Handbook;* O'Brien; Pinckney.

FLORER, Mrs. M. W. [P] Dallas. Exhibited: DAA 1933.

FLURY, Godfrey [P; Comm. A] San Antonio/Moulton/Austin. Birthdate: 1864. Birthplace: Oensingen, Switzerland. Deathdate: 1936. Deathplace: Austin. Studied: Self-taught. Exhibited: Ney Mus., ca. 1936 (memorial). Work: St. Mary's Ch., Praha, Tex. Sources: Flury; *New Handbook.*

FLY, Ben M. [P] Victoria/Houston. Studied: W. H. Stevens; Christoval Camp. Exhibited: AHAE. Sources: Fisk.

FORBIS, Virginia S. [P] Lubbock. Member: Lubbock AA. Exhibited: Lubbock AA 1933. Sources: Wilbanks.

FORD, Arva (Mrs. Vincent) [P] Dallas. Birthdate: 1890. Member: FRAC. Exhibited: FRAC 1932; TAFW 1932–37; DAA; TCE. Sources: PPHM files.

FORD, Mrs. Gus [P] San Antonio. Exhibited: TFWC 1931.

FORD, J. V. [P] Amarillo. Birthdate: 1870. Studied: Self-taught. Exhibited: Amarillo 1932 (solo); Amarillo 1933 (solo). Work: PPHM. Sources: *Amarillo Globe-News;* PPHM files.

FORD, Otha Neil (O'Neil) [Arch.; Pm] Dallas/San Antonio. Birthdate: 1905. Birthplace: Pink Hill, Tex. Deathdate: 1982. Deathplace: San Antonio. Studied: North Texas State College; D. Williams. Member: Amer. Inst. of Arch. Exhibited: DAA 1929, 1931, 1932, 1937. Work: Dallas; San Antonio. Sources: *San Antonio Express; San Antonio Light;* Witte files.

FORSYTH, Constance [P; Pm; T] Austin. Birthdate: 1903. Birthplace: Indianapolis. Deathdate: 1987. Deathplace: Austin. Studied: Butler Univ.; HAI; PAFA; Broadmoor. Member: Dallas Print Soc.; Texas Pm. Exhibited: TFAA; TG; ATPE; PAFA; MFAH; DMFA; KCAI; WFNY. Work: PPHM; HAI; Ball State Univ. Sources: Bywaters Coll.; Farmer; Fielding; Mallett; *New Handbook;* TPan m.; WWWAA.

FOSTER, Cecile [P; T] Levelland/Sudan, Tex. Birthdate: 1905. Birthplace: Hood Co., Tex. Deathdate: 1983. Deathplace: Lubbock. Studied: Dozier; X. Gonzalez; Bisttram; Utter. Member: SSAL; South Plains AG, Lubbock; Lubbock AA. Exhibited: TFAA; WTAE 1939–42; SSAL. Work: PPHM. Sources: Wilbanks.

FOSTER, Grace [P; T] Greenville/Abilene. Birthdate: 1879. Birthplace: Wolf City, Tex. Deathdate: 1931. Deathplace: Hunt Co., Tex. Studied: Hardin-Simmons w/ E. J. Hobbs; Reaugh. Member: SSAL; Hunt Co. FA Assoc. Exhibited: TAFW; West Texas Fair 1926; DWF; Hunt County Fair; TFWC 1931. Sources: Fielding; Fisk; O'Brien; WWWAA.

FOSTER, May [P] Houston/Fort Worth. Exhibited: SACE 1927; AHAE 1927; TAFW 1937. Sources: MFAH files; Witte files.

FOWLER, Evangeline [P; T; Pm] Sherman/Birmingham, Mich. Birthdate: 1850. Birthplace: Kingsville, Ohio. Deathdate: 1934. Deathplace: Birmingham. Studied: ASL; PAFA; Delaye; Chase Summer Sch.; Hillsdale College, Mich.; NYSFAA. Member: SSAL; Detroit Soc. Women PS; Denison AC; Eva Fowler AC, Sherman. Exhibited: TAFW; SACE 1927; SFT 1931; WCE; DWF; Cotton Cent., New Orleans 1885. Work: Hillsdale College, Mich.; Sherman PL. Sources: Fielding; Fisk; Havlice; Mallett; O'Brien; WWWAA.

FOWLER, T. M. [D; Pm] Morrisville, Pa. Work: Witte. Sources: Pinckney.

FOXALL, Horace [S] Dallas. Exhibited: TG 1941S.

FRANCIS, Muriel Wilkins. [S; P; T; Cr] Fort Worth. Birthdate: 1893. Birthplace: Longview, Tex. Studied: Shreveport Sch. of Art; KCAI. Member: FWAA; SSAL; AAPL; Fort Worth AG. Exhibited: TAFW 1935–37; TG; TFAA; SSAL. Sources: DAS; WWWAA.

FRANCOIS, Edgar L. [P] San Antonio. Deathdate: 1919. Deathplace: San Antonio. Studied: France. Sources: San Antonio City Directory 1889–90, 1895–96. Painted landscapes and the Alamo.

FRANK, Goldalee [P] Dallas. Exhibited: DAA.

FRANKE, Helen [P] San Antonio. Exhibited: SALA 1936.

FRANKLIN, Geraldine [P] McKinney. Exhibited: TAFW 1926–29.

FRANKLIN, Ione Ruth [S; T] San Antonio/Commerce. Birthdate: 1893. Birthplace: Poetry, Tex. Deathdate: 1976. Deathplace: San Antonio. Studied: TSCW; Columbia; ASL w/ Zorach and Laurent. Member: Texas Sculpture Group; SSAL. Exhibited: GTPA; TG 1941F, 1944, 1945; SSAL; KCAI 1942. Work: Formerly DMFA. Sources: Bywaters Coll.; DAS; Mallett; *New Handbook;* TPan m., WWWAA.

FRANKLIN, Mary Glenn [P] Houston. Exhibited: AHAE 1942.

FRANKLIN, Mrs. William [P] El Paso. Exhibited: EPWC 1940.

FRASER, Leona [P] Dallas. Exhibited: DAA.

FRASER, Mary Lee [P] El Paso. Exhibited: EPWC 1941.

FRAZER, James [P] San Antonio. Exhibited: SALA 1943; TG 1942, 1943. Work: MAMFW.

FREDERICK, George [P] . Birthdate: 1889. Exhibited: TCE. Work: PPHM.

FREE, Mary Arnold (Mrs. Robert C.) [P; Pm; T] San Antonio. Birthdate: 1895. Birthplace: Pleasant Hill, Mo. Studied: Columbia; KCAI; Snell; Wilomovsky; Braught. Member: Nat. Assoc. Univ. Women; SAAL; Texas WCS. Exhibited: SALA 1935, 1943, 1944; San Antonio Pm 1938, 1941; Witte 1935. Work: Witte. Sources: McAdams; WWWAA; Witte files.

FREEDY, Mrs. I. W. [P] Lamesa, Tex. Member: Lubbock AA. Exhibited: Lubbock AA 1937. Sources: Wilbanks.

FREELAND, Henry C. [P] San Antonio/Galveston. Birthdate: 1821. Birthplace: New York. Deathdate: 1903. Deathplace: San Antonio. Work: Witte. Sources: Steinfeldt.

FREEMAN, Leola (Mrs. Lloyd Freeman) [P; Port. P] El Paso. Birthdate: 1900. Birthplace: Gonzales, Tex. Deathdate: 1989. Deathplace: North Carolina. Studied: PAFA; Garber; Bridgman; Lloyd Freeman. Member: EPAG; EPAA. Exhibited: TAFW 1933, 1936; EPSJ 1934; EPWC; TCE; WTAE 1939–42. Sources: *El Paso Herald-Post;* EPPL; Mallett; O'Brien; Price.

FRETELLIERE, Louise [P; T] San Antonio. Birthdate: 1856. Birthplace: San Antonio. Deathdate: 1940. Deathplace: San Antonio. Studied: Theodore Gentilz. Work: Witte. Sources: Steinfeldt; Utterbeck.

FRITZ, Eleanor Virginia (Mrs. E. B.) [P; T] Fort Worth. Birthdate: 1885. Birthplace: St. Cloud, Minn. Studied: AIC; Dow; E. Neuhaus; A. Hills; H. Hofmann. Member: FWAA; AACFW; Los Angeles AA; SSAL. Exhibited: TAFW 1927–37; TCE. Work: Nash Sch., Fort Worth. Sources: O'Brien; WWWAA

FULLER, Ida Jo [P; T] Greenville. Studied: AIC; Parsons Sch. Member: TFAA. Exhibited: Dallas; San Angelo. Sources: O'Brien.

FULTON, George [P] Houston. Exhibited: AHAE.

FUQUA, Wiley [D] Dallas. Exhibited: DAA 1941.

FUTCH, Bessie Gunter [P] Amarillo. Exhibited: TFWC 1931.

GADBOIS, Henry V. [Comm. A; P] Houston. Birthdate: 1888. Birthplace: St. Eustache, Quebec, Canada. Deathdate: 1975. Deathplace: Houston. Studied: Albany, N.Y. Member: Associated Artists of Houston. Exhibited: Associated Artists of Houston 1940s (solo). Work: PPHM. Sources: Artist's son, Henri V. Gadbois.

GALLAGHER, Richard [P] El Paso. Exhibited: EPWC 1940, 1944, 1945.

GAMBLE, Mrs. L. P. [P] Dallas. Member: FRAC. Exhibited: FRAC 1930. Sources: PPHM files.

GAMMEL, Nora Currie [S] San Antonio/Houston. Birthplace: Aquilla, Tex. Studied: Milford College, Tex.; Houston Art and Stone; H. McNeil. Work: Ft. Sam Houston; Port Lavaca. Sources: Fisk; O'Brien; Witte files.

GANSER, Edna [P] Dallas. Member: FRAC. Exhibited: FRAC; DAA 1930, 1932, 1933; TAFW 1933, 1936; TCE. Sources: Mallett.

GARCIA, Antonio E. [P; T] Corpus Christi/San Diego, Tex. Birthdate: 1901. Birthplace: Monterey, Mexico. Deathdate: 1997. Deathplace: Stuart, Fla. Studied: AIC; W. Adams; B. Anisfield. Member: SSAL; South Texas AL, Corpus Christi; TFAA; Corpus Christi AG. Exhibited: TAFW; TCE; ASET 1937; SFT 1939; TFAA; Corpus Christi Mus.; SSAL. Work: TFWC, Austin; AMST; TAMU-Kingsville. Sources: Bywaters Coll.; WWWAA.

GARDNER, Dan B. [S] Houston. Exhibited: AHAE 1936.

GARLAND, Christine [P; D] Houston. Exhibited: AHAE; ASET. Sources: WWWAA.

GARRET, Mrs. M. K. [P] Fort Worth. Exhibited: TAFW 1928.

GARRETT, Mildred Burrows [P] San Antonio. Member: TFAA. Exhibited: TFAA 1932. Sources: *San Antonio Light;* Witte files.

GARRISON, Elizabeth Howard [P] Belton. Exhibited: TFWC 1931.

GARRISON, Minta H. (Martha, Mrs. J. T.) [P] Houston. Birthdate: 1874. Birthplace: Center, Tex. Studied:

Baylor Female College; E. R. Cherry. Member: NAWPS; TFAA; SSAL; MFAH. Exhibited: TFWC 1931; AHAE; UCE 1; ASET; Texas AL; SSAL 1933. Sources: O'Brien; WWWAA.

GARZA, Delio Flores [P] San Antonio. Exhibited: SALA 1935–37, 1939, 1940; TG 1940. Sources: *San Antonio Light;* Witte files.

GASSLANDER, Karl [P; T] Dallas/Chicago. Birthdate: 1905. Birthplace: Rockford, Ill. Studied: Northwestern; Columbia; C. Martin; A. Heckman; G. J. Cox; A. Storm. Member: Chicago Soc. of Artists. Exhibited: DAA 1930; TSFA 1929; Evanston Women's College 1939. Sources: WWWAA.

GATES, Dr. W. B. [P] Lubbock. Member: Lubbock AA. Exhibited: Lubbock AA 1933. Sources: Wilbanks.

GATEWOOD, Evelyn Mullaney (Mrs. J. R.) [P] Dallas. Birthdate: 1903. Birthplace: Winneshiek Co., Iowa. Studied: C. A. Cumming. Member: FRAC. Exhibited: DAA; FRAC 1932. Sources: PPHM files; WWWAA.

GATTEYS, Allie B. [P] Dallas. Exhibited: DAA 1932, 1933.

GAUTNEY, Loraine D. [P] Houston. Exhibited: AHAE 1931.

GAY, Helen [P] Houston. Exhibited: AHAE.

GAY, Stella [P] Dallas. Exhibited: DAA 1945.

GEESLIN, Lee Gaddis [] Brady, Tex. Exhibited: WTAE 1940.

GENIESSE, Stephen [P] San Antonio. Exhibited: SALA 1943; TG 1941F.

GENIN, Dan [P; Pm] Houston. Exhibited: AHAE 1942; TG 1941S, 1941F.

GENTILZ, Jean Louis Theodore [P; Por. P; T] San Antonio/Castroville. Birthdate: 1819. Birthplace: France. Deathdate: 1906. Deathplace: San Antonio. Studied: L'École Imp. Met. D. Exhibited: Yanaguana (ph.); Centennial Exh. Early Tex. Painters. Work: DRT Lib.; Witte; DMA. Sources: Kendall and Perry bio.; *New Handbook;* O'Brien; Pinckney; Ratcliffe; Steinfeldt; Utterbeck; WWWAA.

GENTILZ, Marie Fargeix [P] San Antonio. Birthdate: 1830. Birthplace: France. Deathdate: 1898. Deathplace: San Antonio? Studied: Theodore Gentilz. Work: Witte. Sources: Kendall and Perry bio.; Steinfeldt; Utterbeck.

GENTLE, Robert "Mac" [Pm] San Antonio. Exhibited: SALA 1943; ATPE 1944.

GENTRY, Nannie Mae [P] Dallas. Birthdate: 1899. Deathdate: 1966. Deathplace: Tarrant County, Tex. Exhibited: DAA 1930–33, 1937; GTPA. Sources: ITD.

GENUNG, Robert [P] El Paso/Los Angeles. Studied: New York; G. Bellow; R. Henri. Member: Calif. AC; FSAA. Exhibited: EPWC. Sources: *El Paso Herald-Post; El Paso Times;* Price; WWWAA.

GERMANY, Pattilou [P] Dallas. Exhibited: DAA 1945.

GEUIEST, Ann [P] San Antonio. Exhibited: SAAL 1924.

GHARIS, Charles Mason Tudor [P] Dallas. Birthdate: 1910. Birthplace: Dallas. Studied: Reaugh; Goff; M. Bonner. Member: FRAC; Dallas AA. Exhibited: TAFW 1936; TCE; DMFA; DAA. Sources: Bywaters Coll.; WWWAA.

GIBBONS, J. E. [P] Dallas. Exhibited: DAA 1930.

GIBSON, Henry Lee [S] Dallas. Birthdate: 1890. Birthplace: Arrington, Kans. Deathdate: 1966. Deathplace: Tarrant County, Tex. Studied: Washburn College w/ R. M. Gage; A. Polaske; AIC. Member: Texas Sculpture Group. Exhibited: DAA 1938; GTPA; SFT 1938; DMFA 1944; ASL of Chicago 1922; Milwaukee AI 1928. Work: Masonic Temple, Wichita, Kans.; Mulvane Mus., Topeka, Kans. Sources: Bywaters Coll.; ITD; WWWAA.

GIDEON, Sadie Cavitt [P; Por. P] Austin. Birthplace: Bryan, Tex. Studied: Hollins College; Fontainebleau; A. Hills. Sources: Fisk; O'Brien.

GIDEON, Samuel Edward [P; W; L; T; Arch.] Austin/Los Angeles. Birthdate: 1875. Birthplace: Louisville, Ky. Studied: MIT; Harvard; Columbia; École BA. Member: TFAA; SSAL; Amer. Inst. of Arch.; Laguna Beach AA. Exhibited: TAFW; SACE 1927, 1928; TAEN (pr.); Grand Central Gall.; SSAL; DMFA; MFAH; FWAM; PAFA (?); TFWC 1931; Witte 1934 (solo); TWF 1917. Work: Stark. Sources: Fielding; Fisk; O'Brien; Samuels; *San Antonio Express; San Antonio Light;* Smith; Witte; WWWAA.

GILBERT, Carrie [P] Galveston? Exhibited: Texas Coast Fair 1895.

GILCHRIST, Mrs. C. F. [P] Fort Worth. Exhibited: TAFW 1932.

GILES, Annie T. [P] Dallas. Exhibited: DAA 1928.

GILES, Fred P. [P] Fort Worth. Exhibited: TAFW 1933–36.

GILES, Lorita [P; Pm] San Antonio. Studied: C. Duer. Member: San Antonio Pm. Exhibited: SALA; TG 1942, 1943; ATPE 1945; SAP 1941; LOC 1944. Work: Witte. Sources: *San Antonio Express; San Antonio Light;* Witte files.

GILLEAN, Mrs. J. A. [P] Dallas. Exhibited: DAA.

GILLESPIE, Sallie Meredith [P; T] Fort Worth. Studied: Newcomb College; Montana Univ.; Philadelphia Sch. of Art. Member: FWPC. Exhibited: TAFW. Sources: Fisk.

GILLUM, Mrs. Don M. [P] Austin. Exhibited: TFWC 1931.

GIRAND, Mrs. W. D. (GIRAUD, Elizabeth M.?) [P] Lubbock. Member: Lubbock AA. Exhibited: Lubbock AA 1933.

GIRAUD, Elizabeth M. (GIRAND, Mrs. W. D.?) [P] Lubbock. Exhibited: WTAE 1942.

GITNICK, Ben [S] Dallas. Member: Texas Sculpture Group. Exhibited: DMFA 1944; DAA 1943.

GJURANOVIC, Mato [P] Galveston. Birthplace: Yugoslavia. Deathdate: 1973. Deathplace: Yugoslavia. Studied: Univ. of Zadar; Venetian Sch. of Art. Exhibited: Galveston 1922 (solo); TAFW 1922, 1925; MFAH; San Antonio; PAFA 1932; Corcoran; Grand Central Gall. Work: RL Sources: Falk PAFA; *Galveston Daily News;* O'Brien; RL; WWWAA.

GLAESER, Edwin Hampton [P; Comm. A] New Ulm, Tex. Birthdate: 1890. Birthplace: Austin Co., Tex. Deathdate: 1979. Deathplace: New Ulm. Studied: Chappell; Broadmoor.

GLASGOW, Octavia [P] El Paso. Exhibited: EPWC.

GLASGOW, Ruth [P] Dallas. Studied: AID. Exhibited: TAFW 1933; DMFA 1935; DAA. Sources: O'Brien.

GLASS, Frances W. [P] Fort Worth. Exhibited: TAFW 1925.

GLASSCOCK, Margaret [S; T] San Antonio. Studied: W. B. Humphries; F. Booth; USC. Exhibited: SALA; TG 1941S; ASET 1937, 1939; TFAA 1938; SSAL; All-Texas Sculptors 1941. Sources: *San Antonio Express; San Antonio Light;* Witte files.

GOATZ, Mary Ruth [P] Waco. Exhibited: WTAE 1940.

GODFREY, Dorothy [Des.] Dallas. Exhibited: DAA 1929.

GOETZ, Gertrude [P] El Paso. Exhibited: TFWC 1931.

GOFF, Lloyd Lhozes [P; Mur. P; T; W] Dallas/Albuquerque/New York. Birthdate: 1908. Birthplace: Dallas. Deathdate: 1982. Deathplace: New York, N.Y. Studied: Reaugh; Simkins; F. Klepper; N. D. Clements; AJ; Acad. Chaumière; ASL w/ Nicolaides, Grosz. Member: FRAC; Klepper AC; ASL; AAPL. Exhibited: FRAC; TAFW; SFT 1931; TCE; GTPA; TPan; NAD 1938; PAFA 1938, 1943; WFNY; Whitney. Work: DMA; PPHM; SMU; MoMA; Whitney. Murals: Cooper, Tex.; Hollis, Okla. Sources: Bywaters Coll.; Falk NAD; Falk PAFA; Fisk; Index to Probate Birth Records; O'Brien; Stewart; WWWAA.

GOLDSTEIN, Louise Marks (Mrs. Maurice) [P] Sherman. Birthdate: 1899. Birthplace: Corsicana, Tex. Studied: Kidd-Key College; Austin College; Belmont College, Tenn.; ASL; Provincetown w/ G. Browne. Member: TFAA; Provincetown AA. Exhibited: TAFW 1928; TCE; SFT; Provincetown AA; AFA 1939. Work: Austin College. Sources: O'Brien; WWWAA.

GOLSON, Mrs. Edward M. [P] San Antonio. Exhibited: SALA 1930.

GONIEWICH, Arthur F. [P] San Antonio. Exhibited: SALA 1940.

GONZALES, Boyer [P] Galveston/Woodstock, N.Y. Birthdate: 1867. Birthplace: Houston. Deathdate: 1934. Deathplace: Galveston. Studied: ASL; Woodstock w/ B. Harrison; Holland; Paris; Florence. Member: TFAA; New York WCC; NAC; Amer. WCS; Washington WCC; Mississippi AA; Salmagundi. Exhibited: Texas Coast Fair 1895; Cotton Carn. 1910–12; Greenville 1924; MFAH 1927;

SACE; SFT; TAFW; Babcock Gall.; LPE. Work: Galveston AL; Witte; RL; Vanderpoel. Sources: Fielding; Fisk; O'Brien; *New Handbook;* Samuels; Smith; Steinfeldt; WWWAA.

GONZALES, Boyer, Jr. [P; T] Austin. Birthdate: 1909. Birthplace: Galveston. Deathdate: 1987. Deathplace: Seattle. Studied: Univ. Virginia; Woodstock; McFee; Kuniyoshi. Member: Woodstock AA; SSAL. Exhibited: SFT 1934; TCE; GTPA; MFAH; ASET; SALA; TG 1940–43; TPan; DMA; SSAL; Corcoran; WFNY; Golden Gate Exposition 1939. Work: Witte; DMA; Univ. Washington. Sources: *New Handbook;* Steinfeldt; WWWAA.

GONZALEZ, Cavier (Xavier?) [P] San Antonio. Exhibited: TFWC 1931.

GONZALEZ, J. Reuben [P] San Antonio. Exhibited: SALA.

GONZALEZ, Xavier [P; T; Mur. P] Alpine/San Antonio/New York. Birthdate: 1898. Birthplace: Andalusia, Spain. Deathdate: 1993. Deathplace: New York, N.Y. Studied: AIC; Arpa; San Carlos Acad., Mexico City. Member: SAAL. Exhibited: TAFW 1930; Witte; SACE; TFWC 1931; GTPA; SALA; WTAE 1939. Work: Witte; MAMFW; DMA; OJAC. Murals: USPO, Hammond, La.; Courthouse, Huntsville, Ala. Sources: Fisk; *New Handbook;* O'Brien; Samuels; Smith; Steinfeldt; WWWAA.

GOODE, Phillip [P] Dallas. Exhibited: DAA 1933.

GOODE, Robert E., Jr. [P] Houston. Exhibited: AHAE.

GOODELL, Mrs. Joe [P] El Paso. Exhibited: EPWC 1937.

GOODWON, Lucy [P] El Paso. Exhibited: EPWC 1936.

GORDON, Allyn [P] Houston. Exhibited: AHAE; ASET; TG 1940.

GORDON, Boris Bernhard [P; Port. P] Houston. Exhibited: Cotton Carn. 1910. Work: TCapitol; MFAH. Sources: *Galveston Daily News.*

GORDON, Clara F. [P] San Antonio. Exhibited: SACE 1927; SALA 1931; Arpa Students, Witte 1928. Sources: *San Antonio Express;* Witte files.

GORDON, Glenn [P] Dallas. Exhibited: DAA 1938.

GORDON, Louise [P] Dallas/Fort Worth. Exhibited: DAA 1943; TG 1943.

GORDON-CUMMING, Mary Elizabeth [P; T] Canyon, Tex. Birthdate: 1878. Birthplace: Dallas Co., Tex. Member: Panhandle-Plains Hist. Soc. Sources: *The Randall County Story.*

GORMAN, Mary Roberta Nichols [Por. P; P] El Paso. Studied: Philadelphia. Exhibited: EPWC; SACE 1928; EPCC. Sources: Price.

GOULD, C. D. [P] Houston. Exhibited: AHAE.

GRACE, Katherine [P] Weimer, Tex. Exhibited: TFWC 1931.

GRAHAM, Mysie (Mrs. Tillghman) [P] Fort Worth. Exhibited: TAFW 1910, 1914.

GRAHAM, Sylvia [D] San Antonio. Exhibited: SALA 1944.

GRANBERRY, C. R. [P] Austin. Birthdate: 1899. Exhibited: GTPA.

GRANBERY, Irene McLarty [P; Pm; S; Des.] Paris, Tex. Birthplace: Henderson, Tex. Studied: ASL w/ DuMond, Olinsky, Mora, Brackman; Acad. Chaumière; A. Dow; Sch. of Industrial and FA, Newark. Member: Nat. Soc. Craftsmen. Exhibited: Solo at Paris, Tyler, Henderson; SFT; Salons of America, Rockefeller Ctr. Sources: O'Brien.

GRANDSTAFF, Harriet Phillips [P; T] Dallas. Birthdate: 1895. Birthplace: Longview. Studied: Reaugh; L. O. Griffith; Anspaugh AS; Columbia. Member: FRAC. Exhibited: FRAC; DAA 1933; SFT 1934. Work: PPHM. Sources: Fisk; Mallett; O'Brien; WWWAA.

GRANT, Florence B. [P] Houston. Exhibited: AHAE.

GRANVILLE, Robert [S] Fort Worth. Exhibited: TG 1941S, 1941F.

GRAVES, E. W. [P] Post, Tex. Exhibited: TFWC 1931.

GRAVES, Mattie Primrose [P] Ysleta, Tex. Exhibited: TAFW 1931–33, 1935.

GRAVES, Milton St. John [P] El Paso. Exhibited: EPWC 1927.

GRAVES, Mrs. Milton St. John [P] El Paso. Exhibited: EPWC; Desert Art Shop, El Paso, 1935. Sources: *El Paso Herald;* EPPL; *El Paso Times;* EPWC scrapbooks.

GRAY, Daisy Gidney [P] Plainview, Tex. Exhibited: TFWC 1931.

GRAY, Estelle Walker [P; T; Cer.] San Antonio. Deathdate: 1950. Deathplace: San Antonio. Studied: TSCW. Member: Daughters of the Amer. Revolution; SAAL; SACG; TFAA. Exhibited: SALA. Sources: *San Antonio Light; San Antonio Teachers' Council News Bulletin;* Witte files.

GRAY, Margaret [P] Cooper, Tex. Exhibited: TAFW 1926, 1930; TFWC 1931.

GRAZIANA, Sante [P; Pm; T] San Antonio/Cleveland, Ohio. Birthdate: 1920. Birthplace: Cleveland. Studied: Cleveland Sch. of Art; Yale. Member: Nat. Soc. Mural Painters. Exhibited: ATPE 1945; Met. 1942; Carnegie 1941; NAD 1942; Cleveland MA 1937–41. Work: Murals: USPOs; Springfield MA. Sources: WWWAA.

GREATHOUSE, Bess [P] Corpus Christi. Exhibited: SSAL.

GREATHOUSE, Carrie (Mrs. G. W.) [P; T] Fort Worth. Birthplace: Allenton/Colorado City, Tex. Studied: AIC; Broadmoor; Reaugh; K. Cherry; F. Neudescher. Member: Dowe AC; FRAC; SSAL; FWAA; TFAA (board); TFWC. Exhibited: TAFW; TFWC 1931. Sources: Fisk, O'Brien; WWWAA.

GREBENAK, Louis Arthur [P; Pm] San Antonio/Cleveland, Ohio. Birthdate: 1913. Birthplace: Wasson, Ill. Studied: P. B. Travis. Exhibited: ATPE 1945; Cleveland MA 1939. Work: Cleveland Board of Education. Sources: WWWAA.

GREEN (GREENE), Ellis [P] San Antonio. Exhibited: SACE 1929; SALA. Sources: Witte files.

GREEN, Abner [P] Houston. Exhibited: AHAE.

GREEN, Katherine [P] Beaumont. Birthdate: 1907. Birthplace: Beaumont. Studied: Rosary College, Ill.; UT w/ R. Everett; J. Barber; A. Hogue. Member: SSAL. Exhibited: TAFW 1936; TCE; ASET 1937.

GREEN, Leona G. [P] San Antonio. Exhibited: TG 1945.

GREEN, Martha Wood [P] Hillsboro. Exhibited: TFWC 1931.

GREEN, Mary Rowena "Rena" Maverick (Mrs. Robert B.) [P; T; W] San Antonio. Birthdate: 1874. Birthplace: Sedalia, Mo. Deathdate: 1962. Deathplace: San Antonio. Studied: Columbia; Provincetown; M. Sterne; C. Martin. Member: SSAL; San Antonio AA; Yanaguana (ph.); Texas State Historical Assoc.; Daughters of the Amer. Revolution; DRT. Exhibited: TAFW 1934; TCE; SALA; TFAA; SSAL 1929, 1940; Witte 1945 (solo). Sources: *New Handbook;* O'Brien; WWWAA.

GREEN, R. H. [S] San Antonio. Exhibited: SALA 1934.

GREEN, Mrs. W. E. [P] El Paso. Exhibited: EPWC 1944.

GREENING, C. R. [P] San Antonio. Exhibited: SALA 1936.

GREER, Aubrey Dale (A. D.) [P; Mur. P; Comm. A] Houston/Austin. Birthdate: 1904. Birthplace: Pondcreek, Okla. Deathdate: 1998. Deathplace: Austin. Studied: St. John's Military Acad., Salina, Kans.; R. Wood; mostly self-taught. Exhibited: Allen Art Galleries, Houston, 1938. Work: Church murals in San Antonio, Brownsville, and Marshall. Sources: Sherwood's Gallery, Houston; *Southwest Art.* Moved to Texas 1928.

GREER, Jefferson Elliott [P; Mur. P; S; Car.; I] Wellington/Bristol, R.I. Birthdate: 1905. Birthplace: Chicago. Studied: Univ. Wisconsin; Chicago Acad. FA; Loyton AI. Exhibited: TAFW 1936; TCE; El Paso (solo); Loyton Art Gall. Work: USPO, Prairie du Chien, Wis. Sources: DAS; Fielding; O'Brien; Samuels; WWWAA.

GREGORY, Jack W. [P] Houston. Birthdate: 1915. Exhibited: AHAE 1937; GTPA.

GRENET, Louis Edward [P; Por. P] San Antonio. Birthdate: 1856. Birthplace: San Antonio. Deathdate: 1922. Deathplace: Paris, France. Studied: ASL; NAD; Bouguereau; Robert-Fleury. Exhibited: Yanaguana (ph.); Paris salons. Work: Witte. Sources: *New Handbook;* O'Brien; Pinckney; Samuels; Steinfeldt; Utterbeck; WWWAA.

GRESHAM, Josephine C. Mann (Mrs. Walter) [P] Galveston. Birthdate: 1844. Birthplace: St. Joseph's Island, Tex. Deathdate: 1933. Deathplace: Galveston? Studied: Self-taught. Exhibited: Texas Coast Fair 1895. Work: Bishop's Palace, Galveston. Sources: RL.

GRIBBLE, Miss [P] Galveston? Exhibited: Texas Coast Fair 1895.

GRICE, (GRISE?) Hendrik [P] Dallas. Exhibited: DAA.

GRIFFITH, John [P; Mur. P] San Antonio/Chicago. Studied: J. Arpa; X. Gonzalez; Chicago. Exhibited: SALA; San Pedro Playhouse 1932; Witte 1933; Witte 1935 (solo). Sources: *San Antonio Evening News; San Antonio Express; San Antonio Light;* Witte files.

GRIFFITH, Mildred [Des.] Dallas. Exhibited: DAA 1929.

GRIGGS, Kate Brown (Catherine Elizabeth Griggs) [P; T] Orange/San Marcos. Birthdate: 1874. Deathdate: 1968. Studied: Coronel Inst., San Marcos. Exhibited: TAFW 1926, 1928. Work: Stark MA. Sources: Stark MA files.

GRIMES, Mrs. E. E. [P] Temple. Exhibited: TFWC 1931.

GRISWOLD, J. C. [D] San Antonio. Exhibited: SALA.

GROCE, John H., Jr. [D] Houston. Exhibited: AHAE.

GROOMS, Mrs. Fred [P; China P] El Paso. Member: EPAG. Exhibited: EPWC 1923, 1935, 1936. Sources: *El Paso Herald;* EPPL; Price.

GROOMS, Mrs. M. O. [P] Rock Springs, Tex. Exhibited: TFWC 1931.

GRUBBS, Kathleen Burkett (Mrs. Carl C.) [P] Fort Worth/Abilene. Studied: Plotkin. Exhibited: TAFW 1930. Sources: Fisk.

GRUBER, Ruth [P] Dallas. Exhibited: TG 1941F, 1944.

GRUNBAUM, Marianne [P] Houston. Exhibited: AHAE 1943.

GUDE, Gerard E. [P] Dallas. Studied: Amsterdam w/ S. Maris, P. Mondrian. Exhibited: TAFW 1917; SFT 1920. Sources: Dallas Hist. Soc. files.

GUDGER, Mureil Ruth [P] El Paso. Exhibited: SACE 1928; EPWC 1935–36. Sources: Witte files.

GUERRA, Alfredo G. [P; I; Des.; S; Mur. P] San Antonio/ Houston/New York. Birthdate: 1908. Birthplace: Coahuila, Mexico. Deathdate: 1987. Deathplace: New York, N.Y. Studied: B. Williams; Arpa; Gonzalez. Member: Villita Art Gall.; Nat. Arts Cl. Exhibited: TCE; Witte; ASET 1937; SALA; TG 1940; TAFW 1934; Witte 1939 (solo). Work: TAM-Kingsville. Sources: O'Brien; *San Antonio Express;* Witte files.

GUERRO, Gustave [P] El Paso. Exhibited: EPWC.

GUGENHEIM, Irma [P] San Antonio. Exhibited: SALA.

GUIDROZ, Emile Samuel [P; Mur. P] Fort Worth. Birthdate: 1906. Birthplace: Welsh, La. Living Fort Worth, 1997. Studied: TCU w/ Cockrell; O. Travis; K. H. Travis; ASL w/ B. Robinson; AIC. Exhibited: DAA 1928; TCE. Work: Fort Worth Central HS. Sources: O'Brien.

GUILBEAU, Honore Cooke [P; Pm] Dallas/Cleveland, Ohio. Birthdate: 1907. Birthplace: Baton Rouge, La. Studied: SMU w/ O. Donaldson; AIC. Member: Cleveland Pm. Exhibited: TCE; HPAG 1930 (solo); DAA; AIC 1930, 1936; Cleveland MA 1936. Work: DMA; AIC. Sources: Falk AIC; O'Brien; WWWAA.

GUILLOT, Ann [P] Dallas. Birthdate: 1875. Birthplace: Kentucky. Studied: D. Garber; W. Robinson; M. Mason; B. M. Peyton. Member: HPSA; FRAC; SSAL; TFAA; DWF. Exhibited: TAFW; DWF 1922; Stoneleigh Court, Dallas 1928; FRAC; SFT 1934; Ney Mus. 1935; TCE; DAA; Lubbock; Wichita Falls. Work: DWF; Seibold Hotel, Fort Worth. Sources: Fisk, Mallett, O'Brien; WWWAA.

GURLEY, Loulie [P] Waco. Exhibited: TG 1941S.

GUTHRIE, Emily. See SMITH, Emily Guthrie

GUZZARDI, Rodolfo [P; T] Houston. Birthdate: 1903. Birthplace: Florence, Italy. Studied: Self-taught. Sources: Nicodemi. Directed Sacred Heart Dominican College art department, Houston.

HAAS, F. W. J. [P] Houston. Exhibited: AHAE.

HACKETT, Nelson G. [P] Fort Worth/Fayette, Mo. Exhibited: TAFW 1910, 1912, 1912. Sources: WWWAA.

HADRA, Ida Weisselberg [P; Por. P] Austin/San Antonio. Birthdate: 1861. Birthplace: Castroville, Tex. Deathdate: 1885. Deathplace: San Antonio. Studied: Duval; Lungkwitz. Work: Witte. Sources: *New Handbook;* Pinckney; Samuels; Steinfeldt.

HAFFNER, Mrs. S. [P] El Paso. Exhibited: EPWC 1936.

HAGARD, Nettie May [S] Dallas. Member: FRAC. Exhibited: FRAC 1932; DAA 1933. Sources: PPHM files.

HAGENDORN, Max [P; Des.; T] Dallas/Sharon, Mass./ Topeka, Kans. Birthdate: 1870. Birthplace: Stuttgart, Germany. Studied: Royal Academy, Stuttgart. Member: Dallas AA; Dallas Painters. Exhibited: LPE (grand pr.); SFT 1908, 1909; TAFW 1910; Cotton Carn. 1911. Work: Munich; Stuttgart; MFA, Boston. Sources: WWWAA.

HAGGART, Mrs. Walter [P] El Paso. Exhibited: EPWC 1927.

HAGNER, Lillie May (Mrs. Ben Saenger) [Pm; P; T; W] San Antonio. Birthdate: 1903. Birthplace: San Antonio. Deathdate: 1985. Deathplace: San Antonio. Studied: Baylor Female College; Witte; Met. Member: Coppini Acad.; San Antonio Conservation Soc.; San Antonio Pm. Exhibited: SALA; TG 1940; ASET 1937, 1938; Witte 1941 (solo); San Antonio Pm 1938. Work: Witte. Sources: Witte files.

HAINES, Marie Bruner [P; Mur. P; Por. P; Pm] College Station, Tex. Birthdate: 1884. Birthplace: Cincinnati, Ohio. Studied: Cincinnati Art Acad.; Pennsylvania Sch. of Industrial Art; AIC; NAD; ASL; Woodstock; Provincetown; Ogunquit, Maine; Taos. Member: SSAL (charter). Exhibited: TAFW; SACE 1928, 1929; DWF 1928; HPAG 1928 (solo); UCE 2; ASET 1937; SSAL 1927. Work: TAMU; MNM; Iowa State Univ. Sources: Fielding; Fisk; Mallett; O'Brien; Samuels; WWWAA.

HAINES, Roberta [P] Dallas. Exhibited: DAA 1928.

HALBARDIER, Mrs. E. W. [P] San Antonio. Exhibited: SALA 1936.

HALE, Isabelle Mayes [P; Cer.] Austin. Birthplace: Brownwood, Tex. Studied: UT w/ S. E. Gideon; OU; Columbia. Sources: O'Brien.

HALEY, Mrs. R. [P] Seagraves, Tex. Exhibited: TFWC 1931.

HALL, Lucille (Mrs. Norman) [P] El Paso/San Antonio. Studied: C. Kay-Scott. Exhibited: EPWC. Sources: Price.

HALL, Margaret de Camp [P] San Antonio. Exhibited: SALA 1940, 1943.

HALTOM, Minnie Hollis [P; Pm; T] San Antonio. Birthdate: 1889. Birthplace: Belton, Tex. Studied: R. Taylor; E. P. McGill; J. Arpa; Met. SFA.; X. Gonzalez; M. Jacobs; B. Wall. Member: SSAL; SAAL; NAWPS; SAAG; TFAA; AAPL. Exhibited: TAFW; TFWC 1931; SAAG 1927; Austin Women's Cl. 1937; SALA 1930; SAAL. Work: Witte. Sources: Fielding; Fisk; Mallett; O'Brien; Smith; Steinfeldt; Witte files; WWWAA.

HAM, G. Suttle [S] Houston. Exhibited: AHAE 1929.

HAMBURG, Dorothy [P] Dallas. Exhibited: DAA 1929.

HAMILTON, Blanche [P] El Paso. Exhibited: EPWC 1942–45.

HAMILTON, J. L. [P] Sinton, Tex. Exhibited: TFWC 1931.

HAMILTON, Willie [P] El Paso. Exhibited: TFWC 1931.

HAMLYN, Edwin [P] El Paso. Exhibited: EPWC 1936.

HAMM, W. Howard [Pm] Houston. Exhibited: AHAE 1938.

HAMMARGREN, Frederick Emmanuel [S] Houston/ Los Angeles. Birthdate: 1892. Birthplace: Orebro, Sweden. Studied: Gothenburg AS, Sweden; Bourdelle in Paris. Member: NSS. Exhibited: AHAE; Chic. Acad. FA; Montclair AM; AAPL. Work: Morton Bldg., Phila; Brooklyn Mus; Newark Mus. Sources: DAS; Fielding; WWWAA.

HAMON, Voila [P] Fort Worth. Exhibited: TAFW 1935.

HANNA, (Mrs.) [P] Galveston? Exhibited: Texas Coast Fair 1895.

HANSEN, Douglas Reid [P; T] Houston/Columbia, Mo. Birthdate: 1900. Birthplace: Jersey City, N.J. Studied: Corcoran; ASL; NAD; R. Reid; B. Sandzen; C. Hawthorn; Broadmoor; Fontainebleau; Vienna. Exhibited: TAFW; AHAE; Houston (solo); SSAL; Toledo Mus.; KCAI; St. Louis Mus. FA. Sources: Fisk; WWWAA.

HANSZEN, O. [P] Dallas. Exhibited: DAA 1933.

HARDIN, Ernest R. [Des.; Dec.; P; Pm] Austin/ Georgetown. Birthdate: 1902. Birthplace: Granger, Tex. Studied: G. E. Browne; W. Adams; AIC; SMU; UT, Austin; Columbia; Southwestern Univ., Ill. Univ. Member:

SSAL. Exhibited: SACE; TAFW; TFWC 1931; UCE 1; TCE; SFT 1939; ASET; TG 1941S. Sources: O'Brien; WWWAA.

HARDINGE, Sarah Ann Lillie [P; T] Guadalupe Co., Tex. Birthdate: 1824. Birthplace: New England. Deathdate: 1913. Deathplace: East Orange, N.J. Studied: Self-taught. Work: Amon Carter. Sources: Ratcliffe; Tyler bio.

HARDMAN, Mary [P] San Antonio. Exhibited: SALA.

HARDWICKE, Lindsey (Mrs. A. S.) [P] Dallas. Member: FRAC. Exhibited: FRAC 1930; DAA 1931; TFWC 1931; TAFW 1937.

HARDY, E. J. [P] Galveston. Exhibited: Cotton Carn. 1910.

HARE, Vida [P] Houston. Exhibited: AHAE.

HARGIS, Mrs. O. D. [P] Lubbock. Member: Lubbock AA. Exhibited: Lubbock AA 1933. Sources: Wilbanks.

HARKEY, Gladys [P] Lubbock. Member: Lubbock AA. Exhibited: Lubbock AA 1933.

HARLACKER, Eula (Mrs. John) [P] El Paso. Exhibited: EPWC; El Paso Centennial Mus. 1937. Sources: *El Paso Herald-Post.*

HARLE, Annie L. [P; T] Abilene/Thorpe Springs/El Paso. Birthplace: Paris, Tex. Deathdate: 1922. Deathplace: Abilene. Studied: Newberry Boarding Sch.; C. Cherry; Bischoff; Lykoff; Met. SFA. Sources: Fisk.

HAROLD, Elizabeth [Des.] Dallas. Exhibited: DAA 1929.

HARPER, Judith [P] San Antonio. Exhibited: SALA 1930, 1931.

HARPER, Roberta Blewett [P; D] Beaumont. Birthdate: 1905. Exhibited: AHAE 1935; DAA 1935; TCE; GTPA.

HARPHAM, Carolyn (Caroline?) Rose [P] San Antonio. Exhibited: SACE 1927; TAFW 1927; SALA. Sources: Witte files.

HARRELL, C. E. (or C. F.) [P] Dallas. Exhibited: SFT 1907; Crawford Gall. 1907.

HARRELL, Elizabeth [P] Agua Dulce, Tex. Exhibited: TAFW 1934–35.

HARRELL, Joi Faye. See CARRINGTON, Joi

HARRIS, Elias B. [P; Por. P] Galveston. Birthdate: 1877. Birthplace: San Francisco. Deathdate: 1954. Deathplace: Galveston. Studied: NAD. Exhibited: SFT 1910; Cotton Carn. 1910–12. Work: RL; Polio Found., Warm Springs, Ga. Sources: RL; Galveston Tribune.

HARRIS, Georgia Maverick [P; T] San Antonio. Birthdate: 1889. Birthplace: San Antonio. Studied: H. L. McFee; H. A. De Young. Member: SSAL. Exhibited: SAAL 1938; TFAA; SALA; TG 1942; SSAL 1938, 1940. Sources: Witte files; WWWAA.

HARRIS, Helen [P] El Paso. Exhibited: EPWC.

HARRIS, Jennie [P; W] Nacogdoches. Birthplace: Nacogdoches. Deathplace: Nacogdoches. Work: Texas State Lib. Sources: O'Brien.

HARRIS, Kenneth [P; Por. P; W] Houston/Galveston. Birthdate: 1904. Exhibited: SALA 1943; TG 1944; RL Work: RL. Sources: *Galveston Daily News;* RL.

HARRISON, Polly [P] Fort Worth. Exhibited: TAFW 1934–36.

HARRISON, Ruth Dunken [P] Dallas. Exhibited: DAA 1942.

HART, Alyce M. [P] Lamesa, Tex. Birthdate: Exhibited: TFWC 1931.

HARTMAN, Donald [P] El Paso. Exhibited: EPWC 1927.

HARTZOG, E. (Miss) [P] Dallas. Birthdate: 1912. Birthplace: Whitesboro, Tex. Studied: Texas Tech; AID. Exhibited: Dallas. Sources: O'Brien.

HARWELL, Jerry, III [P] Fort Worth. Exhibited: TAFW 1932; TFWC 1931.

HARWELL, Jerry, Jr. [P] Fort Worth/Houston. Exhibited: TAFW 1929–31, 1933; AHAE; ASET 1938; TG 1940.

HASTINGS, Daniel [P] Houston. Exhibited: AHAE.

HATFIELD, Karl Leroy [P; Pm] El Paso/Santa Fe. Birthdate: 1886. Birthplace: Jacksonville, Ill. Studied: J. Montgomery; C. Kay-Scott. Member: SSAL; El Paso

AG. Exhibited: EPWC 1935. Sources: Fielding; Price; WWWAA.

HATFIELD, Larie [S] San Antonio. Exhibited: SALA 1934.

HAWKINS, Elva Jane [P] Dallas. Exhibited: TAFW 1930; DAA.

HAWKINS, Rodah [P] Dallas. Exhibited: TSFA.

HAYNES, Cade [P] Pecos. Exhibited: WTAE 1939, 1940.

HAYS, Lena Bentley [P] Abilene. Exhibited: SSAL.

HAZLEWOOD, Dollie [P] Mineral Wells, Tex. Exhibited: TAFW 1930.

HAZLEWOOD, Mrs. G. W. [P] Lubbock. Exhibited: PMS 1932. Sources: Wilbanks.

HEAPS, Belle G. [P] Houston. Exhibited: AHAE; ASET 1938.

HEDDINS, Tincie Hughs. See HUGHS, Tincie

HEDRICK, Lura Ann Taylor. See TAYLOR, Lura Ann

HEESCHE, Ursula H. [P] Houston. Exhibited: AHAE 1944.

HEIRHOLZER, Joan [D] San Antonio. Exhibited: SALA 1944.

HEISLER, Mary [P] Anahuac. Exhibited: TFWC 1931; ASET 1937.

HELFENSTELLER, Veronica (Mrs. H. O.) [P; Pm] Fort Worth. Birthdate: 1910. Birthplace: Fort Worth. Deathdate: 1964. Deathplace: Tucson, Ariz. Studied: FWSFA w/ McVeigh, Sellors, Jolley; SLSFA; CSFAC. Member: TP; SSAL; Calif. WCS; Baltimore WCS; Southern Pm. Exhibited: Fort Worth AL; SFT 1938; TG 1944; ATPE 1941, 1944; TPan; SixTP; SSAL. Work: OJAC; MFAH; MAMFW. Sources: Harris; Mallett; *New Handbook*; TPan m.; *Beyond Regionalism*; Stewart.

HELLER, Ruth S. [P] Houston. Exhibited: AHAE 1943.

HELLMAN, Bertha Louise (Liza) [P; I; Mur. P; C; T] Houston. Birthdate: 1900. Birthplace: La Grange, Tex.

Deathdate: 1976. Studied: Rice; PAFA; Lhote; Vytlacil. Member: SSAL; PAFA. Exhibited: MFAH 1925 (solo); AHAE; TAFW; TWCE; TCE; SFT; SSAL; SACE? Work: MFAH. Mural: USPO, Houston. Sources: Fielding; Houston PL; Mallet; O'Brien; WWWAA.

HENAGAN, Beth Coombes [P] Abilene. Exhibited: WTAE 1939–42.

HENARD, Mildred (Millie) [P] Wellington/San Antonio. Member: Lubbock AA. Exhibited: Lubbock AA 1933; TG 1945. Sources: Wilbanks.

HENDERSON, Dorothy [D] San Antonio. Exhibited: SALA 1933.

HENDERSON, Everett R. [P] Dallas. Exhibited: DAA.

HENDERSON, Norma [Pm] Houston. Exhibited: AHAE 1944.

HENDRICKS, Bernice [P] San Antonio. Exhibited: SALA 1944.

HENDRICKS, Emma Stockman (Mrs. H. G.) [P; T; W] Amarillo/San Antonio. Birthdate: 1868. Birthplace: Solano Co., Calif. Deathdate: 1959. Deathplace: Natalia, Tex. Studied: San Francisco AI; NAD; Broadmoor; Lawson; Cassidy; Arpa; Brunet; Davey. Member: Amarillo AA; SAAL; TFAA; SIA; AFA; SSAL. Exhibited: TSFA; CPE 1927; TAFW; Amarillo 1931 (solo); TFWC 1931; SALA; Texas Tech Mus. 1935. Work: Amarillo PL; PPHM. Sources: Fielding; Fisk; Mallett; O'Brien; Samuels; Smith; WWWAA.

HENKEL, Estella M. [P; Weaver] Dallas. Birthdate: 1889. Birthplace: Fort Worth. Studied: TSCW; Univ. Tennessee. Member: Craft Guild, Dallas. Exhibited: TAFW 1936; TCE; SFT 1939; DAA. Sources: Bywaters Coll.

HENRY, Rebecca Harriett [P; T; Pm] Houston. Birthplace: Tennessee. Studied: Peabody College, Nashville; AIC. Member: SSAL; HAG. Exhibited: TAFW 1928–37; AHAE; SSAL 1933. Sources: O'Brien; WWWAA.

HENRY, William E. [Por. P] Birthdate: 1831. Birthplace: Texas. Sources: Pinckney.

HERMANN, Emil [Por. P; Mur. P] Wichita Falls. Birthdate: 1870. Birthplace: Vienna, Austria. Deathdate: 1966. Deathplace: Wichita Falls. Studied: Royal Acad.,

Vienna; Nat. AI, Budapest; Rembrandt AI, Amsterdam; PAFA. Member: Ohio Brush and Pencil Cl.; Mason. Exhibited: Freer Furniture Company, Wichita Falls, 1919. Work: TCapitol; Wichita Falls HS. Sources: O'Brien; *Wichita Falls Times.*

HERMANN, Wanda de Turczynowicz [P] El Paso. Birthdate: 1908. Birthplace: Krakow, Poland. Studied: Ontario College of Art; Troubetsky; Heatherington. Member: EPAA; Polish AC, Chicago. Exhibited: EPWC. Sources: *El Paso Herald-Post;* EPPL; *El Paso Times.*

HERMON, Lillian Mills [P] Houston. Exhibited: AHAE.

HERNANDEZ, Damaso (Demaso) [P] San Antonio. Exhibited: SALA; TG 1945.

HERNANDEZ, William G. [P] El Paso. Exhibited: EPWC 1942.

HERNDON, Maxwell [P] El Paso. Exhibited: EPWC.

HERRICK, Anne [P] San Antonio. Exhibited: SALA 1944.

HERRINGTON, Walter S. [P] Houston. Exhibited: ASET 1938.

HERTFORD, Estelle Graham (Mrs. J. W.) [P] Galveston. Deathdate: 1946. Deathplace: Galveston. Exhibited: Texas Coast Fair 1895. Sources: RL.

HERWIG, Elgie [P] Houston. Exhibited: AHAE 1945.

HESSER, Yvonne [P] Houston. Exhibited: ASET 1937.

HEWITT, Lea [P] Houston. Exhibited: AHAE.

HIBINO, Tamakichi (Carl) [P] El Paso. Birthdate: 1900. Birthplace: Gifu, Japan. Studied: F. Ellis. Exhibited: TAFW 1932; EPWC 1935, 1937. Sources: *El Paso Herald-Post;* EPPL; *El Paso Times;* Price.

HICKS, Zetha [P] El Paso. Exhibited: EPWC.

HIGGINS, Mrs. C. C. [P] San Antonio. Exhibited: SALA.

HIGGINS, G. Y. [P] Dallas. Member: FRAC. Exhibited: FRAC 1933, 1934. Sources: PPHM files.

HIGGINS, Sophia Shaw [P] San Antonio. Exhibited: SALA.

HIGGINS, William Victor [P] Taos, N.M./San Antonio. Birthdate: 1884. Birthplace: Shelbyville, Ind. Deathdate: 1949. Deathplace: Taos. Studied: AIC; Chicago Acad. FA; Acad. Chaumière; R. Henri. Member: NAD; Taos Soc. of Artists. Exhibited: SFT 1939; AIC; NAD; PAFA; Corcoran. Work: Chicago Union League; DMA; Harwood; MNM; Notre Dame; Santa Fe Railroad, Schaumberg, Ill.; Terre Haute AA. Sources: Dallas Hist. Soc. files; Fielding; Porter bio.; Samuels; WWWAA.

HIGLEY, H. D. [P] San Antonio. Exhibited: SALA.

HILD, Scott Lee [P] Houston. Exhibited: AHAE.

HILL, Mrs. Ben A. [P] Canadian, Tex. Exhibited: TFWC 1931.

HILL, Mrs. Guy P. [P] Mount Vernon, Tex. Exhibited: TFWC 1931.

HILL, Mrs. J. Culver [P] Lubbock. Member: Lubbock AA. Exhibited: Lubbock AA 1933. Sources: Wilbanks.

HILL, Mary Vandenberge [Min. P] Houston. Exhibited: AHAE.

HILL, Nora Livingston [P] Houston. Exhibited: AHAE 1942.

HILL, Robert Jerome [P; Por. P.; Curator; I; Min. P] Dallas/Austin. Birthdate: 1878. Birthplace: Austin. Deathdate: 1942. Deathplace: Dallas. Studied: UT, Downie; ASL; W. A. Clark; Twachtman; W. M. Chase; K. Cox; Bridgman; R. Blum; H. C. Christy. Member: Dallas AA; TFAA; SSAL; FRAC. Exhibited: TAFW; SFT; DWF; DAA; FRAC; SSAL. Work: Stephen F. Austin State Univ., Nacogdoches. Sources: Church; Fielding; Fisk; *New Handbook;* O'Brien; Samuels; Smith; WWWAA.

HILTON, Ethel G. [P] Galveston. Deathdate: 1964. Deathplace: Galveston. Member: Galveston AL (board). Exhibited: Cotton Carn. 1912. Sources: Galveston City Directory, 1919–64; RL.

HINDERLANG, Edna [P] San Antonio. Exhibited: SALA.

HINES, Adrian R. [S] Houston. Exhibited: AHAE 1930.

HINKLE, Gladys Gaffield (Mrs. Stacy) [P] El Paso. Exhibited: EPWC 1927; Turner Art Gall., Denver.

HINNANT, Tom J., Jr. [P; Pm] San Antonio. Exhibited: SALA.

HINSON, Esther [D] Houston. Exhibited: AHAE 1931.

HINTON, Margaret [P; Pm] Houston. Exhibited: AHAE 1945.

HINYARD, Vera Wilson [P] San Angelo. Exhibited: TFWC 1931.

HIRSCH, Grace [D] Houston. Exhibited: AHAE.

HIRST, Sue (Mrs. W. R.) [P] Dallas. Deathdate: 1928. Deathplace: Dallas. Studied: SLSFA; M. Simkins; Reaugh. Member: Dallas AA. Exhibited: SFT 1927; DAA 1928. Work: DMA. Sources: Fisk; O'Brien.

HOBBLE, Eloise [P; Por. P] El Paso. Exhibited: EPWC; EPWC 1940 (solo); El Paso Centennial Mus. 1940 (solo). Sources: *El Paso Herald-Post;* EPPL; *El Paso Times;* Price.

HODGES, Alice Kiefer [P] Houston. Deathdate: 1969. Deathplace: Burleson County, Tex. Exhibited: AHAE 1944. Sources: ITD.

HOETING, I. A. [P] Galveston. Exhibited: Cotton Carn. 1911.

HOFFMAN, Polly (Mrs. Luther) [P; C; Dec.; T] Wichita Falls. Birthdate: 1890. Birthplace: Bryan, Tex. Studied: Pratt Inst.; H. B. Snell; A. Brunet; X. Gonzalez; Columbia; W. Stevens; H. V. Poor. Member: SSAL; TFAA. Exhibited: TFWC 1931; Wichita Falls 1933 (solo); UCE 2; TCE; WTAE 1940; TG 1945; TFAA; SSAL; Texas-Oklahoma Fair. Work: Midwestern State Univ.; First Methodist Ch., First Christian Ch., both Wichita Falls. Sources: Bywaters Coll.; Fielding; O'Brien; WWWAA.

HOGELAND, Eva [P] Beaumont. Exhibited: ASET.

HOGUE, Alexandre [P; Pm; Mur. P; T] Dallas/Tulsa. Birthdate: 1898. Birthplace: Memphis, Mo. Deathdate: 1994. Deathplace: Tulsa. Studied: Reaugh; Minneapolis Inst. Art. Member: LSP; FRAC. Exhibited: FRAC 1929; TAFW; TFWC 1931; TCE; GTPA; ATPE; LSP (all); DAA; SACE 1927; SFT; TG; TPan; WFNY; SSAL; Paris Salon 1938; Carnegie; Corcoran; MoMA; AIC; GGE. Work: DMA; NMAA; PPHM; MFAH; Philbrook; Witte; Gilcrease; Phoenix AM. Sources: Fisk; *New Handbook;*

O'Brien; Philbrook catalogue; Samuels; Smith; Stewart; WWWAA.

HOGUE, Marion N. [P] San Antonio. Exhibited: SAAG 1927.

HOHNSTEDT, Peter Lanz [P; T] Leon Springs/San Antonio/Comfort, Tex. Birthdate: 1872. Birthplace: Urbana, Ohio. Deathdate: 1957. Deathplace: Comfort. Studied: Duveneck. Member: SSAL (charter); New Orleans AA; SSAL; Little Rock AA. Exhibited: TFWC 1931; Witte 1933 (solo), 1936 (solo); SACE 1929 (pr.); TAFW 1930; UCE 1; SALA; Pabst Gall. 1934 (solo). Work: Stark; Torch; Witte. Sources: O'Brien; Steinfeldt; Witte files.

HOLDEN, Mary Helen [P] Dallas. Exhibited: DAA.

HOLLERAN, W. [P] San Antonio. Exhibited: SALA 1934.

HOLLIDAY, Nancy [D] Houston. Exhibited: AHAE 1939.

HOLLINGSWORTH, Willie [P] Fort Worth. Exhibited: TAFW 1933.

HOLLOMAN, Guy W. [P] San Antonio. Exhibited: SALA; TFWC 1931.

HOLMAN, Golda K. [P] Del Rio. Exhibited: TFWC 1931.

HOLMES, Calvin Joseph [P; Des.] Dallas. Birthdate: 1910. Studied: SMU w/ G. Kadel; V. Aunspaugh AS; W. Cole; T. M. Stell; Columbia. Member: DAL. Exhibited: TCE; DMFA; SFT; TFWC; Dallas YWCA. Sources: Bywaters Coll.; O'Brien.

HOLMES, Dwight Clay [P; Mur. P; S; T] Fort Worth/ San Angelo. Birthdate: 1900. Birthplace: Albany, Ore. Deathdate: 1986. Deathplace: San Angelo. Studied: W. L. Dodge; TCU w/ Cockrell, M. Darter, S. Ziegler. Member: FWPC; FWAA; AFA; San Angelo AC; River Art Group; Coppini Acad. Exhibited: TAFW 1925–32, 1933–37; GTPA; SFT. Work: Central Texas Mus., Salado; Coppini Acad.; PPHM; TCU. Sources: Fisk; ITD; O'Brien; PPHM files.

HOLMES, T. C. [P] San Antonio. Exhibited: SAAL 1924.

HOLT, Adelaide E. [P] Houston. Exhibited: AHAE.

HOLT, Percy William [P; T] Galveston. Birthdate: 1883. Birthplace: Mobile, Ala. Deathdate: 1958. Deathplace: Galveston. Studied: ASL w/ Harrison, Carlson; Bellows; Speicher; F. S. Chase; Rosen. Exhibited: Cotton Carn. 1912; TAFW; MFAH 1924 (solo); DWF; SSAL. Work: RL Sources: Fielding; Fisk; O'Brien; RL; Samuels; Smith; WWWAA.

HOLT, Rebecca [P] Fort Worth. Exhibited: TAFW 1937.

HOLTZ, Helmuth Heinrich Diedrich [D] Indianola/Matagorda/New Orleans. Birthdate: 1833. Birthplace: Kappeln, Schleswig. Deathdate: 1915. Deathplace: New Orleans. Sources: *New Handbook*.

HOOD, Dorothy (Mrs. Velasco Maidana) [P; Pm; T] Houston. Birthdate: 1919. Birthplace: Bryan, Tex. Deathplace: Living Houston, 1997. Studied: Rhode Island Sch. of Design; ASL. Exhibited: AHAE 1940. Work: Baylor; MAMFW; MFAH; UT; Rice; TAMU; Witte; Nat. Gall.; Whitney; MoMA; Philadelphia MA. Sources: Bywaters Coll.

HOOKS, Helen Hubbard [Pm.] Dallas. Exhibited: DAA.

HOOPER, Floy (Mrs. C. E.) [P] Lubbock/Dallas. Birthdate: 1898. Member: Lubbock AA; FRAC. Exhibited: SPCCE; TCE; PMS; Lubbock AA 1933; FRAC. Sources: *Art Digest;* Wilbanks; Witte files.

HOOTON, Claude E. [P] Houston. Exhibited: AHAE; TG 1940.

HOPPE, Carl Thomas [P] San Antonio. Birthdate: 1897. Birthplace: San Antonio. Deathdate: 1981. Deathplace: San Antonio. Studied: Arpa; R. Wood; H. Schutter. Member: Coppini Acad.; SAAL; San Antonio P&CC. Exhibited: SAAL 1926; SAAG 1927; Arpa Students, Witte 1928; SALA 1930–36; San Pedro Playhouse 1931; TFWC 1931. Work: PPHM. Sources: PPHM files; Steinfeldt; Witte files.

HOPPE, Louis [P] La Grange, Tex. Birthplace: Germany. Work: Witte. Sources: Pinckney; Ratcliffe; Steinfeldt; Utterbeck.

HOPPIN, Augustus [P; Pm; I] . Birthdate: 1828. Birthplace: Providence, R.I. Deathdate: 1896. Deathplace: Flushing, N.Y. Studied: Brown; Harvard. Work: UT. Sources: Fielding; *New Handbook;* Pinckney.

HORN, Joe Roscoe [P] McKinney. Exhibited: TAFW 1927–29.

HORNBY, Mary [P] San Antonio. Studied: J. Arpa. Exhibited: Arpa Students, Witte, 1928. Sources: Witte files.

HORNE, Eugenie Ligon [P] Orange, Tex. Exhibited: TFWC 1931.

HORNER, Ruth [P] Dallas. Exhibited: DAA 1937; SFT 1939.

HORST, Frank [P] Dallas. Birthdate: 1879. Birthplace: Vienna, Austria. Member: Dallas AA; Allied Artists of Amer. Exhibited: SFT 1922.

HORTON, Mrs. Dwight [P] Dallas. Member: FRAC. Exhibited: FRAC 1933. Sources: PPHM files.

HOSEK, Walter [D] Dallas. Exhibited: DAA 1928.

HOSKINS, Dorothy M. [P] Houston. Exhibited: AHAE 1936.

HOTVEDT, Clarence A. [P; Pm; Des.; T] Fort Worth. Birthdate: 1900. Birthplace: Eau Claire, Wis. Studied: AIC. Member: AACFW; Wichita AG; Prairie Pm; California Pm. Exhibited: TAFW 1933–36. Sources: Fielding; O'Brien; WWWAA.

HOUGHTON, Edna N. [P, T] Lubbock. Studied: Texas Tech. Member: TFAA; South Plains AG, Lubbock. Exhibited: PMS 1932; Century of Progress, Chicago; TFAA 1933–34; Lyme AA 1933. Sources: O'Brien; Wilbanks.

HOULAHAN, Eleanora [P] Galveston. Exhibited: Cotton Carn. 1910. Sources: Galveston City Directory 1908; RL.

HOULISTON, William James, Jr. [P] Houston. Birthdate: 1908. Exhibited: TAFW; TCE; SFT; ASET; MFAH 1938; TG; SSAL. Work: MFAH. Sources: Houston Chronicle; WWWAA.

HOUPY, Henry [P] Dallas. Exhibited: DAA 1933.

HOUSE, Dorothy Denslow [P] Houston. Birthdate: 1899. Exhibited: AHAE 1928–37; TCE. Sources: Mallett; "NTP."

HOUSE, Edith [P] Galveston? Exhibited: Texas Coast Fair 1895.

HOVER, Eleanor Whyte [P] Houston. Exhibited: AHAE 1926.

HOWARD, Dorcas L. (Mrs. A. E.) [P] Fort Worth. Exhibited: TAFW.

HOWARD, Eugenia. See HUNT, Eugenia Howard

HOWE, Bob [P] Dallas. Exhibited: DAA 1942.

HOWELL, Florence [P] Dallas. Member: FRAC. Exhibited: FRAC; TAFW 1935.

HOWELL, Mrs. F. L. (Florence?) Dallas. Exhibited: DAA.

HOWZE, Albert [Pm] Houston. Exhibited: AHAE 1934.

HUBBARD, Bess Bigham (Mrs. Chester A.) [Pm; S; P] Lubbock. Birthdate: 1896. Birthplace: Fort Worth. Deathdate: 1977. Deathplace: Lubbock. Studied: TCU; AFA—Chicago; B. Robinson; Dozier; Zorach; CSFAC; Medellin. Member: SSAL; TSG; TFAA; TP; Dallas Print Soc.; South Plains AG, Lubbock. Exhibited: TFWC 1931; PMS 1932; UCE 2; SPCCE; WTAE; TG 1944; ATPE; DMFA; Ney Mus.; MFAH; Witte; South Plains AG, Lubbock; SSAL; TFAA; Sch. of Amer. Research, Santa Fe; Amer. Assoc. Women Artists. Work: DMA; Longview AM; Ney Mus.; PPHM; TFAA; Texas Tech; CSFAC. Sources: Bywaters Coll.; DAS; Fielding; Harris; Havlice; *New Handbook*; Wilbanks; WWWAA.

HUBBELL, Jack [S] Dallas. Exhibited: DAA.

HUDDLE, Nannie Zenobia Carver (Mrs. William H.) [P; S] Austin. Birthdate: 1861. Birthplace: Mobile, Ala. Deathdate: 1951. Deathplace: Austin. Studied: ASL; Chase; Ney Mus.; Adams. Member: Austin AL; SSAL. Exhibited: TAFW 1926–30; Austin Women's Cl. 1933 (solo); UCE 1; SACE 1927; UCE 1; TFWC 1943 (solo). Work: PPHM; UT (Humanities Research Center and TMM). Sources: Fisk; *New Handbook*; O'Brien; Ratcliffe.

HUDDLE, William Henry [P; Por. P] Austin. Birthdate: 1847. Birthplace: Wytheville, Va. Deathdate: 1892. Deathplace: Austin. Studied: F. Fisher; NAD; ASL w/ Wilmarth; Munich. Work: DMA; TCapitol. Sources: Fisk; *New Handbook*; O'Brien; Pinckney; Ratcliffe; WWWAA.

HUDGINS, Anne G. [P] Houston. Exhibited: AHAE; TG 1943.

HUDSON, Edith Frazier (Mrs. C. E.) [P] Dallas. Birthplace: Centralia, Ill. Member: FRAC; HPSA; SSAL; AAPL. Exhibited: TAFW 1928; FRAC; DAA. Sources: PPHM files; WWWAA.

HUDSON, Jewell Harlan [P] Dallas. Exhibited: DAA 1938.

HUDSON, Ruth [P] Dallas. Exhibited: DAA 1931.

HUDSON, Sarah Dorsey Brown [P; S] Dallas. Birthdate: 1906. Birthplace: Kauffman Co., Tex. Deathdate: 1996. Deathplace: Dallas. Studied: DMFA w/ B. Delabano. Exhibited: DAA.

HUDSON, Winnie B. [P] Dallas. Exhibited: DAA 1928.

HUFSTEDLER, Mrs. E. V. [P] Dallas. Exhibited: DAA 1929.

HUGHES, Ann Louise [S] Dallas. Exhibited: DAA.

HUGHES, Bess [P] McKinney, Tex. Exhibited: TAFW 1926–28; DAA 1929.

HUGHES, Mrs. Maury (Bess?) [S] Dallas. Exhibited: DAA 1932.

HUGHES, Mildred [S] Houston. Exhibited: AHAE 1940; TG 1940, 1942; SSAL.

HUGHS, Tincie (HEDDINS, Tincie Hughs) [P] San Angelo. Birthdate: 1907. Birthplace: San Angelo. Studied: R. Bassett; X. Gonzalez; H. K. Kendall; UT; New Mexico Highlands College. Member: TFAA; San Angelo AC; SSAL. Exhibited: WTAE 1940; SSAL; Studio Guild, N.Y. Work: Murals: Ch. of Christ, San Angelo; County Courthouse, San Angelo. Sources: Bywaters Coll.; WWWAA.

HUIZAR, Pedro [S] San Antonio. Birthdate: 1740. Birthplace: Aguascalientes, Mexico. Work: Mission San Jose, San Antonio. Sources: *New Handbook*.

HUME, Kate [P] Galveston? Exhibited: Texas Coast Fair 1895.

HUNGERFORD, Homer [P] Dallas. Exhibited: SFT 1939; DAA.

HUNT, Eugenia Howard [P] Houston. Birthdate: 1910. Exhibited: TAFW 1936; TCE; AHAE.

HUNT, Mrs. J. A. (or J. H.) [P] El Paso. Exhibited: EPWC.

HUNTER, (Miss) [P] Galveston? Exhibited: Texas Coast Fair 1895.

HUNTER, George Lewis Cope [P] San Antonio. Exhibited: SALA 1939; TG 1940; SSAL.

HUNTER, John Warren [Pm; T; Mur. P; P] San Antonio/Bandera. Birthdate: 1904. Birthplace: London, Tex. Deathdate: 1993. Deathplace: San Antonio. Studied: AIC. Member: San Antonio Pm; SAAL. Exhibited: SALA; TG 1940, 1941S, 1941F; Witte 1941 (solo); TFAA 1941. Mural: USPO, Alice, Tex. Sources: Samuels; Witte files; WWWAA.

HUNTER, Russel Vernon [P; Mur. P.; T; W; Mus. administrator] Farwell, Tex./Texico, N.M./Dallas. Birthdate: 1900. Birthplace: Hallsville, Ill. Deathdate: 1955. Deathplace: Roswell, N.M. Studied: New Mexico Normal; Milliken Univ.; Denver Art Acad.; AIC; S. M. Wright. Member: Panhandle AA; Amarillo AA. Exhibited: Amarillo AA 1933; PPHM 1933; TFWC 1931; GTPA; TSFA 1937; SFT; WFNY; CSFAC; AIC; Corcoran; AFA; MNM 1937. Work: DMA; PPHM; MNM; Norfolk Mus., Va.; Roswell Mus. and Art Center; Virginia Mus. FA; Mural: Ft. Sumner, N.M. Sources: Bywaters Coll.; Havlice; *New Handbook;* O'Brien; Samuels; WWWAA; widow.

HURLOCK, Alba Krueger [P] Houston. Exhibited: AHAE 1943.

HURST, Charles [P] Dallas. Exhibited: DAA 1928.

HUTCHINS, Frederic L. [P; I; A] Houston. Birthdate: 1896. Birthplace: Seattle, Wash. Studied: Graham Univ. Atelier, Colo.; Univ. Penn; Fontainebleau. Exhibited: AHAE 1930. Sources: WWWAA.

HUTCHINS, Roene [P] Fort Worth. Exhibited: TAFW 1937.

HUTCHINS, Mrs. Ross [] Dallas. Exhibited: DAA 1929.

HUTCHINSON, Frank Ray [P] Albany. Exhibited: TFWC 1931.

INGALLIS/INGALLS, Walter [P; Por. P] San Antonio. Birthdate: 1805. Deathdate: 1874. Exhibited: San Antonio 1857. Work: U.S. Capitol. Sources: Pinckney.

INGRAM, Samuel [P] Houston. Exhibited: AHAE 1942; TG 1941S, 1941F.

IRELAND, Irma Thompson [P] El Paso. Exhibited: TFWC 1931.

ISAAC, Dell [P; Pm] Dallas. Exhibited: DAA; TG 1945; ATPE 1945;SSAL.

ISBELL, Hilda M. [P] Houston. Exhibited: AHAE 1936.

IVES, Peggy [P] San Antonio. Exhibited: SALA 1940.

IWONSKI, Carl G. von [P; Por. P.; Ph] Hortonville/New Braunfels/San Antonio. Birthdate: 1830. Birthplace: Hilbersdorf, Silesia, Germany. Deathdate: 1912. Deathplace: Breslau, Silesia, Germany. Studied: Breslau. Exhibited: Yanaguana (ph.). Work: Witte; DRT Lib. Sources: McGuire bio.; *New Handbook;* O'Brien; Pinckney; Steinfeldt.

IZARD, Mrs. V. L. [P] El Paso. Exhibited: EPWC 1942.

JACKMAN, Winifred [P] El Paso. Birthdate: 1896. Exhibited: EPCC; EPPL 1928 (solo). Sources: Price.

JACKSON, Amy Miears [P: Pm; T] Austin/Amarillo/Galveston. Birthdate: 1903. Birthplace: Caldwell Co., Tex. Deathdate: 1970. Deathplace: Lockhart, Tex. Studied: UT; AIC; AFA—Chicago; Amer. Acad. Rome; E. Leon; F. Taubes. Member: TFAA; Amarillo AA; Lubbock AA. Exhibited: TSFA 1931, 1934; Lubbock AA 1933; TFWC 1931; WTAE 1939; SSAL. Work: PPHM; Amarillo Mus. of Art. Sources: *Galveston Daily News;* O'Brien; Wilbanks.

JACKSON, Ann Dealey (Mrs. Rice) [P] Dallas. Birthdate: 1885. Birthplace: Houston. Deathdate: 1960. Deathplace: Dallas. Studied: F. Reaugh; Lasell Junior College, Auburndale, Mass.; Leipzig, Germany. Member: FRAC; Dallas YWCA; DMFA; Dallas Symphony Soc. Exhibited: FRAC 1929, 1933, 1935. Sources: *Dallas Morning News;* PPHM files; family.

JACKSON, Everett Gee [P; I; Pm; T] Mexia, Tex./San Diego, Calif. Birthdate: 1900. Birthplace: Mexia. Studied: TAMC; AIC; San Diego State College; USC. Member: San Diego FA Sch.; Laguna Beach AA; SSAL. Exhibited: TAFW; DWF; Cotton Pal.; SFT; SACE; MFAH 1928 (solo); TCE; AIC; PAFA; Corcoran. Work: MFAH; TAMU; San Diego FA Guild; Kansas Univ.; LA County Mus. of Art; Philadelphia MA. Sources: Bywaters Coll.; Fielding; Fisk; O'Brien; Samuels; WWWAA.

JACKSON, Gene Mercere [Pm] Dallas. Exhibited: DAA 1933.

JACKSON, Katherine [D] San Antonio. Exhibited: SALA 1939.

JACKSON, Rosemary [P] Houston. Exhibited: AHAE 1933.

JACOBS, E. M. [P] Houston. Exhibited: AHAE.

JACOBS, Laura H. (Mrs. William S.) [P] Houston. Sources: Houston Art Directory, 1931.

JAMES, Delwin V. [P] Houston. Exhibited: AHAE.

JAMESON, Clemens [P] Dallas. Exhibited: DAA 1944.

JAMISON, Celia (Mrs. Clifford H. Sankey) [P; T] Denton. Birthdate: 1920. Birthplace: Prosper, Tex. Deathplace: Living Denton, 1997. Studied: TSCW; Iowa Univ.; P. Guston. Member: TFAA; Texas Teachers Assoc. Exhibited: TG 1945; WTAE 1945; FWAA; MFAH 1945; DMFA; KCAI 1942; Weyhe Gall., N.Y. 1945. Work: MAMFW; Iowa Univ. Sources: Bywaters Coll.; Havlice; MAMFW files; WWWAA.

JANGRI, Jose [P] El Paso. Exhibited: EPWC 1936.

JARVIS, J. T. [P] El Paso. Exhibited: EPWC 1940.

JARVIS, Mary [P] Fort Worth. Exhibited: TAFW 1936–37.

JARVIS, W. Frederick [P; T; Cer.] Dallas/San Antonio. Birthplace: Monroe Co., Ohio. Studied: ASL; S. Martin; C. Bullette; A. Schille; F. Mueller in Munich. Member: SSAL; Soc. Independent Artists. Exhibited: TAFW 1923; TSFA 1926; Texas-Oklahoma Fair 1922 or 1924; SALA 1930. Sources: Fielding; Fisk; O'Brien; Samuels; WWWAA.

JEFFREYS, Arthur Bishop [P] Dallas. Birthdate: 1892. Birthplace: Hillsboro, Tex. Studied: Self-taught; W. F.

Jarvis. Member: Dallas AA; Soc. Ind. Artists; Chicago AL. Exhibited: UCE 2. Sources: Fisk; O'Brien.

JEFFRIES, Lucille [P; Pm; T] Dallas/Bolton. Birthdate: 1903. Birthplace: San Luis Potosí, Mexico. Deathdate: 1950. Deathplace: Dallas. Studied: Mary Hardin-Baylor, Belton; Columbia; CSFAC. Member: Texas Pm. Exhibited: DAA; Ney Mus. 1936 (solo), 1941 (solo); Mary Hardin-Baylor 1939 (solo), 1941 (solo); UCE 1; TG; ATPE 1942, 1945; Witte 1943 (solo); ATPE; SSAL. Work: DMA; Corpus Christi PL. Sources: Bywaters Coll.; Harris; O'Brien; TPan m.; Witte files.

JENKINS, John Eliot [P; Por. P; L; T] Houston/Amarillo/Austin. Birthdate: 1868. Birthplace: Onaga, Kans. Deathdate: 1937. Deathplace: Eastland Co., Tex. Studied: Benjamin-Constant; Lefebvre; Monet. Member: Texas AL; Kansas Fed. of Arts. Exhibited: Cotton Carn. 1910; TAFW 1914–15; TWF 1917; Amarillo 1930 (solo); TSFA 1931; TFWC 1931; PPHM 1933. Work: PPHM; TCapitol; Topeka PL; UT? Sources: Amarillo News-Globe; O'Brien; PPHM files; WWWAA.

JENNESS, Velma [P] Lubbock. Member: Lubbock AA. Exhibited: Lubbock AA 1933.

JENNINGS, Jewell [P] San Antonio. Exhibited: TFWC 1931.

JESSEN, Bubi [P; Arch.; Mur. P] Austin. Birthdate: 1908. Deathdate: 1979. Studied: UT. Exhibited: Witte 1932 (solo); ASET 1937; TCapitol 1934. Work: Goliad Mission. Painted PWAP mural, "The Pageant of Texas," which was first hung in the Texas State Capitol in 1934 before being moved to the Goliad Mission for permanent installation.

JESTER, Kathrin [P] Corsicana, Tex. Birthdate: 1910. Studied: Newcomb College w/ E. Woodward; TSCW. Member: TFAA. Exhibited: TAFW 1936; TCE; TFAA. Sources: O'Brien.

JESTER, Martha [P] Dallas. Exhibited: DAA 1935.

JESTER, Ralph [P] Dallas/Hollywood. Birthdate: 1901. Studied: Yale; Fontainebleau; H. Bouchard, Paris. Exhibited: DAA 1929; SFT 1931. Sources: WWWAA.

JEZ, Louise [P] Fort Worth. Studied: TSCWomen. Member: FWAA. Exhibited: TAFW 1928–37.

JOHN, Grace Spaulding [P; W; Mur. P] Houston. Birthdate: 1890. Birthplace: Battle Creek, Mich. Deathdate: 1972. Deathplace: Houston. Studied: SLSFA; AIC; Parsons Sch.; NAD; PAFA; ASL; Hawthorne; Bisttram. Member: HAG (founder); NAWPS; Houston AL; MFAH; Taos AA. Exhibited: Witte; AIC; NAD; PAFA; AHAE; MFAH 1936 (solo); TAFW; ASET; TG 1940. Work: MFAH; PPHM; RL; UT; Rice; Houston PL; MNM; Harwood; Nat. Portrait Gall.; NMWA; LOC; SI. Sources: Fielding; Fisk; Mallett; *New Handbook;* O'Brien; Rose and Kalil; Samuels; Smith; WWWAA.

JOHN, Patricia [P; Harpist; Photog.] Houston. Birthdate: 1916. Birthplace: Canton, Ill. Living Houston, 1999. Studied: Mills College, Calif.; Curtis Inst., Philadelphia; Rice; G. S. John. Exhibited: AHAE 1938; Sch. of Amer. Research, Santa Fe, 1937. Work: No public coll. Sources: Artist.

JOHNSON, Alice Word [D] Houston/Cisco, Tex. Exhibited: AHAE; TFWC 1931.

JOHNSON, Mrs. F. F. [P] Galveston? Exhibited: Texas Coast Fair 1895.

JOHNSON, Ivan E. [P; Pm; T] San Antonio. Exhibited: San Antonio Local Artists Exhibitions 1936, 1938. Sources: Witte files.

JOHNSON, J. C. [P] Post. Exhibited: TFWC 1931.

JOHNSON, Marjorie E. (Marjorie Johnson Lee) [P; Pm] Fort Worth. Birthdate: 1911. Birthplace: Upton Co., Tex. Deathdate: 1997. Deathplace: Fort Worth. Studied: FWSFA; CSFAC; AIC; ASL. Exhibited: TAFW; FWSFA 1939 (solo); ASL. Work: MAMFW: PPHM. Sources: Gillespie and Nail.

JOHNSON, Martha Elizabeth Jane Winsett "Lizbeth" (Mrs. J. F.) [P; T] Canadian, Tex. Birthdate: 1859. Birthplace: Center Grove, Tenn. Deathdate: 1939. Deathplace: Canadian, Tex. Studied: Cincinnati w/ McCoy; Memphis w/ Fugitt and P. Slater; Kansas City; Los Angeles. Exhibited: Nashville, Tenn.; Tennessee State Fair, artist's Canadian, Tex., home. Work: St. Anthony's Hospital Chapel, Amarillo; WCTU Bldg., Canadian. Sources: *Amarillo Sunday News and Globe;* artist's great-grandson. Painted European subjects while living in Texas; moved to Higgins, Tex., 1887; to Canadian, 1889.

JOHNSON, Mary Totten [P] Sherman. Birthdate: 1885. Exhibited: TAFW; TCE.

JOHNSON, Minnie Walaver [P] Austin/Dallas/San Angelo/Wichita Falls. Birthplace: Diana, Tenn. Studied: Reaugh; Brunet; ASL w/ Bridgman; W. Griffith. Member: FRAC; TFAA; SSAL; Laguna Beach AA. Exhibited: FRAC: TAFW; TCE; DWF; DAA; FRAC; Cotton Pal.; TFWC 1931; UCE 2. Work: PPHM. Sources: Fisk; O'Brien.

JOHNSTON, Eliza Griffin [P] China Grove, Tex./Austin. Birthdate: 1821. Birthplace: Fincastle, Va. Deathdate: 1896. Deathplace: Los Angeles. Studied: Philadelphia. Work: DRT Lib. Sources: *New Handbook.*

JOHNSTON, Jessie Margaret [P] Fort Worth. Exhibited: TAFW 1930.

JOLLY, Wade Lytton [P] Fort Worth/Philadelphia. Birthdate: 1909. Birthplace: Philadelphia. Studied: H. Breckenridge; E. Horter; PAFA. Member: Philadelphia Print Cl.; Philadelphia Art Alliance. Exhibited: TAFW; TCE; GTPA. Sources: WWWAA.

JONAH, Horace [P] El Paso. Exhibited: EPCC.

JONES, (Miss) [P] Galveston? Exhibited: Texas Coast Fair 1895.

JONES, C. H. [P] Fort Worth. Exhibited: TAFW 1918.

JONES, Edwin [P] El Paso. Exhibited: EPWC 1937.

JONES, Esther [P] Austin/Dallas. Exhibited: TAFW 1918–20. Sources: WWWAA.

JONES, Jeannette Milam [P] San Antonio. Exhibited: SALA 1936.

JONES, Laura Rose [P] Dallas. Birthplace: Memphis, Tenn. Studied: ASL; Aunspaugh AS; J. Knott; Reaugh. Member: Dallas ASL. Exhibited: TAFW 1922–23. Sources: WWWAA.

JONES, Mrs. Louis C. [P] Fort Worth. Exhibited: TAFW 1935.

JONES, Louise [P] Dallas. Exhibited: DAA.

JONES, Mabel Thorpe [P] Fort Worth. Exhibited: TAFW 1911, 1932, 1933.

JONES, Paul [Pm] San Antonio. Exhibited: SALA 1944; ATPE 1944.

JONES, Ruth M. [P] Fort Worth. Exhibited: TAFW 1926–28.

JONES, Mrs. W. L. [P] Slaton. Member: Lubbock AA. Exhibited: Lubbock AA 1933. Sources: Wilbanks.

JOSSET, Raoul Jean [S; T] Dallas/Chicago/New York. Birthdate: 1898. Birthplace: Burgundy, France. Deathdate: 1957. Deathplace: New York, N.Y. Studied: Lycée Janson, Paris; Sorbonne; École BA w/ Injabert, Bourdelle. Member: Salon d'Automne. Exhibited: TCE (architectural sculpture); GTPA; AIC; NSS; Century of Progress, Chicago; WFNY. Work: Fair Park, Dallas; Refugio; La Grange; Goliad. Sources: Bywaters Coll.; Dallas Hist. Soc. files; DAS; Fielding; Hendricks and Reese; WWWAA.

JOY, Robert C. [P; Por. P] Houston. Birthdate: 1910. Birthplace: Erie, Pa. Deathdate: 1993. Deathplace: Houston. Studied: PAFA. Exhibited: AHAE; MFAH 1933; ASET; TG 1941S; SSAL. Work: TCapitol; MFAH; RL Sources: Bywaters Coll.; MFAH files; WWWAA.

JOYCE, Charles Marita [Pm] Dallas. Exhibited: DAA 1938.

JOYNER, Arista Arnold [P; Pm; W] Arlington, Tex. Birthdate: 1911. Birthplace: Kansas City, Mo. Studied: Gulf Park College, Miss.; Univ. South Dakota; J. Patrick; W. Rosenbauer; M. Rounds; KCAI. Exhibited: SFT 1939; TG 1941F; ATPE 1945. Sources: WWWAA.

JOYNER, Howard Warren [P; Des.; D; T] Arlington, Tex. Birthdate: 1900. Birthplace: Chicago, Ill. Studied: KCAI; Univ. Missouri; Univ. Calif.; Univ. Iowa; École BA; R. Davey; L. Henkora; K. Hudson; J. Despujols; H. Hofmann; R. Braught. Member: FWAA; College Art Assoc.; Dallas AA; Arlington AA; AFA; Delta Phi Delta; Texas Assoc. Art Educators. Exhibited: SFT 1939; TG; Fort Worth; Rockefeller Ctr. 1935; Detroit IA 1931; KCAI 1934. Mural: Univ. Iowa. Sources: Bywaters Coll.; WWWAA.

KAEPPEL, Albert Enno [P] Houston. Exhibited: AHAE 1934.

KAHLDEN, Sarah [P] Houston. Exhibited: AHAE; ASET 1937; TG 1940.

KAMACKER, Frederic [S] Dallas. Exhibited: DAA 1930.

KANE, Thomas [] El Paso. Exhibited: EPWC.

KARGL, Gilard [P; Photog.] San Antonio. Birthdate: 1898. Birthplace: Austria. Deathdate: 1983. Deathplace: San Antonio. Studied: Vienna and Klagenfurt, Austria, with H. Bicker, A. Kolig. Member: San Antonio Pm. Exhibited: SALA; Witte 1935 (solo); Witte 1941 (SAP). Sources: Witte files.

KARL, Mabel Fairfax [S; Pm] Houston/San Diego, Calif. Birthdate: 1901. Birthplace: Glendale, Ore. Deathdate: 1990. Deathplace: San Diego, Calif.? Studied: ASL; L. Lentelli; Pennell; Bridgman; A. Dawson. Member: ASL; AFA. Exhibited: MFAH; AHAE 1932 (pr.), 1934 (purchase pr.); TAFW. Work: MFAH. Sources: Fisk; Hendricks and Reese; Mallett; O'Brien; WWWAA.

KARPER, Mary Nelson [Pm] Dallas. Exhibited: ATPE 1942.

KAY-SCOTT, Cyril [P; Por. P; Mur. P; T] El Paso/San Antonio/Denver. Birthdate: 1879. Birthplace: Richmond, Va. or Westport, Mo. Deathdate: 1940. Deathplace: Denver? Studied: Univ. London; Acad. Colarossi. Work: Denver AM. Sources: O'Brien; Price; WWWAA.

KEATING, Mary Aubrey [P; Pm; Mur. P] San Antonio. Birthdate: 1894. Birthplace: San Antonio. Deathdate: 1953. Deathplace: San Antonio. Studied: Self-taught. Member: SSAL; NAWA; TFAA;. Exhibited: Ney Mus.; SFT; Witte 1943 (solo) 1944 (solo); SSAL; TAFW; TCE; GTPA; SALA; ASET; TG 1941S–45; Coronado Cuarto Centennial Exp., Albuquerque, 1941. Work: Witte. Sources: Bywaters Coll.; Mallet; *New Handbook;* O'Brien; Steinfeldt; TPan m.; WWWAA.

KEEFER, Elizabeth E. See BOATRIGHT, Elizabeth Keefer

KEELEY, Edward [] Dallas. Exhibited: DAA 1932.

KEENER, Anna Elizabeth [P; T; Pm] Dalhart/Clovis, N.M. Birthdate: 1895. Birthplace: Flagler, Colo. Deathdate: 1982. Deathplace: Clovis. Studied: Bethany, Sandzen; AIC; KCAI; Colorado State Teachers College; UNM; Davey. Member: SSAL; AFA. Exhibited: Dallas 1925; TAFW 1927; KCAI; MNM. Sources: Fielding; O'Brien; WWWAA.

KEIDEL, Albert [P] San Antonio. Exhibited: SALA 1934.

KEILLER, Dr. William H. [P] Galveston. Birthdate: 1861. Birthplace: Midlothian, Scotland. Deathdate: 1931. Deathplace: Galveston. Studied: Perth Academy; Univ. of Edinburgh. Exhibited: Cotton Carn. 1910,1911. Sources: RL; UTMB @ Galveston.

KEITH, Jacquelyn [P] Houston. Exhibited: AHAE.

KEITH, James L., Jr. [P] Houston. Exhibited: AHAE 1937.

KELLEY, Edith [P] Dallas. Exhibited: DAA 1932.

KELLOG, Charles [P] El Paso. Exhibited: EPWC 1942.

KELLY, Mrs. A. R. [P] El Paso. Exhibited: EPWC 1941.

KELLY, Dee [Pm] Lubbock. Exhibited: ATPE 1942.

KELLY, Lois Neville [P] Alpine. Exhibited: WTAE 1940.

KELLY, Loucile Jerome [P; T] San Angelo. Birthdate: 1913. Birthplace: San Angelo. Studied: Newcomb College; Sul Ross State. Member: TFAA; SSAL; San Angelo AC; Lubbock AA. Exhibited: GTPA; Lubbock AA 1937; WTAE; TG 1940; SSAL 1939. Sources: Wilbanks; WWWAA.

KELSO, Lillian [P] San Antonio. Exhibited: SALA 1930.

KENDALE (KENDALL?), Evelyn [P] Dallas. Exhibited: DAA 1928, 1931.

KENDALL, Helen King (Mrs. J. Riley) [P] San Angelo. Birthdate: 1895. Birthplace: Kansas. Deathdate: 1946. Deathplace: San Angelo. Studied: Reaugh; Travis; Brunet; Newcomb College; X. Gonzalez. Member: FRAC; San Angelo AC; AFA; TFAA; AAPL. Exhibited: FRAC; Pabst Gall., San Antonio; WTAE 1939–42. Work: Kendall Gall., San Angelo. Sources: O'Brien.

KENDALL, Thelma Graham [P] Abilene. Exhibited: WTAE 1942.

KENNEY, Lillie Vance (Mrs. John W.). [P] San Antonio. Studied: J. Onderdonk. Exhibited: SAAG 1927; Witte 1939. Sources: Witte files.

KEY, Rae Littleton (Mrs. Edmund Jr.) [S] Marshall. Birthplace: Marshall. Studied: AIC. Member: TFAA; SSAL; New Orleans AA; AFA. Exhibited: SFT; East Texas Fair; YWCA, Dallas 1924 (solo). Sources: DAS; Fisk; Harrison County Mus.; H. Key; WWWAA.

KIDD, Hari Matthew [P; Pm] El Paso. Birthdate: 1898. Deathdate: 1964. Deathplace: Tucson, Ariz. Studied: PAFA; E. Thurston. Exhibited: TAFW 1936–37; SFT 1938–39; TCE; WTAE 1939; TG 1940, 1941S; El Paso 1940 (solo); Witte 1941 (solo); El Paso Centennial Mus. 1937; Philadelphia Art Alliance 1939 (solo); PAFA. Work: Philadelphia MA; Allentown Mus., Pa.; La France AM, Frankford, Pa. Sources: *El Paso Herald-Post;* EPPL; *El Paso Times;* Falk PAFA; Price; WWWAA.

KIEFNER, C. H. [P] Houston. Exhibited: AHAE; ASET; TG 1940; SSAL 1939. Sources: WWWAA.

KIESLING, Ninon [P] Houston. Exhibited: TFWC 1931.

KIMBALL, Maria Cage (Mrs. S. H.) [P] Galveston. Birthdate: 1844. Deathdate: 1911. Deathplace: Houston. Exhibited: Texas Coast Fair 1895; Galveston 1897. Sources: RL; Witte files.

KIMMON, Mrs. S. C. [P] Galveston. Exhibited: Cotton Carn. 1912.

KINCHELOE, Marilyn M. [P] Houston. Exhibited: TG 1941F; WFNY.

KING, Clinton Blair [P] Fort Worth/Dallas/Santa Fe. Birthdate: 1901. Birthplace: Fort Worth. Studied: C. W. Hawthorne; NAD; Grand Central Gall.; W. Adams; R. Reid; R. Davey. Member: Fort Worth AG; Philadelphia Watercolor Cl. Exhibited: TAFW; Fort Worth Women's Cl. 1926 (solo); Witte 1934 (solo); FWFCE; SFT 1931; TCE; GTPA; FWAG 1938; DMFA 1939 (solo); NAD; PAFA; AIC; SSAL. Work: TFWC, Austin; MAMFW. Sources: Falk AIC; Falk NAD; Falk PAFA; Fisk; O'Brien; Smith; Witte files; WWWAA.

KING, Grace [P] Houston. Exhibited: AHAE.

KING, J. A. [P] Pampa. Exhibited: TFWC 1931.

KING, J. J. [P] San Antonio. Birthdate: 1860. Birthplace: Carshalton, England. Studied: Self-taught. Exhibited: SALA; TG 1942; Witte 46 (two-person w/ Frank M. Edwards). Sources: *San Antonio Light;* Witte files.

KING, M. A. [P] San Antonio. Exhibited: SALA.

KING, Minnie Clark (Mrs. William) [P] San Antonio/ Waring. Birthdate: 1877. Birthplace: Caldwell, Tex. Studied: Chase; H. Bishop; C. Cox; R. Onderdonk; H. A. McArdle; Arpa. Member: SAAG (director); SAAL. Exhibited: SALA; TFWC 1931; San Antonio Int'l Fair. Work: City Nat. Bank, San Antonio; San Antonio City Auditorium. Sources: Fisk; Smith; WWWAA.

KING, Sally R. [D] San Antonio. Exhibited: SALA.

KING, Walter Gillis [P] Austin/West Caldwell, N.J. Birthdate: 1904. Birthplace: Dewville, Tex. Studied: S. E. Gideon; M. Jacobs; Bridgman. Member: TFAA; SSAL. Exhibited: SACE; TAFW 1927. Work: Austin AL; San Angelo AL; Stark; Tom Green Cty. Courthouse, San Angelo. Sources: Fielding; WWWAA.

KINNEY, Cle [P] Austin. Exhibited: TG 1942.

KINNEY, Mrs. John U. [P] San Antonio. Exhibited: SACE 1928. Sources: Witte files.

KINZBACH, Mary Chandler [P] Houston. Exhibited: AHAE 1943.

KINZINGER, Alice Fish [P] Waco. Birthdate: 1899. Birthplace: Grand Rapids, Mich. Studied: Mich. Univ.; AIC; H. Hofmann; Baylor. Member: TFAA. Exhibited: GTPA; SFT 1938; WTAE 1940; ATPE 1942; Minneapolis Inst. Art. Work: Parker Sch., Chicago. Murals: Grand Rapids public schools. Sources: Fiedling; WWWAA.

KINZINGER, Edmund Daniel [P; S; Pm; T] Waco. Birthdate: 1888. Birthplace: Pforzheim, Germany. Deathdate: 1963. Deathplace: Larboro, N.C. Studied: St. Akad., Mun.; St. Akad., Stut; Acad. Mod., Paris; Iowa Univ. Member: TFAA; SSAL; Amer. Assoc. Univ. Prof. Exhibited: TCE; MFAH; DMFA; SFT 1938; GTPA; ASET; WTAE; TPan.; LSP 1940–41; ATPE; AIC; WFNY; GGE 1939; SSAL. Work: DMA; Witte. Sources: Steinfeldt; Waco Art Ctr. catalogue; WWWAA.

KIRBY, Earleen [P] Sherman. Birthdate: 1910. Birthplace: Denison, Tex. Studied: College of Industrial Arts (now TWU) w/ C. M. Spellman. Exhibited: TFAA 1933. Sources: O'Brien.

KIRKLAND, Forrest [P; T] Dallas. Birthdate: 1892. Birthplace: Mist, Ark. Deathdate: 1942. Deathplace: Dallas. Studied: Sch. of Applied Art, Battle Creek, Mich.; Eisenlohr. Member: Dallas AA; SSAL. Exhibited: TAFW

1922; DAA; SFT 1934; SSAL. Work: Texas Memorial Mus. Sources: Kirkland and Newcomb; O'Brien; Ratcliffe; Samuels; WWWAA.

KIRKSEY, Lola [P] San Antonio. Exhibited: SALA 1944.

KIRKWOOD, Rosa [P] San Antonio. Exhibited: SALA.

KITCHENS, Mrs. Clay [P] Fort Worth. Exhibited: TAFW 1934.

KLEINE, William C. [D] San Antonio. Exhibited: SALA 1933.

KLEINSCHMIDT, Florian A. [P; T; Pm; Arch.] Lubbock. Birthdate: 1897. Birthplace: Mankato, Minn. Studied: Univ. Minn.; Harvard; Fontainebleau. Member: Lubbock AA. Sources: O'Brien; Wilbanks.

KLEPPER, Frank X. E. L. [P; Pm; T] McKinney/Dallas. Birthdate: 1890. Birthplace: Plano, Tex. Deathdate: 1952. Deathplace: McKinney. Studied: AIC; Lachman. Member: Dallas AA; SSAL; TFAA; HPSFA; FRAC. Exhibited: Cotton Carn. 1912; Greenville 1924; FRAC; SACE 1929; TFWC 1931; TAFW; UCE 1, 2; TCE; SSAL; DAA; TFAA; SFT. Work: PPHM; McKinney HS; Plano HS; Vanderpoel. Murals: UPSO, McKinney; Prairie View A&M. Sources: Bywaters Coll.; Fielding; Fisk; New Handbook; O'Brien; Samuels; Smith; WWWAA.

KNEASS, Charles [Por. P; Min. P] Brazoria/Philadelphia. Sources: Pinckney.

KNESSR, Charles [P] San Antonio. Exhibited: SALA 1944.

KNOTT, John F. [Car.; P] Dallas. Birthdate: 1878. Birthplace: Pilsen, Austria. Deathdate: 1963. Deathplace: Dallas. Studied: Holmes Sch. Ill.; Royal Acad., Munich. Member: Philosophical Soc. Texas; Texas State Historical Assoc. Exhibited: TAFW. Sources: Dallas Morning News; New Handbook; O'Brien; WWWAA.

KOCH, Agustus [D; Pm] La Grange. Work: Witte. Sources: Pinckney.

KOENIG, Icie Hardy "Ike" (Mrs. Roy) [P] Kerrville. Birthdate: 1895. Birthplace: Newton, Tex. Deathdate: 1994. Deathplace: Kerrville. Studied: P. Hohnstedt; H. Pohl; Univ. Chicago; Taft Studio. Member: Kerrville AC. (founder); Hill Country Arts Foundation. Exhibited:

Kerrville 1938; Menhard-Taylor Gall., Houston 1940; Women's Fed. Bldg., Austin, 1941; WTAE 1942; Lufkin; Jasper. Sources: Artist's niece; Kerrville Daily Times.

KOENIG, John [P] Houston. Exhibited: AHAE; GTPA.

KOKERNOT, Golda [P] Alpine. Exhibited: WTAE 1939.

KOKES, Rudolph [P] San Antonio. Exhibited: SAAG 1927.

KOONTZ, Gay [S] San Antonio. Exhibited: SALA.

KOUBEK, Jerry [S] Fort Worth. Exhibited: TAFW 1937.

KRAFT, Emma Belle [P] Dallas. Exhibited: TAFW.

KRAKAUER, Gustave [P] El Paso. Exhibited: EPWC.

KRAKAUER, Mrs. Julius [P] El Paso. Exhibited: EPCC.

KRAMER, Alice (Mrs. Everett Spruce) [P] Dallas. Birthdate: 1908. Deathdate: 1975. Deathplace: Austin. Exhibited: DAA; TCE; TAFW 1935; TG 1940. Sources: Mallett; Bywaters "New Texas Painters."

KRAMER, Fred [Arch.; Des.; Pm; T] Dallas. Birthplace: Germany. Studied: Wash. Univ., St. Louis; SLSFA; G. Lerrand; P. Valenti; F. Carpenter; H. Smith. Exhibited: DAA; Sartor. Sources: O'Brien.

KRAUS, Richard [Pm] San Antonio. Exhibited: SALA 1943.

KRIECHBAUM, Ethel (Mrs. J. R.) [P] El Paso. Exhibited: EPWC.

KRISTOFFERSEN, J. K. [P] Dallas. Birthdate: 1877. Birthplace: Denmark. Exhibited: DAA. Sources: O'Brien.

KRITSER, Harriett W. [P] Amarillo. Studied: Univ. of Okla. Exhibited: TSFA; TFWC 1931; SAAG 1927.

KROEKEL, Mrs. Charles A. [P] El Paso. Exhibited: EPWC 1927.

KROLL, Rolfe [P] Dallas. Exhibited: DAA 1937.

KROME, Steve [P] Dallas. Exhibited: DAA 1932.

KRUEGER, Alba [P] Houston. Exhibited: TFWC 1931.

KUNTSCHER, Otto [P; Comm. A] Houston. Birthdate: 1902. Birthplace: Austria. Studied: E. A. Filleau. Exhibited: AHAE 1925. Sources: Fisk; Smith.

KUNZ, Lenore O. [P] Galveston. Exhibited: Cotton Carn. 1912.

KUPFORSCHMID, Sidney John [D] San Antonio. Exhibited: SALA 1944.

KUSIANOVICH, Daniel [P] El Paso. Exhibited: EPWC 1938.

KUTTNER, Walter [P] Houston. Exhibited: AHAE 1943.

LACKEY, Ebba [D] San Antonio. Exhibited: SALA 1934.

LACY, Lucile Land [P; Pm; T] Temple. Birthdate: 1901. Birthplace: Temple. Studied: Mary Hardin-Baylor, Belton; Columbia; Mewhinney. Member: SSAL; Pm Guild; TP; TFAA. Exhibited: TG 1940–43; Pm Guild 1941–45; TFAA 1939–43; SSAL; Ney Mus. 1935 (solo); UCE 1; SFT 1938. Sources: Harris; Mallett; O'Brien; WWWAA.

LACY, Mattie [P; T] Denton. Birthplace: Hutchins, Tex. Studied: TSCW; NYSFAA; Pratt Inst.; Columbia. Exhibited: Sartor; SSAL. Sources: O'Brien.

LACY, Mig [P] San Antonio. Exhibited: SALA 1935.

LACY, Suella [P] Abilene. Exhibited: TFWC 1931; WTAE 1939.

LAFARTHE, (Miss) [P] Galveston? Exhibited: Texas Coast Fair 1895.

LaGOW, Kate Elmore. See ELMORE, Kate L.

LALLIER, Victor [P; Por. P] Dallas. Birthdate: 1912. Birthplace: Fort Worth. Studied: SMU; Claremont (CA) College. Member: Dallas AA. Exhibited: Sartor 1934 (solo); DAA; TCE; TG 1941F, 1944. Work: First Presbyterian Ch., Dallas; SMU; Western States Life, Dallas. Sources: Bywaters Coll.; Havlice; O'Brien; WWWAA.

LAMAR, Mrs. L. M. [P] San Antonio. Studied: J. Arpa. Exhibited: SAAL 1926; Arpa Students, Witte 1928. Sources: San Antonio Express; Witte files.

LAMOND, Allie Douglas [P] Post. Exhibited: TFWC 1931.

LA MOND, Stella Lodge [P; Pm; T] Dallas/Commerce. Birthdate: 1893. Birthplace: Morganfield, Ky. Deathdate: 1968. Deathplace: Dallas. Studied: Peabody College, Nashville; Columbia; Cranbrook; Hogue. Member: AFA; TP (founder); Dallas AA; DAL. Exhibited: TCE; TAFW; SFT; DAA; TG; DMFA; GTPA; ATPE. Work: AMST; DMA; PPHM; Texas Tech. Sources: Bywaters Coll.; Harris; Mallett; *New Handbook;* Stewart; TPan m.; WWWAA.

LAND, Marguerite [P] Baytown. Exhibited: TFWC 1931.

LANDERS, Bertha M. [P; Pm] Dallas. Birthdate: 1911. Birthplace: Winnsboro, Tex. Deathdate: 1996. Deathplace: San Diego, Calif. Studied: Sul Ross State; CSFAC; ASL. Member: TP (founder); TFAA; NMWA (charter). Exhibited: TCE; DAA; TPan; SFT 1939; TG 1941 Spring–45; ATPE; SSAL. Work: DMA; DAM; LOC; Modern Art Mus. of Fort Worth; SAMA; SMU; UT. Sources: Bywaters Coll.; Harris; Mallett; TPan m.; WWWAA.

LANDIS, David M. [Pm] San Antonio. Exhibited: SALA 1943.

LANDON, Winnifred [D] Dallas. Exhibited: SFT 1938.

LANDRUM, Mary Talbot [P] San Benito.

LANDRY, N. R. [P] San Antonio. Exhibited: SAAG 1927. Sources: San Antonio City Directory 1924, 1928; Witte files.

LANE, Joseph [P] Houston/Chicago. Birthdate: 1900. Birthplace: Austin. Studied: F. M. Grant; L. Van Pappelendum; AIC. Exhibited: AHAE 1939; AIC. Murals: Chicago Theatre; Pickwick Restaurant, Chicago. Sources: WWWAA.

LANE, Lilly [P] Bonham.

LANE, Loubeth King [P; T] Dallas/Canyon. Studied: SMU; Univ. Chicago; AIC; PAFA. Sources: O'Brien.

LANGE, Virginia E. [P] Dallas. Exhibited: DAA 1928.

LANGFORD, Ruth Betty [P; Pm; T] Mt. Enterprise, Texas/Los Angeles. Birthdate: Sherman, Tex. Studied: Harding Coll; Iowa Univ.; F. Martin; E. Ganso; P. Guston. Exhibited: TG 1944; Ney Mus. 1943; KCAI 1942; Ark. St. Exh. Work: Hendrix College, Ark. Sources: Bywaters Coll.; Havlice; WWWAA.

LANGHAM, Emily [P; T; S] Houston. Birthdate: 1895. Birthplace: Shepherd, Tex. Studied: Newcomb College; NYSFAA; Arpa. Member: SSAL; TFAA; HAG. Exhibited: TCE; Witte; AHAE. Sources: Fisk; Mallett; O'Brien; Smith; WWWAA.

LANGLEY, Jane [Pm] Dallas. Member: FRAC. Exhibited: FRAC DAA 1933.

LANHAM, Alpha Johnson [P] Midland/Slaton. Birthplace: Johnson Co., Tex. Studied: S. Lee; V. Blundell; A. W. Mack; W. H. Stevens; X. Gonzalez. Exhibited: WTAE 1940–42; SFT; West Texas Fair, Abilene. Sources: Fisk; O'Brien.

LANIER, Fanita (Mrs. Alex Acheson) [P; Pm; Des.] Dallas/Gallup, N. Mex. Birthdate: 1903. Birthplace: Miami, Fla. Studied: ASL; TSCW; École BA. Exhibited: DAA. Work: Federal Bldg., TCE; El Rancho Hotel, Gallup. Sources: WWWAA.

LANSFORD, Henrietta [P] Houston. Exhibited: AHAE 1825.

LARIMORE, Mrs. W. N. [P] Deport. Exhibited: TFWC 1931.

LARKIN, Billy [P] Houston. Exhibited: AHAE 1942.

LARSEN, Andrew [S] Beaumont. Exhibited: SSAL 1941.

LARSEN, Bessie Gage [P] Dallas. Exhibited: TAFW 1936; TCE.

LARSSON, Lesle [P; Por. P; T] San Antonio. Birthdate: 1913. Birthplace: Genoa, Nebr. Deathdate: 1970. Deathplace: San Antonio. Studied: Nebraska State; Chouinard Inst.; ASL. Member: River Art Group; SAAL; Men of Art Guild, San Antonio. Exhibited: San Antonio Local Artists Exhibition 1944. Work: Witte. Sources: Witte files.

LA SELLE, Dorothy Antoinette (Toni) [P; T; Pm] Denton. Birthdate: 1901. Birthplace: Beatrice, Nebr. Deathplace: living Denton, Apr. 1997. Studied: Univ. Neb.; Neb. Wesleyan; Univ. of Chic.; AIC; Calif. SFA, San Fran.; H. Hofmann. Exhibited: GTPA; ATPE 1944, 1945. Work: DMA; MFAH; TWU; Trinity Presb. Ch., Denton; Met. Sources: Dallas Morning News; MFAH; M. Smither.

LAUCK, Blanche M. [P] San Antonio. Exhibited: SALA 1930.

LAUDERDALE, Ursula. [P; T] Dallas/San Antonio. Birthdate: 1880. Birthplace: Moberly, Mo. Studied: ASL; R. Henri; M. Braun; W. DeVoe; Met.; Reaugh. Member: Dallas AA; FWAA; SSAL; AFA; FRAC. Exhibited: SFT; FRAC 1929; SSAL; TAFW; DAA; SALA; TFWC 1931; Greenville 1924; Menger Hotel, San Antonio 1930 (solo). Sources: Fisk; Mallett; O'Brien; Samuels; San Antonio Evening News; Smith; WWWAA; Witte files.

LA VELLE, Edith [P] Big Spring. Exhibited: WTAE 1939.

LAVENDER, Eugenie E. Aubanel (Mrs. Charles) [P] Corpus Christi. Birthdate: 1817. Birthplace: Bordeaux, France. Deathdate: 1898. Deathplace: Corpus Christi. Studied: Paris w/ Delaroche and A. Scheffer. Exhibited: St. Agnes Acad., Corpus Christi; Yanaguana (ph.). Work: Witte; cathedral, Corpus Christi. Sources: Mallett; *New Handbook;* O'Brien; Pinckney; Samuels; Steinfeldt; WWWAA.

LAWRENCE, Harry Zachary [P] Dallas. Birthdate: 1905. Birthplace: Chicago. Studied: F. Klepper; J. Haapenen; A. Cross; Acad. Colarossi; Grand Chaumier w/ A. Lhote. Member: DAL; DPDS; DMFA. Exhibited: TAFW; SFT 1934; TCE; DAA; GTPA. Sources: O'Brien; WWWAA.

LAWRENCE, Kathleen G. (Kay?) [P; Pm] Fort Worth. Exhibited: TAFW; SSAL 1939; GGE 1939.

LAWRENCE, Kay (Kathleen?) [P] Fort Worth. Exhibited: TAFW 1934.

LAWRENCE, S. L. [P] San Antonio. Exhibited: SAAG 1927.

LAWSON, Mamie [P] Dallas. Exhibited: DAA 1929.

LAY, Mrs. Louis [P] El Paso. Exhibited: EPWC 1936.

LAYBURN, Grace E. [P] Houston. Exhibited: AHAE 1942; TG 1943.

LAZENBY, Georgia [P; Pm] San Marcos. Exhibited: SALA 1936; ASET 1938; TG 1940.

LEA, Mary Hornby [P] San Angelo.

LEA, Tom [P; I; Pm; Mur. P; W] El Paso. Birthdate: 1907.

Birthplace: El Paso. Living El Paso, 1999. Studied: AIC w/ J. Norton. Member: Texas Inst. Letters; Nat. Geographic Soc. Exhibited: TG 1940; EPWC; EPSJ; SSAL. Work: DMA; EPMA; TAMU; MNM. Murals: Odessa, Seymour, Dallas, El Paso, Washington, D.C. Sources: Bywaters Coll.; Fielding; Havlice; Samuels; WWWAA.

LEADER, Morris Walton [P] Austin. Birthdate: 1877. Birthplace: Marshall. Deathdate: 1966. Deathplace: Austin. Studied: P. L. Hohnstedt; Edna Collins. Exhibited: SALA 1932; TFAA 1934; Witte 1932; Ney Mus.; UCE 1; UCE 2. Sources: Cook and Roper; O'Brien.

LEARY, Delano [P] Houston. Exhibited: AHAE 1937.

LEAVITT, Clara Waide [P] Slidell. Exhibited: WTAE 1942.

LEBERMAN, Mrs. Henry [P] San Antonio. Exhibited: SAAL 1924.

LEBERMAN, Virginia [P] Austin. Exhibited: TAFW; SACE 1927; UCE 2. Work: TCapitol. Sources: Witte files.

LEDGERWOOD, Ella Ray (Mrs. H. O.) [P; T] Fort Worth. Birthplace: Dublin, Tex. Deathdate: 1951. Deathplace: Fort Worth. Studied: TCU; AFA—Chicago; Henri; Wiles; K. H. Miller. Member: FWAA; AACFW; FW Art Comm.; Art Ed. Assoc. Exhibited: TAFW; DWF; Cotton Carn. 1912; CPE. Sources: Fisk; ITD; Mallett; Smith; WWWAA.

LEDWARD, Mrs. William [P] El Paso. Exhibited: EPWC 1940.

LEE, Amy Freeman [P; L; W] San Antonio. Birthdate: 1914. Birthplace: San Antonio. Studied: UT; Incarnate Word, San Antonio. Member: TFAA; Texas WCS; SAAL; San Antonio River Art Group; AFA; Artists Equity; College Art Assoc. Exhibited: San Antonio Local Artists 1945. Work: Witte; MAMFW; Smith College; Baylor; Baltimore MA; Dallas Republic Nat. Bank. Sources: Fielding; Havlice; Witte files.

LEE, Dean [P] Houston. Exhibited: AHAE; ASET 1937; GTPA.

LEE, L. Valentine [P] Dallas. Exhibited: DAA 1944.

LEE, M. A. [P] San Antonio. Exhibited: SALA 1930.

LEE, Mary Hornby [P] San Antonio. Exhibited: SALA 1934.

LEE, Myrtle [P] Big Spring. Exhibited: WTAE 1942.

LEE, Mrs. R. E. [P] El Paso. Exhibited: EPWC 1936.

LEGGETT, Lucille (Mrs. W. B.) [P] El Paso/Santa Fe. Birthdate: 1896. Birthplace: Tennessee. Studied: El Paso. Exhibited: EPWC; El Paso Centennial Mus. 1937. Sources: *El Paso Herald-Post;* EPPL; WWWAA.

LEHMANN, Theodore [Por. P] Houston/Philadelphia/New Orleans. Birthplace: Germany. Sources: Pinckney.

LeMASTER, Mrs. Pannill [P] Corsicana, Tex. Exhibited: TFWC 1931.

LEMMON, Thetis [P] Denton. Birthdate: 1907. Birthplace: Dallas. Studied: College of Industrial Arts (now TWU); Columbia; C. Martin. Member: Denton AL. Exhibited: TCE; GTPA; TAFW; SFT; DMFA; Denton AL; WTAE; TG. Sources: Mallett; Bywaters "New Texas Painters"; O'Brien; TPan m.; WWWAA.

LENNOX, Martha [P] Clarksville. Exhibited: GTPA.

LENTZ, Richard [P; T] Dallas. Birthdate: 1857. Birthplace: Germany. Studied: Munich. Exhibited: Dallas, 1887. Sources: Church; *New Handbook.*

LERNER, David [P] El Paso. Exhibited: EPWC 1940.

LEROUX, Margaret [D] San Antonio. Exhibited: SALA 1937.

LESLIE, Inez Brickey [P] Dallas. Birthdate: 1891. Birthplace: Dallas. Deathdate: 1969. Deathplace: Kaufman County, Tex. Studied: Reaugh. Member: FRAC. Exhibited: FRAC 1935. Work: PPHM. Sources: Artist's niece; ITD; PPHM files.

LESLIE, Virginia [P; T] Waco/Mineral Wells. Studied: C. H. Chapin; F. Fowler. Sources: O'Brien.

LESTER, William Lewis [P; Pm; T] Dallas/Austin. Birthdate: 1910. Birthplace: Graham, Tex. Deathdate: 1991. Deathplace: Austin. Studied: Travis. Member: LSP; DMFA. Exhibited: DAA; TCE; GTPA; SFT; TG; TPan.; ATPE; Rockefeller; WFNY; AIC 1941, 1942. Work: DMA; Longview AM; MFAH; McNay; Met.; MAMFW; PPHM;

TAMU; PAFA; SMU; UT; Witte. Sources: Carraro thesis; *New Handbook;* O'Brien; WWWAA.

LEVY, Gertrude Lisette [P] Houston. Birthdate: 1924. Exhibited: AHAE 1936.

LEWIS, John F. [P] San Antonio. Exhibited: SALA.

LEWIS, Laura Blocker [P] Marfa/San Antonio/New Orleans. Birthdate: 1915. Birthplace: Manila, Phillipines. Studied: New Orleans AA; X. Gonzalez. Exhibited: WTAE 1939; Witte; TG 1942. Mural: USPO, Eunice, La. Sources: WWWAA.

LEWIS, Lulia M. [P] San Antonio. Exhibited: SALA 1930.

LIEB, Emanuel [P] Galveston? Exhibited: Texas Coast Fair 1895.

LIGHTFOOT, Mary L. [P; Pm] Dallas. Birthdate: 1898. Birthplace: Ravena, Tex. Deathdate: 1970. Deathplace: Paris, Tex. Studied: TWU; Columbia. Member: TP; Dallas Print Society (president, 1943). Exhibited: DAA; TCE; TG; ATPE. Work: PPHM. Sources: Harris; ITD; Mallett; TPan m.

LIGON, Verda [P; Pm] Dallas. Birthdate: 1902. Birthplace: Dallas. Deathdate: 1970. Deathplace: Dallas. Studied: Detroit Inst. FA; SMU; Phoenix AI, New York. Member: Texas Pm (founder); FRAC. Exhibited: DAA; FRAC 1930; TCE; SFT 1938; TG 1941S; ATPE. Work: DMA. Sources: Bywaters Coll.; Harris; ITD; Mallett; "NTP"; TPan m.

LINCOLN, A. [P] Beaumont. Exhibited: TFWC 1931.

LINDSAY, (Miss) [P] Galveston? Exhibited: Texas Coast Fair 1895.

LINGAN, Penelope Bailey [P; Min. P; S; Pm] Houston. Birthdate: 1860. Birthplace: Mt. Mitchel, N.C. Deathdate: 1943. Deathplace: Houston. Studied: Queen's College, Charlotte, N.C.; Newcomb College; AIC. Member: SSAL; TFAA; MFAH; HAG. Exhibited: SFT 1914 (medal); TAFW 1915; AHAE; SSAL. Work: MFAH. Sources: DAS; Fielding; Fisk; Mallett; O'Brien; WWWAA.

LINGUIST, Margaret (Mrs. John) [P] Fort Worth. Exhibited: TAFW.

LINN, Lora [P] Seagraves. Exhibited: TFWC 1931.

LITTLEJOHN, Margaret Martin [P; T] Fort Worth. Birthdate: 1885. Birthplace: Jefferson, Tex. Studied: MFA, Boston; ASL; Chase; J. Carlson; Speicher. Member: FWAA; AACFW. Exhibited: TAFW; Cotton Carn. 1910; SFT 1938; UCE 2. Sources: Fielding; Fisk; Mallett; O'Brien; WWWAA.

LIVINGSTON, George M. [P; Comm. A] Houston. Birthdate: 1903. Birthplace: Marfa, Tex. Deathdate: 1988. Deathplace: Fort Stockton. Studied: Sul Ross State w/ B. Matthaei, M. Vandiver; UT; Chicago Acad. FA. Member: Houston Associated Artists. Exhibited: James Bute Gallery; Houston Associated Artists. Work: Private coll. Sources: Alpine Avalanche; Mus. of the Big Bend, Alpine.

LOBITT, Bertha [P] Galveston. Exhibited: Texas Coast Fair 1895. Sources: RL.

LOCKARD, Robert Ivan [P; T; Pm] Lubbock. Birthdate: 1905. Birthplace: Norton, Kans. Studied: J. F. Helm Jr. Member: SIA; Prairie Water Color Painters. Exhibited: SPCCE; TCE; WTAE 1940; KCAI 1932. Sources: Wilbanks; WWWAA.

LOCKE, Lucie Harris (Mrs. David Roger) [P; T] Corpus Christi. Birthdate: 1904. Birthplace: Valdosta, Ga. Studied: Newcomb College w/ E. Woodward, W. Stevens, X. Gonzalez; Tulane; Witte Mus. Sch. of Art w/ C. Rosen; F. Taubes; O. Travis. Member: South Texas AL, Corpus Christi; TFAA; AAPL; SSAL; AFA; New Orleans AA. Exhibited: UCE 2; TG; Witte 1935 (solo); ASET 1937; SALA; SSAL. Work: Corpus Christi Junior College; Corpus Christi Art Found. Sources: Fielding; O'Brien; *San Antonio Light;* WWWAA; Witte files.

LOCKHART, George [P] Dallas. Exhibited: SFT 1939.

LOCKWOOD, John Ward [P; Pm; Mur. P; T] Austin. Birthdate: 1894. Birthplace: Atchison, Kans. Deathdate: 1963. Deathplace: Ranchos de Taos, N.M. Studied: KU; PAFA; Acad. Ransom, Paris. Member: LSP. Exhibited: GTPA; TG; DMFA/TPE; MFAH 1935 (solo), 1941 (solo); Witte 1935 (solo); HPAG 1935 (solo); TG; ATPE; TPan.; SALA 1943; AIC; Carnegie; CSFAC; Corcoran; DAM; KCAI;PAFA; Whitney; SSAL. Work: DMA; McNay; UT; KU; Met.; Whitney; CSFAC; USPOs, Edinburg and Hamilton, Tex. Sources: Eldredge bio.; Fielding; *New Handbook;* Samuels; WWWAA.

LOMBARDI, A. N. [P] El Paso. Exhibited: EPWC.

LOGGINS, Mrs. R. B. [P] West Columbia. Exhibited: TFWC 1931.

LONG, Eulah Biggers [P] Fort Worth. Exhibited: TAFW.

LONGACRE, Marion [P] San Antonio. Exhibited: SALA 1933.

LONGSHIE, George E. [S] Dallas. Exhibited: DAA 1938.

LOOMIS, Jill S. [P] San Antonio. Exhibited: SALA 1943.

LOOSE, William [P] El Paso. Exhibited: EPWC 1927.

LOPEZ, Pedro [P] San Antonio. Exhibited: TAFW 1922.

LOPEZ, Salvador [P] El Paso. Exhibited: EPWC 1944.

LOPEZ, Viveano [P] San Antonio. Exhibited: SALA 1936.

LOVELADY, Ruth Philpott [P] Abilene. Member: FRAC. Exhibited: SSAL; FRAC 1934.

LOVERT, Reuben [P] El Paso. Exhibited: EPWC 1940.

LOWDON, Elsie Motz [P; Min. P; T] Abilene/New York. Birthdate: 1884. Birthplace: Waco. Deathdate: 1960. Deathplace: Ft. Worth. Studied: Baylor w/ E. Wragg; ASL; Amer. Sch. Min. P. w/ L. F. Fuller. Member: NAWPS; SSAL; TFAA. Exhibited: Cotton Pal. 1915; TAFW '36; NAD; PAFA; Corcoran; NAWPS. Work: NMAA; Met. Sources: Abilene Mus. FA files; Fielding; Fisk; O'Brien; WWWAA.

LOWENSTERN, Virgie. See CLAXTON, Virgie

LUCAS, Ann (Mrs. W. C.) [P] Fort Worth. Exhibited: TAFW; TFWC 1931.

LUCAS, Fannie [P] Houston. Exhibited: AHAE.

LUDEMAN, Henriette (Aletta) [P] Plainview, Tex. Birthdate: 1901. Deathdate: 1977. Deathplace: Plainview. Exhibited: TFWC 1931; WTAE 1942. Sources: Plainview PL.

LUMPKINS, Chester L. [P] Big Spring. Exhibited: WTAE 1942.

LUNGKWITZ, Karl Friedrich Hermann [P; Por. P; T; Ph] New Braunfels/Fredericksburg/San Antonio/Austin.

Birthdate: 1813. Birthplace: Halle-an-der-Saale, Germany. Deathdate: 1891. Deathplace: Austin. Studied: Royal Academy, Dresden. Exhibited: Yanaguana (ph.). Work: Carter; DRT Lib.; MFAH; PPHM; San Antonio PL; TMM; Witte. Sources: McGuire bio.; Fisk; *New Handbook;* O'Brien; Pinckney; Samuels; Steinfeldt; Utterbeck.

LYKES, Genevieve [P] Galveston/Houston. Birthdate: 1885. Birthplace: Pensacola, Fla. Deathdate: 1971. Deathplace: Houston. Studied: Converse College, Spartanburg, S.C. Member: Friends of Art, MFAH. Exhibited: AHAE 1936. Sources: RL.

LYNN, Amy Brewer (Mrs. W. H.) [P; Por.P] Wellington, Tex. Birthdate: 1896. Birthplace: Edom, Tex. Deathdate: 1967. Deathplace: Corpus Christi. Studied: NTSTC; Broadmoor; CSFAC; Christoval; J. Palmer; R. Bassett; A. Brunet. Member: Lubbock AA; TFAA; Amarillo AA; Panhandle Painters Assoc. Exhibited: Ney Mus. 1936 (w/ J. Palmer), 1945 (solo); TSFA; Fort Worth 1945; TFWC. Work: Collingsworth County and Childress County (Tex.) courthouses. Sources: *Austin American-Statesman; The Collingsworth Standard; Denton Record-Chronicle; Fort Worth Star-Telegram; Texian Who's Who;* Wilbanks. Helped found Palo Duro Art Colony; commissioned to paint Iron Mill Ranch subjects.

LYON, L. N., Jr. [P] Houston. Exhibited: AHAE 1934.

LYON, Nicholas [P] Houston. Exhibited: AHAE 1938. Work: USPO, Conroe, Tex. Sources: WWWAA.

LYONS, J. R. [P] Midland. Exhibited: WTAE 1939.

LYONS, Jane Kirk [P] Midland. Exhibited: WTAE 1939.

MacCUISTON, Jacques (Jax) [Miss] [S; P; Pm] Dallas/ Hollywood, Calif. Birthdate: 1906. Birthplace: Texarkana, Tex. Studied: Loyola Univ.; Frolich Sch.; Otis AI; NAD; ASL; R. Aitken; R. Laurent; W. Zorach. Member: Dallas AA; Fed. of Dallas Artists; FRAC; Aunspaugh AS; AFA. Exhibited: DAA 1933. Sources: Bywaters Coll.; DAS; Fielding; WWWAA.

MacDONALD, Mrs. R. H. [P] Fort Worth. Exhibited: TAFW 1918.

MacDONNELL, M. Angela [P] Houston. Birthdate: 1875. Birthplace: Galveston. Deathdate: . Studied: Met. SFA; AIC; Vanderpoel. Member: Galveston AL (founder).

Exhibited: Cotton Carn. 1910; TAFW; AHAE; MFAH 1930 (solo), 1933 (solo). Work: MFAH. Sources: Houston Post; O'Brien; RL.

MacFADDEN, N. [P] San Antonio. Exhibited: TAFW 1926.

MacGREGOR, Mrs. H. F. [P] Galveston? Exhibited: Texas Coast Fair 1895.

MACIAS, E. [P] El Paso. Exhibited: EPWC 1936.

MACK, Alexander Watson [P; S; T] Dallas/San Antonio/Lubbock/Amarillo/Canyon. Birthdate: 1894. Birthplace: Pumpherston, Scotland. Deathdate: 1988. Deathplace: Canyon, Tex. Studied: Herriott-Watt Engin. College; Edinburgh College of Art; D. Alison; H. Lintott; D. M. Sutherland; Royal Acad., London, England. Member: Villita Street Gallery, San Antonio. Exhibited: TFWC 1931; PPHM 1933; Witte 1934; TAFW 1936; TCE; SALA; Villita 1936. Work: PPHM; West Texas A&M Univ., Canyon. Sources: Fisk; O'Brien; PPHM files; Witte files.

MacKAY, Catherine [P] Galveston. Exhibited: Cotton Carn. 1910, 1911. Sources: Galveston City Directory 1905–14.

MACKBEE, Esther [P] Dallas. Exhibited: DAA 1928.

MacKENZIE, M. [P] Fort Worth. Exhibited: TAFW 1918.

MacLEAN, Christina [P] Fort Worth. Birthdate: 1853. Birthplace: Glasgow, Scotland. Studied: Glasgow AS; D. Murray, London; AIC. Exhibited: TAFW. Sources: Fisk; O'Brien; Smith.

MacLEARY, Bonnie (Mrs. Ernest Kramer) [S] San Antonio/ New York. Birthdate: 1890. Birthplace: San Antonio. Deathdate: 1971. Deathplace: Zephyr Hills, Fla. Studied: Chase Sch.; Bougereau; Fraser; AJ; ASL; Mora. Member: AFA; NAWPS; Allied Artists of Amer.; NAC; NAD; AAPL. Exhibited: PAFA; Rochester Memorial Galls; NAC; ARE; NAD. Work: Witte; Baylor Univ.; St. Paul's Episcopal Ch., Waco; SAMA; Children's Mus., Brooklyn; Met; Wesleyan College, Macon, Ga. Sources: DAS; Fielding; Fisk; Hendricks and Reese; *New Handbook;* O'Brien; Smith; WWWAA.

MacNAUGHTON, Mary Hunter [P] Palestine. Exhibited: TFWC 1931. Sources: WWWAA.

MACUNE, Katherine [P] Fort Worth. Exhibited: TFWC 1931.

MADDOX, Maud [P] El Paso. Exhibited: EPWC 1936.

MADDOX, Mrs. Roy G. [P] El Paso. Exhibited: EPWC 1936.

MADDREY, Kate [P] Bonham. Exhibited: TFWC 1931.

MAGILL, Calla Lilly [P] Brownsville, Tex. Exhibited: ASET 1937.

MAHAFFEY, Josephine [P] Fort Worth. Exhibited: TAFW 1937.

MAHER, William H. [Pm] San Antonio. Exhibited: ATPE 1945.

MAHONEY, James Owen, Jr. [P; Pm; Mur. P; T; S] Dallas/Ithaca, N.Y. Birthdate: 1907. Birthplace: Dallas. Deathdate: 1987. Deathplace: Ithaca, N.Y. Studied: SMU; Yale; American Academy in Rome. Member: Nat. Soc. of Mur. P. Exhibited: SFT 1932; DAA; TCE; Grand Central Gall., N.Y. 1935; PAFA 1942. Work: Hall of State, Dallas. Sources: Bywaters Coll.; Falk PAFA; O'Brien; WWWAA.

MALONE, Clotilde Lee [S] Waco. Birthdate: 1860. Birthplace: Nashville, Tenn. Deathdate: 1891. Deathplace: Waco. Studied: Self-taught. Work: Tex. State Capitol. Sources: Hendricks and Reese.

MANN, Kelly [P] El Paso. Exhibited: EPWC 1938.

MANNING, Dorothy [P] Dallas. Exhibited: DAA 1929.

MANSBENDEL, Peter [S; T] Austin. Birthdate: 1883. Birthplace: Basle, Switzerland. Deathdate: 1940. Deathplace: Austin. Studied: Coquier-Roland Sch., Paris. Exhibited: Witte 1930 (solo). Work: SMU; UT. Sources: *New Handbook*; O'Brien; "Peter Mansbendel."

MANZANAREZ, Concepcion [P] El Paso. Exhibited: EPWC 1942.

MAPLES, Barbara Lucile [Pm] Dallas. Birthdate: 1912. Birthplace: Temple. Deathdate: 1999. Deathplace: Dallas. Studied: Mary Hardin-Baylor, Belton; Columbia; CSFAC; TWU. Member: TP; DMFA; Amer. Assoc. Univ. Women; Dallas Print and Drawing Soc. Exhibited: SFT

1938; DAA; TG; DMFA '41 (solo), '43 (solo), '47 (solo); Witte 1942 (solo); SSAL. Work: Belo; Longview AM; PPHM. Sources: Bywaters Coll.; TPan m.; Harris.

MARCOS, (Mrs.) [P] Galveston? Exhibited: Texas Coast Fair 95.

MARFORD (MORFORD), Bessie H. [P] Galveston. Exhibited: Cotton Carn. 1911, 1912. Sources: Galveston City Directory 1903–10.

MARGULES, Adalie. See BRENT, Adalie Margules

MARIETTA, Sister Mary (Mary Isabelle Egerton) [P; T] Austin. Birthdate: 1871. Birthplace: Baltimore. Deathdate: 1949. Deathplace: Columbus, Ohio. Exhibited: TFWC 1931; Driskill Hotel '28. Work: Driskill Hotel, Austin. Sources: Sisters of the Holy Cross, Notre Dame.

MARKHAM, Ruby Stone. See STONE

MARS, Adelaide [P] Dallas. Exhibited: DAA 1929.

MARSHALL, Mary [T] Denton. Birthplace: Greenville, Tex. Studied: St. Mary's College, Dallas; Hamilton College, Lexington, Ky.; Pratt Inst.; Taos. Exhibited: New York Art Ctr.; Art Alliance of Amer. Sources: O'Brien.

MARTIN, Mrs. A. A. [P] El Paso. Exhibited: EPWC.

MARTIN, Beatrice Rawlins "Trix" (Mrs. Harry Martin) [P] Galveston. Exhibited: TAFW 1926. Sources: RL.

MARTIN, Mrs. C. C. [P] George West, Tex. Exhibited: TFWC 1931.

MARTIN, H. [P] San Antonio. Exhibited: SAAL 1924.

MARTIN, Mrs. Howard [P] Weatherford. Exhibited: WTAE 1939.

MARTIN, John Breckenridge [P] Dallas. Birthdate: 1857. Birthplace: Laurel Co., Ky. Deathdate: 1938. Deathplace: Dallas. Studied: Self-taught. Member: Dallas AA. Exhibited: TAFW; SFT 1934; DAA; DMFA 1938 (solo); Sartor 1934 (solo). Work: DMA. Sources: Church; Fisk; *New Handbook*; O'Brien; Samuels; WWWAA.

MARTIN, Jose [S] Dallas. Birthdate: 1891. Birthplace: France. Deathdate: 1984. Deathplace: Dallas. Member:

Tex. Sculp. Group. Exhibited: DMFA 1944. Work: Fair Park, Dallas. Sources: Dallas Hist. Soc. files; Hendricks and Reese.

MARTIN, Lottie E. [P; Pm] Fort Worth. Exhibited: TAFW 1934–37; ATPE 1942.

MARTINEZ, Manuel [P] San Antonio. Exhibited: SALA 1931.

MASCHO, June [P] Dallas/Shreveport, La. Deathplace: Living Shreveport, La. Studied: Reaugh. Member: FRAC. Exhibited: FRAC 1932–34. Work: PPHM. Sources: PPHM files.

MASCHO, Norma (June?) [P] Dallas. Exhibited: DAA.

MASLEY, Alexander Simeon [P; Pm; T; Des.] Austin. Birthdate: 1903. Birthplace: Akeley, Minn. Studied: Minneapolis Sch. of Art; Univ. Minn.; Columbia; Central Sch., London; H. Hofmann Sch., Munich; Design Lab., N.Y.; C. Booth; W. P. Robins. Member: TFAA; Minneapolis AA; Prairie PM. Exhibited: TG; WFNY; Minneapolis Inst. Art; San Francisco MA; AIC; Minnesota State Fair. Sources: WWWAA.

MASSENBURG, Eugenia C. [P; T; Min. P; S] Paris, Texas/Navasota, Tex. Birthdate: 1870. Birthplace: Boston, Bowie Co., Tex. Deathdate: 1951. Deathplace: Navasota. Studied: ASL; Columbia w/ A. Dow; M. Fry; F. B. A. Punch; R. H. Knickles; Granbury Studio, N.Y. Exhibited: Paris (Texas) ca. 1935. Work: Family. Sources: Fisk; O'Brien; Artist's nephew.

MASSEY, Robert [Pm] Dallas. Exhibited: Annual Texas Print Exhibition 1944.

MASSEY, Suwanee [S] Dallas. Exhibited: DAA 1928.

MASSIC, Kathryn [P] Dallas. Exhibited: DAA 1929.

MAST, Clara Glenn [P] Lubbock. Birthdate: 1880. Birthplace: Delaware, Ohio. Deathdate: 1947. Deathplace: Lubbock. Studied: C. Redin. Member: Lubbock AC (founder); TFAA; Lubbock AA. Exhibited: TFWC 1931; PMS 1932; Lubbock AA 1933; UCE 2; SPCCE; WTAE 1942. Sources: Wilbanks.

MASTIN, Mignon [P] Fort Worth. Exhibited: TAFW.

MATHEE, Malzena [P] Houston. Exhibited: AHAE 1937.

MATHEWSON, Thomas C. [P] San Antonio. Exhibited: SALA 1944.

MATHIS, Arthur Jr. [P] San Antonio. Exhibited: SALA.

MATLOCK, Ruth Blanks [P] San Angelo. Birthplace: San Angelo. Studied: A. Brunet; R. Bassett. Exhibited: SFT 1938; WTAE; TFAA. Work: Shannon Mem. Hospital, San Angelo.

MATTHAEI, Beatrice [P; Pm] Houston. Exhibited: TAFW; AHAE; ASET.

MATTHEWS, Harold J. [Pm] Houston. Birthdate: 1897. Birthplace: Waco. Studied: Decatur College; Baylot; Univ. of Kansas. Exhibited: TCE; AHAE.

MATTHEWS, Malvina [P] San Antonio. Exhibited: SALA 1933.

MATTHIES, Frances Glass [P] Fort Worth. Exhibited: TAFW 1932.

MAURER, Julia Ott (Mrs. Joseph M.) [P] Galveston. Birthdate: 1881. Birthplace: Galveston. Deathdate: 1963. Deathplace: Houston. Exhibited: Cotton Carn. 1910. Sources: RL.

MAUZEY, Merritt Thomas [P; Pm; T; W] Dallas. Birthdate: 1898. Birthplace: Clifton, Tex. Deathdate: 1973. Deathplace: Dallas. Studied: F. Klepper; Knott. Member: LSP (Charter). Exhibited: TCE; GTPA; SFT 1938; Ney Mus. (solo) 1942; Witte (solo) 1942; DAA; TG; TPan.; ATPE; LSP; Delphic Studios, New York 1939; Whitney; WFNY; SSAL. Work: DMA; Longview AM; MFAH; PPHM; Witte; MSW; Met; PAFA; Corcoran. Sources: Artist's Notebook; New Handbook; Samuels; Stewart; WWWAA.

MAVERICK, Mrs. Albert [P] San Antonio. Exhibited: SALA 1935.

MAVERICK, Lucy Madison [P] San Antonio. Birthdate: 1883. Studied: Provincetown; A. Dow. Member: Villita Street Gallery. Exhibited: TAFW; SALA; GTPA. Work: SAAL. Sources: O'Brien; WWWAA; Witte files.

MAVERICK, Mary Adams [P] San Antonio. Birthdate: 1916. Studied: Arpa; Nixon. Member: The Attic Studio. Exhibited: SALA 1931. Sources: San Antonio Light; Witte files.

MAVERICK, Mary J. [P] San Antonio. Exhibited: SAAL 1924.

MAXEY, Robert [P] Lubbock. Member: Lubbock AA. Exhibited: Lubbock AA 1937. Sources: Wilbanks.

MAXSON, Peggy [P] Dallas. Exhibited: DAA 1928.

MAXWELL, Mrs. Oliver [P] Dallas. Exhibited: DAA 1929.

MAYER, Marjorie [P] Dallas. Exhibited: DAA 1945.

MAYER, Max [Arch.; P] San Antonio/Little Rock, Ark. Birthdate: 1887. Birthplace: San Antonio. Deathdate: 1947. Deathplace: Little Rock, Ark. Studied: TAMC; École BA. Sources: Goetzmann and Reese.

MAYES, H. H. [P; Por. P] Dallas. Exhibited: DAA.

MAYS, Maxine [Cer.] Dallas. Exhibited: DAA 1938.

McARDLE, Henry Arthur [P; Port. P; T] Independence, Tex. Birthdate: 1836. Birthplace: Belfast, Ireland. Deathdate: 1908. Deathplace: San Antonio. Studied: Belfast w/ Saveur; Maryland Inst. w/ Woodward. Exhibited: Texas Coast Fair 1895. Work: Tex. State Cap. Sources: Fisk; *New Handbook;* O'Brien; Pinckney; Ratcliffe; Samuels; WWWAA.

McATEE, (Mrs.) [P] Galveston? Exhibited: Texas Coast Fair 1895.

McBRIDE, Beatrice Matthaei. See MATTHAEI

McBRIDE, Mrs. E. R. [P] Chico. Exhibited: TFWC 1931.

McBRIDE, Lucille [P] Dallas. Exhibited: DAA 1928.

McCABE, J. Glenn [P; Pm] Fort Worth/Houston. Exhibited: TAFW; AHAE.

McCALL, Dora [P] Dallas. Exhibited: DAA 1933.

McCAMPBELL, Mrs. James B. [S] San Antonio. Exhibited: SALA 1940.

McCAN, James Ferdinand [P] San Antonio/Victoria/Boerne. Birthdate: 1869. Birthplace: County Kerry, Ireland. Deathdate: 1925. Deathplace: San Antonio. Studied: Kensington AS, London. Member: Soc. Tex. A. Exhibited: TAFW 1915. Work: Municipal Auditorium, San Antonio; Nave. Sources: ITD; O'Brien; WWWAA.

McCANN, Charles L. [P] Dallas. Exhibited: TAFW 1931; DAA; Dallas Free Public Art Gallery 1932.

McCARTHY, Lily (Mrs. Victor) [P] Fort Worth. Exhibited: TAFW.

McCLAIN, George M. [P; Pm] Dallas. Birthdate: 1877. Exhibited: TAFW 1936; TCE; SFT 1939; DAA; TG 1940, 1941F.

McCLELLAN, Bowen [P; I] Dallas. Exhibited: DAA 1928.

McCLINTOCK, Mrs. V. H. [P] Paducah. Exhibited: TFWC 1931.

McCLUNG, Florence Elliott White (Mrs. Rufus A.) [P; Pm; T] Dallas. Birthdate: 1894. Birthplace: St. Louis. Deathdate: 1992. Deathplace: Dallas. Studied: SMU; CSFAC; Reaugh; Simkins; Hogue; Travis. Member: SSAL; NAWA; Dallas AA; Pm Guild; TP; FRAC; DAL. Exhibited: FRAC; TFWC 1931; TCE; UCE 1; GTPA; SFT 1939; TAFW; DAA; TG; TPan.; ATPE; PAFA 1937; MoMA; WFNY; SSAL. Work: DMA; PPHM; SMU. Sources: Bywaters Coll.; Fielding; Mallett; *New Handbook;* "NTP"; O'Brien; Samuels; Stewart; TPan m.; WWWAA.

McCOMMON, Frances V. [P] San Antonio. Exhibited: SALA 1931. Sources: *San Antonio Light;* Witte files.

McCORMICK, Mrs. H. P. [P] El Paso. Exhibited: EPWC.

McCULLOUGH, Maxie Thomas [P; Des.; T; Pm] Eastland, Texas/Laguna Beach, Calif. Birthdate: 1874. Birthplace: Forrest City, Ark. Studied: Cincinnati Art Acad.; Academie Julian. Member: Dallas AA; HPSFA; SSAL; TFAA. Exhibited: SACE 1929; SFT. Work: Little Rock MFA. Sources: WWWAA.

McCUTCHEON, Mrs. B. [P] Dallas. Exhibited: DAA 1928.

McDADE, Helen [P] San Antonio. Exhibited: SALA; TG 1944.

McDADE, Ira [P; T] Fort Worth/Pittsburgh, Pa. Birthdate: 1873. Birthplace: Pittsburgh. Studied:

H. Stevens Sch. of Art, Pittsburgh; W. B. Leisser; C. Walters; C. Johns; A. King. Member: Pittsburgh AA. Exhibited: TAFW; TCE. Sources: O'Brien; WWWAA.

McDERMOTT, Cecilia [P] Dallas. Exhibited: TAFW; DAA; Beaumont Fair 1916. Sources: Fisk; WWWAA.

McDONALD, Mary [P] San Antonio. Exhibited: SALA 1936.

McDONALD, Sarah Inglish [P] Stamford. Birthdate: 1900. Exhibited: TAFW; TCE; WTAE.

McDONNELL, M. Angela. See MacDONNELL, M. Angela

McDOWELL, Fritz [P] San Antonio. Exhibited: SALA 1936.

McELRATH, Eva [P] Noelette. Exhibited: TFWC 1931.

McELROY, Michael [P] El Paso. Birthplace: Kilarney Lake, Ireland. Deathdate: 1953. Deathplace: El Paso. Studied: Trinity Univ., Edinburgh. Exhibited: EPWC, WTAE 1942. Sources: *El Paso Herald-Post;* EPPL; *El Paso Times.*

McEVER, Mrs. Thomas F. [P] Slaton. Member: Lubbock AA. Exhibited: Lubbock AA 1933. Sources: Wilbanks.

McFADDEN, Florence N. Glyn-Wells (Mrs. E. E.) [P; Pm] San Antonio. Birthplace: London, Eng. Studied: Armitage; Calif Sch. Design; Arpa. Member: San Antonio A. Gld; San Francisco P&CC; San Francisco AL. Exhibited: TAFW 1929, 1931, 1932; SALA; Witte 1928. Sources: *San Antonio Express;* Witte files; WWWAA.

McFEE, Henry Lee [P; T] Boerne. Birthdate: 1886. Birthplace: St. Louis, Mo. Deathdate: 1953. Deathplace: Claremont, Calif. Studied: ASL. Member: Nat. Inst. of Arts and Letters; Amer. Soc. Painters, Sculptors and Gravers; Woodstock AA. Exhibited: TG 1940; Paris salon; AIC; NAD; PAFA. Work: Witte. Sources: Fielding; Steinfeldt; WWWAA.

McGEE, Will T. [P] Fort Worth. Exhibited: TAFW. Sources: WWWAA.

McGILL, Eloise Polk (Mrs. George) [P; Min. P; T] San Antonio. Birthdate: 1868. Birthplace: Independence, Tex. Deathdate: 1939. Deathplace: San Antonio. Studied: ASL;

Chase; R. J. Onderdonk; R. Reid; R. H. Nicholls. Member: SAAL; SSAL; TFAA; Assoc. of Amer. Women. Exhibited: Texas Coast Fair 95; TWF 1917; TAFW; TWCE; Three Arts Cl. Exh., N.Y. 1928; TCE; UCE 2; SACE; ASET 1937; SALA 1930, 1931. Work: Witte; St. Anselm's Priory, Wash., D.C.; Sacred Heart Ch., Del Rio, Tex. Sources: Fisk; Mallett; O'Brien; Steinfeldt; WWWAA.

McGILL, Leona Leti [P; I; T] Fort Worth. Birthdate: 1892. Studied: AIC. Member: ASL Chicago; SSAL; AACFW. Exhibited: TAFW; TCE. Sources: WWWAA.

McGONIGLE, Ruth G. Y. [D] Houston/Brownsville, Tex. Exhibited: AHAE; ASET.

McGRAW, Hazel Fulton [P] Abilene/Ballinger. Birthdate: 1897. Birthplace: Sherman, Tex. Studied: Hardin-Simmons College; F. Klepper; M. Mauzey; H. A. De Young. Member: AAPL; Texas Pm. Exhibited: WTAE; FWAA; TG; Abilene Mus. FA 1944; ATPE 1945; LOC; Laguna Beach AA. Sources: Harris; WWWAA.

McGUIRE, Jack W. [Car.] San Antonio. Exhibited: SALA 1932. Sources: *San Antonio Express;* Witte files.

McGUIRE, Tom C. [P] San Antonio. Exhibited: SALA 1932.

McINTOSH, Ruby C. (Mrs. R. H.) [P] Abilene. Exhibited: TAFW 1936; WTAE 1939, 1940.

McIVER, Portia Juanita Ragland [P] Dallas. Exhibited: TAFW; DAA.

McKAMY, Marianna [P; Velvet P; I; Cer.] Dallas. Exhibited: DAA.

McKAY, Adelie [P] Dallas. Exhibited: TFWC 1931.

McKEE, Louise [P] Lubbock. Member: Lubbock AA. Exhibited: Lubbock AA. Sources: Wilbanks.

McKENNA, Helen [P; Pm] Houston. Exhibited: AHAE.

McKENNA, William [P] Houston. Deathdate: 1966. Deathplace: Houston. Exhibited: AHAE. Sources: ITD.

McKEON, Hazel [P] Houston. Exhibited: AHAE 1945.

McKINLEY, Catherine Hall [P] Dallas. Exhibited: DAA 1935.

McKINLEY, Frances [P] Dallas. Exhibited: DAA 1929.

McKINNEY, Walter A. [P] San Antonio. Exhibited: SALA 1932.

McLAUGHLIN, Katherine [P] Dallas. Exhibited: TAFW 1930.

McLEARY, Kindred [P; Arch.; Des.; Mur. P; T] Austin/ Pittsburgh, Pa. Birthdate: 1901. Birthplace: Weimar, Tex. Deathdate: 1949. Deathplace: Confluence, Pa. Studied: UT; Fontainbleau w/ Carlu; Paris; Rome. Member: Pittsburgh AA. Exhibited: Pittsburgh AA. Work: MFAH; Westmoreland Mus. of Art, Pa.; USPOs, NYC, Pittsburgh, and Washington, D.C. Sources: Fisk; *New Handbook;* WWWAA; Westmoreland Mus. of Art.

McLEE, Ella Frances [P] Temple. Exhibited: TFWC 1931.

McLELLAN, Henry H., Jr. [P] Fort Worth. Exhibited: TAFW.

McLELLAN, James Lucretius (J. M.) [P] San Antonio. Exhibited: SALA 1934. Sources: Witte files.

McLELLAN, Ralph [P; T; Pm] San Marcos/NYC. Birthdate: 1884. Birthplace: San Marcos, Tex. Studied: MFA, Boston w/ P. Hale, F. W. Benson, E. Tarbell; Mora; ASL. Member: Phila. WC Soc.; Philadelphia Art Alliance; SSAL; TFAA. Exhibited: TAFW 1913; Witte 1930 (solo); Fort Worth, SALA; Galveston; San Antonio; SSAL; NAD; PAFA; AIC; MFA, Boston; SAAL 1926. Work: Southwest Texas State Univ., San Marcos; Sam Houston State Univ., Huntsville. Sources: Fielding; O'Brien; *San Antonio Light;* Witte files; WWWAA.

McLELLAN, Sadie [P] San Antonio. Exhibited: SALA 1936.

McLENDON, Louise [P] Fort Worth. Exhibited: TAFW 1917. Sources: WWWAA.

McLERNON, Nance [S] San Antonio. Exhibited: SALA 1939.

McMAHAN, Peggy L. or C. [P] San Antonio. Exhibited: SALA.

McMATH, Hugh L. [Pm] Austin. Exhibited: ASET.

McMILLAN, Ben [P; Por. P] Dallas. Exhibited: DAA 1928.

McMILLAN, George C. or L. [P] Fort Worth. Exhibited: SFT 1909.

McMILLAN, Mary Jane. See BULLOCK, Mary J. M.
McNAB, Helena [P] Houston. Exhibited: AHAE 1935.

McNABB, Dorothy Horton [P] Dallas. Member: FRAC. Exhibited: FRAC 1941. Sources: PPHM files.

McNAMARA, Tom [S] San Antonio. Exhibited: SALA 1939.

McNAUGHTON, Elizabeth Baskerville [P; Pm] San Antonio. Birthdate: 1906. Birthplace: Los Angeles. Studied: Philadelphia; Los Angeles. Exhibited: TCE; SALA; Witte 1936 (solo). Sources: Witte files.

McNAY, Jessie Marion Koogler Atkinson [P] San Antonio. Birthdate: 1883. Birthplace: DeGraff, Ohio. Deathdate: 1950. Deathplace: San Antonio. Studied: KU; AIC; Bisttram. Exhibited: SALA 1935; TAFW 1935; MacBeth; AWS. Work: McNay. Sources: Burkhalter; *New Handbook;* O'Brien; *San Antonio Light;* Witte files.

McNEEL, Jessie Maverick [D] San Antonio. Exhibited: SALA.

McPHERSON, Mrs. F. E. [P] Dallas. Member: FRAC. Exhibited: FRAC 1941. Sources: PPHM files.

McVEIGH, Blanche [Pm] Fort Worth. Birthdate: 1895. Birthplace: St. Charles, Mo. Deathdate: 1970. Deathplace: Ft. Worth. Studied: SLSFA; AIC; PAFA; ASL; Wash. Univ., St. Louis. Member: SAM; SSAL; Prairie Pm; TP (founder). Exhibited: TCE; TG 1940–45; TFAA; SFT 1938; TAFW; GTPA; NAD; WFNY; SSAL. Work: MAMFW; MFAH; OJAC; PPHM; Rosenberg; Princeton Univ.; Grolier Cl.; PPHM; MFAH; DMA; UT. Sources: Beyond Regionalism; Fielding; Harris; Mallett; *New Handbook;* TPan.m.; WWWAA.

McVEY, Leza S. (Lee?) [S] Austin/Houston/Cleveland, Ohio. Birthdate: 1907. Birthplace: Cleveland, Ohio. Deathplace: living Cleveland 1984. Studied: Cleveland Sch. of Art; CSFAC; Research Studio, Maitland, Fla. Member: Texas Sculpture Group. Exhibited: DMFA 1944; AHAE; SALA 1944; TG 1943, 1944; Southwestern General Exp. Sources: Bywaters Coll.; DAS; Fielding; Houston PL; MFAH; WWWAA.

McVEY, William M. [P; S] Houston/Austin/Cleveland, Ohio. Birthdate: 1905. Birthplace: Boston. Studied: Rice; Cleveland Sch. of Art; Despiau; H. Keller; F. Wilcox; Acad. Colarossi; Acad. Chaumière; Acad. Scandinave, Paris. Member: Texas Sculpture Group; Seven Sculptors; Société Scandinave. Exhibited: AHAE; ASET 1938; TG 1940, 1941S, 1941F; SALA 1944; SSAL. Work: MFAH; San Jacinto Mus.; TMM; Texarkana; Ozona, Texas; playground, Houston. Sources: Bywaters Coll.; DAS; Fielding; Houston PL.; WWWAA.

MEAD, Ben Carlton [P; I; Mur. P] Amarillo/San Antonio/Dallas. Birthdate: 1902. Birthplace: Bay City, Tex. Deathdate: 1986. Deathplace: Santa Ynez, Calif. Studied: AIC w/ J. Rozen, C. Schroeder. Member: Panhandle-Plains Hist. Soc.; Westerners Int'l. Exhibited: TSFA; Amarillo College 1932; Amarillo AA 1933; PPHM 1933; Witte 1931 (solo); TFAA 1932. Work: PPHM; Carson County Square House; Quay County (NM) Courthouse; SAMA; Witte. Sources: New Handbook; PPHM files; Samuels; Witte files; WWWAA.

MEADOWS, Denis [P] El Paso. Exhibited: EPCC.

MEANS, Elliott A. [P; S; Comm. A; I] El Paso/NYC. Birthdate: 1905. Birthplace: Stamford, Tex. Deathdate: 1962. Deathplace: New York, N.Y. Studied: MFA, Boston. Member: Nat. Soc. Illustrators; Salmagundi; Grand Central Gall. Exhibited: EPWC 1938, 1941; EPCC; NAD; PAFA; N.Y. Arch. Lg. 1936; WFNY. Work: USPOs, Suffern, N.Y., and Dexter, Me.; U.S. Printing Office, Washington, D.C. Sources: Bywaters Coll.; El Paso Journal; EPPL; El Paso Times; Falk NAD; Falk PAFA; Price; Samuels; WWWAA.

MEANS, Glenn [P] Dallas. Exhibited: DAA 1935.

MEDELLIN, Octavio [S; P; Pm; T] San Antonio/Dallas/Bandera. Birthdate: 1908. Birthplace: San Luis Potosí, Mexico. Deathplace: Living Bandera, 1997. Studied: SAAI w/ Gonzalez, Arpa; AIC. Member: Villita Art Gall. Exhibited: TAFW 1936; TCE; ASET 1937; Witte 1940 (solo); TG; DMFA 1942 (solo); DAA 1943; SALA; WFNY; SSAL. Work: DMA; PPHM; SAMA. Sources: Hendricks and Reese; O'Brien; Stewart; WWWAA; Witte files.

MEDLIN, Mrs. A. M. [P] Abernathy. Exhibited: TFWC 1931.

MEDRANO, Abdon [P] Dallas. Exhibited: DAA 1933.

MEDRANO, Joaquin [S] Dallas. Birthdate: 1914. Exhibited: TCE; DAA 1941; TG 1941S.

MEISEL, Mrs. H. H. [P] El Paso. Exhibited: EPWC 1940.

MELTON, Felicia Von Briesen [P] El Paso. Exhibited: EPWC.

MELTON, Mrs. Jesse J. (Roxie?) [P] Fort Worth. Exhibited: TAFW 1910. Sources: WWWAA.

MELTON, Roxie (Mrs. Jesse J.?) [P] Fort Worth. Deathdate: 1966. Deathplace: Fort Worth. Exhibited: TAFW 1933. Sources: ITD.

MENDENHALL, Emma [P] Denton/Cincinnati, Ohio. Birthplace: Cincinnati. Studied: Cincinnati Art Acad. w/ Nowottny, Duveneck; AJ; R. H. Nicholls; Snell; Woodbury. Member: Amer. WCS; NAC; Washington WCC; NAWPS. Exhibited: TAFW 1920. Sources: WWWAA.

MENEZES, Harry E. [S] Dallas. Exhibited: DAA 1928.

MEREDITH, Alice Adkins [P; S; Pm; I; T] Dallas. Birthdate: 1905. Birthplace: Dallas. Deathdate: 1992. Deathplace: Dallas. Studied: Reaugh; Simkins; F. Booth; C. Bull; G. Dutch; P. Lemos; P. Carter; G. Bridgman. Member: FRAC; Dallas AA; Klepper AC; TFAA; SSAL. Exhibited: FRAC 1930; SFT 1933; DAA. Sources: O'Brien; WWWAA.

MEROUX, M. [P] San Antonio. Exhibited: SALA 1936.

MERRICK, P. R. [P] Dallas. Exhibited: DAA 1942.

MERRILL, Florence Nicholson "Bobby" [P; Des.; Cr; Comm. A] Dallas. Birthdate: 1907. Birthplace: Champaigne, Ill. Studied: Chicago Acad. FA. Exhibited: DAA?; DMFA?; Dallas Woman's Cl. Sources: O'Brien.

MERRILL, Walter Ralph [Arch.; P] Dallas. Birthdate: 1906. Birthplace: Harvey, Ill. Studied: Univ. Illinois; AIC. Member: Dallas Graphic Arts Soc. Exhibited: DAA. Sources: O'Brien.

METCALF, Louise [P] Houston. Exhibited: AHAE 1935.

MEUSEBACH, Iago [P] Bastrop, Tex. Exhibited: ASET 1937; TG 1941F.

MEWHINNEY, Ella Koepke [P; T] Holland, Tex. Birthdate: 1891. Birthplace: Nelsonville, Tex. Deathdate: 1975. Deathplace: Holland, Tex.? Studied: Texas Presbyterian College; ASL; Broadmoor w/ Davey, Reid. Member: SSAL; TFAA; AFA. Exhibited: TCE; TAFW; TWCE; SACE; SFT; UCE 1; SSAL; DWF 1925; TFWC 1931. Sources: Fielding; Fisk; *Holland's;* Mallett; O'Brien; Waco Art Ctr.; Samuels; WWWAA.

MEYER, Grace Manton [P] Amarillo. Exhibited: WTAE 1939, 1940. Sources: Amarillo City Directory 1939–40.

MEYERS, Jacqueline [D] Marshall, Tex. Exhibited: TG 1943.

MEYERS, Robert W. [D] San Antonio. Exhibited: SALA 1943. Sources: Samuels; Witte files.

MEYER-WALDECK, Kunz [P] Dallas. Birthdate: 1853. Deathdate: 1953. Exhibited: SFT 1910; Dallas Painters 1909.

MEYSENBURG, Virginia C. [P; Pm] Houston. Exhibited: TAFW; TCE; SFT 1939; AHAE.

MILAM, Annie Josephine Nelson (Mrs. R. L.) [P] Fort Worth/Dallas/El Paso/Ennis/Kaufman. Birthdate: 1870. Birthplace: Homer, La. Deathdate: 1934. Deathplace: Ellis Co., Tex. Studied: J. Carlson; Kunz-Meyer; Mt. Lebanon Univ. Member: El Paso AC; AFA. Exhibited: TAFW; Cotton Pal.; DWF; SFT; Southwestern General Exp.; EPCC; EPWC 1927. Sources: Fisk; WWWAA.

MILAM, Lillian (Mrs. W. T.) [P] Lubbock. Studied: Redin. Member: Lubbock AC; Lubbock AA; TFAA. Exhibited: TFWC 1931; Lubbock AA 1933; Childress (solo). Work: First Methodist Ch., Lubbock; First Christian Ch., Lubbock. Sources: Wilbanks.

MILLER, Emily Maverick [P] Austin. Exhibited: TG 1945.

MILLER, Florence Oom [P; Pm] Port Arthur. Exhibited: ASET 1937; ATPE 1945.

MILLER, Grace Ann [P] El Paso. Deathdate: 1977. Deathplace: El Paso. Exhibited: EPWC 1938, 1940. Sources: EPPL; *El Paso Times.*

MILLER, Mrs. Henry [P] Galveston? Exhibited: Texas Coast Fair 1895.

MILLER, Jean Blanc [P; Pm] Houston. Exhibited: AHAE.

MILLER, Jesse [P] Dallas. Exhibited: DAA 1935.

MILLER, Margaret C. [P] Dallas. Exhibited: DAA.

MILLER, Marilyn [P; T] Canyon. Studied: Centenary College; TSCW. Exhibited: Lubbock AA 1937. Sources: West Texas State Teachers College, Canyon, annual; Wilbanks.

MILLER, Olga Schroeder. See SCHROEDER, Olga

MILLER, Robert R. [P] Dallas. Exhibited: DAA 1928.

MILLER, Sallie W. (Dr.) [P] Slaton, Tex. Exhibited: TFWC 1931.

MILLER, Mrs. W. Maurice [P] Gunter, Tex. Exhibited: SFT 1938.

MILLER, Zella [P] Galveston? Exhibited: Texas Coast Fair 1895.

MILLS, Hillis [S] Dallas. Exhibited: DAA 1929.

MILTON, Mrs. Bernett [P] El Paso. Exhibited: EPWC 1936.

MIMS, Louise Holden [P] Dallas. Exhibited: SFT; TG 1940; DAA.

MINTEL, Edwina Krisch. [P; T] San Antonio/Fredericksburg. Birthdate: 1896. Birthplace: San Antonio. Deathdate: 1966. Deathplace: San Antonio. Studied: R. J. Onderdonk; P. Hohnstedt; J. Filippone; J. Arpa; R. Taylor. Member: Fredericksburg AC. Exhibited: SALA 1933, 1934. Sources: ITD; Maguire; Witte files.

MITCHELL, Gladys M. Vinson [P; S] Dallas/Houston. Birthdate: 1894. Birthplace: Albuquerque. Studied: B. Gonzales; E. Eisenlohr. Member: Chicago AG. Exhibited: TAFW; Dallas AA 1916. Work: MNM; Houston AL. Sources: DAS; Fielding; WWWAA.

MITCHELL, Lillian [P] El Paso. Exhibited: EPWC 1936.

MITCHELL, Margaret [P] Dallas. Birthdate: 1909. Exhibited: TCE. Sources: Mallet.

MITCHELL, Maurine R. [P; S] Dallas. Exhibited: DAA.

MITCHELL, Mel [Pm] Dallas. Exhibited: DAA 1929.

MITCHELL, Rena [P] Dallas. Birthdate: Exhibited: DAA.

MITCHELL, Richard [P] Houston. Exhibited: AHAE 1942.

MOELLING, Peter A. [P] Galveston. Birthplace: Bavaria. Exhibited: Chapel Hill, Hempstead, Houston, Huntsville, Independence, Washington (all Texas), 1863.

MOLLHAUSEN, Heinrich Balduin [P; D] . Birthdate: 1825. Birthplace: Bonn, Prussia. Deathdate: 1905. Deathplace: Berlin, Germany. Studied: Self-taught. Work: Smithsonian; Oklahoma State Hist. Soc.; Amon Carter; Staatliches Mus., Berlin. Sources: *New Handbook*; Samuels.

MOMSEN/MOMSON?, Mrs. Leo [P] El Paso. Exhibited: EPWC.

MONICA, Sister M. [P] Houston. Exhibited: AHAE.

MONK, Mattie Lou (Mrs. B. D.) [P] Fort Worth. Exhibited: TAFW.

MONTGOMERY, Fannie E. Bess [P] Houston. Exhibited: AHAE; SALA 1933.

MONTGOMERY, Percy [P] El Paso. Exhibited: EPWC 1927. Sources: EPPL; *El Paso Times*; Price.

MONTMINY, Pierre [P] Austin. Exhibited: TG 1944, 1945.

MOODY, Henry [P] San Antonio. Exhibited: TAFW; Crawford Gall. 1907.

MOORE, C. M. [P] Galveston? Exhibited: Texas Coast Fair 1895.

MOORE, Gwendolyn [P] Fort Worth. Exhibited: TAFW.

MOORE, Harvin [D] Houston. Exhibited: AHAE.

MOORE, John Marcellus ("Tex") [P] Wichita Falls/ Henrietta. Birthdate: 1865. Birthplace: near Fort Worth. Deathdate: 1950. Deathplace: Henrietta. Studied: Self-taught. Exhibited: FWFCE; TAFW 1936, 1937. Work: PPHM; Santa Fe Railroad. Sources: O'Brien; PPHM files; Samuels; WWWAA.

MOORE, P. A. [P] Houston. Exhibited: AHAE.

MOORE, Percy Caruthers [P] Blossom, Tex. Birthdate: 1888. Studied: E. Smith: AIC w/ M. Clute, Krehbiel, H. Pyle, F. Richardson. Exhibited: TAFW. Sources: Fisk.

MOORE, Tom James [P; Pm] Dallas/Hamilton, Mont. Birthdate: 1892. Birthplace: Dallas. Studied: Cincinnati Art Acad. w/ Duveneck; Luks; J. Sloan. Exhibited: WFNY. Sources: Samuels; WWWAA.

MOORE, Mrs. W. L. [P] San Marcos. Exhibited: TFWC 1931.

MORELAND, H. L. [P] Dallas. Exhibited: DAA 1928.

MORENO, Abel [P] Dallas. Exhibited: DAA 1929.

MORGAN, Jean Scrimgeour (Mrs. George D.) [P] Galveston. Birthdate: 1868. Birthplace: Galveston. Deathdate: 1938. Deathplace: Galveston. Studied: Galveston Female Inst.; ASL w/ Beckwith, Chase, Cox, Eakins. Exhibited: Texas Coast Fair 1895; Cotton Carn. 1912. Work: RL Sources: RL.

MORGAN, Portia L. [P] Austin. Exhibited: TFWC 1931.

MORGAN, Mrs. R. D. [P] Mexia, Tex. Exhibited: TFWC 1931.

MORGAN, Theophilous (Theodore) John. [P; T; Pm; W] San Antonio/ Castroville/ Silver Spring, Md. Birthdate: 1872. Birthplace: Cincinnati. Studied: Cincinnati Sch. of Art w/ Lutz, Noble, Meakin, Nowothey, Rebisso, Duveneck. Member: SAAL; SAPAssoc.; SSAL; Soc. of Wash. Artists; Washington AC; NAC; Washington WCC; San Diego AA. Exhibited: SACE. Work: MFAH; Witte; HPSFA; Girl Scout Barracks, San Antonio; Women's Bldg., Harlingen, Tex. Sources: Fielding; WWWAA; Witte files.

MORRIS, Elizabeth H. [P] Houston. Birthdate: 1887. Exhibited: TAFW; TCE; AHAE.

MORRIS, Glory H. [P] Houston. Exhibited: AHAE 1945.

MORRIS, Lena [P] Fort Worth. Exhibited: TAFW 1926.

MORRIS, Martha Wilson [P] Brownwood, Tex. Exhibited: TFWC 1931.

MORRIS, William [P] Houston. Exhibited: AHAE.

MORRISON, Karl R. [P] San Antonio. Exhibited: SALA 1944; ATPE 1944, 1945.

MORRISON, Mary [P] Houston. Exhibited: AHAE 1933.

MORRISON, Olivia Brown. See BROWN, Olivia

MOSE, Carl C. [S] Houston/St. Louis, Mo. Birthdate: 1903. Birthplace: Copenhagen, Denmark. Deathdate: 1973. Studied: AIC; ASL; Beaux Arts Inst. of Design, N.Y.; L. Taft; L. Lentelli; A. Polasek. Member: Soc. Washington Artists; AFA; St. Louis AG; NSS; Nat. Soc. Arts and Letters. Exhibited: AHAE 1944; MFAH (solo). Work: Corcoran; numerous public sculptures in U.S. Sources: Fielding; WWWAA.

MOSELEY, Alice Taylor [P; Min. P; T] Brownwood, Tex. Studied: A. B. Sheppard; H. Payne College; Baylor; AIC; E. N. Casterton; G. Estabrooks; A. A. Fragee; A. P. Walker; M. Mason; Broadmoor. Exhibited: WTAE 1940. Sources: O'Brien.

MOSELEY, Nell [P] Fort Worth. Exhibited: SACE 1927; TAFW. Sources: WWWAA.

MOSES, L. M. [P] San Antonio. Exhibited: SALA 1934.

MOSKOWITZ, Shirley Edith (Mrs. Gruber) [P; T; I; S; Car.] Houston/Oberlin, Ohio. Birthdate: 1920. Birthplace: Houston. Studied: MFAH; Rice; Oberlin College; E. Langham; E. B. Bessell; B. J. Ploger; R. Joy. Member: TFAA. Exhibited: AHAE; TG 1944; TFAA 1945. Sources: WWWAA.

MOTT, Dr. Clifford D. [P] Denison, Tex. Birthdate: 1896. Birthplace: Troy, N.Y. Deathdate: 1977. Deathplace: Denison. Studied: Syracuse Univ.; Middlesex College, Boston. Member: Frank Klepper AC; TFAA. Exhibited: Klepper AC 1945; Sartor 1945 (solo). Sources: Dallas Morning News; Dallas PL; The Denison Herald. Began painting in 1942 after career as doctor of osteopathy.

MOUNT, Esse [P] Dallas. Exhibited: DAA.

MOYER, Marvin [P] Dallas/Manor. Birthdate: 1905. Exhibited: DAA; GTPA; SFT 1939.

MOZLEY, Loren Norman [P; Pm; T; Mur. P] Austin. Birthdate: 1905. Birthplace: Brookport, Ill. Deathdate: 1989. Deathplace: Austin. Studied: Acad. Colarossi; Acad. Chaumière; UNM. Member: Taos AA; SSAL; TFAA; Taos Heptagon; LSP. Exhibited: SFT 1939; TG; LSP 1941; ATPE; TPan; Denver AM 1938; CSFAC 1938; SSAL. Work: Belo; Huntington Gall., UT; DMA; Witte. Murals: Alvin, Tex.; Albuquerque; Clinton, Okla. Sources: Bywaters Coll.; Goetzman and Reese; Havlice; New Handbook; Samuels; Valley House Gall.; WWWAA.

MUELLER, Bertha [P] Houston. Exhibited: AHAE 1927.

MUELLER, Lola Pace (Mrs. Fred E.) [P; Pm] San Antonio. Birthdate: 1889. Birthplace: Atlanta, Ga. Deathdate: 1949. Deathplace: San Antonio. Studied: SAAI; C. Rosen; M. Axley; J. Arpa; H. A. De Young; D. Bergamo; C. Duer. Member: SAAL; SSAL; San Antonio Pm; San Antonio P&CC; TFAA. Exhibited: TFAA; Witte 1943 (solo); Austin Women's Cl.; SALA; TG; ATPE; SSAL; LOC; Carnegie. Work: Witte; TFWC. Sources: WWWAA; Witte files.

MUELLER, Rudolph [P; S] San Antonio. Birthdate: 1859. Birthplace: Saxony, Germany. Deathdate: 1929. Deathplace: San Antonio. Studied: Self-taught. Work: Witte. Sources: Steinfeldt.

MUENCH, Agnes Lilienberg [P; Pm] Houston. Birthdate: 1897. Studied: D. Garber; H. McCarter. Member: SSAL. Exhibited: AHAE; TCE; TAFW; ASET 1937; TG; SSAL. Sources: Houston City Directory 1943–44; WWWAA.

MUENCH, Julian Rhodes [P; S; Mur. P; Por. P] Houston. Birthdate: 1905. Birthplace: Seguin, Tex. Deathdate: 1965. Deathplace: Houston. Studied: PAFA with J. C. Tidden. Member: SSAL. Exhibited: TAFW; TFAA 1928; TAEN; TCE; SSAL. Work: MFAH; Houston PL; UT; Univ. North Texas, Denton; San Jacinto Mus.; Sources: ITD; O'Brien; WWWAA.

MUENCH, Nancy [P] Houston. Exhibited: AHAE 1945.

MULLIS, Phyllis Hass (Mrs. Rex) [P; Des.; I; T] Arlington, Tex. Birthdate: 1900. Birthplace: Sunbury, Pa. Studied: AID; SMU; J. Knott; F. Spicuzza; G. Kadell; J. Eckford. Member: FRAC. Exhibited: SFT 1939; DAA. Sources: WWWAA.

MUMMERT, Sallie Blythe [P] Fort Worth. Birthdate: 1888. Birthplace: Cisco, Tex. Deathdate: 1938. Deathplace: Fort Worth. Studied: Aunspaugh AS; AIC. Member: SIA; FWAA. Exhibited: TAFW; DWF 1916, 1918; SFT 1924, 1926; TCE. Sources: Fisk; ITD; Mallett; WWWAA.

MUNN, I. M. [P] Dallas? Exhibited: Crawford Gall. 1907.

MURFF, Elba Heckel [P; Por. P] Amarillo. Deathplace: Amarillo. Work: PPHM.

MURILLO, Jesus [P; Photog.] Houston. Birthdate: 1895. Birthplace: Morelia, Michoacan, Mexico. Deathdate: 1971. Deathplace: Galveston. Studied: Self-taught. Exhibited: AHAE 1927. Work: Houston PL. Sources: *New Handbook.*

MURPHEY, Mimi [S] Dallas/Albuquerque. Birthdate: 1912. Birthplace: Dallas. Studied: SMU; AID; ASL; Shonnard. Member: Clay Cl., N.Y.; New Mexico AL. Exhibited: TAFW; SFT 1938; DAA; DMFA; SSAL; Brooklyn Mus.; Coronado Cuarto Centennial Exp., Albuquerque. Work: MNM. Sources: DAS; WWWAA.

MURPHY, Mrs. H. B. [P] Dallas. Exhibited: DAA 1928.

MURRAY, Eileen [Pm] Dallas. Exhibited: DAA 1942; ATPE 1944.

MUZZEY, Virginia Reynolds [P] Houston. Exhibited: AHAE.

MYERS, A. [P] San Antonio. Exhibited: SALA 1943.

MYRICK, Bernice Wolfforth (Mrs. R. N.) [P] Lubbock. Exhibited: Plains Mus. Soc. 1932. Sources: Wilbanks.

NABINGER, Dollie [P] Harlingen/Victoria. Birthdate: 1905. Birthplace: Comfort, Tex. Deathdate: 1988. Deathplace: Fredericksburg. Studied: J. F. McCann; ASL; J. Arpa; H. A. De Young. Exhibited: ASET 1937. Sources: Maguire.

NAGLE, Eva (Mrs. E. T.) [P] Austin. Studied: UT. Member: Austin AG; TFAA. Exhibited: Ney Mus.; TFAA; UCE 1, 2. Sources: O'Brien.

NASH, Nancy Kate [P] Fort Worth. Exhibited: TAFW 1925.

NAUGLE, Lela [P] Fort Worth.

NAVE, Royston [P; Por. P] Victoria. Birthdate: 1886. Birthplace: La Grange, Tex. Deathdate: 1931. Deathplace: Harlingen, Tex. Studied: R. Henri; W. Kuhn; I. Wiles; L. Parker. Member: Salmagundi. Exhibited: Cotton Carn. 1910; TAFW; SACE; NAD 1921; PAFA 1921; St. Louis Mus.

FA; Carnegie. Work: Nave Mus; TCapitol; McFaddin-Ward House, Beaumont. Sources: Dawdy; Falk NAD; Falk PAFA; Fielding; Fisk; *New Handbook;* O'Brien; Victoria Regional Mus. Assoc.; WWWAA.

NAYLOR, Alice Stephenson [P; Pm; T] San Antonio. Birthplace: Columbus, Tex. Deathplace: Living San Antonio, 1980. Studied: Witte; SAAI; C. Rosen; E. Ret; A. Dasburg; X. Gonzalez; D. Lutz. Member: SAAL; San Antonio P&CC; San Antonio Pm; TFAA; SSAL. Exhibited: TG; TFAA; SALA; Austin 1942; ATPE 1944, 1945; TFAA 1945 (solo); Witte 1945 (solo); LOC 1943; MNM 1945; Critic's Choice, Cincinnati, 1945. Sources: Fielding; Witte files; WWWAA.

NEIGHBORS, Camille [P] San Antonio. Exhibited: SALA.

NELLI, Cleo [S] Dallas. Exhibited: Confederate Reunion, Dallas, 1925. Work: DMA? Sources: Fisk; O'Brien.

NETTE, Elizabeth [P] San Antonio. Birthdate: 1858. Birthplace: Texas. Deathdate: 1942. Deathplace: San Antonio. Studied: Frankfurt, Germany. Work: Witte. Sources: Steinfeldt.

NEUHEISEL, Cecilia (Mrs. Eric Steinfeldt) [P; Pm; T; Curator] San Antonio. Birthdate: 1915. Birthplace: Montello, Wis. Deathplace: Living San Antonio, 1997. Studied: Witte Mus. Sch.; Univ. Mexico; R. Dugosh; H. L. McFee; C. Merida. Member: SSAL; SAAL; San Antonio Pm. Exhibited: Witte 1937 (solo); TCE; SFT; TAFW; GTPA; ASET; TG; SALA; TFAA 1939; SSAL. Work: Mint MA, South Carolina. Sources: Mallett; WWWAA; Witte files.

NEUMANN, Florence [P] Dallas. Exhibited: DAA.

NEUMANN, Gilbert Franz [P; Pm; Mur. P; Dec.; Des.] San Antonio. Birthdate: 1906. Birthplace: San Antonio. Studied: Arpa; G. Borglum; H. A. De Young; H. Villa. Member: SAAG; SAPC; Laguna Beach AA; Santa Ana AA, Calif.; Fullerton AL, Calif. Exhibited: SACE; San Pedro Playhouse; SALA; TFWC 1931; TAFW 1934. Murals: City Hall, San Antonio; Green Memorial Hospital, San Antonio. Sources: Steinfeldt; WWWAA; Witte files.

NEUSSER, William [P; Por. P] Galveston/New Orleans. Birthdate: 1837. Birthplace: Germany. Deathdate: 1902. Deathplace: New Orleans. Sources: Groce and Wallace; Pinckney; WWWAA.

NEWBERRY, Mrs. J. E. [P] Dallas. Exhibited: DAA.

NEWKIRK, Guyrah [P] San Antonio. Exhibited: SALA 1940.

NEWLAND, Bessie A. [P] Dallas. Member: FRAC. Exhibited: FRAC 1934, 1935. Sources: PPHM files.

NEWLIN, Ora [P] Canyon. Exhibited: TFWC 1931.

NEWMAN, Ellen [P] Galveston. Exhibited: ASET 1938.

NEWMAN, George W., Sr. [P; Pm; I; T] Galveston. Birthdate: 1909. Birthplace: Galveston. Deathdate: 1989. Deathplace: Galveston. Studied: P. Schumann; AIC w/ B. Anisfeld, A. Philbrick, E. Forsberg; TAMC. Member: SSAL; Galveston AL. Exhibited: Galveston AL 1934 (solo); UCE 1; TFAA; MFAH; SSAL. Work: Galveston AL; RL. Sources: Galveston Community Book; *Galveston Daily News;* O'Brien; RL; WWWAA.

NEWTON, J. H. [P] Austin. Exhibited: TFWC 1931.

NEY, Franzisca Bernadina Wilhelmina Elisabet [S] Austin. Birthdate: 1833. Birthplace: Munster, Westphalia. Deathdate: 1907. Deathplace: Austin. Studied: Berlin; Munich; C. Rauch. Exhibited: WCE 1893; LPE 1904; FWFCE (posthumously). Work: NMAA; Ney Mus.; PPHM; TCapitol; Witte; Texas State Cemetery. Sources: DAS; Fielding; Fisk; Hendricks and Reese; Mallett; *New Handbook;* O'Brien; Samuels; WWWAA.

NEYLAND, Watson [P] Liberty, Tex. Birthdate: 1898. Birthplace: Liberty. Studied: Rice w/ Tidden; PAFA; Paris. Exhibited: AHAE; TAFW 1933; Witte 1932 (solo); TFAA; TAEN; SSAL. Sources: Fisk; O'Brien; WWWAA.

NICE, Blanch Heim [P] Houston. Birthdate: 1892. Birthplace: Houston. Studied: SLSFA. Member: SSAL. Exhibited: AHAE; TG; ASET; SFT 1939; SSAL 1941, 1945. Sources: WWWAA.

NICHOLS, Alice Welty [P; T] Canyon. Studied: UT: Pratt Inst.; Columbia. Exhibited: SFT 1938; WTAE 1939. Sources: West Texas A&M Univ. files.

NICHOLS, Mary Roberta. See GORMAN, Mary Nichols

NICHOLS, Nell Brooks [P] Dallas. Exhibited: SFT 1938.

NICHOLS, Perry [P; Mur. P; Des.; T] Dallas. Birthdate: 1911. Birthplace: Dallas. Deathdate: 1992. Deathplace: Dallas. Studied: F. Reaugh; A. Hogue; F. Klepper. Member: DAL; LSP; FRAC. Exhibited: FRAC 1930; TFWC 1931; SFT 1934; TPan; ATPE 1944; DAA; LSP 1938–39; TG 1941S; Sartor 1931 (solo); Thirteen Dallas Artists; TCE; WFNY; SSAL 1942. Work: Belo; DMA; Longview AM. Sources: Bywaters Coll.; Havlice; O'Brien; Stewart; WWWAA.

NICHOLSON, John [P] Ballinger/Abilene. Birthdate: 1916. Exhibited: SFT 1938; GTPA.

NICOLS, Audley Dean [P; Mur. P; I] El Paso. Birthdate: 1875. Birthplace: Pittsburgh. Deathdate: 1941. Deathplace: El Paso. Studied: ASL; Met. SFA w/ Blashfield, Cox, Mowbray. Member: EPAG. Exhibited: SACE; TAFW 1927; EPCC; EPWC; Carnegie. Sources: *El Paso Herald-Post;* EPPL; *El Paso Times;* Fisk; O'Brien; Price; Samuels; WWWAA.

NIENDORFF, Arthur Starr [P] Dallas. Birthdate: 1909. Exhibited: TCE; Thirteen Dallas Artists 1936. Sources: Stewart.

NIES, William A. [Pm] San Antonio. Exhibited: ATPE 1945.

NILSEN, Gurine [P; Comm. A] Galveston. Studied: Aunspaugh AS. Exhibited: TAFW; DWF 1919. Work: RL Sources: Fisk; RL.

NIXON, Wilson K. [P; Por. P] San Antonio. Exhibited: SALA; San Pedro Playhouse 1931; Bright Shawl Gall. 1932. Sources: *Home and Club; San Antonio Light;* Witte files.

NOBLE, Edith Henrietta [P] Dallas. Exhibited: DAA 1943.

NOBLE, Mamie Jones (Mrs. J. V.) [P] Corsicana, Tex. Birthdate: 1874. Exhibited: TAFW; TCE.

NOBLES, Kathryn [P] Dallas. Birthdate: 1910. Exhibited: TCE; DMFA; DAA 1935. Sources: Bywaters Coll.

NOGUEIRA, Juanita [P] Dallas. Member: FRAC. Exhibited: DAA; FRAC.

NORMAN, Lavora (Mrs. A. J.) [P] El Paso. Exhibited: EPWC 1942. Sources: Price.

NORMANN, C. S. [P] Austin. Exhibited: TFWC 1931.

NORMANN, Charles Berkeley (born STIGEN, Normann Zakaus Hansen) [P; Por. P; T] Austin. Birthdate: 1903. Birthplace: Sande, Norway. Deathdate: 1985. Deathplace: Austin. Studied: Eidsfoss SA; Konnerude SA; Yarlsberg SFA; UT. Exhibited: TG 1940; TCE (not in regular exhibition). Work: TCapitol; San Jacinto Mus.; Star of Republic Mus. Sources: Barker; *Heroes of Texas; New Handbook;* Texas State Preservation Board.

NORMANN, Fanny V. [P] Austin. Exhibited: TFWC 1931.

NORTHINGTON, Clarissa Beard [P; Poet] Egypt, Tex. Birthdate: 1880. Birthplace: Egypt. Deathdate: 1979. Deathplace: Egypt. Studied: Self-taught. Exhibited: Witte 1933 (solo); TCE; Ney Mus. Sources: O'Brien; *The Long White Road;* Wharton County Lib.; Witte files.

NORTON, Natalie [P] Houston. Exhibited: AHAE 1935.

NOVICH, Morris [P] San Antonio. Exhibited: SALA.

NOWLIN, Eugenia Campbell [P] Dallas/Pittsburgh. Birthdate: 1908. Exhibited: TAFW 1935; TCE; DAA; TG 1940.

NUHFER, Olive Harriette [P; Mur. P] San Antonio/Pittsburgh. Birthdate: 1907. Birthplace: Pittsburgh. Studied: OU w/ Jacobson; Carnegie; A. Kostellow; N. MacGilvary. Member: SAAL; AAPL; Cordova Cl. Exhibited: SALA; Pittsburgh AA 1936–40. Murals: Westerville, Ohio; Norman, Okla. Sources: WWWAA.

NYSTEL, Mrs. J. P. [P] Abernathy, Tex. Exhibited: TFWC 1931.

O'BRIEN, Erin [P] Beaumont. Exhibited: ASET 1937.

O'BRIEN, Esse Forrester [P] Waco. Exhibited: WTAE 1939.

ODENA, Albert [P] San Antonio. Exhibited: SALA 1932.

O'DONOHOE, Margaret [P] Fort Worth. Exhibited: TAFW 1930.

O'KEEFFE, Georgia Totto [P; T] Amarillo/Canyon/New York, N.Y./Abiquiu, N.M. Birthdate: 1887. Birthplace: Sun Prairie, Wis. Deathdate: 1986. Deathplace: Santa Fe. Studied: AIC; ASL; Columbia w/ Dow. Work: PPHM; DMA; MAMFW; Amon Carter; MFAH; Nat. Gall. of Art;

NMAA; MNM. Sources: Castro bio.; Hoffman bio.; Lisle bio.; *New Handbook;* Samuels.

OLD, Margaret [P] El Paso. Exhibited: EPWC; TG 1941F.

OLINGER, Larry V. [S] San Antonio. Exhibited: SALA 1933.

OLIPHANT, Carol E. [P] Houston. Exhibited: AHAE 1936.

OLIVER, Josephine [P] Dallas. Birthdate: 1908. Birthplace: Terrell, Tex.? Deathdate: 1991. Deathplace: Dallas. Studied: Reaugh. Member: FRAC. Exhibited: Reaugh Studio 1934 (solo). Work: PPHM. Sources: O'Brien.

ONDERDONK, Eleanor Rogers [P; Min. P; Curator; I] San Antonio. Birthdate: 1884. Birthplace: San Antonio. Deathdate: 1964. Deathplace: San Antonio. Studied: ASL w/ H. S. DuMond, L. Fuller, Bridgman, Johansen; Woodstock w/ Carlson. Member: SAAL?; San Antonio Conservation Soc. Exhibited: SAAL 1912; SSAL 1929; SFT. Work: Witte. Sources: Bywaters Coll.; Fielding; Fisk; O'Brien; Smith; Steinfeldt; Steinfeldt bio; *New Handbook;* WWWAA.

ONDERDONK, Robert Jenkins [P; Por. P; T] San Antonio/Dallas. Birthdate: 1852. Birthplace: Catonsville, Md. Deathdate: 1917. Deathplace: San Antonio. Studied: NAD w/ Wilmarth; ASL w/ Shirlaw, Chase, Beckwith. Member: Brass Mug Cl.; SAAL; "Chili Thirteen." Exhibited: Van Dyke Cl. 1887; SFT; TAFW 1911–14, 1916; Cotton Carn. 1910. Work: DMA; Governor's Mansion, Austin; SAMA; Stark; TCapitol; Witte. Sources: Church; Fielding; Fisk; *New Handbook;* O'Brien; Pinckney; Ratcliffe; Samuels; Steinfeldt bio; Steinfeldt; Utterback; WWWAA.

ONDERDONK, Robert Julian [P; Por. P; I; T] San Antonio. Birthdate: 1882. Birthplace: San Antonio. Deathdate: 1922. Deathplace: San Antonio. Studied: R. Onderdonk; ASL w/ Cox, DuMond; Shinnecock w/ Chase. Member: Allied Artists Amer.; Salmagundi; SAAL; Dallas AA. Exhibited: SFT; TAFW; Dallas AA 1916 (solo); Cotton Pal. 1916; Greenville 1924; NAD. Work: Amon Carter Mus.; DMA; DRT Lib.; McNay; MFAH; PPHM; SAAL; SAMA; Stark; TAMU; TFAA; Texas Tech Mus.; Witte. Sources: Fielding; Fisk; O'Brien; Samuels; Steinfeldt bio; Steinfeldt; WWWAA.

ONEAL, Mrs. E. U. [P] Mineral Wells, Tex. Exhibited: TFWC 1931.

OPPERMANN, Emelie [P] San Antonio. Exhibited: SAAG 1927.

ORAM, Sarah H. [P] Dallas. Exhibited: DAA 1928.

ORAVECZ, B. [P] San Antonio. Exhibited: SAAG 1927.

ORREN, Raymond [P] Waco. Exhibited: WTAE 1939.

ORT, William [S] Wichita Falls. Birthdate: 1900. Birthplace: Boerne, Tex. Exhibited: Texas-Oklahoma Fair; HPAG.; DMFA. Work: Witte. Sources: O'Brien.

ORTH, John William [P; Mur. P] Kansas City/Houston/Los Angeles. Birthdate: 1889. Birthplace: Marksteft, Germany. Deathdate: 1976. Deathplace: Santa Ana, Calif. Studied: H. von Habermann. Member: Kansas City SA; P and S of Los Angeles. Work: Kunsthalls, Barmen, Germany. Sources: David Lackey Antiques, Houston; WWWAA.

OSBORNE, Hazel C. [S] Dallas. Exhibited: DAA 1928.

OSTROM, Cora Chambers [P] Eagle Pass, Tex. Birthdate: 1871. Birthplace: Harrison, Ark. Studied: M. Brown; Wells; Arpa. Member: SAAL; SSAL. Sources: Fielding; WWWAA.

OVENDORF, M. [P] Galveston? Exhibited: Texas Coast Fair 1895.

OVERTON, Nan [P] Fort Worth. Deathdate: 1927. Exhibited: TAFW 1922–28. Sources: WWWAA.

OWEN, Elizabeth M. [P] Dallas. Member: FRAC. Exhibited: FRAC 1935. Sources: PPHM files.

OWEN, Michael G., Jr. [S; P; Pm; I; Cr] Dallas/Greenbelt, Md. Birthdate: 1915. Birthplace: Dallas. Deathdate: 1976. Deathplace: Corvallis, Ore. Studied: AID. Member: Soc. Washington Artists; LSP. Exhibited: TCE; GTPA; DAA; DMFA 1937; LSP 1938; Dallas Times-Herald Art Fair 1944; KCAI 1938; WFNY. Work: DMA; SMU. Sources: Bywaters Coll.; Fielding; Havlice; Stewart; WWWAA.

OWEN, Mrs. W. B. [P] Arlington. Member: FRAC. Exhibited: TAFW 1925; TFWC 1931; DAA 1930–32; FRAC. Sources: PPHM files.

OWENS, Annie Laura (Mrs. Harry) [P] Fort Worth. Exhibited: TAFW.

OWSLEY, Mrs. Alvin [Por. P] Dallas. Exhibited: DAA 1928.

PACHL, Delmar Max [Pm; S; Des.; T] Arlington, Texas/Kansas City, Mo. Studied: W. Rosenbauer; T. H. Benton; J. de Martelly; J. Meert; R. Braught; M. W. Hammond. Member: LSP; Co-op Art Assoc., Kansas City. Exhibited: LSP 1941; ATPE 1942,44; TG 1941F; KCAI 1938 (pr.). Sources: WWWAA.

PACKER, Clair Lange (Mr.) [P; I; Car.; Des.] Harlingen/San Antonio. Birthdate: 1901. Birthplace: Gueda Springs, Kans. Studied: W. L. Evans Sch. of Cartooning; H. A. De Young; UNM; M. Sheets; B. Miller; J. Imhof; K. Adams. Member: TFAA; SSAL. Exhibited: ASET 1937; MFAH 1939. Sources: WWWAA.

PAGAN, John L. (Jack) [P] Houston. Birthdate: 1904. Exhibited: TCE; AHAE; SSAL 1936. Sources: Houston City Directory 1942–45; WWWAA.

PAGE, Harvey Linsley [P] San Antonio. Birthdate: 1859. Deathdate: 1934. Deathplace: San Antonio. Studied: J. L. Smithmeyer; R. J. Onderdonk. Exhibited: SACE 1928. Sources: ITD; O'Brien.

PAIGE, Winnie O. [P] Channing. Exhibited: TFWC 1931.

PAINE, Charles R. [P] El Paso. Deathdate: 1974. Deathplace: El Paso. Exhibited: EPWC 1937. Sources: EPPL; *El Paso Times*.

PAINE, Joseph Polley [P; T] San Antonio/Austin/Huntsville. Birthdate: 1912. Birthplace: Llano, Tex. Studied: Texas A&I; ASL; SAAI; KCAI; UT; O'Hara Sch.; New Mexico Highlands College. Member: Bonner Graphic Arts Cl. (San Antonio Pm); Men of AG. Exhibited: SALA; PAFA 1938; San Francisco AA 1938. Work: Witte. Sources: WWWAA; Witte files. Professor of Art Emeritus, Sam Houston State Univ.

PAINTER, James Donald [P] Round Top, Tex. Birthdate: 1906. Birthplace: Louisville, Ky. Deathdate: 1988. Deathplace: Round Top. Studied: Little Rock, Ark.; Chicago; MFAH. Exhibited: MFAH?; DMFA?; Beaumont AM? Sources: *New Handbook*.

PALMER, Hattie Virginia Young (Mrs. Charles F.) [P; T] Houston. Birthplace: Ripley, Ohio. Deathdate: 1935. Deathplace: Houston. Studied: Cincinnati Art Acad. Member: Houston AL; TFAA; SSAL; AAPL. Exhibited:

SACE 1927; MFAH 1927 (solo); HAI; Cincinnati AM; AHAE 1933–34 (special honor, mem.). Sources: Fielding; Fisk; ITD; Smith; WWWAA.

PALMER, Jessie Mae (Mrs. C. E.) [P; S; T] Dallas/Amarillo. Birthdate: 1882. Birthplace: Lawrence, Tex. Deathdate: 1965. Deathplace: Amarillo. Studied: Reaugh; Simkins; J. Carlson; Broadmoor. Member: SSAL; TFAA; FRAC; Amarillo AA. Exhibited: DWF 1924 (medal); FRAC; TFAA 1929–40; Oak Cliff Little Theatre 1931; Ney Mus. 1935 (solo); SFT 1934; TAFW; DAA 1940; TSFA 1931, 1934; Amarillo AA 1933; SSAL. Work: DWF; PPHM. Sources: Fisk; ITD; Mallett; O'Brien; WWWAA.

PANCOAST, Clara Caffrey [P] San Antonio. Birthdate: 1873. Birthplace: Lafayette, La. Deathdate: 1959. Deathplace: San Antonio. Studied: Arpa. Member: SAAL; TFAA; San Antonio P&CC. Exhibited: SACE; TAFW; TFWC 1931; SALA. Work: Witte. Sources: Steinfeldt.

PANCOAST, Martha [D; Pm] San Antonio. Exhibited: SALA 1932.

PARK, Mrs. C. R. [P] Sinton, Tex. Exhibited: TFWC 1931.

PARK, Thelma Booth [P] Dallas. Member: FRAC. Exhibited: FRAC 1929. Sources: PPHM files.

PARKER, Ella Estill [P] Dallas. Exhibited: SFT 1939; DAA 1938.

PARKER, Essa Chauslor [P] Brownsville, Tex. Exhibited: TFWC 1931.

PARKES, Joe, Jr. [Velvet P] Dallas. Exhibited: DAA 1928.

PARKHILL, M. Louise [P] San Antonio. Exhibited: SALA.

PARKINSON, Margaret L. [P] San Antonio. Exhibited: SALA 1935.

PARMELEE, James E. [P] Galveston. Exhibited: Cotton Carn. 1910, 1911. Sources: Galveston City Directory 1910–12.

PARSLEY, Mrs. Charles Howard [P] Plainview, Tex. Studied: TWU; Redin. Exhibited: TFWC 1931. Sources: Wilbanks.

PARSONS, Anna [P] Houston. Exhibited: AHAE.

PASCHAL, Mary D. [P] San Antonio. Exhibited: SALA 1931.

PATTERSON, J. J. [Pm] Fort Worth. Exhibited: TAFW.

PATTERSON, Mary Lou. See THOMAS, M.

PATTERSON, Oriel C. [P] Houston. Exhibited: AHAE 1933.

PATTESON, Helena [P] Dallas. Exhibited: DAA 1938.

PATTESON, John [P] Dallas. Exhibited: DAA 1938.

PAYNE, John Bob [P] San Antonio. Birthdate: 1883. Birthplace: Collierville, Tenn. Deathdate: 1962. Deathplace: San Antonio. Member: Coppini Acad. Work: PPHM. Sources: San Antonio City Directory 1916–18. Landscape painter moved to San Antonio in early 1890s.

PAYNE, Lura Masterson [P; Por. P; Mur. P] Houston. Birthplace: Chenango, Tex. Studied: Newcomb College; AIC w/ A. Serba. Exhibited: AHAEs. Sources: Fisk; Smith.

PAYNE, Mildred [P] El Paso. Exhibited: EPWC 1938.

PEABODY, Rowena [P] El Paso. Exhibited: EPWC 1938.

PEARCE, Mary Blake (Mrs. R. B.) [P; T; I] Dallas. Birthdate: 1890. Birthplace: Cuero, Tex. Studied: M. Washington College; Berlin; Paris; ASL. Member: FRAC. Exhibited: TAFW; DAA; FRAC 1934; TCE. Sources: Fisk; Smith.

PEARSON, Lawrence E. [P; I] Houston. Birthdate: 1900. Birthplace: Bay City, Tex. Studied: MFAH; F. Browne; A. MacDonnell. Member: HAG; Houston Sketch Cl. Exhibited: ASET 1938; AHAE 1940. Sources: WWWAA.

PEEPLES, Nina [P] Dallas. Exhibited: DAA; SFT 1938; GTPA.

PELLET, Anna Minie (Marie Anna) [P] Dallas. Member: FRAC. Exhibited: FRAC 1934, 1935. Sources: PPHM files.

PENDERGRASS, Roger [P] Dallas. Exhibited: DMFA; TG 1941F; DAA. Sources: Bywaters Coll.

PENROD, Viola D. [P] Dallas. Studied: Otis AI. Member: FRAC. Exhibited: FRAC; TAFW; DAA. Sources: Fisk; WWWAA.

PENTENRIEDER, Erhard [D; Pm] San Antonio. Birthdate: 1830. Birthplace: Bavaria. Deathdate: 1875. Deathplace: San Antonio. Work: Amon Carter; Witte. Sources: Pinckney; Witte files.

PERINI, Maxine [P; Des.; T] Abilene. Birthdate: 1911. Birthplace: Houston. Living Abilene, 1994. Studied: Wellesley; AIC; B. Anisfeld. Exhibited: GTPA. Sources: Abilene Mus. FA Mus. files; WWWAA.

PERRY, Gerald F. [P; Cr] El Paso/Ruidoso, N.M. Studied: Iowa and Missouri. Member: FSAA. Exhibited: EPWC; El Paso Community Theater 1941 (solo). Sources: *El Paso Herald;* EPPL; *El Paso Times;* Price.

PERRY, Robert J. [Arch.; P] Dallas. Birthdate: 1908. Birthplace: Vicksburg, Miss. Studied: Cornell; École BA; Princeton. Exhibited: HPAG 1935; DAA 1937; N.Y. Arch. Lg.

PETICOLAS, Alfred Brown [D] Victoria. Birthdate: 1838. Birthplace: Richmond, Va. Deathdate: 1915. Deathplace: Victoria. Studied: Self-taught. Work: Witte; Victoria College Lib.; Arizona Hist. Soc. Sources: Barker Ctr., UT; *New Handbook.*

PETRI, Friedrich Richard [P] Near Fredericksburg. Birthdate: 1824. Birthplace: Dresden, Germany. Deathdate: 1857. Deathplace: Pedernales River near Fredericksburg. Studied: Royal Acad., Dresden. Exhibited: Yanaguana (ph.). Work: Carter; TMM; Witte. Sources: Newcomb bio.; Fisk; O'Brien; Pinckney; *New Handbook;* Samuels; Steinfeldt.

PETTY, Jessie W. (Mrs. Thomas K.) [P; Pm; T] San Antonio/Douglas, Ariz. Birthdate: Navasota, Tex. Studied: Arpa; Gonzalez; De Young; Piazzoni. Member: SSAL; SAAL; San Antonio P&CC; TFAA. Exhibited: SALA; TAFW 1927–29; Arpa Students, Witte 1928. Work: SAAL. Sources: WWWAA; Witte files.

PHELPS, Warren [P] San Antonio. Exhibited: SALA 1939.

PHILLIPS, Carolyn [Pm] Belton, Tex. Exhibited: ATPE 1945.

PHILLIPS, Kenneth Guthrie [P] Temple. Birthdate: 1897. Birthplace: Ilwaco, Wash. Deathdate: 1976. Deathplace: Temple. Studied: Johns Hopkins Medical Sch. w/ M. Brodel; Mayo Clinic. Member: Assoc. of Medical Illustrators. Exhibited: TFWC 1931. Work: Scott and White Memorial Hospital. Sources: Artist's son; *Texas Medicine;* "Wax Medical Moulages."

PHILLIPS, Lenore [P] Dallas. Exhibited: DAA 1931.

PHILLIPS, Virginia East [P] Houston. Exhibited: AHAE 1945.

PICKARD, Kathleen [P] Houston. Exhibited: AHAE 1945.

PIERCE, A. B., Jr. [P] Houston. Exhibited: AHAE. Sources: WWWAA.

PIERCE, Hallie [P] Sabinal, Tex. Exhibited: TG 1945.

PIERCE, Virginia [P] San Antonio. Exhibited: SALA 1934.

PIOTT, Elizabeth [P] Houston. Exhibited: AHAE 1943.

PITTMAN, Beryl [P] Dallas. Exhibited: TAFW 1926.

PITTMAN, Margaret Hallett [P; S] Houston. Exhibited: AHAE 1930.

PITTMAN, Peggy [P] Houston. Exhibited: ASET 1937.

PLOGER, Benjamin John [P; T] Houston. Birthdate: 1908. Birthplace: New Orleans. Studied: Acad. Chaumière; Acad. Colarossi; L'École la Fresque, Paris; W. Adams; E. Woodward. Member: HAG; SSAL; New Orleans AA; New Orleans Art League. Exhibited: TAFW 1936; TCE; AHAE. Work: Flowers Sch., New Orleans. Sources: WWWAA.

PLOTKIN, Peter [P; Por. P; T] Dallas/Abilene. Birthplace: Petrograd, Russia. Studied: Petrograd; Munich. Exhibited: DWF 1928; Abilene 1927. Sources: Fisk.

POHL, Hugo David [P; Pm; I; T; Mur. P] San Antonio. Birthdate: 1878. Birthplace: Detroit. Deathdate: 1960. Deathplace: San Antonio. Studied: J. Melchers; Detroit IA; AJ w/ J. P. Laurens. Member: TFAA; AAPL; Mur. P., Washington. Exhibited: TAFW; Witte 1933 (joint w/ M. Teichmueller); San Antonio 1934 (studio); SALA 1933; NAD. Work: Witte; Int'l Harvester Bldg., Chicago. Sources: Fielding; Fisk; *New Handbook;* O'Brien; Samuels; Smith; Steinfeldt; WWWAA.

POLK, Naomi [P; Poet] Houston. Birthdate: 1892. Birthplace: Houston. Deathdate: 1984. Deathplace: Houston. Studied: self-taught. Sources: *Black History/Black Vision; New Handbook.*

POOL, Eugenia Pope (Mrs. A. E.) [P] Abilene/Big Spring, Tex. Birthplace: Cameron, Tex. Studied: O. Rush; OU; F. Browne; Grand Central Gall., N.Y.; Arpa; D. Dawson-Watson; E. M. Lowdon; H. A. De Young. Member: Lubbock AA. Exhibited: TAFW; West Texas Fair; DWF; Lubbock AA 1936; Snyder, Tex. (solo); Abilene (solo); SSAL. Sources: Fisk; O'Brien; Wilbanks.

PORTER, Fay Lively [S] Dallas. Exhibited: DAA 1928.

PORTERFIELD, Pearl [P] Dallas. Exhibited: DAA 1941–43.

POTHOFF, Lois Helen [P] Dallas. Exhibited: DAA 1943–45.

POYNOR, Mrs. V. E. [P] Fort Worth. Exhibited: TFWC 1931.

PRATHER, Virginia Russ [S; P] Dallas/San Antonio. Birthdate: 1916. Studied: SAAI w/ D. Bergamo; O. Maidarelli. Member: Texas Sculpture Group. Exhibited: GTPA; DAA 1942; TAFW 1936; Witte 1943; SALA 1944–45. Work: Witte. Sources: Bywaters Coll.; *San Antonio Express; San Antonio Evening News.*

PRATT, Henry Cheever [P; Por. P; Min. P] West Texas. Birthdate: 1803. Birthplace: Oxford, N.H. Deathdate: 1880. Deathplace: Wakefield, Mass. Studied: S. F. B. Morse; T. Cole. Work: TMM; Amon Carter. Sources: Fielding; *New Handbook;* Pinckney.

PRESCOTT, Julia [P] Houston. Exhibited: AHAE 1935.

PRESSLY, H. Gilbert [P] Dallas. Studied: Reaugh. Exhibited: DAA 1928. Work: PPHM.

PRESSON, Mrs. W. F. [P; T] Post. Exhibited: TFWC 1931. Sources: Wilbanks.

PRESTOPINO, Gregorio [P; T] San Antonio/Brooklyn. Birthdate: 1907. Birthplace: New York. Studied: NAD. Exhibited: Whitney Mus. American Art; AIC; WFNY; GGE; Corcoran; SACE. Work: Whitney Mus. American Art; MoMA; Walker; Rochester Memorial AG. Sources: Witte files; WWWAA.

PREUSSER, Robert Ormerod [P; T] Houston. Birthdate: 1919. Birthplace: Houston. Deathplace: Cambridge, Mass. Studied: AIC; M. Davidson; Moholy-Nagy; R. J. Wolff. Exhibited: SFT 1938, 1939; AHAE; SAAL 1941; ASET; TG; DMFA 1938; GTPA; KCAI 1936; Rockefeller 1938; WFNY; SSAL. Work: MFAH; PPHM. Sources: WWWAA.

PRICE, Eugenia [P; Min P; T] San Antonio. Birthdate: 1865. Birthplace: Beaumont. Deathdate: 1923. Deathplace: Los Angeles. Studied: SLSFA; AIC; AJ. Member: Alumni AIC; Chicago AC; Chicago Soc. Min. P; TFAA; SAAL. Exhibited: Amer. Soc. Min. P; NAD; San Antonio. Sources: O'Brien; WWWAA.

PRICKETT, William [S] Dallas. Exhibited: DAA.

PRIDEAUX, Mary Donna (Mado) Moore (Mrs. T. R.) [P; S; T] Lubbock. Birthdate: 1888. Birthplace: Lott, Tex. Deathdate: 1967. Deathplace: Lubbock. Studied: Mary Hardin-Baylor; Redin; J. Arpa; E. Gibberd. Member: TFAA; Lubbock AA; South Plains AG (charter). Exhibited: TFWC 1931; PMS 1932; UCE 2; SPCCE; UCE 2; Beaumont 1941. Sources: Artist's scrapbook; Wilbanks.

PRITCHETT, Gloria J. [ ] Dallas. Birthdate: 1910. Exhibited: TAFW 1936; TCE.

PROCTOR, Alexander Phimister [S; P] Denver/New York/Rancho Los Palos, Tex. Birthdate: 1862. Birthplace: Bosanquit, Ontario, Canada. Deathdate: 1950. Deathplace: Palo Alto, Calif. Studied: NAD; ASL; Paris w/ Puech and Injabert. Member: NAD; Soc. of Amer. Artists; Amer. WCS; N.Y. Arch. Lg.; NSS; Nat. Inst. of Arts and Letters; NAC; Amer. Soc. of Animal Painters and Sculptors. Exhibited: WCE; Exp. Universelle, Paris, 1900; LPE; P-PE. Work: Lee Park, Dallas; UT campus; Texas Memorial Mus.; Met.; Brooklyn Mus. Sources: DAS; Fielding; Hendricks and Reese; *New Handbook;* O'Brien; Samuels; WWWAA.

PROCTOR, Jane [P] Houston. Exhibited: AHAE 1945.

PRUITT, C. D. [S] Dallas. Birthplace: Grimes Co., Tex. Studied: TAMC. Exhibited: SFT 1925. Sources: Fisk; O'Brien; Smith.

PRYOR, Nell E. [P; Pm] San Antonio. Studied: Arpa; Fontainebleau w/ E. Leon. Member: SAAL; TFAA. Exhibited: SALA; TFWC 1931, 1933; Arpa Students, Witte 1928; TFAA 1931. Sources: *San Antonio Light;* Witte files.

PUDOR, (Mrs.) [P] Galveston? Exhibited: Texas Coast Fair 1895.

PUGSLEY, Ethel Smith [P] San Antonio. Exhibited: SALA 1944; TG 1945.

PULTE, Frances J. [P] Dallas. Member: FRAC. Exhibited: DAA 1929; FRAC. Sources: PPHM files.

PUTNAM, F. O. [P; Pm] Dallas. Exhibited: DAA.

PUTNAM, Frances M. [P] Houston. Exhibited: AHAE; ASET 1937, 1938.

QUINN, Elizabeth Sugg [P] San Antonio. Exhibited: SALA 1943.

RABA, Ernst [P; Photog.; T] San Antonio. Birthdate: 1874. Birthplace: Friedland, Bohemia. Deathdate: 1951. Deathplace: San Antonio. Studied: A. Neuhauser. Member: Brass Mug Cl.; Beethoven Maennerchor. Exhibited: SALA; Cotton Carn. 1910; SAAG 1927; SAAL 1912, 1926. Work: Witte. Sources: Tichich thesis; Witte files.

RAGLAND, Portia Juanita. See McIVER, Portia

RAHL, Ursula [P] San Antonio. Exhibited: SALA 1930.

RAHR, Gus [P] Dallas. Exhibited: DAA.

RAMOS, Fernando [P; Comm. A] San Antonio. Birthplace: Monterrey, Mexico. Studied: X. Gonzalez. Exhibited: SALA 1931.

RANDALL, Arne [P] Austin. Exhibited: TG 1942.

RANDALL, La Baume Elliott [P] Dallas. Exhibited: TAFW 1920.

RANDLETT, Mamie Randall (Mrs. S. L.) [P; Min. P; Cer.] Dallas/Lancaster, Tex. Studied: ASL; W. M. Chase. Exhibited: SFT? Sources: Fisk.

RANDOLPH, Daisy Ewing [P] Houston. Exhibited: AHAE 1926.

RANDOLPH, Glenna [P] Moran. Exhibited: TFWC 1931. Sources: Wilbanks.

RANK, Mrs. W. A. [P] El Paso. Exhibited: EPWC.

RANKIN, Margaret Fern [P] Fort Worth. Exhibited: TAFW 1928.

RAPHAEL, Frances (Mrs. Nicholas D. Allen) [P] San Angelo/Brooklyn. Birthdate: 1913. Birthplace: San Angelo. Studied: X. Gonzalez; R. Staffel. Member: SSAL. Exhibited: SALA 1934. Sources: WWWAA.

RAPHAEL, Josephine [P] San Antonio. Exhibited: SAAG 1927.

RATLIFF, Blanche Cooley (Mrs. Walter) [P] Fort Worth/ Atlanta, Ga. Birthdate: 1896. Birthplace: Smithville, Tex. Studied: O. B. Jacobson; D. B. Cockrell. Member: FWPC; Les Beaux-Arts, Norman, Okla. Exhibited: TAFW. Work: OU. Sources: Fielding; Fisk; WWWAA.

RAWLINGS, Muriel Peterson [P] San Antonio. Exhibited: SALA 1932.

RAWSON, Phillip N. [P] San Antonio. Exhibited: SALA.

RAY, Alice F. [P] Fort Worth. Deathdate: 1969. Deathplace: Fort Worth. Exhibited: TAFW 1923. Sources: ITD; WWWAA.

RAYL, Edna K. [P] San Antonio. Exhibited: SALA 1933.

REAUGH, Charles Franklin (Frank) [P; T; Inventor] Terrell/Dallas. Birthdate: 1860. Birthplace: Morgan Co., Ill. Deathdate: 1945. Deathplace: Dallas. Studied: SLSFA; AJ. Member: Soc. Western Artists; Dallas AA; AFA. Exhibited: WCE; NAD; PAFA; AIC; LPE; TCE; FWFCE; TAFW; SFT; SFT 1939 (solo); Greenville 1924; Cotton Carn. 1910. Work: DMA; MFAH; PPHM; TAMU; UT; Dallas PL; SMU; Stark; TCapitol; Witte; MFAH; DMA. Sources: Fielding; Fisk; *New Handbook*; O'Brien; Samuels; Smith; Steinfeldt; WWWAA.

REAVIS, Esma Jacobs [P; T; Pm] Greenville. Birthdate: 1900. Birthplace: Corinth, Miss. Studied: College of Industrial Arts (now TWU) w/ M. Marshall; Simkins; Reaugh; F. Klepper; L. O. Griffith. Member: FRAC. Exhibited: TFWC 1931; FRAC; SFT; UCE 1; SSAL. Work: Greenville HS. Sources: O'Brien; WWWAA; Wilbanks.

REDIC, Jack [P] El Paso. Birthdate: 1925. Studied: El Paso Technical Inst. w/ K. Ball. Exhibited: EPWC; Texas College of Mines Mus. 1942 (solo). Sources: *El Paso Herald*; EPPL; *El Paso Times*.

REED, Robert K. [P; Pm] San Antonio. Birthdate: 1906. Birthplace: Cadillac, Mich. Studied: E. Roth, H. A. De Young; A. Naylor. Member: SSAL; TFAA. Exhibited: SALA 1944; San Benito, Tex., 1940 (solo). Sources: Witte files.

REEDER, Edward Dickson [P; Pm; Por. P; T] Fort Worth. Birthdate: 1912. Birthplace: Fort Worth. Deathdate: 1970. Deathplace: Fort Worth. Studied: ASL w/ I. Olinsky; G. Bridgman; W. Adams; W. S. Hayter; New Sch.; Mummert; Gillespie. Member: Fort Worth AA. Exhibited: GTPA; UCE 1, 2; TAFW; TPan; ATPE 1945; SSAL; FWAA; TG; SixTP; Corpus Christi 1945; Dallas Print Soc. 1945; PAFA; CSFAC; Carnegie. Work: DMA; MAMFW; OJAC; CSFAC; Brooklyn Mus.; AIC. Sources: Dickson Reeder retro. catalogue; Fort Worth Star Telegram; *New Handbook*; O'Brien; WWWAA.

REES, Lonnie (Mrs. Terry Shand) [P; Por. P; T] San Antonio. Birthdate: 1910. Birthplace: San Antonio. Deathdate: 1990. Deathplace: San Antonio. Studied: ASL w/ R. Brackman; NAD w/ L. Kroll. Member: SSAL; SAAL; TG. Exhibited: SALA; MFAH; TG; Witte 1939 (solo); ASET; All. Artists of Amer. 1937; NAD 1938; SSAL; Bright Shawl Gall. 1932 (solo). Work: City Council Chambers, San Antonio; Ney Mus.; Witte; UT. Sources: *San Antonio Express; San Antonio Light;* Witte files; WWWAA.

REEVES, Charlotte [P] San Antonio. Exhibited: SACE 1929. Sources: Fisk; Witte files.

REEVES, Elsie [P] El Paso. Birthdate: 1899. Deathdate: 1975. Deathplace: El Paso. Exhibited: EPWC 1942. Sources: EPPL; *El Paso Times.*

REICHERT, Vennie [P] San Antonio. Exhibited: SALA.

REID, Mary [P] Dallas. Member: FRAC. Exhibited: DAA; FRAC.

REIL, W. Gaston [P] Stephenville, Tex. Exhibited: WTAE; TG 1941F.

REINHART, Ida B. (Mrs. E. T.) [P] Houston. Exhibited: AHAE.

REYNOLDS, Alice [P] Dallas. Exhibited: DAA 1929. Work: OJAC.

REYNOLDS, Chang [P] Dallas. Exhibited: DAA 1943.

REYNOLDS, Howard W. [P; Pm] Dallas. Exhibited: DAA 1935.

REYNOLDS, Virginia. See MUZZEY, Virginia R.

RHIND, John Massey [S] New York, N.Y. Birthdate: 1860. Birthplace: Edinburgh, Scotland. Deathdate: 1936. Deathplace: New York, N.Y. Studied: J. Rhind (father); Jules Dalou. Member: NSS; N.Y. Arch. Lg.; NAC; Salmagundi; Allied Artists Amer. Work: RL; Galveston County Courthouse lawn; U.S. Capitol; Newark, N.J.; Trinity Ch., New York, N.Y. Sources: DAS; Fielding; Hendricks and Reese.

RICE, Dama Jones [S] San Antonio. Exhibited: SALA 1940.

RICE, Lucy Wilson (Mrs. C. D.) [P; Port. P] Austin. Birthdate: 1874. Birthplace: Troy, Ala. Deathdate: 1963. Deathplace: Austin. Studied: Mary Hardin-Baylor College; ASL; Grand Central Sch. of Art; W. Adams; G. E. Browne; A. Delecluse; Acad. Chaumière; Acad. Colarossi; Provincetown. Member: SSAL; TFAA; Austin AL; AAPL. Exhibited: DMFA; TAFW; TFWC 1931; MFAH; SSAL; TFAA; Witte. Work: TCapitol; Baylor; PPHM; UT; TAI; San Antonio PL; Southwestern Univ., Georgetown; Southwest Texas State Univ., San Marcos; Texas Medical Sch., Galveston. Sources: Mallett; O'Brien; WWWAA.

RICHARD, Camille [P] Port Arthur. Birthdate: 1897. Exhibited: GTPA.

RICHARDS, Harper [P] Dallas. Exhibited: DAA 1943.

RICHARDS, John H. [D; Pm] Philadelphia/Washington, D.C. Exhibited: Washington, D.C., AA. Sources: Pinckney.

RICHARDSON, Bud [P] El Paso. Exhibited: EPWC 1927.

RICHARDSON, Volney Allen [P; T] Houston. Birthdate: 1880. Birthplace: Attica, N.Y. Studied: Albright AG; ASL; W. M. Chase; E. Dufner; F. V. DuMond; C. W. Hawthorne. Member: Buffalo Soc. Artists. Exhibited: Albright AG; Buffalo Soc. Artists 1935. Sources: WWWAA.

RICHART, Lucille [P] Fort Worth. Exhibited: TAFW.

RICHTER, Will Scott [Pm] Dallas. Exhibited: DAA 1932.

RICKARD, Kathleen [P] Houston. Exhibited: AHAE 1945.

RIDDLE, Martha [P] Dallas. Exhibited: DAA 1928.

RIDLEY, Dr. Ian [P] El Paso. Exhibited: EPWC 1937.

RIEDNER, Ruth [Min. P] San Antonio. Exhibited: SALA 1935.

RILEY, Roy [P] Harlingen. Exhibited: TFWC 1931. Sources: Wilbanks.

RING, Mary [D] Houston. Exhibited: AHAE.

RINSCICA, Vincent [P] Beaumont. Exhibited: TFWC 1931. Sources: Wilbanks.

RIPPETEAU, Hallie Crane (Mrs. J. A.) [P; T] Dallas/El Paso. Birthplace: Independence, Tex. Studied: McArdle; J. Downie; R. Onderdonk; E. Fowler. Member: HPSA; DWF. Exhibited: DAA 1928; TAEN; TFWC 1931; EPSJ 1934; EPWC 1936; UCE 2. Sources: Fisk; O'Brien.

RIVERA, C. Garza [D] Houston. Exhibited: AHAE.

RIVERA, Rafaela [P] San Antonio. Exhibited: SALA 1930; TAFW; TFWC 1931.

ROBBINS, Mrs. W. B. [P] San Antonio. Exhibited: TFWC 1931. Sources: Wilbanks.

ROBERTS, Dorothy [P] San Antonio. Exhibited: SALA 1939; ASET 1938.

ROBERTS, Erie Young [P] Brownwood, Tex. Exhibited: TFWC 1931. Sources: Wilbanks.

ROBERTS, Frank S. [S] Houston. Exhibited: AHAE 1934.

ROBERTS, Hazel [P; T] El Paso. Exhibited: EPCC; SALA; EPWC 1923. Sources: *El Paso Herald-Post*; EPPL; Price.

ROBERTS, Mrs. W. J., Jr. [P] Brenham, Tex. Exhibited: TFWC 1931. Sources: Wilbanks.

ROBERTSON, Fanita Janet [P; Pm; S] Dallas. Exhibited: DAA.

ROBERTSON, H. O. [P; Pm] Dallas. Birthdate: 1887. Birthplace: Marion, Ill. Deathdate: 1970. Deathplace: Dallas? Studied: Self-taught? Member: LSP; FRAC. Exhibited: FRAC 1930; TCE; Dallas AA; DAA; GTPA; TG;

TPan; WFNY; GGE 1939; TAFW 1937; LSP (all); ATPE; SSAL. Work: DMA. Sources: Stewart; WWWAA.

ROBERTSON, Marguerite [P] Galveston. Exhibited: Cotton Carn. 1912.

ROBIN, M. D. [P] San Antonio. Exhibited: SALA 1933.

ROBINSON, C. K. [D] San Antonio. Exhibited: SALA 1935.

ROBINSON, Fern [P] Houston. Exhibited: AHAE.

ROBINSON, F. Leroy [P] Fort Worth. Exhibited: TAFW 1930.

ROBINSON, Jimmie [P] San Antonio. Exhibited: SALA 1934.

ROBINSON, N. B. [P] El Paso. Exhibited: EPWC 1927.

ROBINSON, Thelma Victoria [P; T] Fort Worth. Birthdate: 1900. Studied: TCU. Exhibited: TAFW; TCE. Sources: Fisk.

ROBINSON, Virginia Isabel [P; Pm; T] Canyon. Birthdate: 1894. Birthplace: Adair Co., Mo. Deathdate: 1976. Deathplace: Kirksville, Mo. Studied: Univ. of Mo.; Columbia; Pratt Inst.; Otis AI; CSFAC; Cranbrook. Member: SSAL; Allied Artists of Amer.; Lyme AA; Palo Duro Sch. of Art, Canyon. Exhibited: TSFA 1931; TFWC 1931; TCE; TAFW 1936, 1937; GTPA; TG 1941F; WTAE 1939; ATPE 1942; SSAL. Work: PPHM; West Texas A&M Univ., Canyon. Sources: Fielding; O'Brien; WWWAA.

RODEHAVER, Gladys [P] El Paso. Exhibited: EPWC 1944.

RODRIGUEZ, Dionicio [S] San Antonio. Birthdate: 1891. Birthplace: Toluca, Mexico. Deathdate: 1955. Deathplace: San Antonio. Studied: Self-taught. Work: Brackenridge Park, San Antonio. Sources: Carson and McDonald; Jasper and Turner; *New Handbook*.

ROETTER, Paulus [P; Min. P; T] St. Louis, Mo. Birthdate: 1806. Birthplace: Nuremberg, Germany. Deathdate: 1894. Deathplace: St. Louis. Studied: Nuremberg; Dusseldorf; Munich; Switzerland. Work: UT. Sources: Groce and Wallace; Pinckney.

ROGERMAN, Gertrude [P] Dallas. Exhibited: TAFW 1931; DAA.

ROGERS, Aileen Spencer [P] Fort Worth. Exhibited: TAFW 1915.

ROGERS, Ann B. [P] San Marcos. Exhibited: TG 1942.

ROLAND, Marshall [P] Dallas. Exhibited: DMFA; DAA 1932. Sources: Bywaters Coll.

ROLFE, Walter T. [P] Austin. Exhibited: ASET 1937.

ROMANSKY, Alvin S. [S] Houston. Exhibited: AHAE.

RONEY, Harold Arthur [P; T] Houston/San Antonio. Birthdate: 1899. Birthplace: Sullivan, Ill. Deathdate: 1986. Deathplace: San Antonio. Studied: AIC; Chicago Acad. FA; Glenwood Sch.; J. Folinsbee; H. Leith-Ross; G. Aldrich; D. Dawson-Watson. Member: AAPL; SSAL; TFAA; San Antonio P&CC. Exhibited: AHAE; TFAA; TFWC 1931; Ney Mus. (solo) 1932; SALA; TAFW; ASET; SSAL. Work: Austin PL; PPHM; Southwest Texas State Univ., San Marcos; Witte; Sullivan (IL) PL. Sources: O'Brien; Steinfeldt; WWWAA.

ROOTS, Tom Smith [P] Dallas. Exhibited: TG 1941S.

ROSE, Edwin Lawrence [P] Dallas. Exhibited: TAFW.

ROSE, Martha [P] Dallas. Exhibited: DAA 1928.

ROSEN, Charles [P; I; T] Woodstock, N.Y./San Antonio. Birthdate: 1878. Birthplace: Westmoreland Co., Pa. Deathdate: 1950. Deathplace: Woodstock? Studied: NAD; N.Y. Sch. of Art w/ Chase, DuMond, F. C. Jones. Member: NAD; Amer. Soc. Painters, Sculptors and Gravers; Salmagundi; NAC. Exhibited: TG 1942; SALA 1943–44; NAD; Panama-Pacific Exp.; San Francisco; Corcoran; AIC; PAFA. Work: Witte; Whitney; Minnesota Soc. FA; Duluth FA Assoc.; Univ. Mich. Murals: Beacon, N.Y.; Palm Beach, Fla; Poughkeepsie, N.Y. Sources: Fielding; Steinfeldt; WWWAA.

ROSENBAUM, Caroline [S; Por. P] Dallas/Orlando, Fla. Birthdate: 1896. Birthplace: Bonham, Tex. Studied: AIC. Member: NAWPS; SIA; AAPL. Exhibited: DMFA 1945 (solo); TG 1941S. Work: Hospital for Crippled Children, Galveston. Sources: Bywaters Coll.; WWWAA.

ROSENFIELD, John, III [P; Car.] Dallas. Exhibited: DAA 1941; TG 1941S.

ROSS, Betsy [P] San Antonio. Exhibited: SALA 1944.

ROSS, Sue Robertson (Mrs. Zeno) [P] Fort Worth. Exhibited: TAFW 1919, 1930. Sources: WWWAA.

ROTH, Eleanor [P; Pm] Harlingen, Tex. Studied: H. A. De Young. Exhibited: ASET; ATPE 1945; Witte 1938 (solo). Sources: San Antonio Express; Witte files.

ROTHERMEL, Vera G. [P; Pm; Des.] San Antonio. Birthdate: 1919. Birthplace: San Antonio. Studied: Witte; Univ. of Mexico; SAAI. Member: TFAA; Mill Race Artists. Exhibited: TG 1945; Witte 1945; TFAA 1945; DMFA 1945; LOC 1945; Carnegie 1945. Work: PPHM. Sources: WWWAA.

ROUNTREE, Ralph S. [P; T] Dallas/New York. Birthplace: Stamford, Tex. Studied: SMU; Calif. AS. Exhibited: TAFW 1928; HPAG 1927; YWCA, Dallas 1927 (solo); SFT 1927, 1928, 1934; DAA 1928–29; Sartor; New York AC; MacBeth; Witte 1929 (solo), 1945 (solo). Sources: Fisk; O'Brien; San Antonio Evening News; San Antonio Express; San Antonio Light; Witte files.

ROUTT, Julia Jack [P] Houston. Exhibited: AHAE.

ROWE, Richard S. [Arch.; P] Austin. Birthdate: 1910. Birthplace: Austin. Studied: UT; Fontainebleau; MIT. Exhibited: Ney Mus.; TFAA; Century of Progress, Chicago. Sources: O'Brien; San Antonio Light; Witte files.

ROWNTREE, Madeline B. [P] Houston. Exhibited: AHAE 1936.

RUDMOSE, Zena L. [P] Fort Worth. Exhibited: TAFW. Sources: WWWAA.

RUHLIN, Helena Carlstad [P] Fort Worth. Exhibited: TAFW. Sources: WWWAA.

RUPRECHT, F. D. [S] Dallas. Exhibited: DAA 1928.

RUSS, Virginia Doures. See PRATHER, Virginia Russ

RUSSELL, Duke [P; S] El Paso. Studied: Texas College of Mines. Exhibited: EPWC 1935. Sources: El Paso Herald-Post; EPPL.

RUTLAND, Emily Schwarz [Pm; P] Robstown, Tex. Birthdate: 1890. Birthplace: Williamson Co., Tex. Studied: X. Gonzalez; C. Kay-Scott. Member: SSAL; TFAA; TP; South Texas AL, Corpus Christi; Corpus Christi Art Foundation; Texas WCS. Exhibited: SACE 1929; TCE; TG; ASET; ATPE; Witte 1933 (solo); Delgado Mus., New Orleans; TFWC (Lubbock) 1931; SSAL. Work: SMU; PPHM; Witte; AMST; Whitney. Sources: Bywaters Coll.; Harris; Mallett; O'Brien; TPan m; Wilbanks; WWWAA.

SADDY, Marilyn Wiley [P] Houston. Exhibited: AHAE.

SADLER, Sara [P] Dallas. Studied: Self-taught. Exhibited: 17th DWF; DAA. Sources: Fisk.

SAEGERT, Frieda [P] San Antonio. Exhibited: SALA 1933.

SAEGERT, Mrs. J. F. [P] Seguin. Exhibited: TFWC 1931. Sources: Wilbanks.

SAENGER, Elizabeth Faris "Betty" [P; Des.; I; Por. P] Houston/San Antonio. Birthdate: 1899. Birthplace: San Antonio. Deathdate: 1985. Deathplace: San Antonio. Studied: NYSFAA; MFAH. Member: DRT; Coppini Acad.; SAAL; River Art Group. Exhibited: AHAE 1936. Sources: San Antonio Express; Witte files.

SALINAS, Porfirio, Jr. [P] San Antonio. Birthdate: 1910. Birthplace: Bastrop, Tex. Deathdate: 1973. Deathplace: San Antonio. Studied: Self-taught. Member: TFAA. Exhibited: Dewey Bradford Gall., 1939. Work: MAMFW; PPHM; Stark; TCapitol; LBJ Ranch; Rayburn Lib.; Amarillo HS; TAMU; Witte. Sources: Goddard; New Handbook; Samuels.

SALOMAN, Soloman [P; Por. P] Houston/San Antonio. Exhibited: Cotton Carn. 1911, 1912. Work: RL; Witte; San Antonio Conservation Soc.; Barker Ctr., UT; TCapitol. Sources: O'Brien; Steinfeldt.

SALT, Anastasia (Mrs. W. F.) [P] Fort Worth. Exhibited: TAFW.

SAMPSON, Florence [Pm] Houston. Exhibited: AHAE 1934.

SAMUEL, William G. M. [P] San Antonio. Birthdate: 1815. Birthplace: Missouri. Deathdate: 1902. Deathplace: San Antonio. Studied: Self-taught. Exhibited: San Antonio Int'l Fair 1888. Work: Witte. Sources: New Handbook; Pinckney; Samuels; Steinfeldt; Utterbeck; WWWAA.

SAMUELS, Joyce [P; Pm] Wichita Falls. Exhibited: TG.

SANCHEZ Y TAPIA, Lino [D] Matamoros, Tamaulipas, Mexico. Birthplace: Matamoros. Deathdate: 1838. Deathplace: Matamoros? Studied: Mexico. Sources: Berlandier; New Handbook; Pinckney; Samuels.

SANDEFER, Lucile Gilbert (Mrs. J. D.) [P] Abilene. Studied: Nashville Conservatory Music and Art. Exhibited: West Texas Fair. Sources: Fisk.

SANDERS, Bertha Mae [P] Dallas. Exhibited: DAA 1928.

SANDERS, Hedwyn (Mrs. A. H.) [P] Fort Worth. Birthdate: 1892. Exhibited: TAFW 1927–37; TCE. Sources: Fielding; Samuels.

SANDERS, P. C. (Pedro) [P] San Antonio. Member: Villita Street Gall. Exhibited: SALA; SAAL 1936; Villita Street Gall. 1936. Sources: San Antonio Express; Witte files.

SANDUSKY, William H. [D; Pm] Austin/Galveston. Birthdate: 1813. Birthplace: Columbus, Ohio. Deathdate: 1847. Deathplace: Galveston. Work: Austin PL. Sources: New Handbook; Pinckney.

SANFORD, M. Thomas. See THOMAS, Mary Lou

SARGENT, Betty [P] Dallas. Exhibited: TAFW 1935; DAA 1935. Sources: O'Brien.

SARGENT, Lloyd L. [P; Comm. A; T] Dallas. Birthdate: 1881. Birthplace: Lyndon, Kans. Deathdate: 1934. Deathplace: Dallas. Studied: Chicago Acad. FA. Exhibited: TAFW 1933; Sartor (solo); DMFA (solo); Oak Cliff Sch. of Fine Arts; DAA. Work: DMA. Sources: O'Brien.

SAUNDERS, Hallie L. [P] Galveston. Exhibited: Cotton Carn. 1910. Sources: RL.

SAUNDERS, James [P] Dallas. Exhibited: DAA 1929.

SAUNDERS, Lillian Horsbrugh (Mrs. Guy) [P] Amarillo. Birthdate: 1893. Birthplace: Dickens Co., Tex. Deathdate: 1957. Deathplace: Amarillo. Studied: Pennsylvania Acad. FA; AIC; Taos. Member: Amarillo AA. Exhibited: TSFA. Sources: Amarillo Daily News; artist's family.

SAVAGE, Jane [P] Dallas/San Antonio/Bay City. Birthdate: 1898. Deathdate: 1989. Deathplace: Bay City.

Studied: Reaugh; J. Arpa; X. Gonzalez. Member: Bay City AL. Exhibited: SALA. Work: PPHM. Sources: PPHM files.

SAWYER, Beebe [P] Dallas. Exhibited: DAA 1942–45.

SCHIEFFER, William B. [S] Dallas. Exhibited: SFT 1939; DAA 1937.

SCHIWETZ, Berthold, Jr. ("Pete" or "Tex") [S] Houston. Birthdate: 1909. Birthplace: Cuero, Tex. Deathdate: 1971. Deathplace: Dexter, Mich. Studied: TAMC; MFAH w/ W. McVey; Cranbrook. Exhibited: AHAE; ASET 1938. Work: TAMU; Flint Mus., Mich.; Cleveland AM; City Park, Philadelphia. Sources: *Buck Schiwetz' Texas; New Handbook.*

SCHIWETZ, Edward Muegge ("Buck") [P; Pm] Houston. Birthdate: 1898. Birthplace: Cuero, Tex. Deathdate: 1984. Deathplace: Cuero. Studied: TAMC; J. Doctoroff; G. Cahoon. Exhibited: TCE; AHAE; HPSA (solo); Ney Mus. (solo); TFWC 1931; TG; ASET 1937–39; Philadelphia Watercolor Exh.; PAFA; Palace Legion Honor, San Francisco; SSAL. Work: MFAH; DMA; MAMFW; Humanities Research Center, UT; PPHM; TAMU; Witte. Sources: *New Handbook;* O'Brien; Pruett and Cole bio.; Samuels; WWWAA.

SCHIWETZ, Ruby Lee (Mrs. Edward M.) [S] Houston. Deathplace: Kerrville. Exhibited: AHAEs. Work: MFAH. Sources: Pruett and Cole.

SCHIWETZ, Theodore ("Ted") [S] Houston. Exhibited: AHAE. Sources: *Buck Schiwetz' Texas;* Pruett and Cole.

SCHMALZ, J. P. [P] Dallas. Exhibited: TG 1941F.

SCHMARD, Roberta [S] San Antonio. Exhibited: SALA 1934.

SCHMIDT, Tillie [P] Houston. Exhibited: AHAE 1926.

SCHMITT, Harold W. [P] Austin. Exhibited: TFWC 1931. Sources: Wilbanks.

SCHOEFIELD, Mary E. [P] Dallas. Exhibited: DAA 1929.

SCHOENBERGER, Edward T. [D; Pm] San Antonio. Exhibited: SALA 1944; TG 1944; ATPE 1944, 1945.

SCHOENFELDT, Henry H. [S] Dallas. Exhibited: TG 1944; DAA.

SCHOFIELD, Lillian Wells [P] Houston/Dallas. Exhibited: AHAE 1926; DAA.

SCHOTT, Arthur Carl Victor [P] Washington, D.C. Birthdate: 1814. Birthplace: Stuttgart, Wurtanberg. Deathdate: 1875. Deathplace: Washington, D.C. Work: Witte. Sources: *New Handbook;* Pinckney; Samuels.

SCHOW, May [P; T] Dallas/Huntsville/Fort Worth. Birthdate: 1895. Birthplace: Texas. Deathdate: 1976. Deathplace: Huntsville. Studied: College of Industrial Arts (now TWU); Columbia; Hofmann; Hogue; M. Sheets; F. Martin. Exhibited: DAA 1934; TAFW; TCE. Sources: Mallett.

SCHRECK, Horst [P; Pm; Mur. P] El Paso. Birthdate: 1885. Birthplace: Herisau, Switzerland. Exhibited: EPSJ 1934; EPWC. Sources: O'Brien; Price; Samuels; WWWAA.

SCHROEDER, Olga [P] San Antonio. Exhibited: SALA.

SCHUBART, Eva Maria [P] San Antonio/Galveston. Birthdate: 1919. Birthplace: Switzerland. Studied: P. R. Cook; Acad. of Applied Arts, Munich. Exhibited: SALA 1938. Sources: *Texas Week;* Witte files.

SCHUBART, Fred C. [P] San Antonio. Birthplace: Germany. Studied: E. Verstraeten. Exhibited: SACE 1929; SALA 1933. Sources: Witte files.

SCHUBART, Imelda [P] San Antonio. Birthdate: 1925. Birthplace: Mexico. Studied: P. R. Cook; Acad. of Applied Arts, Munich. Exhibited: SALA 1938. Sources: *Texas Week;* Witte files.

SCHUCHARD, Carl [I; Engraver] Fredericksburg. Birthdate: 1827. Birthplace: Hesse-Cassel, Germany. Deathdate: 1883. Deathplace: Corralitos, Chihuahua, Mexico. Studied: Freiburg Sch. of Mines. Sources: *New Handbook;* Samuels.

SCHUHARDT, Ernest [P] San Antonio. Studied: J. Arpa. Exhibited: Arpa Students, Witte 1928. Sources: Witte files.

SCHULTZ, M. Frances [P] Wichita Falls. Exhibited: UCE 2.

SCHULTZ, Mrs. R. H. [P] El Paso. Exhibited: EPWC 1941.

SCHUMANN, Paul R. [P; T] San Antonio/Galveston. Birthdate: 1876. Birthplace: Reichersdorf, Germany. Deathdate: 1946. Deathplace: Galveston. Studied: J. Stockfleth. Member: SSAL; Galveston AL; TFAA; New Orleans AA. Exhibited: TAFW 1923–37; SSAL, Houston, 1926; DWF; ASET 1937; West Texas Fair, San Angelo; Cotton Pal.; Cotton Carn. 1910–12. Work: Galveston AL; Southwest Texas State Univ., San Marcos; PPHM; Vanderpoel; Witte. Sources: Fisk; *Galveston Daily News;* O'Brien; RL; Samuels.

SCHUSTER, Mrs. Frank [P] El Paso. Exhibited: EPWC 1936.

SCHUTTER, H. [P; T] San Antonio. Exhibited: SALA 1930.

SCHWARTZ, Irving [Pm] El Paso. Birthdate: 1895. Birthplace: El Paso. Deathdate: 1989. Deathplace: El Paso. Studied: E. Cahero; X. Gonzalez; Columbia. Exhibited: DFPAG 1934; EPSJ 1934; EPWC 1935–37, 1940–42; Philadelphia Soc. Etchers 1934, 1935. Work: EPMA. Sources: EPMA files; EPPL; *El Paso Times;* O'Brien; Price.

SCHWARTZ, Mrs. Morris [P] Austin. Birthplace: Bryan Co., Indian Territory. Studied: College of Industrial Arts (now TWU); UT; S. E. Gideon; S. C. Gideon. Exhibited: SFT; TFAA; Century of Progress, Chicago. Sources: O'Brien.

SCHWARTZ, Sandra [P] Austin. Birthdate: 1899. Exhibited: UCE 2; GTPA.

SCHWEERS, Lyda A. (Mrs. A. H.) [P] Hondo. Birthplace: Houston. Studied: J. Arpa; H. A. De Young; M. Cook; Univ. Lauderdale; SAAI. Member: SAAL; Houston AL; TFAA; Dallas AL; MFAH; Nat. Soc. Arts and Letters. Exhibited: TFWC 1931. Sources: Wilbanks.

SCOTT, Helen Nina [D] Houston. Exhibited: AHAE.

SCOTT, Nell Elizabeth [P; T] El Paso. Birthdate: 1892. Birthplace: Red Oak, Iowa. Deathdate: 1936. Deathplace: Waco. Studied: Sul Ross State; Columbia. Member: NAWPS. Exhibited: EPWC 1935; AIC 1934; NAWPS 1936. Sources: Falk AIC; *El Paso Herald;* EPPL; *El Paso Times;* Price.

SCOTT, Robert Gillam [P] Austin/New Orleans. Birthdate: 1907. Birthplace: St. Johns, Mich. Studied: Harvard; Yale. Member: SSAL; Amer. Assoc. Univ. Profs. Exhibited: TG; SSAL; Detroit Inst. of Art. Sources: WWWAA.

SCOTT, T. E. [P] El Paso. Exhibited: EPWC 1927.

SCOTT (SCUTT?), Winifred [Por. P; I] El Paso. Birthplace: Douglaston, N.Y.? Studied: Columbia; ASL; W. Woolsey. Member: Studio Cl., N.Y.; Salon of Seven, N.Y.; Kappa Pi; Douglaston AL. Exhibited: EPWC. Sources: Price.

SCRIMGEOUR, Mary E. Jones (Mrs. Charles) [P] Galveston. Birthplace: Yazoo City, Miss. Deathdate: 1946. Deathplace: Galveston. Studied: Hollins Inst., Roanoke, Va. Exhibited: Cotton Carn. 1910. Sources: *Galveston Daily News;* RL.

SCRUGGS, Margaret Ann. See CARRUTH, Margaret Ann Scruggs

SCUTT, Winifred. See SCOTT (SCUTT?), Winifred

SEARCY, Creola [P] Fort Worth. Exhibited: TAFW 1935.

SEARS, Mary Eula [P] Merkel, Tex./Abilene. Exhibited: WTAE; TG 1940.

SEEWALD, Margaret [Mur. P; Pm; C] Amarillo. Birthdate: 1896. Birthplace: Amarillo. Living Amarillo, 1999. Studied: AIC w/ A. Philbrick. Member: SSAL; TFAA; Amarillo AA. Exhibited: TSFA 1931; Lubbock AA 1933; PPHM 1933; Chicago Soc. Etchers 1933. Work: Llano Cemetery, Amarillo; PPHM. Sources: Fisk; Mallett; O'Brien; WWWAA.

SELLORS, Evaline Clark [S] Fort Worth. Birthdate: 1903. Birthplace: Fort Worth. Deathdate: 1995. Deathplace: Fort Worth. Studied: Washington Univ.; PAFA; C. Grafley; A. Laessle. Member: FWSFA. Exhibited: Amer. Art Today, N.Y., 1939; TCE; TAFW; SFT 1938; TG 1940, 1941S; WFNY. Work: DMA; MAMFW; OJAC; PPHM. Sources: Bywaters Coll.; Fisk; Gillespie and Nail; Mallett; "NTP"; TPan m.

SETON, Lulu L. [P] Lubbock. Member: Lubbock AA. Exhibited: Lubbock AA 1933. Sources: Wilbanks.

SETTOON, Baldwin E. [Pm] Houston. Exhibited: AHAE.

SEWALL, Blanche Harding (Mrs. Cleveland) [P] Houston. Birthdate: 1889. Birthplace: Fort Worth. Studied: J. C. Tidden; F. Wagner. Member: SSAL. Exhibited: TAFW; AHAE. Sources: Fisk; WWWAA.

SHACKELFORD, George E. [P] Houston. Exhibited: AHAE 1939.

SHAFFER, Conway [P] Houston. Exhibited: AHAE 1931.

SHAND, Terry, Jr. [P] San Antonio. Exhibited: SALA 1944; TG 1943.

SHANNON, Aileen Phillips (Mrs. Edmund G.) [P] El Paso/Las Cruces, N.M. Birthdate: 1888. Birthplace: Gillsburg, Mich. Studied: PAFA; Chicago Acad. FA; W. Chase; W. Adams; T. Martin; Paris. Member: NAWA; SSAL; AAPL; Mississippi AA; San Francisco AA. Exhibited: EPWC 1938; Women Painters Amer., Wichita Falls 1938; Rockefeller Ctr., 1938; Federal Sch., N.M. 1933, 1939. Work: Mississippi. AA; New Mexico State College; Brannigan Lib., Las Cruces, N.M. Sources: WWWAA.

SHANNON, Sara [P] Fort Worth. Exhibited: TG.

SHAPARD, Mary [P] Waco. Exhibited: WTAE; SSAL.

SHARON, Jessie M. (Mrs. S. Clifford Sharon) [P] Fort Worth? Exhibited: TAFW 1911.

SHARP, Florence C. [P] Dallas. Exhibited: SFT 1938.

SHARP, Florence S. [P] Dallas. Member: FRAC. Exhibited: FRAC 1929; DAA 1932. Sources: PPHM files.

SHARP, Mrs. L. W. [P] Dallas. Exhibited: DAA.

SHARP, Minnie Lee [S; P] Houston. Exhibited: AHAE; SSAL 1939. Sources: WWWAA.

SHARP, V. [P] Dallas. Exhibited: DAA 1929.

SHAW, Lois Hogue (Mrs. Elmer) [P; Min. P; T] Abilene/Sweetwater. Studied: Baylor College, Belton; AIC w/ Foresberg, Welsh; ASL w/ F. D. Steele. Exhibited: West Texas Fair 1926; TFWC 1931; WTAE; TG 1945; SSAL.

SHAW, Nell [P] San Angelo. Birthplace: San Angelo. Studied: X. Gonzalez; W. H. Stevens; A. Brunet; O. Travis; G. E. Browne. Exhibited: TFWC; TFAA 1933–34. Sources: O'Brien.

SHEAN, Annie [P] Galveston? Exhibited: Texas Coast Fair 1895.

SHELTON, G. Harris [P; I; Des.] El Paso. Birthdate: 1894. Birthplace: Ohio. Deathdate: 1973. Deathplace: El Paso. Studied: Cahero; G. Frederick; I. Summers. Member: TFAA; EPAA. Exhibited: EPWC; WTAE 1939; TCE (Catholic Exh.); EPWC 1942 (solo); TFWC 1931. Sources: *El Paso Herald-Post*; EPPL; *El Paso Times*; Price.

SHEPARD, Anne Blake [P; S; T] Brownwood, Tex. Birthplace: Bellville, Tex. Exhibited: SFT 1909; Cotton Carn. 1911. Sources: O'Brien.

SHEPHERD, Jim [D] Houston. Exhibited: AHAE 1939.

SHEPLER, Ira D. [P] San Antonio. Exhibited: SALA; TFWC 1931. Sources: Richard Plumly Fine Art, San Antonio.

SHIELDS, Susanna Taylor [P] San Antonio. Birthdate: 1915. Birthplace: San Antonio. Studied: Corcoran; SAAI w/ C. Rosen. Exhibited: SALA 1944. Work: SAMA. Sources: *North San Antonio Times*; Witte files.

SHIPP, Aloys Gossage [P] Sherman. Birthdate: 1898. Exhibited: GTPA; SFT 1938.

SHOCKLEY, Pearle [P] Fort Worth/Dallas. Member: FRAC. Exhibited: TAFW 1924; DAA; FRAC 1934. Sources: PPHM files.

SHORE, Clover Virginia [P] Lott/Fort Worth. Birthdate: 1908. Birthplace: Durango, Tex. Deathdate: 1981. Deathplace: Fort Worth. Studied: Self-taught; George Peabody College, Nashville. Exhibited: WTAE 1940, 1942. Work: Abilene Christian Univ. Sources: Artist's son.

SHORES, Charles [P] El Paso. Exhibited: EPWC 1936.

SHUNNEY, Andrew [P] Dallas. Exhibited: DAA 1943.

SHURTLEFF, Stella Hope [P] Houston. Deathdate: 1963. Studied: Kidd-Key College, Sherman; AIC; UT; Columbia. Member: TFAA; Austin AL; Houston AL. Sources: O'Brien.

SIEVERS, Albert [D] San Antonio. Birthdate: . Exhibited: SALA 1938.

SIMKINS, Martha E. [P; T] Dallas/Woodstock. Birthdate: 1869. Birthplace: Monticello, Fla. Deathdate: 1969. Deathplace: Los Angeles Co., Calif. Studied: ASL; K. Cox; S. Mobray; Chase; C. Beaux; Snell; Sargent; E. Carlsen. Member: ASL; SSAL; NAWPS; FRAC. Exhibited: Corcoran Gall. of Art; NAD; Paris Salon 1927; FRAC 1929; SFT; TAFW; TCE; MFAH 1926 (solo); DAA 1928, 1933; TG 1941S. Work: DMA; Hockaday Sch.; Oak Cliff SFA; SMU; UT. Sources: Bywaters Coll.; Church; Dawdy; Fisk; Mallett; *New Handbook;* Smith; WWWAA.

SIMMANG, Charles [Medallist; S; Pm] San Antonio. Birthdate: 1874. Birthplace: Serbin, Tex. Studied: Karl Stubenrach. Member: AFA; SAAL. Work: Witte. Sources: O'Brien; Smith; WWWAA.

SIMMONS, Bernice [S; Des; D; P] Dallas. Exhibited: DAA.

SIMMONS, Gladys [P] Galveston. Exhibited: Cotton Carn. 1912. Sources: Cotton Carn. catalogue.

SIMMONS, Dr. L. E. [P] Perryton, Tex. Exhibited: TFWC 1931. Sources: Wilbanks.

SIMON, Jewel W. [P; S; Pm] Houston. Birthdate: 1911. Birthplace: Houston. Studied: Atlanta Univ.; Colorado Univ. Member: Nat. Conference of Artists; Amer. Assoc. Univ. Women. Exhibited: Houston, 1934–39. Work: Atlanta Univ.; Carnegie; Univ. Chicago; Univ. Maryland. Sources: Cederholm.

SIMPSON, Dow [P] Dallas. Exhibited: TG; DAA; SSAL.

SIMPSON, J. H. [P] Dallas. Exhibited: DAA 1928.

SIMPSON, Mrs. James Wesley [P] Dallas. Member: FRAC. Exhibited: FRAC 1933. Sources: PPHM files.

SIMPSON, Wallace Everett [P; I] Fort Worth/Dallas. Birthdate: 1880. Birthplace: Moweaqua, N.Y. Deathdate: 1969. Deathplace: Eastland County, Tex. Studied: F. Reaugh. Member: Fort Worth AA. Exhibited: TAFW; DAA 1933. Sources: ITD; O'Brien; WWWAA.

SIMS, Ruth [P] Houston. Exhibited: AHAE 1938.

SINGLETARY, Olga [P] Dallas. Exhibited: SSAL.

SKINNER, Frances Johnson [P; T] Dallas/Houston. Birthdate: 1902. Birthplace: Dallas. Deathdate: 1983. Deathplace: Houston? Studied: MFA, Boston; Chouinard

Inst.; Spruce. Member: TFAA; SSAL; NAWA; FRAC. Exhibited: FRAC 1930; DAA; TAFW; TCE; SFT; TG; TPan; AHAE; PAFA 1938; KCAI; SSAL. Work: DMA; MFAH; Dallas public schools. Sources: Bywaters Coll.; Falk PAFA; Mallett; TPan m.; WWWAA.

SKIPWORTH, Lucile [P] El Paso. Exhibited: EPWC.

SLATER, Elsie McElroy (Mrs. H. D.). [P] El Paso. Exhibited: EPSJ 1934. Sources: *El Paso Herald;* EPPL.

SLAUGHTER, Avery [P] Dallas. Exhibited: DAA 1933.

SLAUGHTER, Clyde Laura [P] Amarillo. Exhibited: WTAE 1939.

SLIMP, Helen Ferne (Mrs. Chester A.) [P; Pm] San Antonio. Birthdate: 1890. Birthplace: Crozet, Va. Studied: E. Lawson; F. Ellis; G. Cassidy; R. Davey; H. De Young. Exhibited: SAAG 1927; SALA; TFWC 1931; Witte 1936 (solo). Work: Witte. Sources: Witte files.

SLOAN, Jas. Blanding [P; Pm; I; T] Corsicana/Chicago. Birthdate: 1886. Birthplace: Corsicana. Studied: Chicago Acad. FA; B. J. O. Nordfeldt; G. Senseney. Member: Chicago Soc. Etchers. Exhibited: TAFW 1914–17; DAA 1937. Work: Witte. Sources: WWWAA.

SLOAT, Blanche A. [P] Denton. Exhibited: TAFW 1918.

SMART, Frank Ellis [P] Dallas. Exhibited: DAA 1937; SFT 1939.

SMEDES, Elizabeth H. [P] Houston. Exhibited: AHAE 1931.

SMITH, Mrs. A. B. [P] Wellington. Exhibited: TFWC 1931. Sources: Wilbanks.

SMITH, Alexa (Mrs. J. T.) [P] San Antonio. Birthplace: Millersburg, Ky. Studied: Baylor; Arpa; Dawson-Watson; R. Taylor; De Young; Wall. Exhibited: UCE 2; SACE 1927; SSAL; TFAA; TFWC; TAFW; SAAG 1927; Arpa Students, Witte 1928; San Pedro Playhouse 1931 (two-person w/ Hoppe). Sources: O'Brien.

SMITH, Alice Akin [P] Houston. Exhibited: TFWC 1931. Sources: Wilbanks.

SMITH, Amanda Fern [P] San Antonio. Exhibited: SALA 1930; TFWC 1931.

SMITH, Ellen Harrison [S] San Antonio/Dallas. Birthplace: New Orleans. Studied: TCU. Exhibited: DAA; HPSA. Sources: Fisk; O'Brien.

SMITH, Emily Guthrie (Mrs. Tolbert C.) [P; T] Fort Worth. Birthdate: 1909. Birthplace: Fort Worth. Deathdate: 1986. Deathplace: Fort Worth. Studied: College of Industrial Arts (now TWU); OU; ASL; R. Brackman. Member: SSAL; TFAA; FWAA; Dallas AA; Taos AA; Pastel Soc. Amer.; Nat. Soc. Arts and Letters. Exhibited: TAFW 1936; TG; FWAA; SSAL; TFAA; Salamagundi. Work: DMA; Longview AM; MAMFW; OJAC; TCapitol; MAMFW; Texas Tech; OJAC; TAMU; TWC; TCU. Sources: Bywaters Coll.; Gillespie and Nail; New Handbook; O'Brien; TPan m.; WWWAA.

SMITH, Erwin Evans [Ph; S] Bonham, Tex. Birthdate: 1886. Birthplace: Honey Grove, Tex. Deathdate: 1947. Deathplace: Bonham. Studied: L. Taft; B. L. Pratt. Work: DMA; LOC. Sources: Fisk; New Handbook; O'Brien; Samuels.

SMITH, Fay [P] Wellington, Tex. Exhibited: WTAE 1942.

SMITH, Frances M. [P] Wellington, Tex. Exhibited: WTAE 1942.

SMITH, Gean [P] Galveston. Birthdate: 1851. Birthplace: New York. Deathdate: 1928. Deathplace: Galveston. Studied: Self-taught. Exhibited: TAFW 1925–28. Work: TCapitol. Sources: Galveston Tribune; ITD; RL; Samuels; WWWAA.

SMITH, Helen [S] San Antonio. Exhibited: SALA 1932.

SMITH, Jane [P] San Antonio. Exhibited: SALA.

SMITH, Jean [P] Houston. Exhibited: AHAE 1929.

SMITH, Jessie Stubblefield [P] Fort Worth. Exhibited: TAFW 1935.

SMITH, Louise [P] Galveston? Exhibited: Texas Coast Fair 1895.

SMITH, Lowell [P] El Paso. Exhibited: EPWC 1945.

SMITH, Mary Loving [Pm] Fort Worth. Exhibited: TAFW 1933.

SMITH, Olive H. (Olive Haley) [P] San Antonio. Deathdate: 1969. Deathplace: San Antonio. Exhibited: SALA. Sources: ITD; PPHM.

SMITH, Robin Artine [P; Des.] Dallas. Birthdate: 1903. Birthplace: Warren, Ark. Studied: AIC; Northwestern; H. Ropp; E. O'Hara. Member: Dallas AA; TFAA NAWA. Exhibited: DAA; TG; FRAC; Klepper AC; TFAA 1945; SSAL; Amer. WCS 1945; NAWA. Sources: WWWAA.

SMITH, Ruth Connerly [P] San Antonio. Exhibited: SALA 1944.

SMITH, Sarah M. [P] Fort Worth/Philadelphia. Exhibited: TAFW; SSAL, Montgomery, Ala., 1938, San Antonio, 1939. Sources: WWWAA.

SMITH, Virginia [P] El Paso. Exhibited: EPWC 1935; El Paso Centennial Mus. Sources: El Paso Herald-Post; EPPL.

SMITH, Winston [P] Dallas. Exhibited: DAA 1931.

SNEED, Mary (Mrs. R. H.?) [P] Dallas. Exhibited: DAA 1932.

SNEED, Mrs. R. H. (Mary?) [P] Dallas. Exhibited: DAA 1929.

SNODGRASS, Libby [P] San Antonio. Exhibited: SALA 1933.

SNOWDEN, Chester Dixon [P; I; T] Houston. Birthdate: 1900. Birthplace: Elgin, Tex. Deathdate: 1984. Deathplace: Houston. Studied: UT; Cooper Union; ASL; Grand Central Gall.; Univ. Houston; Chouinard Inst., Los Angeles. Member: SSAL. Exhibited: AHAE; TG; ASET; Corcoran. Work: MFAH. Sources: Archives of Amer. Art Journal; Torch Energy files; WWWAA.

SOLER Y MANONELLES, Urbici Jose Franceso [S; T] El Paso. Birthdate: 1890. Birthplace: Farran, Lerida, Spain. Deathdate: 1953. Deathplace: El Paso. Studied: Barcelona; Hildebrand; Bourdelle. Exhibited: EPWC 1945. Work: Cristo Rey, El Paso; EPMA; EPPL. Sources: Hendricks and Reese; New Handbook.

SORRENSON, Ella [P] Houston. Exhibited: Cotton Carn. 1912. Sources: Cotton Carn. catalogue.

SOUTHWICK, (Miss) [P] Galveston? Exhibited: Texas Coast Fair 1895.

SPAULDING, Florence S. [P] Dallas. Exhibited: DAA 1933.

SPAULDING, Grace. See JOHN, Grace Spaulding

SPEAR, W. [P; Pm] San Antonio. Exhibited: SALA 1938.

SPEARS, Lena [P] Houston/Dallas. Exhibited: AHAE; DAA 1931.

SPEED, Rosalie [P; Des.] Dallas. Birthdate: 1907. Birthplace: Dallas. Studied: Aunspaugh AS; SMU; TWU. Member: TFAA; SSAL; DAL; FRAC. Exhibited: FRAC 1930; TAFW; TCE; SFT 1938; DAA; GTPA; TG. Sources: Bywaters Coll.; Mallett; Bywaters, "New Texas Painters"; TPan m.; WWWAA.

SPEER, Anniola [P] Fort Worth. Exhibited: TAFW.

SPELLMAN, Coreen Mary [P; Pm; T] Denton. Birthdate: 1905. Birthplace: Forney, Tex. Deathdate: 1978. Deathplace: Denton. Studied: TWU; Columbia; ASL; Iowa; C. Martin; K. H. Miller; Vytlacil. Member: SSAL; Denton AL; Pm Guild; TP (founder). Exhibited: SACE 1929; TAFW; TCE; GTPA; SFT; WTAE; DMFA 1932 (solo), 1943 (solo); Witte 1933 (solo); MFAH 1933 (solo); TPan; TG; ATPE; SSAL. Work: Belo; Brooklyn Mus.; City of Forney; DMA; Joslyn Mus.; Ney Mus.; PPHM; Tyler MA. Sources: Bywaters Coll.; Fielding; Harris; Mallett; *New Handbook*; "NTP"; O'Brien; TPan m.; WWWAA.

SPENCE, Julia [Interior Des.] Dallas. Exhibited: DAA 1928.

SPENCER, Henry Cecil [P; Por. P; I; W; T] Ballinger/ Chicago/College Station. Birthdate: 1903. Birthplace: Mangum, Okla. Studied: Baylor; TAMC; E. Blumenschein; ASL w/ Romanovsky. Member: SSAL; Amer. Inst. Draftsmen. Exhibited: TAFW 1928; ASET 1937. Work: Baylor. Sources: Fisk; Smith; WWWAA.

SPENCER, Icy [P] Dallas. Exhibited: SFT 1939; DAA 1938; TG 1941F.

SPIGENER, H. Walton [P] Post. Exhibited: TFWC 1931. Sources: Wilbanks.

SPIVEY, Pauline [P] Dallas. Exhibited: DAA 1938.

SPRAGUE, Harold C. [P] Fort Worth. Exhibited: TAFW.

SPRUCE, Everett [P; Pm.; T] Dallas/Austin. Birthdate: 1908. Birthplace: Conway, Ark. Living Austin, 1997. Studied: AID, Travis, Stell. Member: LSP; TFAA. Exhibited: DAA; TCE; GTPA; SFT; TAFW; TG; TPan; ATPE; LSP; MoMA; AIC; Rockefeller; WFNY. Work: CSFAC; DMA; MAMFW; MFAH; TAMU; OJAC; PPHM; Met.; MoMA; Nelson; PAFA; SMU; UT; Witte. Sources: Carraro thesis; Fisk; O'Brien; Samuels; WWWAA.

SQUYRES, Willie [P] Fort Worth. Exhibited: TAFW 1924.

STAFFEL, Rudolf [P; Cer.; T] San Antonio/New Orleans/ Philadelphia. Birthdate: 1911. Birthplace: San Antonio. Deathplace: Living Philadelphia, 1997. Studied: J. Arpa; H. Hofmann; AIC w/ L. Ripman, L. Van Papelbaum. Exhibited: TAFW; GTPA; ASET 1937; SALA. Sources: "American Potters"; O'Brien.

STAINBROOK, Dr. M. A. [P] Lubbock. Member: Lubbock AA; Plains Mus. Soc. (Charter). Exhibited: Lubbock AA 1933. Sources: Wilbanks.

STALEY, Mary Louise [P] San Antonio. Exhibited: SALA 1936.

STALLINGS, Pearl S. (Mrs. Henry) [P] Brownwood, Tex. Exhibited: TFWC 1931; WTAE 1940.

STANBERRY, Mrs. W. T. [P] Amarillo. Exhibited: TSFA 1931. Sources: Amarillo newspapers.

STANFORD, J. Elizabeth [P] Houston. Exhibited: AHAE.

STANFORD, Minnie M. [P] San Antonio. Exhibited: SALA 1936, 1938.

STANLEY, John Mix [P; Por. P] Washington, D.C./Detroit. Birthdate: 1814. Birthplace: Canandaigua, N.Y. Deathdate: 1872. Deathplace: Detroit. Studied: Self-taught. Exhibited: Smithsonian. Work: NMAA; Amon Carter; Stark; Detroit IA; Phoenix AM; Denver PL. Sources: Dawdy; Goetzmann and Reese; Kinietz; *New Handbook*; Ratcliffe; Samuels.

STANLEY, Mack [P] Houston. Exhibited: AHAE 1943.

STANLEY, Madeleine [P] Houston. Exhibited: TG 1944; AHAE 1945.

STANSBURY, Florence E. [S] Houston. Exhibited: AHAE 1931.

STARCALA, John J. [S] Houston. Exhibited: AHAE 1933.

STEARMAN, Mrs. W. C. [P] Dallas. Exhibited: DAA 1928.

STEDMAN, Myrtle Kelly [P; W; Des.] Houston/Santa Fe. Birthdate: 1908. Birthplace: Charleston, Ill. Living Santa Fe, 1999. Studied: F. Browne; W. Stedman. Member: HAG; TFAA. Exhibited: AHAE. Sources: *New Mexico* Magazine, Apr. 97; WWWAA.

STEDMAN, Rosabel [P] Houston. Exhibited: AHAE 1925.

STEDMAN, Wilfred Henry [P; S; Pm; I; T; Arch.] Houston/Santa Fe. Birthdate: 1892. Birthplace: Liverpool, England. Deathdate: 1950. Deathplace: Santa Fe. Studied: Minneapolis Inst. Art; SAL; Broadmoor; G. Goetch; L. Phoenix; H. Dunn; L. Mora; F. DuMond. Member: HAG; TFAA. Exhibited: AHAE; Ch. of Christ, Houston. Sources: DAS; Fielding; *New Mexico* Magazine, Apr. 97; WWWAA.

STEEN, Mary (Mrs. Hugh) [P] El Paso. Exhibited: EPWC 1944, 1945. Sources: EPPL; *El Paso Times.*

STEINFELDT, Cecilia. See NEUHEISEL, Cecilia (Mrs. Eric Steinfeldt)

STEINFELDT, Eric [P] San Antonio. Birthdate: 1917. Birthplace: San Antonio. Deathplace: Living San Antonio, 1997. Studied: H. L. McFee. Exhibited: SALA 1940. Sources: Cecilia Steinfeldt.

STELL, Thomas M., Jr. [P; Por. P] Dallas. Birthdate: 1898. Birthplace: Cuero, Tex. Deathdate: 1981. Deathplace: San Antonio. Studied: Rice; ASL; NAD w/ Bridgman, G. Luks, C. Hawthorne; Columbia. Member: LSP. Exhibited: TAFW; SFT 1928; DAA; TCE; LSP 1938; ATPE 1944; SALA; 48 States Competition; GGE 1939. Work: DMA. Murals: Forest Ave. HS, Dallas; USPOs, Perry, Okla., and Teague and Longview, Tex. Sources: *New Handbook;* O'Brien; Stewart; WWWAA.

STELZIG, Frances [P] Houston. Exhibited: AHAE 1938.

STEPHENS, Julia Margurite [P] Houston. Exhibited: AHAE 1940.

STEPHENS, Mrs. M. A. [P] Galveston? Exhibited: Texas Coast Fair 1895.

STEPHENS, Seth H. [P] San Antonio. Exhibited: SALA 1943.

STERNE, J. J. [P] San Antonio. Exhibited: SALA.

STERNE, Stella M. [P] San Antonio. Exhibited: SALA.

STEVENS, Harrison [P] Dallas. Exhibited: DMFA; HPAG. Sources: Bywaters Coll.

STEVENS, Kelly Haygood [P; T] Mexia, Tex. Birthdate: 1896. Birthplace: Mexia. Studied: Texas Sch. for the Deaf; Gallaudet; Corcoran; Trenton Sch. Industrial Arts; Paris; Acad. Colarossi; NYSFAA; LSU. Member: SSAL; TFAA; Salon Int'l des Arts Silencieux. Exhibited: TFWC 1931; UCE 1; TCE; TAFW 1937; Herzog Gall., Houston (solo); TFAA; SSAL. Sources: O'Brien; Samuels; *San Antonio Light;* WWWAA; Witte files.

STEVENS, Lawrence Tenney [S; P; Pm; T] Tulsa. Birthdate: 1896. Birthplace: Boston, Mass. Deathdate: 1972. Deathplace: Tulsa ? Studied: Amer. Acad., Rome; Grafly; B. L. Pratt; Tufts Univ. Member: NSS; N.Y. Arch. Lg.; Soc. of Medallists. Exhibited: PAFA; N.Y. Arch. Lg.; NAD; MFA, Boston. Work: Fair Park, Dallas; Brooklyn Mus.; Brookgreen Sculpture Garden, S.C. Sources: Dallas Hist. Soc. files; DAS; Fielding; Hendricks and Reese.

STEVENS, Walter [P] Dallas. Exhibited: TAFW; DAA.

STEVENS, William [Por. P] Austin. Sources: Pinckney.

STEVENSON, Louise A. [P] Houston. Exhibited: AHAE.

STEVENSON, Orissa [P] Houston. Exhibited: AHAE; ASET.

STEWART, William P. [P; S] Austin. Exhibited: TG 1941F.

STILLMAN, Ary [P] Houston. Birthdate: 1891. Birthplace: Russia. Deathdate: 1967. Deathplace: Houston. Studied: AIC; NAD; ASL. Exhibited: AHAE 1935. Work: MFAH; New Britain MA, Conn.; Sioux City AC, Iowa. Sources: ITD; WWWAA.

STOCKFLETH, Julius [P; Por. P] Galveston. Birthdate: 1857. Birthplace: Wyk, Denmark. Deathdate: 1935. Deathplace: Wyk. Studied: Painter in Wyk. Exhibited: Texas Coast Fair 1895; Cotton Carn. 1911. Work: RL; Stark. Sources: Fisk; McGuire; *New Handbook.*

STOCKHAM, Eva H. [P] Dallas. Exhibited: DAA 1933.

STOCKWELL, Mrs. Walter [P] El Paso. Exhibited: EPWC 1936.

STOKES, Pauline [P] Dallas. Member: FRAC. Exhibited: FRAC 1930; SFT 1939. Sources: PPHM files.

STOLLEIS, Miss L. [P] Cuero, Tex. Exhibited: TFWC 1931. Sources: Wilbanks.

STONE, Catherine [D] Houston. Exhibited: AHAE 1936.

STONE, Jesse R. [P] Houston. Exhibited: AHAE.

STONE, Mildred B. [P] Houston. Exhibited: AHAE. Sources: WWWAA.

STONE, Ruby Dempsey (Mrs. James P. Markham, Jr.) [P] Dallas/Houston. Birthdate: 1900. Deathdate: 1993. Deathplace: Houston. Studied: AID w/ Travis; NAD w/ Kroll; ASL w/ Lucioni; Hofmann. Exhibited: SFT 1933 TAFW; DAA; TCE; AHAE; GTPA; ASET 1937. Sources: Bywaters Coll.; Mallett; O'Brien; WWWAA.

STOREY, Boude E. [P] Dallas. Exhibited: DAA 1928.

STOREY, Evelyn Erwin (Mrs. Boude) [P; Pm] Dallas. Member: FRAC. Exhibited: DAA 1928; FRAC; SFT 1939; ATPE 1945.

STOREY, Jackson Gray [P] Cotulla, Tex. Birthdate: 1902. Birthplace: San Marcos. Deathdate: 1978. Deathplace: Cincinnati, Ohio. Studied: TAMC; AIC. Exhibited: San Marcos; Midland; San Antonio.

STORM, Birdie [P] Dallas? Exhibited: Crawford Gall. 1907.

STORM, Mark [P] Houston. Exhibited: AHAE 1943.

STOUT, Mary Jane [P] Houston. Exhibited: AHAE 1942.

STOUT, Myron S. [P] San Antonio. Exhibited: SALA 1931. Work: MFAH. Sources: *San Antonio Light;* Witte files.

STOVALL, Ida Harrington [P] Plainview, Tex. Birthdate: 1885. Deathdate: 1943. Deathplace: Hale Co., Tex. Studied: Carl Redin. Exhibited: TFWC 1931. Work: PPHM. Sources: Wilbanks; Plainview PL.

STOVALL, Winona Young [P] BrownwoodColeman, Tex. Exhibited: WTAE.

STOY, Frances Baskette [P] Houston. Exhibited: AHAE 1926.

STRACHN, Hal [P] Lubbock. Exhibited: Plains Mus. Soc. 1932. Sources: Wilbanks.

STRAHALM, Franz (Frank) [P; Mur. P; T] Dallas. Birthdate: 1879. Birthplace: Vienna, Austria. Deathdate: 1935. Deathplace: Dallas. Studied: Hamburg AS, Germany. Member: Dallas AA; SIA; New York AC; SSAL. Exhibited: TAFW; SFT 1931, 1934; DAA 1928–32. Work: Ney Mus. Mural: Dallas Power and Light Company. Sources: Fisk; O'Brien; Samuels.

STRAIN, Ella [P] El Paso. Exhibited: EPCC.

STRAITON/STRATON, Betty [P] Dallas. Exhibited: DAA.

STRAND, Charlotte [P] San Antonio. Exhibited: SALA 1940.

STRANGE, James [Por. P] Austin's Colony, Harris Co. Birthdate: 1786. Birthplace: Scotland? Sources: Pinckney.

STRANGE, Olive B. [P] Temple. Exhibited: TFWC 1931. Sources: Wilbanks.

STREET, Mrs. J. C. [P] El Paso. Exhibited: EPWC.

STREET, Lois [P] Houston. Exhibited: AHAE.

STREETMAN, Christine Norman (Mrs. Sam, Jr.) [S; Dec.; Des.] Houston. Birthdate: 1903. Studied: MFAH; Rice; N.Y. Sch. Interior Design; TSCW. Exhibited: AHAE; ASET?; TG 1943. Work: MFAH. Sources: WWWAA.

STRIMBAN, Jack J. [P; Pm] San Antonio. Exhibited: SALA 1944.

STROHMEYER, August F. [S; T] Dallas. Birthplace: Wheeling, W. Va. Studied: Apprenticed to father. Exhibited: DAA; SFT; HPAG; Sartor. Work: Petroleum Bldg., Houston; Highland Park Methodist Ch., Dallas; Hilton Hotel, Lubbock. Sources: O'Brien.

STRONG, Grace [P] Fort Worth/El Paso. Exhibited: TAFW; EPWC 1936.

STUART, Carrie M. [P] Mercedes, Tex. Exhibited: TFWC 1931. Sources: Wilbanks.

STUART, Mrs. S. A. [P; Por. P] Galveston. Sources: Pinckney.

SUGGS, Tom [P] Dallas. Exhibited: DAA 1933. Work: PPHM.

SULAICA, Anthony R. [P] San Antonio. Deathdate: 1968. Deathplace: San Antonio. Exhibited: SALA.

SULLIVAN, C. F. [S] Dallas. Exhibited: DAA 1933.

SULLIVAN, Edna (Mrs. J. P.) [P] Brownwood, Tex. Exhibited: TAFW 1929.

SUMMERHILL, Marinel [P] Monahans, Tex. Exhibited: WTAE 1940.

SURGINER, Elizabeth [P] San Antonio. Exhibited: SALA 1940.

SUTTON, Dorothy [P] Dallas. Exhibited: DAA 1930.

SUTTON, Mrs. W. B. [P] Dallas. Member: FRAC. Exhibited: FRAC 1933, 1934. Sources: PPHM files.

SWADEK, Joy [P] Dallas. Member: FRAC. Exhibited: FRAC 1941. Sources: PPHM files.

SWANLUND, D. C. [P] San Antonio. Exhibited: SALA 1943.

SWANN, James [P; Pm; Comm. A; I] Amarillo/Dallas. Birthdate: 1905. Birthplace: Merkel, Tex. Studied: Sul Ross State; A. Keener; E. Keefer; F. Klepper. Member: TFAA; SSAL; HPSFA; Dallas AA. Exhibited: TAFW; TCE; DAA; SFT; TFAA; HPAG (solo); PPHM (solo); Amarillo (solo); Lubbock (solo); Ney Mus. (solo); Sherman (solo); SSAL. Work: Sherman PL; MAMFW. Sources: O'Brien.

SWEARINGEN, Mrs. W. E. [P] El Paso. Exhibited: EPWC 1943.

SWEETLAND, Dana Warner [P] San Antonio. Exhibited: SALA 1933.

SWIFT, Mrs. Charles [P] Santa Rosa, Tex. Exhibited: TFWC 1931.

SWINDELL, Jessie Volah [P] Denton. Exhibited: WTAE 1939.

SWYERS, Amelia M. [P] San Antonio/Nueces Co., Tex. Deathdate: 1971. Deathplace: Nueces Co. Exhibited: SALA 1933.

TAKSA, Desha Milcinovic. See DESHA

TALLEY, Thomasina [P] San Antonio. Exhibited: SALA 1937. Sources: *San Antonio Light;* Witte files.

TARPLEY, Myra [Pm] Houston. Exhibited: ASET 1937.

TARVER, Nell H. (Mrs. Charles) [P] Dallas. Studied: Aunspaugh AS. Exhibited: TAFW.

TATE, Blanche [P] Dallas. Member: FRAC. Exhibited: FRAC 1934. Sources: PPHM files.

TATE, Claire [P; T; Comm. A] Abilene. Birthplace: Abilene. Studied: E. M. Lowdon; KCAI; Broadmoor; ASL; Christoval w/ O. Travis, W. Stevens, X. Gonzalez; N.Y. Sch. of Art. Exhibited: TAFW 1925; WTAE 1939; HPAG; West Texas Fair. Sources: Fisk.

TATE, Mrs. J. Waddy [P] Dallas. Member: FRAC. Exhibited: DAA 1928; FRAC 1932.

TAUCH, Waldine Amanda [S; T; P] San Antonio. Birthdate: 1892. Birthplace: Schulenberg, Tex. Deathdate: 1986. Deathplace: San Antonio. Studied: P. Coppini. Member: SSAL; Soc. of Women Sculptors; NAWA; NAWPS; AAPL. Exhibited: Witte; NSS 1931; NAD. Work: Baylor; Buckner's Ranch, Burnet; Coppini-Tauch Studio; Howard-Payne; Love Field; PPHM; UT; Witte. Sources: Hutson bio.; Bywaters Coll.; DAS; Fielding; Fisk; Hendricks and Reese; O'Brien; Smith; WWWAA.

TAYLOR, A. Hinkle [P] Houston. Exhibited: AHAE; TG 1941F.

TAYLOR, Edgar D. [P] Austin. Exhibited: TG 1941 Spring 1944.

TAYLOR, Harry [P] Fort Worth. Exhibited: TAFW 1919.

TAYLOR, Lura Ann [Pm] Dallas. Birthdate: 1906. Birthplace: Smithville, Mo. Deathdate: 1990. Deathplace: Dallas. Studied: SMU; TWU. Member: TP (founder); Dallas Pm Guild; Dallas AA; Texas Artists Group; Dallas Print

Soc. Exhibited: TCE; DAA; SFT 1939; TG 1941S; ATPE 1942, 1944. Sources: Bywaters Coll.; Harris; O'Brien.

TAYLOR, Rolla Sims [P; T; Pm] San Antonio. Birthdate: 1872. Birthplace: Galveston. Deathdate: 1970. Deathplace: San Antonio. Studied: Cuero Inst.; Arpa; J. Onderdonk; SAAL. Member: TFAA; SAAL; AFA. Exhibited: Cotton Carn. 1910; TAFW; SAAG 1927; SACE; SAAL 1928; Witte; TFWC 1931; ASET 1937; SALA 1930–37, 1944; TFAA. Work: Witte; PPHM; RL. Sources: Fisk; O'Brien; PPHM files; Samuels; Steinfeldt.

TEEL, Lewis, Jr. [P; S; T] El Paso. Studied: Provincetown, Mass. w/ C. Martin; Texas College of Mines; Columbia. Exhibited: EPWC. Sources: *El Paso Herald-Post;* EPPL; *El Paso Times;* EPWC scrapbooks.

TEEL, Lewis Woods [P; I] El Paso. Birthdate: 1883. Birthplace: Clarksville, Tex. Deathdate: 1960. Deathplace: Long Beach, Calif. Studied: Mostly self-taught. Member: Salmagundi; TFAA; FSAA; EPAG; EPAA; Nat. Soc. Arts and Letters. Exhibited: TAFW; SACE 1928; TFWC 1931; EPSJ 1934; EPWC; WTAE 1939–42. Work: PPHM. Sources: EPPL; Fisk; O'Brien; PPHM files; Samuels; WWWAA.

TEESDALE, Christopher Hugh [P] Cleburne, Tex. Birthdate: 1886. Birthplace: Eltham, Kent, England. Studied: C. Teesdale (uncle); Oxford; Royal Military College. Member: FWPC; SSAL; TFAA; AAPL; Cleburne AA (founder). Exhibited: TAFW; DWF; TFWC 1931; HPAG (solo); SSAL; World's Fair, Chicago 1933. Work: Cleburne public schools; Cleburne Masonic Temple. Sources: Fielding; Fisk; O'Brien.

TEICH, Frank [S] Llano, Tex. Birthdate: 1856. Birthplace: Lobenstein, Thüeringen, Germany. Deathdate: 1939. Deathplace: Llano. Studied: Nuremberg; Dresden w/ Schilling. Work: Pioneer Park, Dallas; TCapitol. Sources: Hendricks and Reese; *New Handbook;* O'Brien.

TEICHMUELLER, Minnette [P; T; Mur. P] San Antonio/New Braunfels. Birthdate: 1872. Birthplace: La Grange, Tex. Studied: SHNS; San Antonio Art Acad.; Pohl. Exhibited: Witte 1933 (joint w/ Pohl); in studio; SALA. Work: White House, Washington, D.C.; Witte. Mural: USPO, Smithville, Tex. Sources: *San Antonio Light;* Steinfeldt; WWWAA; Witte files.

TENNANT, Allie Victoria. [S] Dallas. Birthdate: 1898. Birthplace: St. Louis. Deathdate: 1971. Deathplace: Dallas. Studied: Aunspaugh AS; ASL w/ Bridgman and McCartan; Kunz-Meyer. Member: NSS; Dallas AA; SSAL; Texas Sculpture Group. Exhibited: DWF 1919 (pr.); DAA; TCE; SFT; GTPA; TG 1941S; AIC; KCAI; WFNY; PAFA. Work: DMA; Hockaday Sch.; McMurry College, Abilene; Brookgreen Sculpture Garden, S.C. Sources: DAS; ITD; Fielding; Fisk; Hendricks and Reese; Mallett; O'Brien; Smith; Stewart; TPan m.; WWWAA.

THARSILLA, Sister M. (Mary Tharsilla Fuchs) [P; Pm; T] San Antonio. Birthdate: 1912. Birthplace: Westphalia, Tex. Living San Antonio, 1997. Studied: Our Lady of the Lake College; Columbia; AIC w/ C. Pougialis, R. Lifvendahl. Member: SAAL; TWCS; Texas Art Ed. Assoc.; Nat. Art Ed. Assoc. Exhibited: SALA; TG 1945. Sources: The artist; WWWAA. Taught, Our Lady of the Lake College, 1942–91; sculpture studio at college named for her in 1996.

THEBO, Anne Noble (Mrs. A. V.) [P] Temple. Exhibited: TFWC 1931.

THIELEPAPE, William Carl August [Por. P; Photog.] San Antonio. Birthdate: 1814. Birthplace: Wabern, Kurhessen, Germany. Deathdate: 1904. Deathplace: Chicago. Work: Witte. Sources: Albrecht; O'Brien; Utterbeck; Witte files.

THOMAS, Frances E. [P] Dallas. Exhibited: TAFW; DAA. Sources: Fisk.

THOMAS, Knox Thurman [P] Lubbock. Birthdate: 1903. Deathdate: 1954. Deathplace: Lubbock. Studied: Redin; A. Hammond; N. Piper; West Texas State College, Canyon. Member: South Plains AG; TFAA; Lubbock AA. Exhibited: TFWC 1931; PMS 1933; Lubbock AA 1933. Work: Texas Tech; First Federal Savings, Lubbock. Sources: ITD; Wilbanks.

THOMAS, M. (Mary Lou Thomas Patterson Sanford) [Por. P; P] Wichita Falls/Abilene/Taos, N.M. Birthdate: 1899. Birthplace: Sulphur Springs, Tex. Deathdate: 1989. Deathplace: Taos. Studied: SMU. Exhibited: West Texas Fair 1926; Texas-Oklahoma Fair 1927; TFWC 1931. Work: Blumenschein Home Mus., Taos; PPHM. Sources: Fisk; O'Brien; PPHM files.

THOMAS, Stephen Seymour [P; Por. P] San Augustine, Texas/Paris/New York, N.Y./ La Crescenta, Calif. Birthdate: 1868. Birthplace: San Augustine, Tex. Deathdate: 1956. Deathplace: La Crescenta. Studied: ASL; W. Chase; C. Beckwith; AJ w/ Lefebvre, Benjamin-Constant; École BA. Member: Los Angeles AA; Paris Soc. Amer. P; Pasadena AS. Exhibited: Paris salons; WCE; Exp. Universelle, Paris, 1900; Pan-American Exp., Buffalo, N.Y.; PAFA. Work: DMA; MFAH; San Jacinto Mus.; White House; Syracuse; Univ. Calif. Sources: Fielding; Fisk; *New Handbook;* O'Brien; Pinckney; Samuels; WWWAA.

THOMPSON, Charles [P] San Antonio. Exhibited: SALA 1940.

THOMPSON, Cornelia [P] Dallas. Exhibited: DAA.

THOMPSON, Elaine Trulove [P] Alvarado, Tex. Exhibited: TAFW 1927.

THOMPSON, Eloise Reid [P] Dallas/Houston. Birthdate: 1900. Birthplace: Dallas. Deathdate: 1986. Deathplace: Houston. Studied: Aunspaugh AS; OU; ASL w/ Bridgman, Nicolaides. Member: FRAC. Exhibited: FRAC; AHAE 1935–37; DAA 1931–33. Work: Houston Mus. of Natural Science. Sources: Houston Mus. of Natural Science; Sutton.

THOMPSON, May Beth [P] Dallas. Exhibited: DAA 1935.

THOMPSON, William [D] Dallas. Deathdate: 1968. Deathplace: Dallas. Exhibited: DAA. Sources: ITD.

THOMS, P. A. [P] Dallas. Exhibited: DAA 1928.

THOMSON, Adele Underwood [P, T] Corpus Christi. Birthdate: 1887. Birthplace: Grosbeck, Tex. Studied: AIC; Newcomb College; Tulane; E. A. Holmes; W. Stevens; X. Gonzalez. Member: SSAL; TFAA; Corpus Christi Art Foundation; South Texas AL. Exhibited: TFAA; Corpus Christi Art Foundation. 1945; SSAL. Sources: WWWAA; Witte files.

THOMSON, Mrs. H. H. [P] Ballinger. Exhibited: TFWC 1931.

THRASH, Rozella C. [P] Dallas. Exhibited: DAA 1935.

THURMOND, Ethel Dora [P; T] Victoria. Birthdate: 1905. Birthplace: Victoria. Deathdate: 1988. Deathplace: Victoria. Studied: UT; Sul Ross State; Univ. Colo.; X. Gonzalez; P. Ninas; J. Woeltz. Member: TFAA; SSAL; Victoria AL. Exhibited: SALA; TFAA 1935; TG; Texas-Oklahoma Fair; ASET; MFAH 1938; SSAL. Mural: Victoria HS. Sources: WWWAA.

THURSTON, Eugene Boufanti [P; Car.; Pm] El Paso. Birthdate: 1896. Birthplace: Memphis, Tenn. Deathdate: 1993. Deathplace: El Paso. Studied: Federal Sch., Minneapolis; Texas Western; UT; TAMC. Member: EPAA (founder); SSAL; EPAG; FSAA; Nat. Soc. Arts and Letters; EPAA. Exhibited: TAFW; SACE 1927; EPWC; El Paso Centennial Mus. 1937. Work: EPMA; PPHM; UTEP Lib. Sources: Artist's daughter; *El Paso Herald-Post; El Paso Times;* EPPL; O'Brien; Price.

THURSTON, Fannie Wallace Palmer "Fern" [P] El Paso. Birthdate: 1870. Birthplace: Crystal Springs, Miss. Deathdate: 1956. Deathplace: El Paso. Studied: Emma B. Thurston (mother-in-law); Dey de Ribcowski; X. Gonzalez; R. Taylor. Member: Del Norte AG; EPAG; EPAA; EPWC. Exhibited: EPWC 1927, 1935–37, 1940–45. Work: PPHM; TCapitol; UTEP Lib. Sources: Artist's granddaughter; *El Paso Herald-Post;* EPPL; Price; artist's granddaughter.

TIDDEN, Agnes Lilienberg. See MUENCH, Agnes Lilienberg Tidden

TIDDEN, John Clark [P; T; I] Houston. Birthdate: 1889. Birthplace: Yonkers, N.Y. Studied: PAFA. Member: SSAL. Exhibited: TAFW 1925; AHAE 1925; TWF 1917. Work: MFAH; Penn State Univ.; University Cl., Houston. Sources: Fielding; WWWAA.

TIDWELL, James T. [S] Dallas. Exhibited: DAA 1928.

TILSON, Beryl [P] Dallas. Exhibited: DAA.

TIPTON, Joe Celia (Mrs. Thomas B.) [P] Dallas. Birthdate: 1895. Birthplace: Mixon East, Tex. Deathdate: 1996. Deathplace: Dallas. Studied: F. Reaugh; Bud Riggs; Western Colo. Sch. Art. Member: FRAC (founder, president). Exhibited: FRAC. Sources: *Dallas Morning News.*

TIRADO, Tom Vick [P] Houston. Exhibited: AHAE 1940.

TITSWORTH, Sarah [P] Dallas. Exhibited: DAA 1931.

TITTLE, Juanita (Mrs. C. E. Pollard) [P; T] Abilene. Birthdate: 1909. Birthplace: Trent, Tex. Deathdate: 1994. Deathplace: Abilene. Studied: Abilene Christian College; H. A. De Young; E. Eisenlohr; Reaugh; O. Travis; W. Lester; E. Spruce; R. Wood; J. G. Smith. Member: Abilene Mus. FA; Texas WCS. Exhibited: WTAE. Work: Abilene Mus. FA. Sources: Abilene Mus. FA files; *Abilene Reporter-News;* Wilbanks.

TOBERMAN, Mrs. M. S. [P] San Antonio. Exhibited: TFWC 1931.

TOCKER, Mrs. Phillip [P] El Paso. Exhibited: EPWC 1935.

TODD, Viola L. [P] San Antonio. Exhibited: SALA; TG 1945.

TOLAR, Harriett [P] Houston. Exhibited: AHAE 1942.

TONKIN, Linley Munson [P; Pm] Denison/ McAllister, Okla./Taos, N.M. Birthdate: 1877. Birthplace: Sherman, Tex. Deathdate: 1932. Deathplace: Dallas. Studied: ASL; J. Carlson; I. Wiles; C. Carleton. Member: Assoc. Oklahoma Artists; SSAL; Chicago Soc. Etchers; Calif. Pm; Prairie Pm. Exhibited: TAFW; SSAL, San Antonio, 1929; Harwood; Tennessee State Fair; Oklahoma State Fair; Univ. of Tulsa 1932. Sources: O'Brien; WWWAA.

TOOLEY, Marvin P. [P] Dallas. Exhibited: DAA 1945.

TOOMEY, Anne [D] Dallas. Exhibited: DAA 1933.

TOWNSEND, Elizabeth [D] San Antonio. Exhibited: SALA.

TOWNSEND, Gerry [P] San Antonio. Exhibited: SALA 1939.

TOWNSEND, Thurmond [S] Dallas. Exhibited: SFT; DAA.

TRACY, Elizabeth (Mrs. Pierre Montminy) [P; Mur. P] Austin. Birthdate: 1911. Birthplace: Boston. Studied: Radcliffe. Member: Guggenheim Foundation 1941. Exhibited: TG 1944–45; Phillips 1936; Golden Gate Exposition 1939; Worcester 1938; Corcoran 1939. Murals: USPOs, Milton, Mass., Downers Grove, Ill., and Kennebunkport, Me. Sources: WWWAA.

TRACY, Helise (Helice?) [P] Castroville, Tex. Exhibited: SACE 1929. Sources: Witte files.

TRAMMELL, Mildred [P] Fort Worth. Exhibited: TAFW.

TRANTHAM, Harrell E. [P; Pm] Abilene. Birthdate: 1900. Birthplace: Caps, Tex. Studied: Hegg Studio, Fresno, Calif. Member: TFAA; SSAL; Abilene Mus. FA; San Joaquin Valley AA. Exhibited: Abilene Woman's Forum 1928; WTAE; TG; ATPE 1944; Fort Worth Art Gall.; SSAL. Work: MAMFW. Sources: Fisk; WWWAA.

TRANTHAM, Ruth Newberry (Mrs. Harrell) [P] Canyon/Abilene. Birthdate: 1903. Birthplace: Caps, Tex. Member: SSAL; TFAA; Abilene Creative Art Ctr. Exhibited: WTAE 1942; TG; Fort Worth 1944; Abilene 1945. Sources: Fisk; WWWAA.

TRAVIS, Diane [P] Houston/Dallas/New Orleans/Tulsa. Birthdate: 1892. Birthplace: New York, N.Y. Studied: H. Giles; A. Stillman. Member: SSAL; Oklahoma Northwest AA; New Orleans AA. Exhibited: AHAE; SFT 1939; DAA 1935; PAFA 1932, 1933. Sources: WWWAA.

TRAVIS, Kathryne Hail [P] Dallas. Birthdate: 1894. Birthplace: Ozark, Ark. Deathdate: 1972. Deathplace: Ruidoso, N.M. Studied: AIC; AFA—Chicago; Cincinnati AM; Bellows; R. Davey. Member: SSAL; DMFA; HPSA. Exhibited: SFT; TAFW; DAA 1928, 1929; TCE; Greenville 1924; TFAA 1928. Sources: Bywaters Coll.; Fisk; Mallet; O'Brien; Smith; WWWAA.

TRAVIS, Olin Herman [P; T; Mur. P; Port. P; Pm] Dallas. Birthdate: 1888. Birthplace: Dallas. Deathdate: 1975. Deathplace: Dallas. Studied: Aunspaugh AS; R. J. Hill; Reaugh; AIC. Member: DAA; LSP. Exhibited: TAFW; SFT; Dallas (solo) 1926; DAA; HPAG (solo) 1929; SSAL 1932; Denver Art Mus. (solo) 1933; MoMA 1933; AID (solo) 1934; DMFA (solo) 1940; TAEN; TCE; GTPA; ATPE 1944–45; TFAA 1928; Greenville 1924; LSP 1938, 1940; TG 1943, 1944; TPan. Work: Belo; PPHM; DMA. Murals: Hall of State, Dallas; Love Field. Sources: Fisk; *New Handbook;* O'Brien; Samuels; Smith; WWWAA.

TRENTHAM, Eugene [P; T; Mur. P] Austin. Birthdate: 1912. Birthplace: Gatlinburg, Tenn. Studied: C. M. Kassler. Exhibited: TG; TPan; Denver AM; Corcoran; GGE; WFNY; MoMA 1941; PAFA 1942; Whitney 1942; AIC 1943. Work: Denver AM. Murals: Denver; O'Neill, Nebr. Sources: Falk AIC; Falk PAFA; WWWAA.

TREUTHARDT, L. [P] Georgetown, Tex. Exhibited: TFWC 1931.

TRIMBLE, A. M. [P] Galveston. Exhibited: TG 1940; ASET 1937.

TRIPLETT, Gertrude Myrick (Mrs. Chas. C.) [P] Lubbock/George West, Tex. Deathdate: 1968. Deathplace: Harris Co. Member: Lubbock AA. Exhibited: TFWC 1931; PMS 1932; Lubbock AA 1933; SPCCE. Sources: ITD; Wilbanks.

TROTTER, Lillian Carter (Mrs. Charles) [P] Dallas. Deathdate: 1968. Deathplace: Dallas. Member: FRAC. Exhibited: TAFW 1937; DAA; FRAC. Sources: ITD; PPHM files.

TROWBRIDGE, Caroline A. [P] Dallas. Exhibited: SFT 1908.

TRUITT, Una B. (Mrs. J. J.) [P; T] Houston. Birthdate: 1896. Birthplace: Joaquin, Tex. Studied: Univ. of Houston; J. O. Mills; P. Tate. Member: Houston AC; Assoc. of Artists of Houston. Exhibited: TFWC 1931; SFT; MFAH 1938, 1939; AHAE. Work: Nacogdoches Coll. FA. Sources: WWWAA.

TRUKA, Elizabeth [P; S] San Antonio. Exhibited: SALA.

TSANOFF, Katherine [P; Pm] Houston. Exhibited: AHAE; TG 1943; ATPE.

TUBB, Clodine [P] Dallas. Exhibited: DAA 1929.

TUCKER, John J. [Por. P] San Luis, Tex./Cincinnati/Philadelphia. Birthplace: Texas. Studied: Cincinnati Gall. FA w/ Franks; Italy. Sources: Groce and Wallace; Pinckney.

TUPPER, Margaret Wright (Mrs. C. H.) [P; Por. P] San Antonio. Studied: Arpa. Exhibited: SACE; SAAG 1927; Arpa Students, Witte 1928; TFWC 1931; SALA; UCE 1; GTPA; TAFW; ASET 1937. Sources: Fisk; Witte files.

TURNER, Agatha [P] Lubbock. Member: Lubbock AA. Exhibited: Lubbock AA 1933. Sources: Wilbanks.

TURNER, C. J. [P] Houston. Exhibited: AHAE 1927.

TURNER, Grace [P; S] Dallas. Exhibited: TAFW 1934; DAA.

TURNER, Harvey W. [P] El Paso. Deathdate: 1971. Deathplace: El Paso. Exhibited: EPWC 1943. Sources: ITD.

TURNER, Ida L. [Min. P] Fort Worth. Exhibited: TAFW.

TURNER, Miss Joe [P] Fort Worth. Exhibited: TAFW 1930.

TURNER, John H. [P] San Antonio. Deathdate: 1971. Deathplace: San Antonio. Exhibited: SALA 1930. Sources: ITD.

TURNER, Josephine [P] Fort Worth. Exhibited: TAFW 1932.

TURNER, Leslie [I] Wichita Falls/Tobe, Colo. Birthdate: 1900. Birthplace: Cisco, Tex. Studied: SMU w/ O. Donaldson; J. Knott; AIC. Sources: Fielding; Fisk; Smith; WWWAA.

TURNER, Mrs. Ralph [S] . Member: Texas Sculpture Group. Exhibited: DMFA 1944. Sources: Bywaters Coll.

TURNLEY, Lucille [P] Amarillo. Exhibited: TFWC 1931.

TUTT, May [P] Amarillo. Exhibited: TFWC 1931.

TYLOR, Stella T. Elmendorf [P; S] San Antonio/Oak Park, Ill./Madison, Wis. Birthdate: 1885. Birthplace: San Antonio. Studied: TSCW; R. Henri; UT; Columbia. Member: Wisconsin P and S. Exhibited: TAFW. Sources: DAS; Fielding; O'Brien; WWWAA; Witte files.

TYNES, Mrs. W. A. [P] Dallas. Exhibited: DAA 1931.

UHLER, Ruth Pershing [P; T] Houston. Birthdate: 1898. Birthplace: Gordon, Pa. Deathdate: 1967. Deathplace: Houston. Studied: Philadelphia Sch. of Design for Women; J. Charlot; L. Seyffert; Snell AS. Member: HAG; SSAL. Exhibited: AHAE; ASET; TAFW; TAEN; TFWC 1931; TG 1940; TFAA; SSAL. Work: MFAH; PPHM. Sources: Bywaters Coll.; Fisk; ITD; Mallett; O'Brien; Smith; WWWAA.

ULLMAN, Mrs. N. C. [S] Dallas. Exhibited: DAA 1928.

UMLAUF, Charles (Karl Julius) [S; T] Austin. Birthdate: 1911. Birthplace: South Haven, Mich. Deathdate: 1994. Deathplace: Austin. Studied: AIC w/ A. Polasek; Chicago Sch. Sculpture w/ V. Norman. Member: Texas Sculpture Group; Sculptors Guild; Artists Equity. Exhibited: DMFA 1944; TG 1942, 1943–45; Corcoran; AIC; WFNY. Work: Umlauf Sculpture Garden, Austin; DMA; MFAH; OJAC; Witte; McNay; Fort Worth AC; Met; Krannert AM; Univ. Illinois; Oklahoma AC. Sources: Bywaters Coll.; DAS; Valley House Gall.

UNDERWOOD, Laura [P] Galveston? Exhibited: Texas Coast Fair 1895.

UNDERWOOD, Maude R. [P] DeLeon, Tex. Exhibited: TG 1944.

UNDERWOOD, Ruth K. [P] Dallas. Member: FRAC. Exhibited: FRAC. Work: PPHM. Sources: PPHM files.

UNDERWOOD, Mrs. W. L. [P] Post, Tex. Exhibited: TFWC 1931. Sources: Wilbanks.

URBACH, Amelia [P] San Antonio/Dallas. Birthplace: Norfolk, Va. Deathdate: 1969. Deathplace: San Antonio. Studied: AID. Member: TFAA. Exhibited: AIC 1940; TPan; TG; TFAA; DAA; TCE; SFT; GTPA; SALA; SSAL. Work: DMA. Sources: Bywaters Coll.; ITD; Mallet; "NTP"; TPan m.; WWWAA.

UTTER, Bror [P; T] Fort Worth. Birthdate: 1913. Birthplace: Fort Worth. Deathdate: 1993. Deathplace: Fort Worth. Studied: FWSFA; Colorado College, Colorado Springs. Member: Fort Worth AA; Texas WCS. Exhibited: TG; ATPE 1941; SixTP; TCU; Whyte Gall., Washington, D.C.; SSAL. Work: MAMFW; OJAC; Denver AM. Sources: Bywaters Coll.; Gillespie and Nail.

VALENA, Sister Mary [P] El Paso. Exhibited: EPWC.

VALENTINE, Edward [P; Por. P; T] San Antonio. Studied: AJ. Exhibited: SALA; Witte 1933 (solo). Sources: *San Antonio Express; San Antonio Light;* Witte files.

VALENTINE, Ramona [P] Lubbock. Member: Lubbock AA. Exhibited: Lubbock AA 1933. Sources: Wilbanks.

VALENTINE, Wilma Davis [P] Austin. Exhibited: ASET 1938.

VALERO, Jesus Rodriquez [P] San Antonio. Exhibited: SALA.

VALLEE, Lorin [P; S] Houston. Exhibited: AHAE; ASET 1937.

VANCE, Helen Blesi [P; Comm. A] San Antonio. Birthdate: 1915. Exhibited: TAFW; GTPA; ASET 1937; SALA. Sources: *San Antonio Express;* Witte files.

VANCE, Katherine Hinton [P] San Antonio. Exhibited: SALA 1940.

VAN DEMARK, (Mrs.) [P] Galveston? Exhibited: Texas Coast Fair 1895.

VANDRUFF, Olive Freda [P; Comm. A; T] San Antonio/Kerrville/Clarendon. Birthdate: 1908. Birthplace: Martin's Ferry, Ohio. Deathplace: Living, Clarendon, 1998. Studied: Univ. Chicago; F. C. Hibbard; E. Giesbert; E. H. Hibbard. Member: Coppini Acad. Exhibited: PPHM; San Antonio 1932. Work: PPHM; Stark. Sources: Artist; Kovinick and Kovinick; PPHM files.

VAN MELDERT, Leon [P] Houston. Exhibited: AHAE 1929.

VANTINE, Emma Hawkins [P] Dallas. Exhibited: TFWC 1931.

VAUGHAN, Ernest W. [P; Comm. A] Fort Worth. Birthplace: Big Spring, Tex.? Studied: AIC. Exhibited: TAFW. Sources: O'Brien.

VENNING, Mary Laura E. (M. Lauryl) [P] Fort Worth. Exhibited: TAFW.

VERMILLION, Harriett [P] Dallas. Exhibited: DAA 1928.

VERNON, Rhea J. [P; Comm. A] Abilene/Lubbock. Studied: P. Plotkin; A. Brunet. Exhibited: TSFA 1923; PMS 1932, Lubbock. Sources: O'Brien; Wilbanks.

VINCENT, Jay J. [P] Fort Worth. Exhibited: TAFW.

VISSER, Evelyne [P] Dallas. Exhibited: DAA.

VOGEL, Donald S. [P; Pm; T] Dallas. Birthdate: 1917. Birthplace: Milwaukee, Wis. Living Dallas, 1997. Studied: Corcoran; AIC. Member: Painters of Texas; "The Eight"; Fed. of Dallas Artists. Exhibited: DAA; TG; DMFA 1941 (solo); Witte 1942 (solo); TPan; ATPE; SixTP; Carnegie 1941; Nat. Gall. of Art 1941; Artists for Victory, Metropolitan 1942; PAFA 1941; AIC 1940. Work: DMA; Witte; OJAC; MAMFW. Sources: Artist; Bywaters Coll.; WWWAA.

VOGEL, Hildegarde [P] Dallas. Exhibited: DAA 1944–45.

VOGT, Augusta [P] Dallas. Exhibited: TG; DAA; SSAL 1944.

VON ZELL, Fredda [P] El Paso. Exhibited: EPWC 1944.

VORSE, Virginia [P] Houston. Exhibited: AHAE 1936.

VOSPER, S. C. P. [S] Austin. Work: UT, "Texas Memorial to Honored Dead." Sources: O'Brien.

WADE, Ted [P; Pm] San Antonio. Birthdate: 1913. Birthplace: Germany. Studied: California SFA. Member: Amer. Medical Arts Assoc.; Amer. Etchers and Pm Assoc. Exhibited: SALA 1944; ATPE 1944; Witte 1943 (solo); GGE. Work: Witte. Sources: *San Antonio Evening News; San Antonio Express; San Antonio Light;* Witte files.

WAGGENER, Gertrude [S] Dallas. Exhibited: DAA.

WAGGONER, Harry [P] El Paso. Birthdate: 1896. Birthplace: Chicago? Deathdate: 1955. Deathplace: El Paso. Member: Nat. Soc. Arts and Letters. Exhibited: EPWC 1935. Work: Cooper-Union. Sources: Price.

WAGNER, Charles Pennell [P] Mission, Tex. Exhibited: ASET 1938.

WAGNER, Emma S. [P] San Antonio. Exhibited: SALA 1930.

WAGNER, Reta [P] Houston. Exhibited: AHAE 1939.

WAHL, Nina E. [P] Weslaco, Tex. Deathdate: 1971. Deathplace: Hidalgo County, Tex. Exhibited: TFWC 1931. Sources: ITD.

WAHLBERG, Phillip L. [P] Galveston/Houston. Exhibited: Cotton Carn 1910. Sources: Galveston City Directory 1910–14.

WALKER, Dickman [S] Houston. Exhibited: AHAE; TG 1943.

WALKER, Hanna (Mrs. W. Phil) [P] Luling/San Antonio. Studied: Arpa; X . Gonzalez; De Young. Exhibited: TAFW 1927; SAAG 1928; Arpa Students, Witte 1928; SACE; SALA; TFWC 1931; Bright Shawl Gall. 1932 (solo); UCE 2; SSAL; HPSA;. Sources: Fisk; O'Brien; Witte files.

WALKER, Jack [P] El Paso. Exhibited: EPWC 1940.

WALKER, Lissa Bell [Mur. P; P; T] Dallas/Plainview/Boston. Birthplace: Forney, Tex. Studied: NYSFAA; Reaugh; Hagendorn. Member: NAC; Dallas AA; FRAC (founder). Exhibited: FRAC; Mass. Horticultural Soc. Work: Monticello Hotel, Charlottesville, Va. Sources: Fisk; Wilbanks; WWWAA.

WALKER, Lonnie French (Mrs. Rich) [P] Fort Worth/San Antonio. Exhibited: TAFW; SALA; Witte 1937 (solo). Sources: *San Antonio Express; San Antonio Light;* Witte.

WALKER, Maurine [P] San Antonio. Exhibited: SALA 1939.

WALKER, Tecla [P] Dallas. Exhibited: DAA 1945.

WALKER, William Aiken [P; Por. P] Galveston/Charleston, S.C. Birthdate: 1838. Birthplace: Charleston. Deathdate: 1921. Deathplace: Charleston. Studied: Dusseldorf; largely self-taught. Exhibited: San Antonio 1876. Work: RL; SAMA; Witte. Sources: Pinckney; Seibel bio; Steinfeldt.

WALL, Bernhardt [P; Pm; W; T] San Antonio/Houston. Birthdate: 1872. Birthplace: Buffalo, N.Y. Studied: ASL; J. F. Brown; H. Reuterdahl; W. Auerbach-Levy. Member: SAAL (founder); Texas State Hist. Soc; Missouri State Hist. Soc.; Sierra Madre AG, Calif. Exhibited: AHAE; Witte 1936 (solo); Laguna Beach AA; Chicago Soc. Etchers. Work: Many U.S. libraries; Witte. Sources: *San Antonio Express;* O'Brien; Samuels; WWWAA; Witte files.

WALL, Emma Sims (Mrs. Lawrence A.) [P] Abilene/Dallas/Weatherford, Tex. Birthplace: McKinney?, Tex. Studied: B. Lowry; Fair Mont Seminary. Member: Abilene Woman's Forum. Sources: Fisk.

WALLER, Mary (Mrs. Harold B.) [P] Dallas. Exhibited: TAFW; DAA 1928. Sources: WWWAA.

WALLER, Virginia [S] Dallas. Exhibited: DAA 1928.

WALMSLEY, Elizabeth Harter (Mrs. Donald) [P, Pm; T] Dallas. Birthdate: 1900. Birthplace: Barberton, Ohio. Deathdate: 1993. Deathplace: Dallas. Studied: Washington Univ.; TWU; CSFAC; Bethany College. Member: TP. Exhibited: DAA; TG; SFT 1934; Sartor 1932–33 (solo); LSP 1945; ATPE 1945. Work: PPHM. Sources: Bywaters Coll.; Harris; Mallet; O'Brien; TPan m.

WALMSLEY, Katherine (WANSLEY, Kate?) [P] Dallas. Exhibited: DMFA. Sources: Bywaters Coll.

WALTON, Madeleine [P] Houston. Exhibited: AHAE 1937.

WALTON, Mary Ann [D] Houston. Exhibited: AHAE 1939.

WANSLEY, Kate [P] Fort Worth. Exhibited: SACE 1927; TAFW. Sources: FWPL; Witte files.

WARD, Mrs. W. B. [P] Fort Worth. Exhibited: TAFW 1925.

WARLICK, Mildred [P] Dallas. Birthdate: 1905. Birthplace: Marshall, Tex. Studied: M. Baldwin College, Virginia; SMU. Exhibited: DAA; TG. Sources: Bywaters Coll.

WARNER (WERNER?), Richard [P] San Antonio. Exhibited: SALA.

WARNER, William Riddle [P] El Paso/New Mexico. Exhibited: TAFW; EPWC 1935.

WARREN, Mallory Page [P; Por. P; T] San Antonio. Birthplace: Mobile, Ala. Studied: Our Lady of the Lake College; X. Gonzalez; G. Urmston; Fontainebleau. Exhibited: Witte; Our Lady College (solo); TAFW 1936; TCE; UCE 1; ASET 1937; SALA. Sources: O'Brien; *San Antonio Light;* Witte files.

WATERHOUSE, C. Ewing [Pm; P; Arch.] El Paso. Birthdate: 1905. Birthplace: El Paso. Studied: H. Roberts. Exhibited: EPSJ 1934; EPWC 1927; EPPL 1924 (solo). Work: EPPL. Sources: EPWC scrapbooks; Price.

WATKINS, Florence Ament (Mrs. Sam) [P; W] El Paso. Member: Nat. Soc. Arts and Letters; EPAG. Exhibited: EPWC 1927. Sources: *El Paso Herald-Post;* EPPL.

WATKINS, Mrs. W. J. [P] Fort Worth. Exhibited: TAFW 1912.

WATKINS, Sue [P] Temple. Exhibited: TFWC 1931.

WATSON, Maggie Joe (Mrs. Alexandre Hogue) [P] Dallas. Deathdate: 1988. Deathplace: Tulsa. Exhibited: TAFW 1935; DAA.

WATSON, Margaret L. [P] Galveston. Exhibited: Cotton Carn. 1911, 1912.

WATSON, Marguerite Thompson [P; D] Houston. Exhibited: AHAE; SSAL.

WATSON, Mary M. Green [P] Gregory, Tex. Exhibited: TFWC 1931.

WATTS, Beulah [P] Lufkin. Birthdate: 1873. Birthplace: Homer, Tex. Deathdate: 1941. Deathplace: Lufkin. Studied: Self-taught. Work: Mus. of East Texas, Lufkin. Sources: Fisk; Mus. of East Texas, Lufkin.

WATTS, Margaret [P] Dallas. Member: FRAC. Exhibited: FRAC 1929. Sources: PPHM files.

WEATHERRED, Mary Betty [P] Houston. Exhibited: AHAE.

WEATHERRED, Rosemary [P] Houston. Exhibited: AHAE.

WEBB, Esther Elizabeth [P; T] Dallas. Birthplace: Denver. Studied: Aunspaugh AS; TSCW. Exhibited: TAFW; DAA. Sources: O'Brien.

WEBB, Frank Sexton [Pm] Dallas. Exhibited: TG; DAA; ATPE 1944; DMFA 1945 (solo).

WEBB, Margaret Lee [P] Houston. Exhibited: AHAE 1943.

WEBER, Mrs. John E. [P] Fort Worth. Exhibited: TAFW 1937.

WEBSTER, Alfred Thomas [P] Galveston. Birthdate: 1864. Birthplace: London. Deathdate: 1924. Deathplace: Galveston. Member: Galveston AL. Exhibited: Cotton Carn. 1910–12. Sources: RL; *Galveston Daily News.*

WEBSTER, Mary [P] Dallas. Exhibited: DAA 1928.

WEEKLEY, Mary [P] Fort Worth. Exhibited: TAFW 1920.

WEIS, Frederic S. [P] Houston. Exhibited: AHAE 1931; MFAH? Sources: Houston City Directory 1942; WWWAA.

WEISBERG, Marie L. [P] Dallas. Birthdate: 1921. Exhibited: TAFW 1937; GTPA; DAA.

WEISE, Paul R. [P] Dallas. Exhibited: TAFW; DAA 1929. Sources: WWWAA.

WEISSER, Leonie Oelkers (Mrs. Fred W.) [P] San Antonio/New Braunfels. Birthdate: 1890. Birthplace: Guadalupe Co., Tex. Studied: College of Industrial Arts, Texas; Southwestern Univ.; J. E. Jenkins; R. J. Onderdonk. Member: SSAL; SAAL; TFAA. Exhibited: SACE; SAAL 1926; SAAG 1927; TFWC; SALA; TAFW; UCE 2; SSAL. Sources: O'Brien; WWWAA.

WEITZ, Anne [P] San Antonio. Exhibited: SALA 1944.

WELLS, Mrs. Wallace W. [P] Lubbock. Member: Lubbock AA. Exhibited: Lubbock AA 1933. Sources: Wilbanks.
WELLS, Willie Sheets [P] Fort Worth. Exhibited: TAFW.

WELMAKER, Ethel [P; T] Lubbock/Amarillo. Member: Lubbock AC. (charter); Amarillo AA. Exhibited: TFWC 1931. Sources: Wilbanks.

WEST, Georgette (George Etta) Rees [S; P; T] San Antonio. Birthdate: 1882. Birthplace: Kerr Co., Tex. Deathdate: 1959. Deathplace: Kerrville. Studied: TSCW; Chicago Acad. FA; Witte. Member: Art Industries Cl., San Antonio. Exhibited: SALA; San Pedro Playhouse 1932; Menger Hotel 1933. Work: Witte. Sources: Barton Ellison (grandson); *San Antonio Light;* Witte files.

WEST, Maud S. [P] Dallas/Houston/Santa Fe. Member: Southwest Artists, Houston; SSAL; TFAA. Exhibited: TFWC 1931; TAFW 1935; DAA 1935; AHAE; ASET 1938. Sources: MFAH files; WWWAA.

WESTMORELAND, Vivian [P] Dallas. Member: FRAC. Exhibited: FRAC. Sources: PPHM files.

WEYSS, John E. [D] . Birthdate: 1820. Deathdate: 1903. Deathplace: Washington, D.C.

WHEATLEY, Helen Margaret (Huntoon) [Pm; Comm. A] Ft. Worth. Birthdate: 1900. Birthplace: Fairbury, Nebr. Deathdate: 1932. Deathplace: Fargo, N.D. Studied: Europe; AIC; PAFA w/ D. Garber. Exhibited: TAFW. Sources: O'Brien.

WHEELER, Ellie (Mrs. A. C.) [P; S; Pm] San Antonio/ Poteet, Tex. Birthplace: Boston. Studied: Arpa; Dawson-Watson. Exhibited: SAAL 1926; SACE 1927; SAAG 1927; SALA; TFWC 1931; UCE 2 TFAA;. Sources: O'Brien; Witte files.

WHEELER, Florence [P] Galveston? Exhibited: Texas Coast Fair 1895.

WHEELER, Hughlette ("Tex") [S] Alhambra/Santa Monica, Calif. Birthdate: 1900. Deathdate: 1955. Deathplace: Christmas, Fla. Studied: Chicago. Exhibited: FWFCE. Sources: Samuels; WWWAA.

WHEELER, Lucille [P] Houston. Exhibited: AHAE.

WHISENHANT, Paul [D] Houston. Exhibited: AHAE.

WHITE, (Mrs.) [P] Galveston? Exhibited: Texas Coast Fair 1895.

WHITE, Carrie Harper [P] Legion, Tex. Birthdate: 1875. Birthplace: Detroit. Deathdate: 1969. Deathplace: Harris County, Tex. Studied: Cleveland SA; N.Y. Arch. Lg.; Sch. Applied Design, N.Y.; Arpa. Exhibited: SALA 1934. Sources: ITD; O'Brien.

WHITE, Mrs. E. A. [P] El Paso. Exhibited: EPWC 1944.

WHITE, Ila Mae (Mrs. H. C.) [P] Sudan. Member: Sudan AC. (charter); Lubbock AA. Exhibited: WTAE 1939; Lubbock AA 1937. Sources: Wilbanks.

WHITE, J. F. [P] Houston. Exhibited: AHAE 1925.

WHITE, Jessie Aline (Mrs. George R. Angell) [P; C; W] Fort Worth/Dallas. Birthdate: 1889. Birthplace: Wessington, S.D. Studied: Minneapolis Sch. of Art; AIC; ASL. Member: Dallas AA; SSAL; TFAA. Exhibited: DAA; TFWC 1931; SSAL; TAFW; SFT; Sartor 1933; TCE; TG 1940. Sources: Bywaters Coll.; Mallett; O'Brien; WWWAA.

WHITE, Lena [P] Dallas. Member: FRAC. Exhibited: DAA 1929.

WHITE, Lloyd Y. [P] Houston. Exhibited: AHAE 1927.

WHITE, Lula [P] Dallas. Exhibited: DAA 1928.

WHITE, Mattie B. Haywood [P; T] Austin. Birthdate: 1867. Birthplace: Tennessee. Deathdate: 1951. Deathplace: Austin. Studied: Walden Univ. Sources: *New Handbook.*

WHITE, Norman Robinette [P] San Antonio. Exhibited: SALA.

WHITE, Ralph [P; Pm; S; T] Austin. Birthdate: 1921. Birthplace: Minneapolis. Deathplace: Living Austin, 1997. Studied: Minneapolis SA; Pratt Inst.; Univ. Minnesota. Exhibited: Minneapolis Inst. Art 1943 (Texas drawings). Work: UT; SAMA; AMST; Austin PL. Sources: Artist; Goetzmann and Reese.

WHITE, Rena [P] El Paso. Exhibited: EPWC 1943.

WHITE, Victoria [P] Dallas. Exhibited: DAA.

WHITEHOUSE, Eula [P; T] El Paso/Austin/Electra, Tex. Birthdate: 1892. Birthplace: Cleburne, Tex.. Deathdate: 1974. Deathplace: Dallas. Studied: UT. Member: Ornithological Soc. of Texas; World Wildlife Fund; Nat. Audubon Soc. Exhibited: SSAL 1945. Sources: *New Handbook*.

WHITING, Daniel Powers [D] New York. Birthdate: 1808. Studied: West Point. Work: Amon Carter; New York Hist. Soc. Sources: Groce and Wallace; Pinckney.

WHITTING, G. W. [P] Galveston. Exhibited: Cotton Carn. 1911.

WICKES, M. J. [P] San Antonio. Exhibited: TFWC 1931.

WIER, Mattie [P] Houston. Exhibited: AHAE; ASET 1938. Sources: WWWAA.

WIESNER-ORTH, Steffi [P] Houston. Exhibited: AHAE.

WILBURN, Tee [D; I] Dallas. Exhibited: DAA.

WILDER, Mildred Morrill [P] George West, Tex. Exhibited: TFWC 1931.

WILDMAN, Caroline Lax [P] Houston/Bellaire. Birthplace: Hull, England. Deathdate: 1949. Deathplace: Harris Co., Tex. Exhibited: AHAE; SSAL; San Antonio 1939; ASET. Sources: WWWAA.

WILDMAN, Louis [P] Rockdale. Exhibited: TFWC 1931.

WILKINSON, Edward [P; S; Arch.; Dec.; T; W] Houston. Birthdate: 1889. Birthplace: Manchester, England. Studied: Rice; Chillman; Tidden. Exhibited: SACE; TAFW; AHAE. Work: TCapitol; Houston PL. Sources: Fielding; WWWAA.

WILLCOX, Rayte [P] Fort Worth. Exhibited: TAFW 1912.

WILLET, Oaul B. [P] San Antonio. Exhibited: SALA 1931.

WILLHITE, Jean Wagner [P] Dallas. Exhibited: DAA 1945.

WILLIAMS, Mrs. Ben [P] Post, Tex. Exhibited: TFWC 1931. Sources: Wilbanks.

WILLIAMS, David [P; Pm] Dallas. Exhibited: DAA.

WILLIAMS, Elinor (Mrs. J. H. Thompson) [P] Lamesa, Tex. Exhibited: TFWC 1931. Sources: Wilbanks.

WILLIAMS, Helen P. Carnell [P] Fort Worth. Exhibited: TAFW.

WILLIAMS, Katherine [P] San Antonio. Exhibited: SALA 1936.

WILLIAMS, Marian G. [P] Houston. Exhibited: AHAE.

WILLIAMS, Ramond Hendry [P; S; T] Lubbock. Birthdate: 1900. Birthplace: Ogden, Utah. Studied: M. Frazer; C. J. Martin; W. Varnum; A. Archipenko; AIC; Univ. Chicago. Member: Utah AG; Lincoln AG; Texas Tech AI. Exhibited: Texas Tech 1939 (solo); WTAE 1940; TG 1940. Sources: Wilbanks; WWWAA.

WILLIAMS, Ronald [P; S; T] Denton. Birthdate: 1910. Birthplace: Monett, Mo. Studied: Paris; Univ. Colorado; Columbia; Univ. Chicago; NYU; Univ. Bruxelles. Member: Western Artists Assoc. Exhibited: TAFW 1936; TG 1941S. Sources: Bywaters Coll.; O'Brien.

WILLIAMSON, Clara McDonald [P] Iredell, Tex. Birthdate: 1875. Birthplace: Iredell. Deathdate: 1976. Deathplace: Dallas. Studied: Self-taught. Exhibited: DAA 1945–50; TG 1946; DMFA 1948 (solo); Ney Mus. 1948 (solo). Work: Belo; DMA; Longview AM; A. Carter; Wichita AM; MoMA. Sources: Vogel bio.

WILLIS, William Stephen, Jr. [P] Fort Worth. Studied: Self-taught. Exhibited: TAFW 1937.

WILLS, Le Becca [P] Sweetwater, Tex. Exhibited: WTAE 1940.

WILLS, Mary Motz [P] Abilene. Birthdate: 1875. Birthplace: Wyethville, Va. Deathdate: 1961. Deathplace: Abilene. Studied: ASL w/ Chase, Twachtman, DuMond; Pa. Sch. of Industrial. Art. Member: SSAL. Exhibited: Amer. Mus. Natural History; Witte 1935 (solo); TCE (special); Montgomery Mus., Ga.; Mint Mus., Charlotte, N.C. Work: TMM; Witte. Sources: *New Handbook*; Steinfeldt.

WILLSON, Robert [S] Handley, Tex. Exhibited: SFT 1938.

WILSON, Douthitt [P] Dallas/Fort Worth. Exhibited: SFT; TG; DAA. Work: DMA.

WILSON, Gay (Mrs. Ralph Turner) [Pm] Waco. Exhibited: TG 1941F.

WILSON, Grace Louise [P] Fort Worth. Exhibited: TAFW.

WILSON, Hazel Marie (Mrs. Buford). [P] El Paso. Birthplace: Chicago. Studied: AIC; De Ribcowsky; C. Kay-Scott; X. Gonzalez. Exhibited: EPWC; El Paso Centennial Mus. 1917; EPWC (solo); Sun Carnival; SSAL. Sources: *El Paso Herald-Post;* EPPL; *El Paso Times;* O'Brien; Price.

WILSON, John B. [Pm] San Antonio. Studied: Harvard; Exeter. Exhibited: SALA 1935. Sources: *San Antonio Express;* Witte files.

WILSON, John M. [P] San Antonio. Exhibited: SAAG 1927.

WILSON, Loma [P] San Angelo. Exhibited: TG 1941F; WTAE 1942.

WILSON, Madge [P] Houston. Exhibited: AHAE.

WILSON, Milam D. [P] Houston. Exhibited: AHAE 1937.

WILSON, Robert, Jr. [P; S] Austin/Dallas. Exhibited: TAFW 1927; DAA.

WILSON, Sybil [P] Fort Worth. Exhibited: TG 1945.

WIMER, Cecile Janin [P] San Antonio. Exhibited: SALA; TAFW 1930.

WINANS, Judith H. [S] Dallas. Exhibited: TAFW 1937; DAA 1938.

WINFIELD, James H. [P] Bartlett, Tex. Exhibited: TFWC 1931.

WINGO, Ross [P] Kress, Tex. Studied: Redin. Exhibited: TFWC 1931. Sources: Wilbanks.

WINGO, Mrs. Ross [P] Kress, Tex. Exhibited: TFWC 1931. Sources: Wilbanks.

WINGO, Mrs. T. M. [P] El Paso. Exhibited: EPWC.

WINN, James Buchanan, Jr. (Buck) [P; Mur. P] Dallas/Wimberley, Tex. Birthdate: 1905. Birthplace: Celina, Tex. Deathdate: 1979. Deathplace: Wimberley. Studied: Berninghaus; F. Carpenter; Washington Univ.; AJ. Member: Acad. Applied Sciences; Amer. Inst. of Arch.; Philo-

sophical Soc. of Texas. Exhibited: Dallas Public Art Gall. 1932 (Dallas Nine); SFT 1930, 1931, 1934; DAA 1929–30, 1933. Work: PPHM. Murals: Texas State Bldg., Village Theatre, and Dallas Power and Light Company, Dallas; Texas Memorial, Gonzales; River Oaks Theatre, Houston. Sources: *New Handbook;* WWWAA.

WINN, Mrs. Robert [P] Dallas. Exhibited: DAA 1941.

WINNE, Betty [P] Houston. Exhibited: AHAE.

WINSTEAD, Mrs. Maurice [P] Houston. Exhibited: ASET 1937.

WISE, Vera [P; Pm; T] El Paso. Birthplace: Iola, Kans. Studied: Willamette Univ., Ore.; Chicago Acad. FA; KCAI w/ Benton. Member: NAWA; TFAA; SSAL. Exhibited: TFAA; WTAE 1942; ATPE; Fort Worth 1942; EPWC; KCAI; Denver Art Mus.; NAWA; Amer. WCS; SSAL. Sources: EPPL; *El Paso Herald-Post; El Paso Times;* Price; WWWAA.

WITHERSPOON, Mary Eleanor [P; Min. P] Fort Worth. Birthdate: 1905. Birthplace: Gainesville, Tex. Studied: L. Langace; M. Welsh. Member: Brooklyn Soc. Min. P. Exhibited: TAFW 1930–37; Old Lyme, Conn.; Pennsylvania Soc. Min. P; Amer. Soc. Min. P; Brooklyn Soc. Min. P. Work: OJAC. Sources: O'Brien; WWWAA; Witte files.

WITT, Mrs. D. A. [P] Lubbock. Member: Lubbock AA. Exhibited: Lubbock AA 1933. Sources: Wilbanks.

WITTIG, G. Walter [P] Galveston. Birthdate: 1887. Birthplace: Galveston. Deathdate: 1964. Deathplace: Galveston. Exhibited: Cotton Carn. 1910. Sources: RL.

WITTING, Annie Lee [P] San Antonio. Studied: J. Arpa. Exhibited: Arpa Students, Witte 1928. Sources: Witte files.

WOELTZ, Julius [P; Mur. P] San Antoni/Alpine/New Orleans. Birthdate: 1911. Birthplace: San Antonio. Deathdate: 1956. Deathplace: San Antonio. Studied: X. Gonzalez; AJ; AIC. Exhibited: Witte 1933 (solo); GTPA; TG; TPan.; ASET 1937; SALA; WFNY. Work: Amarillo MA; Art Mus. of Southeast Texas, Beaumont. Murals: Amarillo, Alpine, and Elgin, Tex. Sources: *American-German Review;* Bywaters Coll.; O'Brien; WWWAA; Witte files.

WOFFORD, Doris [P] San Antonio. Exhibited: SAAG 1927.

WOLFFGRAM, Hertha [P] Dallas. Exhibited: TAFW 1936.

WONNER, Paul [P; Pm; T] San Antonio. Birthdate: 1920. Birthplace: Tucson, Ariz. Studied: California College of Arts and Crafts; ASL; Univ. California, Berkeley. Exhibited: ATPE 1945; M. H. De Young; Guggenheim; MoMA; Denver AM; AIC; Whitney. Work: Univ. Nebraska; Oakland AM; Guggenheim; San Francisco MA; NMAA. Sources: Fielding.

WOOD, Mrs. Guy N. [P] Vernon, Tex. Exhibited: WTAE 1942.

WOOD, Jewel [P] El Paso. Exhibited: EPWC 1942.

WOOD, Mildred [P] Houston. Exhibited: AHAE 1936.

WOOD, Norma Lynn [P] Houston. Exhibited: AHAE. Sources: WWWAA.

WOOD, Robert W. [P; T] San Antonio. Birthdate: 1889. Birthplace: Sandgate, England. Deathdate: 1979. Deathplace: Bishop, Calif. Studied: South Kensington Sch.; Arpa. Member: Coppini Acad. Exhibited: SACE 1928; SALA 1930. Work: Stark; Witte. Sources: Samuels; Steinfeldt; WWWAA.

WOOD, Seth V. [P] San Antonio. Studied: Dallas SFA. Member: Villita Street Gall. Exhibited: SALA; Bright Shawl Gall.; Villita Street Gall. 1936. Work: Witte. Sources: Southwester; Witte files.

WOOD, Mrs. William [P] Lockney, Tex. Exhibited: TFWC 1931. Sources: Wilbanks.

WOODRUFF, Alice C. [P] Houston. Exhibited: AHAE.

WOODS, J. Edward [P] San Antonio. Exhibited: SALA.

WOODS, Nora [P] Boerne. Exhibited: TFWC 1931.

WOOLDRIDGE, Lessi Ellen [P; S; T] San Antonio. Birthdate: 1907. Birthplace: Austin. Deathdate: 1989. Deathplace: Carmel, Calif. Studied: R. Onderdonk; E. Onderdonk; ASL w/ Bridgman, A. Lewis, A. Goldthwaite, Henri; Columbia; Nat. Acad. Mexico w/ Merida, O. Martinez. Member: SAAL; Southwest Craft Ctr.; McNay; Witte. Exhibited: GTPA; Witte; Plaza Hotel and San Pedro Playhouse, San Antonio; SALA. Sources: O'Brien; Witte files.

WOOLEY, Pauline [P] Dallas. Exhibited: DAA 1928.

WOOLLEY, G. Livingston [P] Dallas. Exhibited: DAA 1945.

WORK, Maud Estelle [P] Dallas. Birthdate: 1888. Deathdate: 1943. Exhibited: TCE; TAFW; DAA. Work: PPHM. Sources: Mallett. Only artist with more than one work in TCE.

WORTHINGTON, Christine D. [P] Houston. Exhibited: AHAE.

WORTHINGTON, Virginia Lewis [P; C] San Antonio. Birthdate: 1915. Studied: Newcomb College. Member: SSAL; Rio Grande Group. Exhibited: GTPA; ASET 1938; TG 1940; SALA; SSAL, Montgomery, Ala. 1938; Cincinnati AM. Sources: *San Antonio Express*; WWWAA; Witte files.

WORTHMAN, Harry [P; Por. P; Mur. P] San Antonio/ Houston. Exhibited: SALA 1943. Sources: *The Southern Artists*.

WRAGG, Eleanor T. [P; Min. P; Pm; T] Waco/Stoney Creek, Conn. Studied: ASL. Member: Carolina AA. Exhibited: TAFW 1911; Cotton Carn. 1910, 1912; New York Min. Soc. Sources: O'Brien.

WRAY, Pearl [P] Breckenridge, Tex. Exhibited: TFWC 1931.

WRIGHT, Carroll [P] Houston. Exhibited: AHAE 1930.

WRIGHT, Dudley [P] El Paso. Exhibited: EPWC.

WRIGHT, Gladys Yoakum [P] Fort Worth. Exhibited: TAFW 1919. Sources: WWWAA.

WRIGHT, Reba [P] San Antonio. Exhibited: SALA.

WRIGHT, Silas A. [P] Houston. Exhibited: AHAE 1938.

WRIGHT, Thomas Jefferson [Por. P] Houston. Birthdate: 1798. Birthplace: Mt. Sterling, Ky. Deathdate: 1846. Deathplace: Mt. Sterling. Studied: T. Sully; M. Jouett. Work: TCapitol; California Hist. Soc. Sources: *New Handbook*; Pinckney; Samuels.

WRIGHT, Vela [P] Celeste, Tex. Exhibited: TFWC 1931.

WUESTE, Louisa Heuser [P] San Antonio/Eagle Pass, Tex. Birthdate: 1805. Birthplace: Gummersbach, Germany. Deathdate: 1874. Deathplace: Eagle Pass. Studied: Dusseldorf Acad. Exhibited: Yanaguana (ph.). Work: Witte. Sources: Mallett; *New Handbook;* O'Brien; Pinckney; Samuels; Steinfeldt; Utterbeck.

WUNTCH, Freddie [P] Houston. Exhibited: ASET 1938.

YANDELL, Dagley [D] Houston. Exhibited: AHAE.

YARBROUGH, Vivian Sloan Daggett [P] Fort Worth. Birthdate: 1893. Birthplace: Whitesboro, Tex. Studied: Broadmoor; R. Davey; E. Lawson; J. Sloan; R. Reid; S. B. Mummert. Member: SIA; SSAL; TFAA; AACFW; FWPC. Exhibited: TFAA; TFWC 1931; SFT 1934; SSAL; Sartor (solo); TAFW; Denver Art Mus. Sources: Bywaters, "New Texas Painters"; Fisk; Mallett; O'Brien; WWWAA.

YARD, Pense Cook (Mrs. George N.) [P] Alvin/Galveston. Birthdate: 1877. Birthplace: La Grange, Tex. Deathdate: 1957. Deathplace: Galveston. Member: DRT. Exhibited: Cotton Carn. 1912. Sources: *Galveston Daily News;* RL.

YATES, Jean Perry [P] Houston. Exhibited: AHAE 1938.

YATES, J. Gordon [S] Houston. Exhibited: AHAE.

YOUNG, Edith [P] Galveston. Exhibited: Cotton Carn. 1910.

YOUNG, Pearl [P] San Antonio. Exhibited: SALA 1936.

YOUNG, Mrs. R. L. [P] Laredo. Exhibited: TFWC 1931.

YOUNGER, Yucola [P] San Antonio. Exhibited: SALA 1940.

YTURIAGA, Enrique [P] El Paso. Exhibited: EPWC 1938.

ZACK, Peter [P] San Antonio. Exhibited: SALA 1933.

ZEMAN, Edith [P] San Antonio. Exhibited: SALA 1933.

ZIEGLER, Rosa Hildebrand (Mrs. Henry) [P] Galveston. Birthdate: 1869. Deathdate: 1947. Exhibited: Texas Coast Fair 1895. Sources: RL.

ZIEGLER, Samuel Peters [P; Pm; T] Fort Worth. Birthdate: 1882. Birthplace: Lancaster, Pa. Deathdate: 1967. Deathplace: Fort Worth. Studied: PAFA w/ Chase, T. Anshutz, H. Breckenridge. Member: SSAL; AAPL; FWAA; TFAA; AFA; Salmagundi. Exhibited: TAFW; San Angelo; TAEN; TFAA; TCU; SFT 1924; West Texas Exposition; SSAL 1929. Work: Fort Worth Univ. Cl.; FWAM; TCU; FWPL. Sources: Fielding; Fisk; ITD; *New Handbook;* O'Brien; Samuels; Smith; WWWAA.

ZIMMERAN, S. F. [P] Dallas. Exhibited: DAA 1928.

ZUBER, Mamie G. [P] Dallas. Member: FRAC. Exhibited: FRAC 1931–34; 1941. Sources: PPHM files.

ZWEIG, Irene Ormsby [P] San Antonio. Exhibited: SALA.

ZWEINER, Charles L. [P] Houston. Exhibited: AHAE 1942.

PLATES

1. LUCIEN ABRAMS
South of France   n.d.
Oil on canvas, 21 x 25 in.
Collection of Drs. Mary and Mike Arno

2. LLOYD L. ALBRIGHT
The Cross of the Martyrs   1930
Oil on Masonite, $23\frac{7}{8}$ x $30\frac{1}{8}$ in.
Panhandle-Plains Historical Museum, Canyon, Texas; gift of Mrs. Jim Hess and Ariel Kemish

3. GEORGE R. ALLEN
Portrait of Nancy Lea   n.d.
Oil on canvas, $26\frac{5}{8}$ x $32\frac{1}{8}$ in.
Harris County Heritage Society, Houston, Texas

4. C. HARVI ALTHEIDE
Untitled   1934
Oil on canvas, 16 x 20 in.
Collection of Charles Stevens

5. *JOSE ARPA*
Sloping Hills   1926
Oil on canvas, 24 x 34 in.
The Barrett Collection

6. *REVEAU BASSETT*
Dallas Skyline   1927
Oil on canvas, 12 x 16 in.
A. H. Belo Corporation Foundation

7. *FORREST BESS*
Bread and Potatoes
ca. 1938
Oil on canvas, 16 x 18 in.
The Museum of Fine Arts,
Houston; gift of Forrest Bess

8. MURRAY BEWLEY
Against the Sky   1920s
Oil on canvas, 24 x 20 in.
Rainone Galleries, Inc., Arlington, Texas

10.   KATHLEEN
BLACKSHEAR
*Mamie at the
Window   1930*
Oil on canvas, 36 x 30 in.
*Collection of Mr. and Mrs.
William J. Terrell*

9. GEORGE BIDDLE
Negro Quarter, San Antonio   1940
Oil on canvas, 25 x 30 in.
Fred R. Kline & Co., Santa Fe, New Mexico

12. RUTH SIMON BODE
Sunlight and Shadows   n.d.
Oil on canvas, 18 x 22 in.
Collection of Edward C. Bode

11. FLORA BLANC
Portrait of Bill (Bill Bomar)   1940
Oil on canvas, 30 x 24 in.
Collection of Bill and Mary Cheek

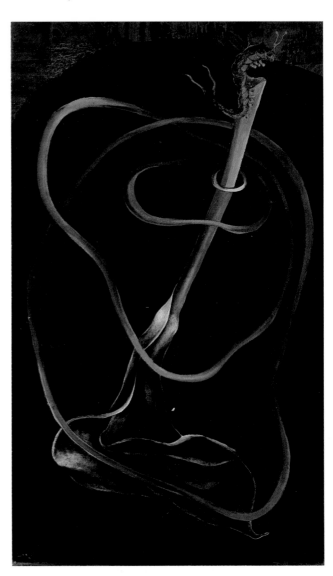

13. BILL BOMAR
*Persistence above Dark
Water   1945*
Oil on canvas, 30 x 18 in.
*Modern Art Museum of
Fort Worth*

14. HALE BOLTON
Untitled 1917
Oil on canvas, 28 x 37 in.
Collection of Robert T. Brousseau

15. E. L. BOONE
West Texas Mountains 1930s
Oil on canvas, 24 x 32 in.
Collection of Ed Prohaska

17. CHARLES T. BOWLING
Turtle Creek 1937
Oil on Masonite, 8 x 10 in.
Collection of Ed Prohaska

16. MINNIE BOWLES
Bluebonnets on Boles Farm Place, Grand Prairie,
Texas 1920s
Pastel on paper, 8 x 5 in.
Rainone Galleries, Inc., Arlington, Texas

18. OLIVE BRACK
Ingleside, Texas   1911-12
Oil on canvas, 12 x 18 in.
Collection of David Lackey

19. FREDERIC BROWNE
Untitled [Hermann Park]   1930s
Oil on canvas, 25 x 21 in.
Collection of Stuart Haynsworth

20. GAITHA BROWNING
Mission San Jose, San Antonio   1937
Oil on canvasboard, 12 x 16 in.
Panhandle-Plains Historical Museum, Canyon, Texas;
gift of Donald A. Drefke

21. ADELE BRUNET
Foot Bridge at Christoval   n.d.
Oil on canvas, 22 x 28 in.
Collection of Bob and Linda Rork

22. H. D. BUGBEE
The Cattleman   1934
Oil on canvas mounted on wall, 78 x 144 in.
Panhandle-Plains Historical Museum, Canyon, Texas; Public Works of Art Project

24. JERRY BYWATERS
Texas Subdivision   1938
Oil on board, 20 x 24 in.
Collection of Jason Schoen, New Orleans, Louisiana

23. MARIE HAINES BURT
Wet Roofs—Galveston   n.d.
Oil on panel, 30 x 24 in.
Collection of Russell Tether

26. HARRY CARNOHAN
Windmill   n.d.
Pastel on paper, 10 x 15 in.
Collection of Bob and Linda Rork

25. MAURINE CANTEY
Girl in a Rain Coat   n.d.
Oil on board, 14 x 11 in.
Collection of Mr. and Mrs. Edward J. Denari

27. GEORGIE CARR
Sophie   n.d.
Oil on canvas, 21 x 18 in.
*Collection of Mary Rhodes
Gibson*

28. MAUDEE LILYAN CARRON
#1 Magic Script   1944
Watercolor on paper, $11\frac{1}{2}$ x 9 in.
Collection of David Lackey

29. DOUGLAS CHANDOR
Portrait of G. B. Dealey   1939
Oil on canvas, 37 x 31 in.
A. H. Belo Corporation Foundation

30. ALICE CHILTON
Untitled   n.d.
Oil on canvas, 16 x 22 in.
Collection of Mr. and
Mrs. Saverio Giammalva

31. *E. RICHARDSON CHERRY*
Memorial Day in Houston   1925
Oil on canvas, 30 x 36 in.
Collection of Ralph Plemons

32. *VIRGIE CLAXTON*
Rocks and Surf, Galveston Coast   n.d.
Oil on canvas, 12 x 14 in.
Collection of Robert G. Richardson

33. *F. A. CLOONAN*
San Antonio River
n.d.
Oil on canvas, 24 x 28 in.
Collection of Drs. Mary
and Mike Arno

36. PAUL RODDA COOK
Untitled   n.d.
Oil on canvas, 20 x 16 in.
Collection of Drs. Mary
and Mike Arno

(BELOW LEFT) 34. ALICE MELINDA
COBB
Untitled [Hanging Fish]   n.d.
Oil on board with rope,
$23\frac{1}{2}$ x 14 in.
Collection of Willetta Stellmacher

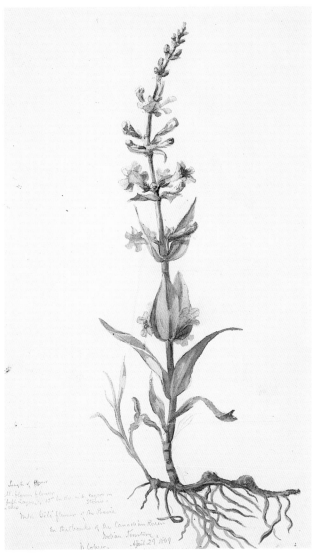

35. VINCENT COLYER
*Wild Gili Flower of the Prairie on the Banks of
the Canadian River, Indian Territory   1869*
Watercolor on paper, $13\frac{5}{8}$ x $8\frac{1}{8}$ in.
Museum of Fine Arts, Houston; Bayou Bend Collection; museum purchase with funds provided by the Finger Family in honor of Nanette Finger at "One Great Night in November, 1996"

115

38. MOLLIE CROWTHER
Untitled   n.d.
Oil on board, 8 x 12 in.
Collection of Charles Stevens

37. REID CROWELL
Portrait of a Black Cowboy   n.d.
Oil on canvas, 22 x 18 in.
The Torch Collection of Torch Energy Advisors Incorporated

39. THEODORE SAINT-
AMANT CUNNINGHAM
The Old School House,
Waco, Texas   n.d.
Watercolor on paper,
12 x 14 in.
Rainone Galleries, Inc.,
Arlington, Texas

40. FRED DARGE
Shearing Season   n.d.
Oil on canvas, 24 x 30 in.
Collection of Jason Schoen,
New Orleans, Louisiana

41. LORENE DAVID
The Battery, Eastport   1936
Watercolor, 24$\frac{1}{4}$ x 30$\frac{7}{8}$ in.
Art Museum of Southeast
Texas, Beaumont, Texas

117

42. JESSIE DAVIS
Fair Park Lightnin'   n.d.
Oil on canvas, 26 x 26 in.
Collection of George and Beverly Palmer

43. VELMA DAVIS
Grain Shock   n.d.
Oil on canvasboard,
14 x 20 in.
Collection of Bill and
Mary Cheek

44. DAWSON DAWSON-WATSON
Lui-même   1935
Oil on canvas, 21 x 16 in.
Collection of Charles Stevens

45. DAWSON DAWSON-WATSON
Landscape   n.d.
Oil on board, 15½ x 13 in.
The Frank H. Wardlaw Collection of Texas
Art, Texas A&M University Press

46. HARRY ANTHONY DE YOUNG
Untitled   1930
Oil on canvas, 45 x 55 in.
Collection of Robert T. Brousseau

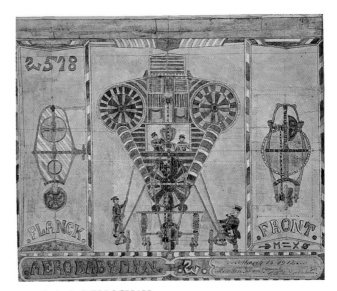

47. C. A. A. DELLSCHAU
Aero Babymyn   1912
Watercolor and ink on wood pulp paper mounted on cardboard
16 x 19 in.
Courtesy of the Witte Museum, San Antonio, Texas

48.   JOHN DOUGLASS
The Builders   n.d.
Oil on Masonite, 32 x 28 in.
Collection of Mr. and Mrs. John K. Sterling

49. OTIS DOZIER
Roadrunner and Cactus   1925
Oil on canvas, 20 x 16 in.
The Barrett Collection

50. SANTA DURAN
Portrait of Jose Arpa   1925
Oil on board, 24 x 18 in.
Collection of Charles Stevens

52. *EDWARD G. EISENLOHR*
June Fields   1915
Oil on canvas, 24 x 36 in.
The Barrett Collection

51. *EMILY EDWARDS*
The Toilet of Cinderella
n.d.
Color block print, 14 x 11½ in.
Courtesy of the Witte
Museum, San Antonio,
Texas

53. *INEZ STAUB ELDER*
Geranium   1935
Oil on canvas, 28 x 24 in.
Collection of Bill and Mary Cheek

54. *FREMONT ELLIS*
Valley of the Gods   n.d.
Oil on canvas, 61 x 80 in.
(framed)
El Paso Museum of Art;
gift of Mr. and Mrs. James
A. Dick Estate

55. *BERLA IYONE*
EMEREE
At the Studio   1920s
Oil on canvas, 13 x 17 in.
Rainone Galleries, Inc.,
Arlington, Texas

56. J. B. ERWIN
Fugue   1944
Watercolor on paper,
21 x 28 $\frac{1}{2}$ in.
Collection of the artist

57. LOUIS EYTH
Ranger Encampment
ca. 1880s
Oil on canvas, 24$\frac{1}{2}$ x 36$\frac{1}{2}$
in. State Preservation
Board, Austin, Texas

58. E. A. FILLEAU
Untitled   n.d.
Oil on board, 12$\frac{1}{2}$ x 28 in.
Collection of Charles and
Catherine Attal

59. GODFREY FLURY
Untitled   n.d.
Oil on board, 20 x 24 in.
Collection of Charles and Catherine Attal

60. MARIE GENTILZ
Phalenes-Nocturna-Sphinx-Crepuscularia n.d.
Watercolor with pencil on paper, 6 x 7 in.
Daughters of the Republic of Texas Library,
San Antonio, Texas

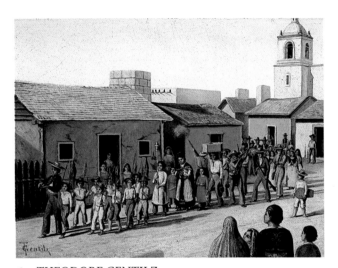

61. THEODORE GENTILZ
Entierro de un Angel   n.d.
Oil on canvas, 7½ x 10 in.
Private collection

62. LLOYD GOFF
*Construction near Tower
Petroleum Building (Dallas)
n.d.*
Oil on canvas, 30 x 24 in.
*Collection of Robert T.
Brousseau*

63. *LOUISE MARKS GOLDSTEIN*
Beauty Salon   n.d.
Oil on canvas, 24 x 20 in.
Beth and David Dike Collection, Dallas

64. *BOYER GONZALES*
Campeche Fisherman Taking on Provisions   n.d.
Watercolor, 9½ x 13 in.
Rosenberg Library, Galveston, Texas

65. *EDWARD GRENET*
The Corner of My
Studio   n.d.
Oil on canvas, 12 x 9½ in.
Collection of Robert T.
Brousseau

67. IDA WEISSELBERG HADRA
San Antonio River at St. Mary's Street Bridge   n.d.
Oil on canvas, 24 x 30 in.
Courtesy of the Witte Museum, San Antonio, Texas

66. EMIL GUIDROZ
Downtown Fort Worth   n.d.
Oil on canvas, 10 x 8 in.
Beth and David Dike Collection, Dallas

68. EMMA HENDRICKS
Palo Duro Canyon,
Panhandle of Texas   1936
Oil on canvas, 25 x 28 in.
Panhandle-Plains
Historical Museum,
Canyon, Texas;
gift of Susan Nelson

126

69. EMIL HERMANN
Mount Moran, Wyoming
1932
Oil on canvas, 18 x 22 in.
Collection of Konrad Shields
and Wes Miller

70. R. JEROME HILL
White Rock Lake   1926
Oil on canvasboard, 12 x 18 in.
Collection of Robert T. Brousseau

71. POLLY HOFFMAN
Untitled   n.d.
Oil on board, 18 x 20 in.
Private collection

72. ALEXANDRE HOGUE
Drouth Stricken Area 1939
Oil on canvas, 30 x 42¼ in.
Dallas Museum of Art, Dallas
Art Association purchase

73. PETER HOHNSTEDT
Untitled n.d.
Oil on canvas, 21¼ x 27¼ in.
Collection of Mr. and Mrs. Saverio Giammalva

74. DWIGHT C. HOLMES
Twin Mountains, San Angelo, Texas n.d.
Oil on panel, 12 x 16 in.
Collection of David Lackey

128

75. PERCY HOLT
Craig Valley #29   n.d.
Oil on canvasboard, 8 x 10 in.
Rosenberg Library, Galveston, Texas

76. CARL T. HOPPE
Texas Fire Wheels   1926
Oil on canvas, 15 x 21 in.
Collection of Glenn Lewallen

77. NANNIE HUDDLE
Bluebonnets (Lupinus texensis)   ca. 1920–36
Watercolor, 11 x 15 3/4 in.
Courtesy of the Texas Memorial Museum, accession #970-104

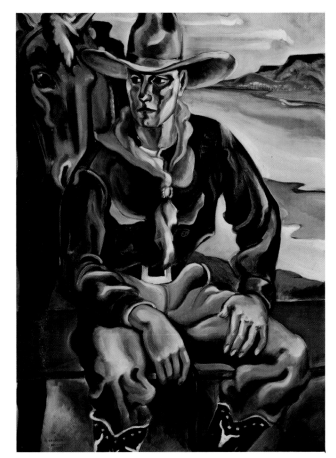

78. R. VERNON HUNTER
Cowman   ca. 1930s
Oil on canvas, 38 x 28 in.
Panhandle-Plains Historical Museum, Canyon, Texas;
gift of Skillman C. Hunter

79. *CARL G. VON IWONSKI*
Theatre at Old Casino Club   ca. 1860
Oil on canvas, 9½ x 14 in.
Courtesy of the Witte Museum, San Antonio, Texas

80. *EVERETT GEE JACKSON*
Dinner Time   n.d.
Oil on canvas, 18 x 18 in.
Collection of Bill and Mary Cheek

81. *W. FREDERICK JARVIS*
Evening Light   1919
Oil on canvas, 16 x 20 in.
Collection of Bill and Mary Cheek

82. *JOHN ELIOT JENKINS*
Untitled   n.d.
Oil on canvas, 18 x 26 in.
Collection of Charles and Catherine Attal

84. MINNIE JOHNSON
Untitled   n.d.
Oil on canvas, 18 x 22 in.
Collection of Charles and Catherine Attal

83. GRACE SPAULDING JOHN
Patterns (Ruth)   1932
Oil on linen, 60 x 54 in.
Museum of Fine Arts, Houston;
gift of Patricia John Keightley

85. W. GILLIS KING
Untitled   n.d.
Oil on canvas, 18 x 20 in.
Collection of Charles and Catherine Attal

86. EDMUND KINZINGER
Two Mexican Children   1938
Oil on canvas, 32 x 26 in.
Courtesy of the Witte Museum, San Antonio, Texas

87. FORREST KIRKLAND
Wash Day—Galveston   ca. 1930
Watercolor, 9¾ x 12 in.
Courtesy of the Texas Memorial Museum, accession #2203-1

89. BERTHA LANDERS
Mining Town   1930
Oil on Masonite, 18 x 24 in.
Collection of Kenneth M. Hamlett

88. LUCILE LAND LACY
Portrait of a Woman   n.d.
Oil on canvasboard, 24 x 18 in.
Collection of David Lackey

90. URSULA LAUDER-
DALE
Untitled   n.d.
Oil on canvas, 24 x 20 in.
*Collection of Robert T.
Brousseau*

91. TOM LEA
Portrait of Sarah   1939
Oil on canvas, 39 x 37 in. (framed)
El Paso Museum of Art, gift of IBM Corporation

92. M. WALTON LEADER
Three Elms   n.d.
Oil on canvas, 30 x 36 in.
Collection of Bill and Mary Cheek

93. VIRGINIA
LEBERMAN
Untitled   n.d.
Oil on canvas, 16 x 25 in.
*Collection of Charles and
Catherine Attal*

94. MARJORIE
JOHNSON LEE
The Old House   1944
Oil on canvas, 30 x 20 in.
*Beth and David Dike
Collection, Dallas*

95. WILLIAM LESTER
The Rattlesnake Hunter   1939
Oil on Masonite, 19 x 24 in.
Gift of the Senior Class of 1939, S.M.U.; University Art Collection,
Southern Methodist University, Dallas

96. MARGARET LITTLEJOHN
Untitled [Landscape]   n.d.
Oil on canvas, 15 x 20 in.
Collection of Robert T. Brousseau

98. HERMANN
LUNGKWITZ
Swenson's Ruin—Austin
n.d.
Oil on academy board,
$10\frac{3}{8}$ x $14\frac{3}{8}$ in.
Collection of Russell Tether

97. LUCIE LOCKE
Cinderland Cedar
1937
Oil on panel, 16 x 12 in.
Collection of Russell Tether

99. PETER MANSBENDEL
Untitled   n.d.
Painted plaster high relief,   11 x 55 in.
Collection of Charles and Catherine Attal

100. SISTER M. MARIETTA
Untitled   n.d.
Oil on board, 20 x 25 in.
Private collection

101. EUGENIA C.
MASSENBURG
Little Sister   1889
Pastel, 19 x 16 in.
Collection of Rivers
A. Patout Jr.

102. FLORENCE
McCLUNG
Swamp King   1938–39
Oil on canvas, 20 x 24 in.
Beth and David Dike
Collection, Dallas

103. ELOISE POLK
McGILL
*Cock Fight, near
El Paso   1890s*
Oil on canvas, 13 x 18 in.
*Rainone Galleries, Inc.,
Arlington, Texas*

104. MARION KOOGLER McNAY
Navajo Women Weaving   n.d.
Watercolor on paper, $15\frac{3}{4}$ x $22\frac{3}{4}$ in.
*McNay Art Museum, bequest of Marion Koogler McNay, San
Antonio, Texas*

105. WILLIAM McVEY
Texas Natural Resources   1937–38
Limestone, 66 x 100 in.
*Courtesy of the Texas Memorial Museum, University of Texas,
Austin, Texas*

106. MARGARET MITCHELL
Magnolia Bud   n.d.
Pastel, 19 x 18 in.
Collection of Bill and Mary Cheek

107. JEAN SCRIMGEOUR MORGAN
Bedroom—810 Post Office   n.d.
Oil on canvas, 14 x 18 in.
Rosenberg Library, Galveston, Texas

108. SALLIE BLYTHE MUMMERT
Untitled   n.d.
Oil on canvas, 34 x 36 in.
Collection of Mr. and Mrs. Saverio Giammalva

109. AUDLEY DEAN NICOLS
West Texas Desert Scene   1924
Oil on canvas, 14 x 20 in.
Collection of Bill and Mary Cheek

110. GURINE NILSEN
1502 Market—Galveston   n.d.
Watercolor, 12½ x 18 in.
Rosenberg Library, Galveston, Texas

111. JULIAN ONDERDONK
Near San Antonio   n.d.
Oil on canvas, 30 x 40 in.
San Antonio Museum of Art

112. ROBERT [JENKINS] ONDERDONK
The Alamo   n.d.
Watercolor on paper, 7½ x 10 in.
McNay Art Museum

113. JOHN WILLIAM ORTH
Man with Sunburned Face and Forearms   n.d.
Oil on canvas, 30 x 24 in.
Collection of David Lackey

114. JACK PAGAN
Montrose Boulevard, Houston, Texas   1942
Watercolor on paper, 14 x 10¾ in.
Collection of David Lackey

116. RICHARD PETRI
Fort Martin Scott   1850
Oil and pencil on canvas, 16½ x 23 in.
Courtesy of the Texas Memorial Museum

115. CLARA C.
PANCOAST
*Still Life with Clay
Pots   n.d.*
Oil on canvas, 18 x 24 in.
*Collection of Charles
Stevens*

139

119. ROBERT PREUSSER
Composition No. 1   ca. 1940
Casein and tempera on paper, 21¾ x 14¾ in.
The Museum of Fine Arts, Houston; Sixteenth Annual
Houston Artists Exhibition, Museum Purchase Prize, 1940

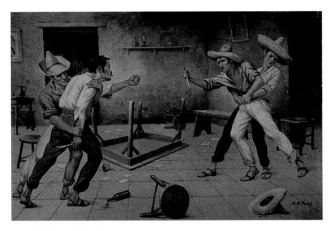

117. HUGO POHL
Hot Blood   n.d.
Oil on board, 10 x 16 in.
Private collection

118. H. C. PRATT
View of West Texas Ranch, El Paso County   1853
Oil on canvas, 30⅛ x 50¼ in.
Courtesy of the Texas Memorial Museum

120. FRANK REAUGH
The Approaching Herd   1902
Oil on canvas mounted on Masonite, 23¼ x 48½ in.
Panhandle-Plains Historical Museum, Canyon, Texas;
Frank Reaugh Estate

122. HAROLD RONEY
Summer Landscape   n.d.
Oil on board, 9 x 12 in.
Collection of Bob and
Linda Rork

121.   LUCY W. RICE
Cowboy   1930
Oil on canvas, 30 x 22 in.
Courtesy of the Texas
Memorial Museum

141

123. *PORFIRIO SALINAS*
Road to Hondo   1940
Oil on canvas, 30 x 36 in.
United Pawn Collection

124. *PAUL SCHUMANN*
Fishermen and Skiff: Galveston Beach Scene   n.d.
Oil on Masonite, 12 x 16 in.
Rosenberg Library, Galveston, Texas

125. *PAUL SCHUMANN*
Untitled   n.d.
Oil on canvas, 30 x 40 in.
Collection of Drs. Mary and Mike Arno

142

127. FRANCES SKINNER
Lewellyn 1940
Oil on Masonite, 23¾ x 19¾ in.
Dallas Museum of Art, Kiest Fund Purchase Prize, Twelfth
Annual Dallas Allied Arts Exhibition, 1941

126. MARTHA SIMKINS
Grandmother 1920s
Oil on canvas, 20 x 16 in.
Rainone Galleries, Inc.,
Arlington, Texas

128. EMILY GUTHRIE
SMITH
Young Mulatto 1942
Oil on canvas,
30½ x 20½ in.
Dallas Museum of Art, Lida
Hoe Memorial Fund

129. CHESTER SNOWDEN
Chinese Junk   n.d.
Oil on canvas, 24½ x 32 in.
Collection of David Lackey

131. HENRY CECIL
SPENCER
Near Taos   n.d.
Oil on canvasboard,
18 x 13 in.
Collection of David Lackey

130. COREEN MARY SPELLMAN
Road Signs   1936
Oil on canvas, 28 x 36 in.
*Dallas Museum of Art, gift of Helen, Mick, and Thomas
Spellman*

132. EVERETT SPRUCE
Green Hillside 1942
Oil on Masonite,
16¼ x 24 in.
The Museum of Fine Arts,
Houston; museum purchase
with funds provided by the
Houston Friends of Art

133. CECILIA NEUHEISEL
STEINFELDT
Still Life
1940
Oil on canvas, 24 x 30 in.
Panhandle-Plains Historical
Museum, Canyon, Texas;
gift of the artist

134. TOM STELL
Untitled n.d.
Oil on Masonite, 20 x 50 in.
Collection of Robert T.
Brousseau

135. *JULIUS STOCKFLETH*
Galveston Wharf Scene   n.d.
Oil on canvas, 21½ x 31 in.
Rosenberg Library, Galveston, Texas

136. *RUBY STONE*
Nude Study—Three Women   n.d.
Oil on canvas, 19 x 15 in.
Collection of David Lackey

137. *FRANZ STRAHALM*
Bluebonnets in the Hill Country   n.d.
Oil on canvas, 16 x 36 in.
Collection of Robert T. Brousseau

146

138. ROLLA TAYLOR
West Texas Oil Field   n.d.
Oil on canvas, 24 x 30 in.
Collection of Bob and
Linda Rork

139. LEWIS TEEL
Wind Swept West Texas
n.d.
Oil on canvasboard,
22 x 28 in.
Collection of Bill and Mary
Cheek

140. ELOISE REID THOMPSON
Crossvine   n.d.
Watercolor, $11\frac{1}{2}$ x $9\frac{5}{8}$ in.
Gift of the Artist, Houston Museum of Natural Science

147

141. EUGENE
THURSTON
Sandia Mountains   n.d.
Oil on canvas, 21 x 29 in.
Collection of Holly and
Sanford C. Cox Jr.

142. FERN THURSTON
After Glow   n.d.
Oil on board, 12 x 16 in.
Collection of Holly and Sanford C. Cox Jr.

143. KATHRYNE HAIL TRAVIS
Zinnias and Brass   n.d.
Oil on canvas, 29 x 30 in.
Collection of Bill and Mary Cheek

144. OLIN TRAVIS
Mayor of Hoover City (Texas)   1929
Oil on canvas, 32 x 30 in.
The Barrett Collection

145. MARGARET WRIGHT TUPPER
San Antonio Morning   n.d.
Oil on canvas mounted on board, 7 x 9 in.
The Torch Collection of Torch Energy Advisors Incorporated

146. RUTH PERSHING
UHLER
Earth Rhythms No. 3   1935
Oil on canvas,
$25\frac{1}{4}$ x $30\frac{3}{8}$ in.
The Museum of Fine Arts,
Houston; Twelfth Annual
Houston Artists Exhibition,
Museum Purchase Prize,
1936

147. CHARLES UMLAUF
Dancing Figures   1938
Ceramic, height 27 in.
Collection of Mr. and Mrs.
Eric Steinfeldt

148. DONALD VOGEL
Evening   ca. 1943
Oil on canvas, 29½ x 40 in.
Dallas Museum of Art, Kiest Memorial Purchase Prize,
Fifteenth Annual Dallas Allied Arts Exhibition, 1944

149. HANNA WALKER
Peacock Military Institute   1923
Oil on canvas, 16 x 22 in.
Collection of Charles Stevens

150. WILLIAM AIKEN
WALKER
*SouthernCotton
Picker   1880s*
Oil on canvas, 7 x 13 in.
*Rainone Galleries, Inc.,
Arlington, Texas*

151. BEULAH WATTS
*First Capitol of Texas—
Columbia   1936
Watercolor and ink on
paper, 5 x 6 in.
Museum of East Texas,
Lufkin, Texas*

152. CARRIE HARPER
WHITE
*Watkins Ranch (Built in
1867)—Rio Frio, Texas
1927
Oil on canvas, 16 x 20 in.
The Torch Collection of
Torch Energy Advisors
Incorporated*

153. CLARA McDONALD WILLIAMSON
*Get Along Little Dogies   1945
Oil on canvas,
$26\frac{3}{4}$ x $39\frac{3}{4}$ in.
Dallas Museum of Art,*

154. MARY MOTZ WILLS
*Mexican Hat   ca. 1920–36
Watercolor, $10\frac{7}{8}$ x $6\frac{1}{2}$ in.
Courtesy of the Texas
Memorial Museum,
University of Texas, Austin*

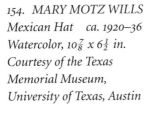

155. ROBERT WOOD
Pink Buka   *n.d.*
Oil on canvas, 24 x 30 in.
Collection of Dr. Charles
Russo

156. SAMUEL ZIEGLER
Untitled   *n.d.*
Oil on canvas, 20 x 24 in.
Collection of Robert T. Brousseau

157. MAMIE G. ZUBER
Portrait of Louis-Philippe d'Orleans   *n.d.*
Oil on canvas, $29\frac{1}{4}$ x $24\frac{1}{8}$ in. [oval]
French Legation Museum, Austin, Texas

TABLES

Annual Houston Artists Exhibition Index, 1925-31

Artist's Name	1925	1926	1927	1928	1929	1930	1931
ANDREWS, M. Virginia					X		X
ARMSTRONG, Amos Lee							X
ATCHISON, Alice						X	
AUGUSTIN, Genevieve H.						X	X
AYARS, Beulah Schiller					X	X	X
BAILEY, Carden					X	X	X
BESSELL, Evelyne Byers	X	X	X	X	X	X	X
BLACKSHEAR, Kathleen						X	
BODET, Marjorie Lockman							X
BRISBINE, Margaret	X	X	X	X	X	X	X
BROWN, Olivia					X	X	X
BROWN, Susan					X		
BROWNE, Frederic		X	X	X	X	X	X
BRYAN, Katharine McGown						X	X
BRYAN, Mary Alice						X	
CHERRY, E. R.	X	X	X	X	X	X	X
CHILLMAN, Jas., Jr.	X	X	X				
CLAXTON, Virgie	X		X	X	X	X	X
CLEMONS, Callie	X				X	X	
COSTELLO, E. J.			X	X	X	X	
CRAVENS, Leila Groce						X	
CREW, Grace	X				X		X
DAVIDSON, Ola McNeill	X	X	X	X		X	X
DAVIS, Helen C.	X	X	X	X	X	X	X
DIEMAN, Clare	X			X	X	X	X
DUHIG, W. G.						X	X
EPHRAIM, Eleanor						X	X
ESCHER, Erwin	X						
FAIN, Hazel Barr							X
FILLEAU, E. A.		X				X	
FISCHER, Florence	X						
FISHER, May					X		
FLY, Ben M.						X	X
FOSTER, May			X				X
GAUTNEY, Loraine D.					X		X
GOODE, Robert E., Jr.		X	X				X
HAAS, F. W. J.		X					
HAM, Dr. G. Suttle					X		
HANSEN, Douglas R.	X	X	X	X			X
HASTINGS, Daniel						X	X
HELLMAN, Bertha Louise	X	X	X	X	X	X	X
HENRY, Rebecca			X	X	X	X	X
HERMON, Lillian Mills							X
HILL, Mary Vandenberge						X	X
HINES, Adrian R.						X	
HINSON, Esther							X
HOLT, Adelaide E.		X	X				X
HOOTON, Claude E.					X	X	X
HOUSE, Dorothy D.				X	X	X	X
HOVER, Eleanor Whyte		X				X	X
HOWARD, Eugenia						X	
HUTCHINS, Frederic L.	X				X	X	X
JOHN, Grace Spaulding	X	X	X	X	X	X	X
KAHLDEN, Sarah					X	X	X
KARL, Mabel Fairfax			X	X			X
KEEFER, Elizabeth E.	X				X		
KUNTSCHER, Otto	X						
LANGHAM, Emily	X	X	X	X	X	X	X
LANSFORD, Henrietta	X					X	
LINGAN, Penelope	X	X	X	X	X	X	X
LUCAS, Fannie		X		X			X
MacDONNELL, M. Angela	X	X					
MATTHAEI, Beatrice			X	X	X	X	X
McKENNA, Helen						X	X
McKENNA, William							X
McVEY, William E.					X		
MILLER, Jean Blanc						X	X
MONICA, Sister M.		X		X	X		X

Annual Houston Artists Exhibition Index, 1925-31, Continued

Artist's Name	1925	1926	1927	1928	1929	1930	1931
MUELLER, Bertha			X				
MUENCH, Agnes Lilienberg					X		X
MUENCH, Julien Rhodes		X	X				X
MURILLO, J.							
PAGAN, John L.							X
PALMER, Hattie Virginia	X	X	X	X	X	X	
PAYNE, Lura M.	X	X		X			
PITTMAN, Margaret Hallett						X	
RANDOLPH, Daisy Ewing		X					
REINHART, Ida B. (Mrs. E. T.)			X	X			
RIVERA, C. Garza				X	X		X
RONEY, Harold A.		X	X	X			
SCHIWETZ, E. M.						X	X
SCHMIDT, Tillie		X					
SCHOFIELD, Lilian Wells		X					
SCOTT, Helen Nina		X					X
SCOTT, William		X					
SETTOON, Baldwin E.							X
SEWALL, Blanche Harding	X						
SHAFFER, Conway							X
SMEDES, Elizabeth H.							X
SMITH, Jean					X		
STANSBURY, Florence E.							X

Artist's Name	1925	1926	1927	1928	1929	1930	1931
STEDMAN, Rosabel	X						
STEDMAN, Wilfred	X						X
STEVENSON, Louise A.	X	X			X	X	X
STONE, Jesse R.			X		X		
STONE, Mildred B.							X
STOY, Frances Baskette		X					
STREET, Lois					X		X
TIDDEN, Agnes (also MUEN	X	X	X				
TIDDEN, John Clark	X						
TURNER, C. J.			X				
UHLER, Ruth Pershing	X	X	X	X			X
VAN MELDERT, Leon					X		
WEATHERRED, Mary Betty				X	X	X	
WEIS, Frederic S.							X
WEST, Maud S.		X	X	X	X	X	
WHEELER, Lucille		X		X			X
WHITE, J. F.	X						
WHITE, Lloyd Y.			X				
WILKINSON, Edward				X			X
WOODRUFF, Alice C.		X				X	
WRIGHT, Carroll						X	
YATES, J. Gordon					X		X

Artist's Name	1933	1934	1935	1936	1937	1938	1939	1940
ADAMS, Clarie	X							
ADAMSON, Alma Calista							X	X
ALLEN, Virginia			X					
ANDRE, Joan						X		
ARMSTRONG, Daniel L., Jr.		X	X					
ARRANTS, Edward B.	X							
AYARS, Beulah Schiller	X	X	X	X	X	X		X
BAGNELL, E. W.	X	X						
BAILEY, Carden	X	X	X	X	X	X	X	X
BAKER, William H.					X			
BAXTER, Henry							X	
BECKSMITH, Louise Veach					X			
BENJAMIN, Anne Cleveland								X
BESS, Forrest							X	
BESSELL, Evelyne Byers	X	X	X	X	X			X
BEST, Margaret			X	X	X	X		
BLACK, Nell					X			
BLACKSHEAR, Kathleen		X	X	X	X			
BOONE, G.		X						
BOWLES, Ray Earnest, Jr.						X	X	
BRISBINE, Margaret		X	X	X	X			
BROWN, Hamilton		X						
BROWN, John H.		X	X	X				
BROWN, Olivia	X							
BROWNE, Amelie N.		X						
BROWNE, Frederic	X	X	X	X	X	X	X	X
BRUBAKER, Harley	X	X	X			X		
BUFFINGTON, Ralph M.					X			
BULLINGTON, Maida P.			X					
BUNJES, Emil					X			X
BURGE, A. Lee				X				
BURTON, Caroline		X						
BYRNES, Olive Audrey								X
CALHOUN. Harold							X	
CAMPBELL, James I.		X						
CARLSON, Nione							X	
CARRON, Maudee Lilyan					X	X	X	X
CASHMAN, John					X			
CAVITT, Mary					X			
CHARLTON, Frances		X	X					
CHARLTON, Gene		X	X	X	X	X	X	X
CHERRY, E. R.	X	X	X	X	X	X		
CHILDRESS, Doris							X	X
CHRISTIANSON, Stanley H.	X	X						
CLAXTON, Virgie	X	X	X	X	X	X	X	X
CLEARY, W. P.	X							
COCHRAN, Billy						X		
COCKRELL, Marie								X

Artist's Name	1933	1934	1935	1936	1937	1938	1939	1940
COLE, Elsie W.				X				
COLE, Ross						X		
COLEY, Elizabeth Thomson				X	X		X	
CONNOR, Barbara		X	X	X	X			X
CONTRERAS, Theones		X	X		X			
COOK, Margot					X			
CRABB, Bob				X	X	X		X	X
CREW, C. C.				X				
CRITTENDEN, Ethel S.		X	X	X	X			
CRUM, Dorothy			X	X				
CUMMINS, Sascha M.			X	X		X		
DAVIDSON, Ola McNeill	X	X	X	X	X	X	X	
DAVIS, Helen C.	X	X	X	X	X	X	X	
DAVIS, Maude Frances								X
DAVIS, Ralph				X				
DAVIS, Redwood			X					
DAVIS, Russel							X	
DAY, Agnes N.								X
DICKSON, Melvin	X							
DIXON, Mildred Wood					X			
DOLEJSKA, Frank						X	X	
DUHIG, Camilla F.				X				
DYER, Laura								X
EINFELDT, George		X	X	X	X	X		
ELLEDG, Pearl					X			
EMIG, Adolph P.						X	X	X
EPHRAIM, Eleanor E.				X	X			
FALL, Frieda Kay						X		
FARQUHARSON, Thelma A.			X					
FERGUSON, W. B., III								X
FILSON, Genevieve				X	X	X		X	X
FLANAGAN, Jack Key								X
FULTON, George		X	X					
GARDNER, Dan B.				X				
GARLAND, Christine				X	X	X	X	X	X
GARRISON, Minta H.	X	X	X	X	X	X		
GAY, Helen				X	X			
GORDON, Allyn				X	X	X		X	
GOULD, C. D.								X
GRANT, Florence B.							X	
GREGORY, Jack W.					X			
GROCE, J. H., Jr.							X	
HAAS, F. W. J.	X	X	X					
HAMM, W. Howard						X		
HAMMARGREN, Frederick								X
HARE, Vida					X			
HARPER, Roberta Blewitt			X					
HARWELL, Jerry, Jr.							X	X

Artist's Name	1933	1934	1935	1936	1937	1938	1939	1940
HASTINGS, Daniel	X	X						
HEAPS, Belle G.				X		X		X
HELLMAN, Bertha Louise	X	X	X	X	X			
HENRY, Rebecca	X	X	X	X			X	
HERMON, Lillian Mills				X				
HEWITT, Lea				X	X	X		
HILD, Scott Lee	X	X						
HIRSCH, Grace		X	X					
HOLLIDAY, Nancy							X	
HOOD, Dorothy								X
HOOTON, Claude E.	X							
HOSKINS, Dorothy M.					X			
HOULISTON, William J., Jr.			X	X	X	X	X	X
HOUSE, Dorothy D.	X	X	X	X	X			
HOWZE, Albert		X						
HUGHES, Mildred								X
HUNT, Eugenia Howard	X	X	X	X		X		X
ISBELL, Hilda M.					X			
JACKSON, Rosemary	X							
JACOBS, E. M.					X	X		
JAMES, Delwin V.	X	X			X	X		
JOHN, Grace Spaulding	X	X	X	X		X	X	
JOHN, Patricia						X		
JOHNSON, Alice Word					X	X		
JOY, Robert	X	X	X	X		X	X	X
KAEPPEL, Albert Enno		X						
KAHLDEN, Sarah	X	X	X	X	X		X	X
KARL, Mabel Fairfax	X	X	X	X	X			
KEITH, Jacquelyn			X		X	X	X	
KEITH, James L., Jr.					X			
KIEFNER, C. H.					X	X	X	
KING, Grace		X						X
KOENIG, John				X	X			
LANE, Joseph							X	
LANGHAM, Emily	X	X	X	X	X	X		X
LEARY, Delano					X			
LEE, Dean				X	X	X	X	
LEVY, Gertrude Lisette				X				X
LINGAN, Penelope	X	X	X	X				
LYKES, Genevieve				X				
LYON, L. N., Jr.		X						
LYON, Nicholas						X		
MacDONNELL, M. Angela	X	X	X	X	X		X	X
MARKHAM, Ruby Stone (also STONE)				X	X			
MATHEE, Malzena					X			
MATTHAEI, Beatrice	X	X	X	X	X	X		
MATTHEWS, Harold J.				X	X	X		
McBRIDE, Beatrice Matthaei (also MATTHAEI)							X	X

Artist's Name	1933	1934	1935	1936	1937	1938	1939	1940
McCABE, J. Glenn			X					
McGONIGLE, Ruth G. Y.		X			X			
McKENNA, Helen	X	X	X	X				
McKENNA, William	X	X	X	X				
McNAB, Helena			X					
McVEY, Leza						X	X	
McVEY, William E.		X			X	X	X	
METCALF, Louise			X					
MEYSENBURG, Virginia C.		X		X	X	X		
MONTGOMERY, Fannie E. Bess		X	X	X		X		
MOORE, Harvin		X	X					
MOORE, P. A.				X	X			
MORRIS, Elizabeth H.	X		X	X				
MORRISON, Mary	X							
MORRISON, Olivia Brown (also BROWN)		X	X					
MOSKOWITZ, Shirley				X	X		X	X
MUENCH, Agnes Lilienberg	X	X	X	X	X		X	X
MUENCH, Julian Rhodes	X	X	X					
MUZZEY, Virginia Reynolds								X
NEYLAND, Watson		X	X					
NICE, Blanch Heim	X	X	X	X	X	X	X	X
NORTON, Natalie			X					
OLIPHANT, Carol E.					X			
PAGAN, John L. (Jack)		X	X	X	X		X	
PALMER, Hattie Virginia*	X	X						
PARSONS, Anna			X	X	X			
PATTERSON, Oriel C.	X							
PEARSON, Lawrence E.							X	
PIERCE, A. B., Jr.						X	X	X
PLOGER, Benjamin John					X	X	X	
PRESCOTT, Julia			X					
PREUSSER, Robert		X	X	X	X	X	X	X
PUTNAM, Frances M.					X	X	X	
REYNOLDS, Virginia (also MUZZEY)				X	X	X	X	
RING, Mary		X	X	X				
ROBERTS, Frank S.		X						
ROBINSON, Fern					X	X		
ROUTT, Julia Jack				X	X	X	X	
ROWNTREE, Madeline B.				X				
SAENGER, Betty				X				
SAMPSON, Florence		X						
SCHIWETZ, B., Jr. (Pete)						X	X	
SCHIWETZ, E. M.	X	X	X	X	X	X	X	X
SCOTT, Helen Nina	X			X				
SETTOON, Baldwin E.		X						
SEWALL, Blanche Harding		X						
SHACKELFORD, George E.							X	
SHARP, Minnie Lee	X	X	X	X			X	

Artist's Name	1933	1934	1935	1936	1937	1938	1939	1940
SHEPHERD, Jim							X	
SIMS, Ruth						X		
SNOWDEN, Chester			X	X	X		X	X
SPEARS, Lena		X	X	X				
STANFORD, J. Elizabeth			X	X	X			
STARCALA, John J.	X							
STEDMAN, Myrtle	X	X	X	X				
STEDMAN, Wilfred	X	X						
STELZIG, Frances						X		
STEPHENS, Julia Marguerite								X
STEVENSON, Louise A.	X							
STEVENSON, Orissa	X							
STILLMAN, Ary			X					
STONE, Catherine				X				
STONE, Mildred B.	X	X	X	X		X	X	
STONE, Ruby							X	
STREETMAN, Christine Norman		X	X	X		X		X
THOMPSON, Eloise Reid			X	X	X			
TIRADO, Tom Vick								X
TRAVIS, Diane							X	X
TRUITT, Una B.			X	X	X	X	X	X
UHLER, Ruth Pershing	X	X		X	X	X	X	X
VALLEE, Lorin				X	X		X	X
VORSE, Virginia				X				
WAGNER, Reta							X	
WALL, Bernhardt				X	X			
WALTON, Madeleine					X			
WALTON, Mary Ann							X	
WATSON, Marguerite Thompson							X	
WEATHERRED, Rosemary			X	X				
WEST, Maud S.							X	
WHISENHANT, Paul				X	X	X		
WIER, Mattie		X	X	X	X	X	X	X
WIESNER-ORTH, Steffi	X	X	X	X				
WILDMAN, Caroline Lax		X	X	X	X	X	X	
WILLIAMS, Marian G.	X	X	X	X				
WILSON, Madge								X
WILSON, Milam D.					X			
WINNE, Betty								X
WOOD, Mildred				X				
WOOD, Norma Lynn				X	X	X	X	
WORTHINGTON, Christine D.				X	X			
WRIGHT, Silas A.						X		
YANDELL, Dagley				X	X			
YATES, Jean Perry						X		

* Special honor, memorial.

Artist's Name	1942	1943	1944	1945
ALDEN, Lowell		X	X	X
ALEXANDER, Martha Ray				X
AYARS, Beulah Schiller		X		
BAILEY, Carden	X		X	
BAKER, Estes			X	X
BARTLAM, Virginia Newsom	X		X	X
BELL, Mary Elizabeth			X	X
BELL, Nona				X
BESSELL, Evelyne Byers	X			X
BEVAN, Haddie Fulton				X
BILLFALDT, Jeanne				X
BILLFALDT, Patye			X	
CALDWELL, Esther		X		
CARLSON, Nione			X	X
CHARLTON, A. R.				X
CHARLTON, Gene	X	X	X	X
CHERRY, E. R.	X	X	X	X
CHILDRESS, Doris		X		X
CIMAREC, G. W.		X		
CLARK, Sydney George				X
CLARKE, Lucy Milby		X	X	X
CLAXTON, Virgie	X	X		X
COCHRAN, Adelaide		X		
COCKRELL, Marie	X	X		
COLEY, Elizabeth Thomson		X		
COMBS, Arthur		X		
COMBS, W. A.			X	
CONKLIN, Orville W.	X			
CONNOR, Barbara	X			X
CRABB, Bob		X		
CRATE, Herbert L.		X		
CRITTENDEN, Ethel S.		X		
CUMMINGS, Ben H.				X
CURTIS, Frances				X
DAVIS, Maude Frances	X			
DAY, Agnes N.		X		
DREYER, Margaret Webb			X	X
DREYER, Martin		X	X	X
DUFFY, Rebecca				X
DYER, Laura	X			
EINFELDT, George				X
EMIG, Adolph P.			X	X
EPHRAIM, Eleanor E.	X			
FILSON, Genevieve	X			
FLACK, Jack		X		
FLANAGAN, Jack Key	X	X	X	X
FRANKLIN, Mary Glenn	X			
GENIN, Dan	X			

Artist's Name	1942	1943	1944	1945
GOODE, Robert E., Jr.				X
GOULD, C. D.	X			
GRANT, Florence B.		X	X	X
GREEN, Abner	X	X		
GROCE, John H., Jr.	X			
GRUNBAUM, Marianne		X		
HAMMARGREN, Frederick	X			
HARE, Vida	X			
HEAPS, Belle G.		X		X
HEESCHE, Ursula H.			X	
HELLER, Ruth S.		X		
HENDERSON, Norma			X	
HENRY, Rebecca	X	X		
HERWIG, Elgie				X
HILL, Nora Livingston	X			
HINTON, Margaret				X
HODGES, Alice Kiefer			X	
HOULISTON, William J., Jr.	X	X	X	
HUDGINS, Anne G.			X	X
HUNT, Eugenia Howard		X	X	
HURLOCK, Alba Krueger		X		
INGRAM, Samuel	X			
JOHNSON, Alice Word	X			X
JOY, Robert		X		
KAHLDEN, Sarah	X	X		
KINZBACH, Mary Chandler		X		
KUTTNER, Walter		X		
LARKIN, Billy	X			
LAYBURN, Grace	X			
McKEON, Hazel				X
MEYSENBURG, Virginia C.		X		
MITCHELL, Richard	X			
MOORE, P. A.			X	X
MORRIS, Glory H.				X
MORRIS, William			X	X
MOSE, Carl C.			X	
MOSKOWITZ, Shirley		X	X	X
MUENCH, Agnes L.	X	X	X	X
MUENCH, Nancy				X
MUZZEY, Virginia Reynolds	X			
NICE, Blanch Helm	X	X	X	X
PAGAN, John S. (Jack)	X	X	X	X
PHILLIPS, Virginia East				X
PIERCE, A. B., Jr.	X			
PIOTT, Elizabeth		X		
PREUSSER, Robert Ormerod	X	X	X	
PROCTOR, Jane				X
RICKARD, Kathleen				X

Artist's Name	1942	1943	1944	1945
ROMANSKY, Alvin S.			X	X
ROUTT, Julia Jack		X		
SADDY, Marilyn Wiley			X	X
SCHIWETZ, B., Jr.		X		
SCHIWETZ, Edward M.		X	X	X
SCHIWETZ, Ruby Lee		X	X	X
SCHIWETZ, Ted				X
SKINNER, Frances		X	X	X
SNOWDEN, Chester	X	X		X
STANLEY, Mack		X		
STANLEY, Madeleine				X
STEVENSON, Orissa	X			
STORM, Mark		X		
STOUT, Mary Jane	X			
STREETMAN, Christine Norman			X	X

Artist's Name	1942	1943	1944	1945
TAYLOR, A. Hinkle	X	X		
TOLAR, Harriett	X			
TRUITT, Una B.	X	X		
TSANOFF, Katherine			X	X
VALLEE, Lorin	X			
WALKER, Dickman			X	X
WATSON, Marguerite Thomp	X	X		X
WEBB, Margaret Lee		X		
WEIS, Frederick	X	X		
WIER, Mattie	X	X	X	X
WILDMAN, Caroline Lax			X	X
WILSON, Madge	X	X	X	
WINNE, Betty		X		
WOOD, Norma Lynn			X	
ZWEINER, Charles L.	X			

Artist's Name	1937	1938	1939
ALLBRITTON, H. J.	X		
ANDRE, Joan	X	X	
ASTIN, John H.		X	
AYARS, Beulah S.	X		
BAILEY, Ben P., Jr.	X		
BAILEY, Carden		X	X
BERKOWITZ, Rosalie	X		
BESS, Forrest		X	
BESSELL, Evelyne Byers		X	
BIRD, Laura Lee	X		
BLACKSHEAR, Kathleen	X		X
BLAIR, Catherine Stone	X		
BOATRIGHT, Elizabeth Keefer		X	
BOHN, Mildred Knight		X	
BRAND, Frances Christian		X	
BRISBINE, Margaret	X		
BROCK, Gene H.		X	
CARRON, Maudee Lilyan	X		
CAVAZOS, Humberto		X	
CHARLTON, Gene		X	
CHILDRESS, Doris		X	
CLARK, Mary Lee		X	
CLAXTON, Virgie	X	X	
COCKRELL, Marie	X		
COLLINS, Edna	X		
COMPTON, Carl Benton		X	
COMPTON, Mildred Norris	X		
COOK, Paul Rodda	X		
CORBETT, Nancy D.	X	X	
COX, Abbe Rose	X		
CRABB, Bob	X	X	
CRITTENDON, Ethel Stuart	X	X	
CRONIN, Marie		X	
CUMMINS, Sascha		X	
DAVID, Lorene	X	X	
DAVIDSON, McNeill	X	X	
DAVIS, Helen C.	X		
DAVIS, Russel F.		X	
DECKERT, Verna	X	X	
DENE, Pierre		X	
DILL, Frank C.	X		
DOLEJSKA, Frank	X	X	
DONOP, Edna Bierschwale		X	
DUGOSH, Ruby Evelyn	X	X	X
DURST, Frances			X
EINFELDT, George	X	X	
EMIG, Adolph P.	X	X	
EVERETT, Raymond	X		

Artist's Name	1937	1938	1939
FILSON, Genevieve Winnifred	X	X	
FINNEY, C. J.	X	X	
GARCIA, Antonio E.	X		
GARLAND, Christine	X	X	
GARRISON, Minta	X	X	
GLASSCOCK, Margaret	X		
GONZALES, Boyer, Jr.	X	X	
GORDON, Allyn	X	X	
GREEN, Katherine	X		
GUERRA, Alfredo	X		
HAGNER, Lillie May	X	X	
HAINES, Marie	X		
HARDIN, Ernest R.	X	X	
HARWELL, Jerry, Jr.		X	
HEAPS, Belle G.		X	
HEISLER, Mary	X		
HERRINGTON, Walter S.		X	
HESSER, Yvonne	X		
HOGELAND, Eva	X	X	
HOULISTON, William James	X	X	
JESSEN, Bubi	X		
JOHN, Grace	X	X	
JOY, Robert	X	X	
KAHLDEN, Sarah	X		
KEATING, Mary A.	X	X	
KIEFER, C. H.		X	
KINZINGER, Edmund	X	X	X
LAZENBY, Georgia		X	
LEE, Dean	X		
LOCKE, Lucie H.	X		
MAGILL, Calla Lilly	X		
MATTHAEI, Beatrice	X	X	
McGILL, E. P.	X		
McGONIGLE, Ruth Young	X	X	
McMATH, Hugh L.	X	X	
McVEY, William M.		X	
MEDELLIN, Octavio	X		
MEUSEBACH, Iago	X		
MILLER, Florence Oom	X		
MUENCH, Agnes L.	X		
NABINGER, Dollie	X		
NEUHEISEL, Cecilia	X	X	
NEWMAN, Ellen		X	
NEWMAN, George W.	X	X	
NICE, Blanch Heim	X	X	
O'BRIEN, Erin	X		
PACKER, C. L.	X		X
PEARSON, Lawrence E.		X	

Artist's Name	1937	1938	1939
PITTMAN, Peggy	X		
PREUSSER, Robert	X	X	
PUTNAM, Frances M.	X	X	
RAPHAEL, Frances	X		
REES, Lonnie	X	X	X
ROBERTS, Dorothy		X	
ROLFE, Walter T.	X		
RONEY, Harold	X		
ROTH, Eleanor	X	X	
RUTLAND, Emily	X		X
SCHIWETZ, B., Jr.		X	
SCHIWETZ, E. M.	X	X	X
SCHUMANN, Paul R.	X		
SNOWDEN, Chester	X	X	
SPENCER, H. C.	X		
STAFFEL, Rudolf	X		
STEVENSON, Orissa	X	X	
STONE, Ruby	X		
TARPLEY, Myra	X		

Artist's Name	1937	1938	1939
TAYLOR, Rolla	X		
THURMOND, Ethel	X	X	
TRIMBLE, A. M.	X		
TUPPER, Margaret Wright	X		
UHLER, Ruth Pershing	X	X	
VALENTINE, Wilma Davis		X	
VALLEE, Lorin	X		
VANCE, Helen Blesi	X		
WAGNER, Charles Pennell		X	
WARREN, Mallory Page	X		
WEST, Maud S.		X	
WHISENHANT, Paul	X		
WIER, Mattie		X	
WILDMAN, Caroline Lax	X	X	
WINSTEAD, Mrs. Maurice	X		
WOELTZ, Julius	X		
WORTHINGTON, Virginia	X		
WUNTCH, Freddie		X	

Cotton Carnival Exposition, 1910-12

Artist's name	1910	1911	1912
ADRIANCE, Ethel		X	
ARNOLD, H. R.	X		
ARPA, Jose	X		X
BAEZINGER (BAEZNER), A.	X		
BEWLEY, Murray			X
BLANTON, Daisy			X
CHAMBODUT, Marie H.		X	
CHARLESTON, F.			X
CHASE, Carrie A.	X		
CLAIBORNE, Madge		X	
COLEMAN, Roi Clarkson			X
CRONIN, Marie	X		
CUPRIEN, F. W.	X	X	
CURRIE, D. K.	X		
DAVIS, Margaret Tolar	X		X
DE PEILLON , Jeanne	X	X	
DUNLAP, Ellen L.			X
EASTON, Mrs. Alex (Mary C. F.)	X		
EDWARDS, Mrs. K. J.	X		
EISENLOHR, E. G.	X		X
ENGELMEYER, Louis	X	X	X
GONZALES, Boyer	X	X	X
GORDON, Boris Bernhard	X		
HAGENDORN, Max		X	
HARDY, E. J.	X		
HARFORD, Bessie		X	
HARRIS, Elias B.	X	X	X
HILTON, Ethel			X
HOETING, I. A.	X	X	
HOLT, Percy W.			X
HOULAHAN, Eleanora	X		
JENKINS, John E.	X	X	
KEILLER, Dr. Wm. H.	X	X	
KIMMON, Mrs. S. C.			X
KLEPPER, Frank X. E. L.			X
KUNZ, Lenore O.			X
LEDGERWOOD, Ella Ray			X
LITTLEJOHN, Margaret M.	X		
MacDONNELL, M. Angela	X		
MacKAY, Kathrine (Catherine)	X	X	
MARFORD, Bessie		X	
MAURER, Mrs. J. M. (Julia Ott)	X		
MORFORD (MARFORD), Bessie			X
MORGAN, Mrs. George D. (Jean S.)			X
NAVE, Royston	X		
ONDERDONK, Robert	X		
PALMER, Mrs. C. F. (Hattie)	X	X	
PARMLEE, J. M.	X		
RABA, Ernst	X		
REAUGH, Frank	X		
ROBERTSON, Marguerite			X
SALOMON, S.		X	X
SAUNDERS, Hallie L.	X		
SCHUMANN, Paul	X	X	X
SCRIMGEOUR, Mrs. Chas. (Mary E.)	X		
SHEPARD, Anne Blake		X	
SIMMONS, Gladys			X
SORRENSON, Ella			X
STOCKFLETH, Julius		X	
TAYLOR, Rolla	X		
WAHLBERG, P. L.	X		
WATSON, Margaret L.			X
WEBSTER, A. T.	X	X	X
WHITTING, G. W.		X	
WITTIG, G. Walter'	X		
WRAGG, Eleanor T.	X		X
YARD, Mrs. George N. (Pense)			X
YOUNG, Edith	X		

Artist's Name	1928	1929	1930	1931	1932	1933	1935	1937	1938
ADAMS, Eleanor		X							
ADDIS, Elsinore M.	X								
ADDIS, Wm. H.	X								
ADKINS, Alice		X	X			X			
AKIN, Elizabeth				X					
ANDERSON, Fern	X								
ANDERSON, H.	X								
ANDRESS, Annie Lee		X							
ANKENEY, John S.				X	X	X			
ANTON, Angelina	X								
AUSTIN, Dorothy						X	X		X
BARKER, H. A.						X			
BASSETT, Reveau	X	X		X	X				
BATSEL, Lawrence				X					
BELL, Gerald		X							
BELSTERLING, Mrs. Ed	X								
BETHEL, Julia	X	X	X	X					
BISHOP, Travis	X								
BONNER, Julia M.	X								
BONNER, Mrs. M.						X			
BOOTH, Nell									X
BORN, Annette	X	X							
BOWLES, Minnie				X	X	X			
BOWLING, Charles T.			X	X	X	X	X	X	X
BOYER, Mrs. Josephine		X							
BRADFORD, Mary Katherine				X					
BRADY, Marie	X								
BRANNIN, Mrs. E. B.						X			
BREWSTER, Stanley H.			X						
BROAD, Thomas D.		X		X	X	X			
BROOKS, Helen							X		
BROOKS, James						X			
BROOKS, Mary Nell								X	X
BROWN, Elbert								X	
BROWN, Kenneth								X	
BRUCE, Granville					X				
BRUNET, Adele Laure				X	X	X			X
BRYAN, Ralph	X				X				
BUCHANAN, Laura		X	X	X	X	X		X	X
BUSTER, Mrs. C.	X								
BUVENS, Ethel	X	X							
BYWATERS, Jerry	X	X	X	X	X	X	X	X	X
CAHOON, Guy F.	X	X							
CAMPBELL, W. Edward						X		X	
CANTEY, Maurine						X			
CARNOHAN, Harry						X	X		
CARR, Bess							X	X	X
CASEY, William									X

Dallas Allied Arts Exhibition Index, 1928-38, Continued

Artist's Name	1928	1929	1930	1931	1932	1933	1935	1937	1938
CATHART, Mary	X								
CAVE, Mrs. Bertha					X	X			
CHAMBERLAIN, Johnnie									X
CHERRY, Eunice L.			X		X				
CHIPLEY, Mrs. L. P.					X				
CLACK, Clyde			X		X				
CLARKSON, Florence	X								
COLE, William				X					
CONERLY, Ruth	X	X							
COOK, Mary		X							
COOPER, H. R.						X			
CORDER, Mrs. Flora		X	X						
CORNELL, Wellington		X							
COUSE, Lucile		X							
COX, Clark	X			X	X				
COX, Thelma								X	
CRENSHAW, Mrs. James	X								
CROSBY, Kathryn O.	X								
CROWELL, Reid						X	X		X
CRUM, Dorothy Rea		X	X	X	X	X			
CULWELL, B. L.									X
CUSACK, Charles	X								
DANNA, J. B.					X				
DARGAN, Margaret	X	X	X	X	X	X			
DARGE, Fred								X	X
DAVIS, Jessie		X	X	X	X	X	X	X	
DAVIS, Velma			X	X			X		
DEAL, L. Kate					X				
DEANE, G. M.				X	X		X		
DEVEREUX, Joy	X								
DEWITT, Minnie A.						X			
DIAL, Dan									X
DIGGINS (DIGINS? DIGINGS?), Loraine			X		X	X			
DILLARD, Mrs. W. D.					X	X			
DODSON, Helen M.							X		
DONNELL, Lucretia								X	
DONOHUE, Margaret					X				
DOOLITTLE, Leda S.								X	X
DORSETT, Modesta		X							
DOUGLASS, John			X	X	X	X	X	X	
DOYLE, Mary									X
DOZIER, Otis	X	X	X	X	X	X	X	X	
DRIVER, Rose R.					X	X	X	X	X
DUDLEY, Wilburine		X							
DUGGER, Ruth		X							
ECKFORD, Jessiejo	X	X	X				X		X
EDGE (EDE?), Marian					X	X			
EISENLOHR, E. G.	X	X	X	X	X	X	X	X	

Artist's Name	1928	1929	1930	1931	1932	1933	1935	1937	1938
ELDER, Inez Staub	X	X	X	X	X	X	X	X	
ELLIOTT, William C.					X	X	X	X	X
ENSOR, Rettie Kelly		X							
FALL, Frieda Kay		X							
FALL, Mrs. C. G.	X								
FALL, Willie K.		X				X			
FICKLIN, Jack		X							
FIRMIN, A. E. (Bert)						X			
FISHER, John V.					X	X			
FLEMING, Margaret							X		
FLORER, Mrs. M. W.						X			
FORD, Arva				X	X				
FORD, O'Neil		X		X	X			X	
FRANK, Goldalee		X	X						
FRASER, Leona				X					X
GANSER, Edna			X			X			
GASSLANDER, Karl			X						
GATEWOOD, Evelyn						X	X		
GATTEYS, Allie B.						X	X		
GENTRY, Nannie Mae			X	X	X	X		X	
GHARIS, Charles						X	X		
GIBBONS, J. E.			X						
GIBSON, Harry Lee									X
GILES, Annie T.	X								
GILLEAN, Mrs. J. A.	X	X							
GLASGOW, Ruth				X	X	X	X		
GODFREY, Dorothy		X							
GOFF, Lloyd	X	X	X	X	X				
GOODE, Phillip						X			
GORDON, Glenn									X
GRANDSTAFF, Harriett						X			
GRIFFITH, Mildred		X							
GUIDROZ, Emile	X								
GUILBEAU, Honore				X	X				
GUILLOT, Ann		X	X			X			
HAGARD, Nettie May						X			
HAINES, Roberta	X								
HAMBURG, Dorothy		X							
HANSZEN, O.						X			
HARDWICKE, Lindsey				X					
HAROLD, Elizabeth		X							
HARPER, Roberta Blewett							X		
HAWKINS, Elva J.	X	X							
HENDERSON, Everett R.	X	X	X	X	X				
HENKEL, Estella M.							X	X	
HILL, R. Jerome	X	X		X		X			
HIRST, Sue	X								
HOGUE, Alexandre	X	X	X	X	X	X	X	X	X

Artist's Name	1928	1929	1930	1931	1932	1933	1935	1937	1938
HOLDEN, Mary Helen	X	X							
HOOPER, Mrs. C. E. (Floy)			X		X	X			
HORNER, Ruth								X	
HOSEK, Walter	X								
HOUPY, Henry						X			
HOWELL, Mrs. F. L.					X	X			
HUBBELL, Jack					X	X	X		
HUDSON, Edith (Mrs. C. E.)	X	X			X	X			
HUDSON, Jewel Harlan									X
HUDSON, Ruth				X					
HUDSON, Sarah Dorsey						X	X		
HUDSON, Winnie B.	X								
HUFSTEDLER, Mrs. E. V.		X							
HUGHES, Ann Louise	X	X							
HUGHES, Bess		X							
HUGHES, Mrs. Maury					X				
HUNGERFORD, Homer						X			X
HURST, Charles	X								
HUTCHINS, Mrs. Ross		X							
JACKSON, Gene Mercere						X			
JESTER, Martha							X		
JESTER, Ralph		X							
JOHNSON, Minnie W.		X	X	X	X	X	X		
JONES, Louise							X		X
JOYCE, Charles Marita									X
KAMACKER, Frederic			X						
KEELEY, Edward					X				
KELLEY, Edith					X				
KENDALE (KENDALL?), Evelyn	X			X					
KIRKLAND, Forrest		X		X	X	X	X	X	
KLEPPER, Frank	X	X	X	X			X	X	
KRAMER, Alice							X	X	X
KRAMER, Fred					X	X			
KRISTOFFERSEN, J. K.					X	X			
KROLL, Rolfe								X	
KROME, Steve					X				
LA MOND, Stella L.								X	
LALLIER, Victor						X	X		
LANDERS, Bertha M.									X
LANGE, Virginia E.	X								
LANGLEY, Jane						X			
LANIER, Fanita						X		X	
LAUDERDALE, Ursula	X	X							
LAWRENCE, Harry				X		X	X	X	
LAWSON, Mamie		X							
LESTER, William			X	X	X	X	X	X	X
LIGHTFOOT, Mary	X	X						X	
LIGON, Verda		X		X	X	X	X	X	X

Artist's Name	1928	1929	1930	1931	1932	1933	1935	1937	1938
LONGSHIE, George E.									X
MacCUISTON, Jacques						X			
MACKBEE, Esther	X								
MAHONEY, J. O.	X	X							
MANNING, Dorothy		X							
MARGULES, Adalie Brent								X	
MARS, Adelaide		X							
MARTIN, J. B.	X		X			X	X	X	X
MASCHO, Norma	X	X							
MASSEY, Suwanee	X								
MASSIC, Kathryn		X							
MAUZEY, Merritt								X	X
MAXSON, Peggy	X								
MAXWELL, Mrs. Oliver		X							
MAYES, H. H.		X			X				
MAYS, Maxine									X
McBRIDE, Lucille	X								
McCALL, Dora						X			
McCANN, Charles L.				X	X				
McCLAIN, George M.								X	X
McCLELLAN, Bowen	X								
McCLUNG, Florence		X	X	X	X	X	X	X	X
McCUTCHEON, Mrs. B.	X								
McDERMOTT, Cecelia	X		X						
McGREGOR, George									
McIVER, Mrs. P. R.	X	X							
McKAMY, Marianna		X		X					
McKINLEY, Catherine Hall							X		
McKINLEY, Frances		X							
McMILLAN, Ben	X								
MEANS, Glenn							X		
MEDRANO, Abdon						X			
MENEZES, Harry E.	X								
MEREDITH, Alice					X				
MERRILL, Bobby				X	X	X	X		
MERRILL, Ralph				X		X			
MILLER, Jesse							X		
MILLER, Margaret C.	X								
MILLER, Robert R.	X								
MILLS, Hillis		X							
MIMS, Louise Holden								X	X
MITCHELL, Maurine R.	X	X							
MITCHELL, Mel		X							
MITCHELL, Rena	X	X							
MORELAND, H. L.	X								
MORENO, Abel		X							
MOUNT, Esse							X		X
MOYER, Marvin									X

Artist's Name	1928	1929	1930	1931	1932	1933	1935	1937	1938
MULLIS, Phyllis Haas								X	
MURPHEY, Mimi					X	X	X		
MURPHY, Mrs. H. B.	X								
NEUMANN, Florence				X	X				
NEWBERRY, Mrs. J. E.		X							
NICHOLS, Perry	X	X		X	X	X	X		X
NOBLES, Kathryn Helm							X		
NOGUEIRA, Juanita				X	X				
NOWLIN, Eugenia C.							X	X	X
ORAM, Sarah H.	X								
OSBORNE, Hazel C.	X								
OWEN, Mike							X	X	X
OWENS, Mrs. W. B.			X	X	X				
OWSLEY, Mrs. Alvin	X								
PARKER, Ella Estill									X
PARKES, Joe, Jr.				X					
PATTESON, Helena									X
PATTESON, John									X
PEARCE, Mary Blake (Mrs. R. B.)	X		X			X			
PEEPLES, Nina				X	X	X	X		X
PENROD, Viola	X	X	X	X	X	X			
PERRY, Robert J.								X	
PHILLIPS, Lenore				X					
PORTER, Fay Lively	X								
PRESSLY, H. G.	X								
PRICKETT, William	X	X							
PULTE, Frances		X							
PUTNAM, F. O.	X	X	X		X				
RAHR, Gus						X	X		
REID, Mary P.									
REYNOLDS, Alice		X							
REYNOLDS, Howard W.							X		
RICHTER, Will Scott					X				
RIDDLE, Martha	X								
RIPPETEAU, Hallie C.	X								
ROACH, Mariana									X
ROBERTSON, Fanita		X	X	X					
ROBERTSON, H. O.			X	X	X	X	X	X	X
ROGERMAN (RODGERMAN?), Gertrude				X	X				
ROLAND, Marshall					X				
ROSE, Martha	X								
ROUNTREE, Ralph S.	X	X							
RUPRECHT, F. D.	X								
SADLER, Sara			X	X					
SANDERS, Bertha Mae	X								
SARGENT, Betty							X		
SARGENT, Lloyd L.					X	X	X		
SAUNDERS, James		X							

Artist's Name	1928	1929	1930	1931	1932	1933	1935	1937	1938
SCHIEFFER, William B.								X	
SCHOEFIELD, Mary E.		X							
SCHOFIELD, Lillian W.	X		X		X	X			
SCHOW, May							X		
SCRUGGS, M. A.	X	X	X		X		X		
SHARP, Florence S.					X				
SHARP, Mrs. L. W.	X		X						
SHARP, V.		X							
SHOCKLEY, Pearl	X	X			X	X			
SIMKINS, Martha	X					X			
SIMMONS, Bernice	X	X				X			
SIMPSON, J. H.	X								
SIMPSON, Wallace						X			
SKINNER, Francis J.				X	X	X	X	X	X
SLAUGHTER, Avery						X			
SLOAN, J. Blanding								X	
SMART, Frank Ellis								X	
SMITH, Ellen H.	X								
SMITH, Winston				X					
SNEED, Mary C.					X				
SNEED, Mrs. R. H.		X							
SPAULDING, Florence S.						X			
SPEARS, Lena				X					
SPEED, Rosalie		X	X	X	X	X	X	X	X
SPENCE, Julia	X								
SPENCER, Icy									X
SPIVEY, Pauline									X
SPRUCE, Everett	X	X	X	X	X	X	X	X	X
STEARMAN, Mrs. W. C.	X								
STELL, Thomas M., Jr.	X	X				X	X	X	X
STEVENS, Walter	X	X	X						
STOCKHAM, Eva H.						X			
STONE, Ruby	X	X	X		X		X		
STOREY, Boude E.	X								
STOREY, Evelyn (Mrs. Boude)	X			X	X				X
STRAHALM, Franz	X	X	X	X	X				
STRAITON (STRATON?), Betty	X	X							
STROHMEYER, A. F.	X	X	X		X				
SUGGS, Tom						X			
SULLIVAN, C. F.						X			
SUTTON, Dorothy			X						
SWANN, James							X	X	
TATE, Mrs. J. Waddy	X								
TAYLOR, Lura Ann				X	X	X		X	
TENNANT, Allie V.	X	X	X				X		
THOMAS, Frances E.	X	X	X						
THOMPSON, May Beth							X		
THOMPSON, Cornelia	X	X				X			

Artist's Name	1928	1929	1930	1931	1932	1933	1935	1937	1938
THOMPSON, Eloise Reid				X	X	X			
THOMPSON, William	X			X		X			
THOMS, P. A.	X								
THRASH, Rozella C.							X		
TIDWELL, James T.	X								
TILSON, Beryl							X	X	
TITSWORTH, Sarah				X					
TOOMEY, Anne						X			
TOWNSEND, Thurmond									X
TRAVIS, Diane							X		
TRAVIS, Kathryne Hail	X	X							
TRAVIS, Olin H.	X	X	X		X	X	X		X
TROTTER, Lillian C.		X	X	X	X	X			
TUBB, Clodine		X							
TURNER, Grace		X	X		X	X			
TYNES, Mrs. W. A.				X					
ULLMAN, Mrs. N. C.	X								
URBACH, Amelia	X	X			X	X		X	X
VERMILLION, Harriett	X								
VISSER, Evelyne						X		X	
VOGT, Augusta									X
WAGGENER, Gertrude	X	X							
WALLER, Mary M.	X								
WALLER, Virginia	X								
WALMSLEY, Elizabeth H.					X	X	X		
WATSON, Maggie Joe							X		
WEBB, Esther	X	X	X	X			X		
WEBSTER, Mary	X								
WEISBERG, Marie							X		X
WEISE, Paul R.		X							
WEST, Maud S.							X		
WHITE, Jessie Aline	X	X	X	X	X	X	X	X	X
WHITE, Lena		X							
WHITE, Lula	X								
WHITE, Victoria	X	X							
WILBURN, Tee					X	X			
WILLIAMS, David		X			X				
WILSON, Douthitt	X	X							
WILSON, Robert		X	X		X				
WINANS, Judith H.									X
WINN, Buck		X	X			X			
WOOLEY, Pauline	X								
WORK, Maud	X	X	X	X	X	X		X	
ZIMMERAN, S. F.	X								

Dallas Allied Arts Exhibition Index, 1939-45

Artist's Name	1939	1940	1941	1942	1943	1944	1945
AKIN, Elizabeth					X		
ANDREWS, Golda					X		
ANTON, Mrs. F.							X
AUSTIN, Dorothy			X				
BEARD, Evelyn						X	X
BEARDEN, Ed				X	X	X	X
BEVERLEY, E. N.	X*		X				
BOWLING, Charles T.	X*	X*	X	X	X	X	X
BRAKE, Dorothy Hawkins				X	X		
BRECKENRIDGE, Dorothy							X
BRENT, Adalie Magules				X	X	X	
BRODNAX, Ethel May				X	X	X	X
BROWNE, Jean Calerdine							X
BRYANT, William H.						X	X
BUCHANAN, Laura					X		
BYWATERS, Jerry	X*		X	X	X	X	X
CARR, Bess			X				
CHENEY, F. Michael						X	X
CLACK, Clyde C.				X		X	X
CROCKETT, Grace						X	X
CROWELL, Reid			X			X	
DAILEY, Modena Stroud							X
DARGE, Fred			X	X	X	X	X
DARVER, Capt. A.					X		
DAUGHERTY, Bob							X
DAVIS, Jessie						X	
DAVIS, Velma			X				
DIAL, Dan	X*	X*					
DOYLE, Mary							X
DOZIER, Otis	X*	X*	X	X	X		
DU BOIS, Donald					X		
EISENLOHR, Edward G.			X		X	X	
ELDER, Inez Staub							X
ELLIOTT, William			X	X	X		
ELLIS, John Bryant				X			
EUBANK, Lydia				X	X	X	X
FALL, Frieda Kay			X	X	X	X	
FERNEAU, J.			X				
FUQUA, Wiley			X				
GAY, Stella							X
GERMANY, Pattilou							X
GITNICK, Ben					X		
GORDON, Louise					X		
GRICE (GRISE?), Hendrik							X
HARRISON, Ruth Dunken				X			
HOGUE, Alexandre			X	X	X		
HOWE, Bob				X			
HUNGERFORD, Homer				X	X	X	X
ISAAC, Dell					X	X	
JAMESON, Clemens				X	X	X	X
JEFFRIES, Lucille	X*	X*	X	X	X	X	X
KLEPPER, Frank					X	X	X
LA MOND, Stella L.			X		X	X	X
LALLIER, Victor			X	X	X	X	X
LANDERS, Bertha	X*	X*	X	X	X	X	X
LEE, L. Valentine						X	
LESTER, William	X*	X*	X	X	X	X	
LIGHTFOOT, Mary			X	X		X	
LIGON, Verda			X	X			X
MAPLES, Barbara			X	X	X	X	X
MAUZEY, Merritt		X*	X	X	X	X	X
MAYER, Marjorie							X
McCLAIN, George M.	X*						
McCLUNG, Florence			X	X	X	X	X
MEDELLIN, Octavio					X		
MEDRANO, Joaquin			X				
MERRICK, P. R.				X			
MOYER, Marvin			X				

Dallas Allied Arts Exhibition Index, 1939-45, Continued

Artist's Name	1939	1940	1941	1942	1943	1944	1945
MURRAY, Eileen				X			
NICHOLS, Perry		X*	X	X			X
NOBLE, Edith Henrietta					X		
NOWLIN, Eugenia C.			X			X	
PEEPLES, Nina	X*		X	X?			
PENDERGRASS, Roger			X	X	X		
PORTERFIELD, Pearl			X	X	X		
POTHOFF, Lois Helen					X	X	X
PRATHER, Virginia Russ				X			
REYNOLDS, Chang					X		
RICHARDS, Harper					X		
ROBERTSON, H. O.			X		X		X
ROSENFIELD, John, III			X				
SAWYER, Beebe				X	X	X	X
SCHOENFELDT, Henry H.			X		X	X	
SHUNNEY, Andrew					X		
SIMPSON, Dow			X	X	X	X	X
SINGLETARY, Olga							X
SKINNER, Frances		X*	X	X			
SMITH, Artine					X	X	X

Artist's Name	1939	1940	1941	1942	1943	1944	1945
SPEED, Rosalie		X*	X	X	X		X
SPRUCE, Everett		X*	X	X			
TAYLOR, Lura Ann				X		X	X
TENNANT, Allie			X				
TOOLEY, Marvin P.							X
TOWNSEND, Thurmond			X	X			
TRAVIS, O. H.			X				
URBACH, Amelia	X*	X*	X				
VOGEL, Donald S.				X	X	X	X
VOGEL, Hildegarde						X	X
VOGT, Augusta					X	X	
WALKER, Tecla				X	X		X
WALMSLEY, Elizabeth			X	X	X	X	X
WARLICK, Mildred					X	X	
WEBB, Frank S.				X	X	X	
WILLHITE, Jean Wagner							X
WILLIAMSON, Clara M.							X
WILSON, Douthitt		X*	X				
WINN, Mrs. Robert			X				
WOOLLEY, G. Livingston							X

* Special honors, P

176 DICTIONARY OF TEXAS ARTISTS

El Paso Woman's Club Exhibition, 1927-45

Artist's Name	1927	1935	1936	1937	1938	1940	1941	1942	1943	1944	1945
ACEVES, Bartolo			X								
ACEVES, Jose		X	X	X		X	X	X		X	
ACOSTA, Manuel						X					
AINSA, Marion	X										
AKIN, Horace										X	
ALBRIGHT, Frell									X		
ALFEREZ, Enrique			X								
ANDERSON, Florence M. (Mrs. S. S.)		X	X				X	X		X	
AUGUR, Ruth	X										
BAILEY, Mary Laws				X							
BAILEY, Mrs. Charles			X								
BALL, Kate (Mrs. Preston)		X	X	X	X		X	X	X	X	X
BARRETT, Robert										X	
BEAUBIEN, K. G.			X								
BERLON, Charles											X
BIGGERS, Mrs. N. L.					X						
BINKLEY, Betty			X				X				
BISHOP, Dr. Ida	X										
BISHOP, J. W.			X								
BLAKE, Beth		X									
BLINEBEERY, Frances									X		
BOONE, E. L.		X	X	X	X	X	X	X	X	X	X
BRENDLEY, Eleanor					X						
BRETZ, Mrs. L. N.										X	
BRICE, Louise							X				
BROOKS, F. S.				X							
BROOKS, Shelby			X								
BUCKANOU, Ella			X								
BURK, Robert	X										
BURLINGHAM, Hilda							X		X		
CAHERO, Emilio Garcia		X									
CAMPOS, Ruben Lara						X	X				
CANTRELL, Vivian (Mrs. Steve)								X		X	
CARLSON, Robert											X
CARROL, Ed W.			X		X	X	X				
CHERRY, Phyllis					X						
CISNEROS, Jose					X	X	X	X			
CLEAVELAND, James						X	X	X			X
CLICK, O'Bera					X						
CONGDON, Mrs. W. L.		X	X				X				
CONTRERAS, Jose						X					
CRAIG, Camille Kibler			X	X		X	X				
CRAIG, Mrs. R. C.			X								
CREWS, Seth Floyd	X	X	X	X	X	X	X	X		X	X
CUNNINGHAM, Mrs. E. N.						X	X		X	X	
DAVIS, Mrs. Lynn B.			X								
DEAN, Douglas					X						
DENTON, Lois		X	X	X	X	X	X				

Artist's Name	1927	1935	1936	1937	1938	1940	1941	1942	1943	1944	1945
DIAZ, Ricardo			X								
DOUGLAS, Richard										X	
EDWARDS, Mrs. Wiley M.		X	X	X			X				
ELLIOTT, Jouett Fall	X										
ELLIS, Fremont		X									
EMEREE, Berla Iyone	X	X	X	X	X	X	X	X		X	X
ERLICH, Jake		X	X	X							
FINDLEY, Mrs. H. F.			X								
FRANKLIN, Mrs. William						X					
FRASER, Mary Lee							X				
FREEMAN, Leola		X		X	X	X	X	X		X	
GALLAGHER, Richard						X				X	X
GENUNG, Robert		X		X	X	X		X	X	X	
GLASGOW, Octavia		X		X		X	X	X			
GONZALEZ, P. Carrillo		X		X		X	X	X	X		X
GOODELL, Mrs. Joe				X							
GOODWON, Lucy			X								
GORMAN BLACK, Mary Nichols	X			X				X			
GRAVES, Milton St. John	X										
GRAVES, Mrs. Milton		X			X						
GRAVES, Mrs. S.			X								
GREEN, Mrs. W. E.										X	
GROOMS, Mrs. Fred		X	X								
GUDGER, Muriel		X	X								
GUERRO, Gustave		X		X		X	X				
HAFFNER, Mrs. S.			X								
HAGGART, Mrs. Walter	X										
HALL, Lucille (Mrs. Norman)		X	X	X		X	X		X	X	
HAMILTON, Blanche								X	X	X	X
HAMLYN, Edwin			X								
HARLACKER, Mrs. John	X		X			X	X	X	X		X
HARRIS, Helen					X	X	X				
HARTMAN, Donald	X										
HATFIELD, K. L.			X								
HERMANN, Wanda						X	X	X			X
HERNANDEZ, William G.								X			
HERNDON, Maxwell		X	X								
HIBINO, Carl T.		X		X							
HICKS, Zetha			X			X	X				
HINKLE, Mrs. Stacy	X										
HOBBLE, Eloise						X	X	X	X	X	X
HUNT, Mrs. J. A. (J. H.)		X	X								
IZARD, Mrs. V. L.								X			
JANGRI, Jose			X								
JARVIS, J. T.						X					
JONES, Edwin				X							
KANE, Thomas								X	X		X
KELLOG, Charles								X			

El Paso Woman's Club Exhibition, 1927-45, Continued

Artist's Name	1927	1935	1936	1937	1938	1940	1941	1942	1943	1944	1945
KELLY, Mrs. A. R.							X				
KIDD, Hari		X	X	X		X	X		X	X	
KRAKAUER, Gustave		X	X	X							
KRIECHBAUM, Ethel (Mrs. J. R.)						X	X	X			X
KROEKEL, Mrs. Charles A.	X										
KUSIANOVICH, Daniel					X						
LAY, Mrs. Louis			X								
LEA, Tom		X	X	X		X	X	X			
LEDWARD, Mrs. William						X					
LEE, Mrs. R. E.			X								
LEGGETT, Lucille (Mrs. W. B.)			X		X	X	X		X		
LERNER, David						X					
LOMBARDI, A. N.		X	X	X						X	
LOOSE, William	X										
LOPEZ, Salvador										X	
LOVERT, Reuben						X					
MACIAS, E.			X								
MADDOX, Mrs. Roy G. (Maud)			X								
MANN, Kelly					X						
MANZANAREZ, Concepcion								X			
MARTIN, Mrs. A. A.						X	X	X		X	
MARTIN, Keith				X							
McCORMICK, Mrs. H. P.						X					X
McELROY, Michael								X		X	X
MEANS, Elliott					X		X				
MEISEL, Mrs. H. H.						X					
MELTON, Felicia Von Briesen					X	X	X	X		X	
MILAM, Annie	X										
MILLER, Grace Ann					X	X					
MILTON, Mrs. Bernett			X								
MITCHELL, Lillian			X								
MOMSEN (MOMSON), Mrs. Leo		X					X				
MONTGOMERY, Percy	X										
NICOLS, Audley Dean	X	X				X					
NORMAN, Mrs. A. J.								X			
OLD, Margaret									X	X	X
PAINE, Charles					X						
PAYNE, Mildred					X						
PEABODY, Rowena					X						
PERRY, Gerald				X	X	X					
RANK, Mrs. W. A.		X	X								
REDIC, Jack								X	X	X	X
REEVES, Elsie								X			
RICHARDSON, Bud	X										
RIDLEY, Dr. Ian				X							
RIPPETEAU, Hallie Crane			X								
ROBINSON, N. B.	X										
RODEHAVER, Gladys										X	

Artist's Name	1927	1935	1936	1937	1938	1940	1941	1942	1943	1944	1945
RUSSELL, Duke		X									
SCHRECK, Horst		X	X	X	X	X	X	X			
SCHULTZ, Mrs. R. H.							X				
SCHUSTER, Mrs. Frank			X								
SCHWARTZ, Irving		X	X	X		X	X	X			
SCOTT, Maj. T. E.	X										
SCOTT, Nell		X									
SHANNON, Aileen					X						
SHELTON, G. Harris		X	X	X			X	X			X
SHORES, Charles			X								
SKIPWORTH, Lucile										X	X
SMITH, Lowell											X
SMITH, Virginia		X									
SOLER, Urbici											X
STEEN, Mary										X	X
STOCKWELL, Mrs. Walter			X								
STREET, Mrs. J. C.		X	X			X					
STRONG, Grace			X								
SWEARINGEN, Mrs. W. E.									X		
TEEL, Lewis Woods	X	X	X	X	X	X	X	X		X	X
TEEL, Lewis, Jr.		X		X	X	X	X				
THURSTON, Eugene	X	X	X	X	X	X	X	X		X	X
THURSTON, Fern	X	X	X	X		X	X	X	X	X	X
TOCKER, Mrs. Phillip		X									
TURNER, Harvey									X		
VALENA, Sister Mary					X	X	X				
VON ZELL, Fredda										X	
WAGGONER, Harry		X									
WALKER, Jack						X					
WARNER, William R.		X									
WATKINS, Mrs. Sam	X										
WHITE, Mrs. E. A.										X	
WHITE, Rena									X		
WILSON, Hazel (Mrs. Buford)		X	X	X	X		X			X	
WINGO, Mrs. T. M.		X	X			X					
WISE, Vera					X	X	X	X			
WOOD, Jewel								X			
WRIGHT, Dudley		X	X								
YTURIAGA, Enrique					X						

ANKENEY, John S.
AUSTIN, Dorothy
BALTZELL, Marjorie
BLACKSHEAR, Kathleen
BOATRIGHT, Elizabeth Keefer
BOWLING, Charles T.
BRISAC, Edith M.
BROOKS, James
BROWN, Don
BROWN, Kenneth
BROWNE, Frederic
BUCHANAN, Laura
BURTON, Caroline
BURTON, Lura Mae
BYWATERS, Jerry
CANADAY, John
CARR, Bess
CHARLTON, Gene
CHERRY, E. R.
COOK, Margot
CRABB, Bob
CROWELL, Reid
DARGE, Fred
DAVID, Lorene
DAVIDSON, Ola McNeill
DAVIS, Jessie
DEANE, Granville M.
DELLENEY, Marie
DOUGLASS, John
DOZIER, Otis
EAST, Pattie R.
ECKFORD, Jessiejo
EISENLOHR, E. G.

ELDER, Inez Staub
ENSER, John F.
FISH, Alice (KINZINGER)
FRANKLIN, Ione
GARY, Cecil Fern
GENTRY, Nannie Mae
GIBSON, Henry Lee
GOFF, Lloyd
GONZALES, Boyer, Jr.
GONZALEZ, Xavier
GRANBERRY, C. R.
GREGORY, Jack W.
HARDIN, Ernest R.
HARPER, Roberta
HOGUE, Alexandre
HOLMES, Dwight C.
JOLLY, Wade
JOSSET, Raoul
KEATING, Mary Aubrey
KELLEY, Loucile
KING, Clinton
KINZINGER, Edmund
KOENIG, John
LA MOND, Stella Lodge
LACY, Lucile Land
LASELLE, Dorothy A.
LAWRENCE, Harry
LEE, Dean
LEMMON, Thetis
LENNOX, Martha
LESTER, William
MARGULES, Adalie
MAUZEY, Merritt

MAVERICK, Lucy
McCLUNG, Florence
McVEIGH, Blanche
MERRILL, W. Ralph
MOYER, Marvin
NEUHEISEL, Cecilia
NICHOLSON, John
OWEN, Michael
PEEPLES, Nina
PERINI, Maxine
PREUSSER, Robert
REEDER, Dickson
RICHARD, Camille
ROBERTSON, H. O.
ROBINSON, Isabel
RUSS, Virginia
SCHWARTZ, Sandra
SCRUGGS, Margaret Ann
SHIPP, Aloys Gossage
SPEED, Rosalie
SPELLMAN, Coreen Mary
SPRUCE, Everett
STAFFEL, Rudolf
STONE, Ruby
TENNANT, Allie Victoria
TRAVIS, Olin
TUPPER, Margaret W.
URBACH, Amelia
VANCE, Helen Blesi
WEISBERG, Marie L.
WOELTZ, Julius
WOOLDRIDGE, Lessi Ellen
WORTHINGTON, Virginia

Lone Star Printmakers Exhibition, 1938-41

Artist's Name	1938	1939	1940	1941	Artist's Name	1938	1939	1940	1941
BASSETT, Reveau	X		X	X	LESTER, William	X	X	X	X
BOWLING, Chas. T.	X	X	X	X	LOCKWOOD, Ward			X	X
BROWN, Don			X	X	MAUZEY, Merritt	X	X	X	X
BYWATERS, Jerry	X	X	X	X	MOZLEY, Loren				X
CARNOHAN, Harry	X				NICHOLS, Perry	X	X		
DOUGLASS, John	X	X	X	X	OWEN, Mike	X			
DOZIER, Otis	X	X	X	X	PACHL, Delmar				X
EISENLOHR, E. G.	X	X	X	X	ROBERTSON, H. O.	X	X	X	X
ELLIOTT, William			X	X	SPRUCE, Everett	X	X	X	X
HOGUE, Alexandre	X	X	X	X	STELL, Thomas M., Jr.	X			
KINZINGER, Edmund			X	X	TRAVIS, Olin	X		X	

Artist's Name	1927	1928	1929	Artist's Name	1927	1928	1929
ALLEN, Clarence	X			HARPHAM, Carolyn Rose	X		
ALTHEIDE, Harvi C.		X		HELLMAN, Bertha Louise	X		
ARPA, Jose	X	X+	X	HOGUE, Alexandre	X		
BACHOFEN, Max Alben			X	HOHNSTADT, Peter Lanz			X
BELL, Mrs. A. J.	X	X	X	HUDDLE, Nannie	X		
BLACKMON, T. Lawson		X+	X	JACKSON, Everett Gee	X	X	
BROCKMAN, Marie	X			KING, Gillis	X		
BRUCE, Granville T.			X	KINNEY, Mrs. John		X	
BRYAN, W. E.	X	X		KLEPPER, Frank			X
CHERRY, E. R.	X	X		LEBERMAN, Virginia	X		
CHRISTIANSON, Carl		X		McCLEARY, Kindred		X	
COLEMAN, Mrs. W. P.	X			McCULLOUGH, Max			X
COLLINS, Edna		X		McGILL, Eloise Polk	X	X	
COOK, Paul Rodda	X	X	X	MEWHINNEY, Ella K.	X	X	X
COSGROVE, Suzanna			X	MORGAN, Theo. J.		X+	X
CREWS, Seth Floyd	X	X	X	MOSELEY, Nell	X		
CROCKER, Edna Earl	X	X		NAVE, Royston	X	X	
CRONIN, Marie			X	NEUMANN, Gilbert	X		X
CROWTHER, Mrs. W. L.	X			NICHOLS, Mary Roberta		X	
DAVIDSON, Ola McNeill		X	X	NICOLS, Audley Dean	X	X+	X
DAWSON-WATSON, Dawson	X	X	X	PAGE, Harvey L.		X	
DAWSON-WATSON, Edward			X	PALMER, Jessie	X		
DeYOUNG, Harry A.			X	PALMER, Mrs. H. V.	X		
DIAZ, Emilio G.		X		PANCOAST, Clara C.		X	X
DOWNIE, Janet	X			PRESTOPINO, Gregorio			X
ECKFORD, Jessiejo			X	REEVES, Charlotte			X
EDSTROM, Miriam I.		X		RUTLAND, Emily			X
EDWARDS, Emily			X	SCHUBART, Fred C.			X
EISENLOHR, E. G.	X	X	X	SMITH, Alexa	X		
EMEREE, Berla Ione	X	X		SPELLMAN, Coreen Mary		X	X
ENSER, John F.	X		X	TAYLOR, Rolla	X	X	
EVERETT, Raymond	X			TEEL, Lewis Woods		X	
FLETCHER, Vallie	X			THURSTON, Eugene	X		
FOSTER, M.	X			TRACY, Helise (Helice?)			X
FOWLER, Eva	X			TUPPER, Margaret W.	X	X	X
GIDEON, Samuel E.	X	X		WALKER, Mrs. Phil			X
GONZALES, Boyer	X	X		WALKER, Mrs. W. P.	X	X	
GONZALEZ, Xavier			X	WANSLEY, Kate	X		
GORDON, Mrs. Clara F.	X			WEISSER, Mrs. Fred W.	X	X	X
GREEN, Ellis			X	WHEELER, Ellie	X		
GUDGER, Mureil Ruth		X		WILKINSON, Edward	X	X	
HAINES, Marie		X	X	WOOD, Robert		X	
HARDIN, Ernest R.	X						

San Antonio Local Artists Exhibition, 1930-36

Artist's Name	1930	1931	1932	1933	1934	1935	1936
ADAMS, Carleton W.			X				
ALTHEIDE, C. Harvi	X						X
ANGELL, Mrs. C. Roy				X	X		
ANTHONI, Lillian Prescott			X	X	X	X	X
ARPA, Jose	X			X			
ATKINSON, Marion Koogler						X	
BACHOVEN, Max		X	X				
BARNARD, Herbert							X
BELL, Blanche C.	X	X	X	X	X		
BENEDICT, Clifford L.				X			
BENNETT, Bertha				X	X	X	X
BENSON, Olive				X			
BENZAQUIN, Gold			X	X	X		
BERKOWITZ, Rosalie	X		X	X	X	X	
BETTER, Gladys B.			X				
BIERSCHWALE, Edna H.	X	X	X	X	X		
BITTER, Marion M. (Mrs. F. W.)		X			X		
BLAKE, Viola					X		
BODE, Ruth Simon	X	X					
BONNER, Mary				X	X		X
BRIGGS, Mae							X
BROBECK, Irvin	X	X					
BROUGHTON, Willie Riddle							X
BROWN, George C.						X	
BUCKLEY, Eleanor Ann	X						X
BUENZ, Fred J.		X					
CALDWELL, Marjorie				X			
CALHOUN, Mrs. M.	X			X			
CAMPBELL, Orville A.	X						
CANADAY, John				X			
CARDENAS, Edward		X	X	X			
CARR, Georgia							X
CARRINGTON, Joi Harrell		X					
CARSON, Miss M.		X					X

Artist's Name	1930	1931	1932	1933	1934	1935	1936
CARTTER, Myrtle					X		
CASE, Mrs. M. R.						X	
CASKEY, Lucile				X			
CHAPMAN, Joseph P.						X	
CHILTON, Alice	X						
CHRISTENSEN, Andrew		X	X	X	X	X	X
CLARK, Mary Lee							X
CLOONAN, F. A.	X			X	X	X	
COCKE, Bessie	X	X					X
COLEMAN, Florence			X				
COLEMAN, Mrs. W. P.	X						
COOK, Paul Rodda						X	
COONEY, Mary Wheeler	X		X	X	X	X	X
CORDER, Ruth		X					
COSGROVE, Suzanna	X	X					X
COWDEN, Mary S.						X	
CULMER, Lessi Wooldridge						X	
DALSEIMER, Rosalie	X	X					
DARGE, Fred					X		
DAVENPORT, Jack						X	
DAVIS, Martha	X						
DAWSON-WATSON, Edward				X		X	X
DAY, Hallie		X			X		
de BRECEDA, A. R.	X						
De YOUNG, Harry Anton				X	X	X	
DIEDRICH, B. H.				X			
DIXON, Tola		X		X	X		
DUGOSH, Ruby Evelyn				X	X	X	X
DURAN, Santa			X	X	X	X	X
EARNEST, Billy				X	X	X	X
EDWARDS, Emily					X	X	
EDWARDS, Frank M.						X	
EDWARDS, Mrs. O. D.	X						
EIGNUS, Everett			X				

San Antonio Local Artists Exhibition, 1930-36, Continued

Artist's Name	1930	1931	1932	1933	1934	1935	1936
ELLET, Lois						X	
ELLISON, Gussie	X	X					
ENSER, John	X	X	X				
FARIS, Polly					X		
FILIPPONE, J. C.	X		X	X	X		X
FLETCHER, Vallie				X			
FRANKE, Helen							X
FREE, Mrs. R. C.						X	
GARZA, Delio Flores						X	X
GLASSCOCK, Margaret							X
GOLSON, Mrs. Edward M.	X						
GONZALEZ, J. Reuben					X		X
GONZALEZ, Xavier		X		X	X		
GORDON, Clara F.		X					
GRAY, Estelle							X
GREEN, R. H.							
GREEN, Rena Maverick	X	X		X	X	X	X
GREENE, Ellis				X	X		
GREENING, C. R.		X					
GRIFFITH, John			X	X			
GRISWOLD, J. C.	X	X		X	X	X	X
GUERRA, Alfredo			X				
GUGENHEIM, Irma		X	X	X	X	X	
HAGNER, Lilly May		X				X	X
HALBARDIER, Mrs. E. W.					X		X
HALTOM, M. Hollis	X						
HARDMAN, Mary				X	X	X	
HARPER, Judith	X	X					
HARPHAM, Carolyn Rose	X	X	X	X	X		
HATFIELD, Larie	X				X		
HENDERSON, Dorothy				X			
HENDRICKS, Emma							X
HERRELL, Joi Faye						X	
HIGGINS, Mrs. C. C.		X		X			

San Antonio Local Artists Exhibition, 1930-36, Continued

Artist's Name	1930	1931	1932	1933	1934	1935	1936
HIGGINS, Sophia Shaw	X					X	
HINDERLANG, Edna		X			X		
HINNANT, Tom J., Jr.		X	X	X			
HOHNSTEDT, Peter	X		X				
HOLLERAN, W.					X		
HOLLOMAN, Guy W.	X	X	X	X	X		
HOPPE, Carl	X	X	X	X	X	X	X
JARVIS, W. F.	X						
JOHNSON, Ivan E.							X
JONES, Jeanette Milam							X
KARGL, Gillard			X	X	X		
KEATING, Mary Aubrey		X	X	X		X	X
KEIDEL, Albert					X		
KELSO, Lillian	X						
KING, M. A.				X	X		X
KING, Mrs. Wm.	X		X				
KING, Sally R.						X	X
KIRKWOOD, Rosa				X	X		
KLEINE, William C.				X			
KOONTZ, Gay			X				X
LACKEY, Ebba					X		
LACY, Mig						X	
LAUCK, Blanche M.	X						
LAUDERDALE, Ursula		X			X	X	X
LAZENBY, Georgia							X
LEADER, M. W.			X				
LEE, M. A.	X						
LEE, Mary Hornby					X		
LEWIS, John F.					X	X	
LEWIS, Lulia M.	X						
LOCKE, Lucie H.	X	X	X	X	X	X	
LONGACRE, Marion				X			
LOPEZ, Viveano						X	X
MACK, Alexander Watson					X		X

Artist's Name	1930	1931	1932	1933	1934	1935	1936
MAVERICK, Lucy						X	X
MAVERICK, Mary Adams		X					
MAVERICK, Mrs. Albert						X	
McCOMMON, Frances V.		X					
McDONALD, Mary							X
McDOWELL, Fritz							X
McFADDEN, Florence G.		X					
McFADDEN, Mrs. E. A.	X						
McFADDEN, Mrs. E. E.			X				
McGILL, Eloise Polk	X	X					
McGUIRE, Jack W.			X				
McGUIRE, Tom C.			X				
McKINNEY, Walter A.			X				
McLELLAN, J. M.					X		
McLELLAN, Jas. Lucretius	X	X					X
McLELLAN, Ralph		X			X		
McLELLAN, Sadie							X
McMAHAN, Peggy L.	X		X	X			
McNAUGHTON, Elizabeth B.			X	X	X	X	X
MEDELLIN, Octavio			X		X	X	
MEROUX, M.							X
MILLER, Olga Schroeder							X
MINTEL, Edwina				X	X		
MONTGOMERY, Bess				X			
MOSES, L. M.					X		
MUELLER, Lola	X					X	
MUELLER, Mrs. Fred		X					
NcNEEL, Jessie Maverick							X
NEIGHBORS, Camille	X	X	X				
NEUHEISEL, Cecilia			X			X	X
NEUMANN, Gilbert	X	X	X	X	X	X	X
NIXON, Wilson K.	X	X					
NOVICH, Morris	X	X	X	X		X	X
NUHFER, Olive		X	X		X		X
ODENA, Alfred			X				X
OLINGER, Larry V.		X		X			
PANCOAST, Clara	X	X	X	X			X
PANCOAST, Martha	X	X	X		X		
PARKHILL, M. Louise				X	X		X
PARKINSON, Margaret L.						X	
PASCHAL, Mary D.		X					
PETTY, Jessie W.	X	X	X	X	X		
PIERCE, Virginia					X		
POHL, Hugo D.		X		X		X	
PRYOR, Nell	X	X	X			X	
RABA, Ernst	X	X	X	X		X	X
RAHL, Ursula	X						
RAMOS, Fernando		X					
RAPHAEL, Frances					X		
RAWLINGS, Muriel Peterson							
RAWSON, Phillip N.			X				
RAYL, Edna K.		X		X	X	X	
REES, Lonnie	X	X	X		X	X	X
REICHERT, Vennie				X	X	X	X
RIEDNER, Ruth						X	X
RIVERA, Rafaela	X						
ROBIN, M. D.				X			
ROBINSON, C. K.						X	
ROBINSON, Jimmie					X		
RONEY, Harold A.	X	X	X	X	X	X	
SAEGERT, Frieda			X	X			
SANDERS, P. C. (Pedro)				X	X	X	X
SAVAGE, Jane	X	X					
SCHMARD, Roberta					X		
SCHUBART, F. C.				X			
SCHUTTER, H.	X						
SHEPLER, I. D.	X	X	X		X	X	X
SLIMP, Helen Fern	X	X			X	X	X

San Antonio Local Artists Exhibition, 1930-36, Continued

Artist's Name	1930	1931	1932	1933	1934	1935	1936
SMITH, Amanda	X						
SMITH, Helen			X				
SMITH, Jane	X	X	X				
SMITH, Mrs. J. T. (Alexa)	X	X	X	X	X		
SMITH, Olive H.		X	X				
SNODGRASS, Libby				X			
STAFFEL, Rudolf			X		X	X	
STALEY, Mary Louise							X
STANFORD, Minnie M.							X
STERNE, J. J.	X	X	X	X			
STERNE, Stella M.		X	X	X	X	X	
STOUT, Myron S.		X					
SULAICA, Anthony				X	X	X	
SWEETLAND, Dana Warner				X			
SWYERS, Amelia				X			
TAYLOR, Rolla	X	X	X	X	X	X	X
TEICHMUELLER, Minnette	X	X		X			
THURMOND, Ethel					X	X	
TODD, Viola L.			X			X	X
TOWNSEND, Elizabeth	X		X	X	X	X	X
TUPPER, Margaret Wright	X			X	X	X	X
TURNER, John H.	X						
VALENTINE, Edward	X			X			
VALERO, Jesus Rodriguez					X	X	
VANCE, Helen Blesi		X					
WAGNER, Emma S.	X						X

Artist's Name	1930	1931	1932	1933	1934	1935	1936
WALKER, Evelyn	X	X					
WALKER, Hannah (Mrs. Phil)	X	X	X		X	X	X
WALKER, Lonnie French						X	X
WARNER, Richard J.		X					
WARREN, Mallory Page		X				X	
WEISSER, Leonie Oelkers		X		X	X		X
WERNER, Richard						X	
WEST, Georgette		X	X	X			
WHEELER, Ellie	X		X	X			X
WHEELER, Mrs. A. C.		X					
WHITE, Carrie Harper					X		
WILLET, Oaul B.		X					
WILLIAMS, Katherine							X
WILSON, John B.						X	
WIMER, Cecile Janin	X		X		X		
WOELTZ, Julius		X	X	X	X		X
WOOD, Robert	X		X	X			
WOOD, Seth V.					X	X	
WOODS, J. Edward			X	X			
WOOLDRIDGE, Lessi Ellen	X		X		X		X
WORTHINGTON, Virginia							X
WRIGHT, Reba		X	X				
YOUNG, Pearl							X
ZACK, Peter				X			
ZEMAN, Edith				X			
ZWEIG, Irene Ormsby	X	X		X			

San Antonio Local Artists Exhibition, 1937-44

Artist's Name	1937	1938	1939	1940	1942	1943	1944
ACHNING, Estellyn			X	X			
ADAIR, Lucie						X	X
ADDIE, Gordon					X		
ALSUP, Katherine				X			
ALTHEIDE, Harvi	X						
ANDERSON, Anne							X
ANKROM, Francis		X					
ASHLEY, James F.						X	X
AXLEY, Martha		X				X	X
BARTEL, Arthur							X
BARTHA, Maria							X
BARTON, Martha				X			
BEACHMAN, Charles M.			X				
BECKER, Frederick W.	X			X			
BENNETT, Bertha	X			X		X	X
BERGAMO, Dorothy J.				X		X	X
BERKOWITZ, Rosalie			X	X		X	
BLACK, Harding	X	X	X	X			
BLACKMON, T. Lawson		X		X	X	X	
BODE, Ruth Simon	X						X
BOLTON, Grant						X	
BOYLES, Allan K.		X					
BRAND, Frances Christian	X	X	X	X	X	X	
BRIGGS, Mae	X						
BROWN, Mary Johnson							X
BURNSIDE, Erial	X						
CALDWELL, Marjorie						X	X
CARR, Georgia						X	X
CARRINGTON, Joi Harrell	X						
CARTTER, M. Gillett							X
CASKEY, Lucile				X		X	
CHASE, Susan B.		X	X				
CHERRY, E. R.		X	X				
CIAMPA, Anthony							X

Artist's Name	1937	1938	1939	1940	1942	1943	1944
CLARK, Lorena			X	X		X	X
CLARK, Mary Lee		X	X	X			X
CLEMMER, Thelma						X	
CLOONAN, F. A.						X	
COCKE, Bessie	X			X			
COLEMAN, Florence			X				
COMITO, Nicolas							X
CONTOIS, Isabel						X	
COOK, Paul Rodda	X	X		X			
COSGROVE, Suzanna	X						
COVERT, Lucile	X					X	
CULMER, Lessi Woolridge			X	X			
DE BROUILETTE, Francois			X	X		X	X
DE BROUILETTE, M. Henard				X			
DEAL, Homer T.							X
DECKERT, Verna		X					
DROUT, Rosalind M.				X			
DUER, Clara					X		
DUGOSH, Ruby Evelyn	X		X	X			X
DUMUTH, Werner							X
DURST, Frances			X				
EDMENSON, Fannie Mae							X
ENGELKING, R. S.			X				
FARNSWORTH, Otis		X	X	X			
FAUSETT, William Dean						X	
FEATHER, Henrietta Gibson		X					
FEIGERLE, Franz							X
FICKESSEN, Dot	X						
FITZGERALD, Elsie Luthy				X			
FRAZER, James						X	
FREE, Mary Arnold						X	X
GARZA, Delio Flores	X		X	X			
GENIESSE, Stephen						X	
GENTLE, Robert						X	

San Antonio Local Artists Exhibition, 1937-44, Continued

Artist's Name	1937	1938	1939	1940	1942	1943	1944
GILES, Lorita							X
GLASSCOCK, Margaret	X		X	X			
GONIEWICH, Arthur F.		X		X			
GONZALES, Boyer, Jr.	X	X	X				
GRAHAM, Sylvia							X
GRAY, Estelle		X		X			
GREEN, Rena Maverick	X	X	X	X	X	X	X
GRISWOLD, J. C.							X
HAGNER, Lilly May	X						
HALL, Margaret de Camp				X		X	X
HARRIS, Georgia M.		X		X		X	
HARRIS, Kenneth						X	
HEIRHOLZER, Joan							X
HENDRICKS, Bernice							X
HENDRICKS, Emma			X				
HERNANDEZ, Damaso				X			X
HERRICK, Anne							X
HIGLEY, H. D.		X	X				
HOHNSTEDT, Peter		X		X			
HUNTER, George			X				X
HUNTER, Warren		X	X	X			
IVES, Peggy				X			
JACKSON, Katherine			X				
JOHNSON, Ivan		X					
JONES, Paul							X
KARGL, Gilard					X		
KEATING, Mary Aubrey	X	X	X	X		X	
KING, J. J.	X	X	X			X	
KIRKSEY, Lola							X
KNESSR, Charles							X
KRAUS, Richard						X	
KUPFORSCHMID, Sidney John							X
LANDIS, David M.						X	
LARSON, Lesle							X

Artist's Name	1937	1938	1939	1940	1942	1943	1944
LEROUX, Margaret	X						
LEWIS, Joun						X	
LOCKE, Lucie H.				X			
LOCKWOOD, Ward						X	
LOOMIS, Jill S.						X	
MATHEWSON, Thomas C.							X
MAVERICK, Lucy	X				X		
McCAMPBELL, Mrs. James B.				X			
McDADE, Helen						X	X
McLELLAN, James Lucretius	X	X		X			X
McLELLAN, Ralph	X						
McLERNON, Nancy			X				
McNAMARA, Tom			X				
McNAUGHTON, Elizabeth	X						
McNEEL, Jessie Maverick	X						
McVEY, Leza							X
McVEY, William M.							X
MEDELLIN, Octavio	X	X	X	X			
MEYERS, Robert W.						X	
MORRISON, Karl R.							X
MUELLER, Lola	X	X	X	X	X	X	X
MYERS, A.						X	
NAYLOR, Alice				X		X	X
NEUHEISEL, Cecilia	X	X	X	X	X	X	X
NEUMANN, Gilbert	X						
NEWKIRK, Guyrah				X			
PAINE, Joseph Polley		X	X				
PANCOAST, Clara C.	X					X	
PHELPS, Warren			X				
PRATHER, Virginia Russ						X	X
PUGSLEY, Ethel Smith							X
QUINN, Elizabeth Suggs						X	
REED, Robert							X
REES, Lonnie	X	X	X	X	X	X	X

San Antonio Local Artists Exhibition, 1937-44, Continued

Artist's Name	1937	1938	1939	1940	1942	1943	1944
REICHERT, Vennie		X					
RICE, Dama Jones				X			
ROBERTS, Dorothy			X				
ROBERTS, Hazel			X	X			
RONEY, Harold A.	X	X			X	X	X
ROSEN, Charles					X	X	X
ROSS, Betsy							X
SCHOENBERGER, Edward T.							X
SCHROEDER, Olga	X						
SCHUBART, Eva Maria		X					
SCHUBART, Imelda		X					
SHAND, Terry, Jr.						X	X
SHIELDS, Susanna							X
SIEVERS, Albert		X					
SLIMP, Helen Fern					X		
SMITH, Ruth Connerly							X
SPEAR, W.		X					
STAFFEL, Rudolf	X						
STANFORD, Minnie		X					
STEINFELDT, Eric				X			
STELL, Tom			X	X			
STEPHENS, Seth H.			X		X	X	
STERNE, Stella M.					X	X	
STRAND, Charlotte				X			
STRIMBAN, Jack J.							X

Artist's Name	1937	1938	1939	1940	1942	1943	1944
SURGINER, Elizabeth				X			
SWANLUND, D. C.						X	
TALLEY, Thomasina	X						
TAUCH, Waldine		X		X			
TAYLOR, Rolla	X						X
THARSILLA, Sister M.						X	X
THOMPSON, Charles				X			
TODD, Viola L.				X		X	
TOWNSEND, Gerry			X				
TRUKA, Elizabeth						X	X
TUPPER, Margaret Wright	X	X					
URBACH, Amelia	X					X	X
VANCE, Helen	X						
VANCE, Katherine Hinton				X			
WADE, Ted							X
WALKER, Maurine			X				
WEITZ, Anne							X
WEST, Georgette					X		
WHEELER, Ellie			X			X	X
WHITE, Norman Robinette		X				X	X
WOELTZ, Julius	X						X
WORTHINGTON, Virginia	X		X	X			
WORTHMAN, Harry						X	
YOUNGER, Yucola				X			

Southern States Art League, 1924-39 (Texas only)

Artist's Name	1924	1925	1929	1933	1939
ARMSTRONG, Voyle N.	X				
AUGUR, Ruth Monro			X		
BELL, Mrs. A. J.			X		
BROCKMAN, Dorothy			X		
BROWN, Don					X
BULLOCK, Mary Jane McLean					X
CHERRY, E. R.	X	X	X	X	
CHILLMAN, James, Jr.		X			
CLARK, Minnie (Mary) Lee					X
CLAXTON, Virgie			X	X	X
COLLINS, Edna			X		
COOK, Paul Rodda			X		
COSGROVE, Suzanna			X		
COX, Abbie Rose					X
CRONIN, Marie			X		
DAVID, Lorene					X
DAVIDSON, Ola McNeill			X	X	
DAVIS, Helen Cruikshank				X	
DAWSON-WATSON, Dawson			X		
DAWSON-WATSON, Edward				X	
EAST, Pattie R.			X	X	
ECKFORD, Jessiejo			X	X	
EISENLOHR, E. G.	X	X			
EMIG, Adolph P.					X
ENSER, John			X		
EVERETT, Raymond			X		X
FISH, Margaret			X		
FLETCHER, Vallie			X	X	X
FOWLER, Eva			X	X	
FRITZ, Eleanor			X		
GARCIA, Antonio E.					X
GARRISON, Minta H. (Mrs. J. T.)				X	
GIDEON, Samuel E.			X		
GILLESPIE, Sallie Meredith				X	

Artist's Name	1924	1925	1929	1933	1939
GONZALES, Boyer	X				
GONZALES, Boyer, Jr.					X
GONZALEZ, Xavier			X		X
GREEN, Rena M.			X		X
GUILLOT, Ann				X	X
HAINES, Marie		X		X	X
HARRIS, Georgia M.			X		
HELLMAN, Bertha Louise			X	X	
HENRY, Rebecca			X	X	
HILL, Mary Vandenberge			X		
HOFFMAN, Polly			X		
HOGUE, Alexandre				X	
HOHNSTEDT, Peter L.			X		X
HOLT, Percy William		X			
HOULISTON, William James					X
HUDSON, Edith				X	
JACKSON, Everett Gee			X		
JOHN, Grace Spaulding	X	X			
KELLY, Loucile					X
KIEFNER, C. H.					X
KIRKLAND, Forrest				X	
KLEPPER, Frank	X	X		X	
LAUDERDALE, Ursula	X				
LAWRENCE, Kathleen					X
LINGAN, Penelope	X		X		
LOCKE, Lucie H.				X	X
LOWDEN, Elsie Motz				X	
McCLUNG, Florence					X
McCULLOUGH, Max			X		
McGILL, Eloise Polk	X		X		
McKENNA, Helen				X	
McNAY, Marian					
MEWHINNEY, Ella K.			X	X	X
MORGAN, Theo. J.			X	X	X

Southern States Art League, 1924-39 (Texas only), Continued

Artist's Name	1924	1925	1929	1933	1939
MUELLER, Lola					X
MUENCH, Julian R.			X		
NEUHEISEL, Cecilia					X
NICE, Blanch Heim					X
NOBLE, Mamie (Mrs. J. V.)			X	X	
ONDERDONK, Eleanor			X		
PALMER, Hattie V.			X		
PALMER, Jessie A.				X	
PANCOAST, Clara C.			X		
PETTY, Mrs. Thos. K.			X		
POOL, Eugenia Pope			X		
RATLIFF, Mrs. Walter B.	X				
REEDER, Dickson					X
REES, Lonnie					X
RICE, Lucy			X		
ROBINSON, Isabel				X	
RONEY, Harold A.				X	
RUTLAND, Emily				X	
SCHUMANN, Paul R.			X	X	
SEEWALD, Margaret				X	
SHARP, Minnie Lee					X

Artist's Name	1924	1925	1929	1933	1939
SMITH, Alexa			X		
SMITH, Sarah					X
TATE, Claire		X			
TAYLOR, Rolla			X		
TEESDALE, Christopher H.	X		X		
TENNANT, Allie Victoria				X	
THOMAS, M.				X	
THURMOND, Ethel					X
TIDDEN, Agnes Lilenberg	X		X		
TIDDEN, John Clark	X		X		
TUPPER, Margaret W.			X		
UHLER, Mrs. Ruth Pershing	X	X	X		
WALKER, Mrs. Phil			X		
WEISSER, Mrs. Fred W.			X	X	
WEST, Maud S.			X		
WHITE, Jessie Aline			X		X
WILDMAN, Caroline Lax					X
WILSON, Loma					X
YARBROUGH, Vivian Sloan			X	X	
ZIEGLER, Samuel P.			X		

Southern States Art League, 1940-45 (Texas only)

Artist's Name	1940	1941	1943	1944	1945
ACHNING, Estellyn	X	X	X	X	X
ALDEN, M. Lowell				X	
ASTIN, John Heard	X				
BEARDEN, Ed				X	
BERKOWITZ, Rosalie	X				
BOMAR, Bill		X			
BOWLING, Charles T.	X	X			
BRAND, Frances Christian	X	X			
BRISAC, Edith M.	X			X	
BROWN, Don		X			
BYWATERS, Jerry	X			X	
CARR, Georgie		X			X
CARTTER, M. Gillett				X	
CHARLTON, Gene		X			
CHERRY, E. R.		X			
CLACK, Clyde C.				X	
CLARK, Lorena		X			
CLARK, Minnie (Mary) Lee	X				
CLAXTON, Virgie	X	X			
COOK, Paul Rodda	X				
COX, Abbe Rose		X			
CROCKETT, Grace				X	
DAILEY, Modena Stroud					X
DAVID, Lorene	X	X	X		
DOZIER, Otis	X				
DRIVER, Rose Buford	X	X			
EAST, Pattie R.	X	X	X	X	
FARNSWORTH, Otis	X				
FEARING, Kelly				X	
FILSON, Genevieve Winnifred		X			
FOSTER, Cecile		X			

Artist's Name	1940	1941	1943	1944	1945
LACY, Lucile Land		X	X	X	X
LANDERS, Bertha				X	
LARSEN, Andrew		X			
LAWRENCE, Kathleen		X	X		X
LEA, Tom	X				
LINGAN, Penelope	X				
LOCKE, Lucie H.			X	X	X
LOCKWOOD, Ward	X				
LOVELADY, Ruth Philpott			X		
MAPLES, Barbara				X	
MAUZEY, Merritt			X	X	X
McCLUNG, Florence		X	X	X	X
McVEIGH, Blanche		X		X	X
McVey, William M.		X			
MEDELLIN, Octavio	X	X			
MEWHINNEY, Ella K.		X	X	X	X
MOZLEY, Loren				X	
MUELLER, Lola	X	X	X	X	
MURPHEY, Mimi			X	X	X
NEUHEISEL, Cecilia	X	X	X		
NICE, Blanche Heim		X		X	X
PALMER, Jessie A.				X	
PREUSSER, Robert O.		X			
REEDER, Dickson				X	X
REES, Lonnie	X				
ROBERTSON, H. O.		X			
RONEY, Harold A.				X	
SCHIWETZ, Edward M.	X				
SCOTT, Robert Gilliam					X
SHAPARD, Mary			X		
SHAW, Lois Hogue					X

Southern States Art League, 1940-45 (Texas only), Continued

Artist's Name	1940	1941	1943	1944	1945
FRANKLIN, Ione R.				X	
GARCIA, Antonio E.	X				
GLASSCOCK, Margaret	X	X			
GREATHOUSE, Bess					X
HAYS, Lena Bentley					X
HELFENSTELLER, Veronica	X	X	X		
HOULISTON, William James		X			
HUBBARD, Bess Bigham					X
HUGHES, Mildred	X	X			
HUGHS, Tincie	X	X			
HUNTER, George Lewis Cope	X				
ISAAC, Dell				X	X
JACKSON, Amy					X
JEFFRIES, Lucille				X	
JOY, Robert		X			
KEATING, Mary Aubrey	X	X			
KELLY, Loucile	X		X		
KING, Clinton		X			
KINZINGER, Edmund		X			
SIMPSON, Dow					X
SINGLETARY, Olga					X
SKINNER, Frances			X	X	
SMITH, Emily Guthrie			X	X	X
SMITH, Robin Artine				X	X
SPELLMAN, Coreen Mary				X	
THOMSON, Adele Underwood					X
TRANTHAM, Harrelle		X			X
UHLER, Ruth Pershing		X			
URBACH, Amelia	X				
UTTER, Bror					X
VOGT, Augusta				X	
WATSON, Marguerite Thompson				X	
WHITE, Jessie Aline	X				
WHITEHOUSE, Eula					X
WILDMAN, Caroline Lax	X		X	X	
WISE, Vera				X	X
WORTHINGTON, Virginia	X				

State Fair of Texas Exhibition, 1901-20

Artist's Name	1901	1906	1907	1908	1909	1910	1913	1920
ABRAMS, Lucien				X	X			
ARPA, Jose	X							
BOCK, Charles P.				X	X	X		
BOLTON, Hale W.								X
BROWN, Tom			X					
CASTELUCHO, Claudio				X				
CRONIN, Marie							X	
CUPRIEN, Frank						X		
EISENLOHR, E. G.		X			X	X	X	X
GONZALES, Boyer					X	X	X	X
GRIFFITH, L. O.					X			
GUDE, G. E.								X
HAGENDORN, Max				X	X			
HARRELL, C. E.			X					
HARRIS, Elias B.						X		
KUNZ-MEYER					X	X		
LAUDERDALE, Ursula								X
McMILLAN, Geo. L.					X			
ONDERDONK, Julian			X	X	X		X	X
ONDERDONK, Robert	X		X	X	X	X	X	
REAUGH, Frank	X		X	X	X		X	X
SHEPARD, Anne Blake					X			
SIMKINS, Martha							X	
TRAVIS, Olin H.								X
TROWBRIDGE, Caroline A.				X				

Artist's Name	1921	1922	1923	1924	1925	1926	1927	1928	1929	1930
ABRAMS, Lucien			X							
BASSETT, Reveau				X		X	X	X		X
BEWLEY, Murray		X	X	X		X		X		
BONNER, Mary						X				
BRUNET, Adele								X		
CUPRIEN, Frank			X	X		X	X	X		
DAVIS, Jessie								X		
ECKFORD, Jessiejo		X	X	X		X	X	X		X
EISENLOHR, E. G.		X	X	X		X	X	X		X
HILL, R. Jerome		X		X				X		
HOGUE, Alexandre								X		
HORST, Frank		X								
KLEPPER, Frank						X	X	X		X
LAUDERDALE, Ursula			X			X	X	X		
MUMMERT, Sallie Blythe				X		X				
REAUGH, Frank		X	X	X		X	X	X		X
ROUNTREE, Ralph							X	X		
SIMKINS, Martha				X		X	X	X		X
STELL, Thomas M.								X		
TENNANT, Allie							X	X		X
TRAVIS, Kathryne H.			X			X	X	X		X
TRAVIS, Olin H.		X	X	X		X	X	X		
WHITE, Jessie Aline								X		

Artist's Name	1931	1932	1933	1934	1935	1936	1937	1938	1939
ALBRIGHT, Lloyd L.									X
ANKENEY, John S.	X			X					
AUSTIN, Dorothy	X			X					X
BAILEY, Carden									X
BASSETT, Reveau	X			X					
BESSELL, Evelyne Byers								X	
BEVERLY, E. N.									X
BEWLEY, Murray	X								
BLACKSHEAR, Kathleen								X	X
BOATRIGHT, Elizabeth Keefer								X	
BONNER, Mary								X	
BOWLING, Charles T.				X				X	X
BRISAC, Edith M.								X	X
BRUCE, Granville				X					
BRUNET, Adele Laure	X			X					X
BRUSH, Maurine									X
BUCHANAN, Laura	X			X				X	X
BYWATERS, Jerry	X		X	X				X	X
CARNOHAN, Harry				X					
CARR, Bess									X
CHARLTON, Gene									X
CHERRY, E. R.	X			X					X
COOK, Paul Rodda									X
CRABB, Bob								X	
CROWELL, Reid								X	X
CULWELL, B. L.									X
DARGE, Fred									X
DAVIS, Jessie	X			X				X	X
DAWSON-WATSON, Dawson				X					
DEANE, Granville M.								X	
DeBORD, Marjorie Evelyn								X	X
DELLENEY, Marie								X	
DIAL, Dan								X	
DOLEJSKA, Frank								X	X
DOUGLASS, John				X					
DOZIER, Otis			X	X				X	
DRIVER, Rose									X
DUGOSH, Ruby Evelyn									X
ECKFORD, Jessiejo	X			X					
EISENLOHR, E. G.	X		X	X				X+	X
ELDER, Inez Staub				X				X	X
ELLIOTT, William				X					
ENSER, John F.				X					
FALL, Frieda Kay									X
FISHER, Frank									X
FOWLER, Eva	X								
GARCIA, Antonio E.									X
GIBSON, Harry Lee								X	

Artist's Name	1931	1932	1933	1934	1935	1936	1937	1938	1939
GOFF, Lloyd	X								
GOLDSTEIN, Louise Marks								X	X
GONZALES, Boyer, Jr.	X							X	X
GRANDSTAFF, Harriett				X					
GUILLOT, Ann				X					
HARDIN, Ernest R.									X
HELFENSTELLER, Veronica								X	
HELLMAN, Bertha Louise									X
HENKEL, Estella M.									X
HIGGINS, Victor									X
HILL, R. Jerome	X			X					
HOGUE, Alexandre	X		X	X				X	
HORNER, Ruth									X
HOULISTON, William James								X	X
HUNGERFORD, Homer									X
HUNTER, R. Vernon			X	X					
JESTER, Ralph	X								
JOYNER, Arista A.									X
JOYNER, Howard W.									X
KEATING, Mary Aubrey								X	X
KIDD, Hari								X	X
KING, Clinton	X								
KINZINGER, Alice Fish								X	
KINZINGER, Edmund								X	
KIRKLAND, Forrest				X					
KLEPPER, Frank	X		X	X					X
LA MOND, Stella Lodge								X	X
LACY, Lucile Land								X	
LANDERS, Bertha M.									X
LANDON, Winnifred								X	
LAWRENCE, Harry Z.				X					
LEMMON, Thetis								X	X
LESTER, William			X					X	X
LIGON, Verda								X	
LITTLEJOHN, Margaret Martin								X	
LOCKHART, George									X
MAPLES, Barbara								X	
MARGULES, Adalie								X	
MARTIN, J. B.				X				X	X
MATLOCK, Ruth Blanks								X	
MAUZEY, Merritt								X	X
McCLAIN, George M.									X
McCLUNG, Florence								X	X
McVEIGH, Blanche								X	
MEWHINNEY, Ella K.				X				X	X
MEYSENBURG, Virginia C.									X
MILLER, Mrs. W. Maurice								X	
MIMS, Louise Holden								X	X

Artist's Name	1931	1932	1933	1934	1935	1936	1937	1938	1939
MOYER, Marvin									X
MOZLEY, Loren									X
MULLIS, Mrs. Rex									X
MURPHEY, Mimi								X	
NEUHEISEL, Cecilia								X	X
NICE, Blanch Heim									X
NICHOLS, Alice Welty								X	
NICHOLS, Nell Brooks								X	
NICHOLS, Perry				X					
NICHOLSON, John								X	
PALMER, Jessie				X					
PARKER, Ella Estill									X
PEEPLES, Nina								X	
PREUSSER, Robert								X	X
REAUGH, Frank				X					X+
ROUNTREE, Ralph				X					
SCHIEFFER, William B.									X
SCRUGGS, Margaret Ann				X					
SHARP, Florence C.								X	
SHIPP, Aloys Gossage								X	
SIMKINS, Martha	X			X					
SKINNER, Frances								X	X
SMART, Frank									X
SPEED, Rosalie								X	X
SPELLMAN, Coreen Mary								X	X
SPENCER, Icy									X
SPRUCE, Everett			X					X	X
STELL, Thomas			X	X					
STEVENS, Kelly H.				X				X	X
STOKES, Pauline									X
STONE, Ruby			X						
STOREY, Evlyn									X
STRAHALM, Franz	X			X					
STROHMAYER, A. F.	X			X					
TAYLOR, Lura Ann									X
TENNANT, Allie Victoria	X		X	X					X
TOWNSEND, Thurmond								X	X
TRAVIS, Diane									X
TRAVIS, Kathryne Hail	X								
TRAVIS, Olin Herman	X		X	X					X
TRUITT, Una								X	
URBACH, Amelia								X	X
WALMSLEY, Elizabeth				X					
WHITE, Jessie Aline				X				X	
WILLSON, Robert								X	
WILSON, Douthitt								X	X
WINN, James Buchanan, Jr. (Buc	X			X					
YARBROUGH, Vivian				X					

Artist's Name	1910	1911	1912	1913	1914	1915	1916	1917	1918	1919	1920
ABRAMS, Lucien				X	X		X	X			
ANDERSON, Margaret							X				
ANDERSON, Mrs. Marvin C.							X				
BAILEY, Mynnye Moly				X	X		X			X	X
BARSE, Mrs. Robert		X									
BEWLEY, Murray	X	X	X	X		X	X				X
BLOOMFIELD, James									X		
BOCK, Charles Peter	X			X							
BOLTON, Hale William					X	X			X	X	
BOUCHARD, Thomas											X
BRADFORD, G. R.									X		
BROOKS, Mabel H.				X	X	X					
BROWN, Donnell							X				
BROWN, Tom Linn	X	X	X	X	X	X		X			X
BRYAN, W. E.		X		X							
BUCHANAN, Laura							X				
CHERRY, E. R.		X			X	X		X	X	X	X
CLANCY, Eliza R.										X	
COCKRELL, Dura Brokaw		X		X	X	X	X	X	X	X	X
CONNER, Mrs.							X				
CRAWFORD, Dorsey Gibbs										X	
CRONIN, Marie					X						X
CUPRIEN, Frank W.		X									
DARTER, Mary Sue							X		X	X	X
DAVID, Selim A.	X										
DAWSON-WATSON, Dawson								X	X	X	X
DOKE, Sallie George (Mrs. Fred)						X	X	X			X
DORAN, Robert C.									X		
DOUGLAS, Lucile				X							
DUNLAP, Ellen L.			X	X	X						
ECKFORD, Jessiejo							X	X	X	X	X
EISENLOHR, E. G.	X		X	X	X	X	X	X	X	X	X
ELMENDORF, Stella			X	X	X	X					
FOWLER, Eva (Evangeline)		X		X	X	X			X		X
GONZALES, Boyer			X	X	X	X	X	X	X		
GRAHAM, Mysie (Mrs. Tillghma	X				X						
GREATHOUSE, Mrs. G. W.						X					
GUDE, Gerard E.									X		
HACKETT, Nelson G.	X		X	X							X
HAGENDORN, Max	X										
HILL, R. Jerome								X	X	X	
JENKINS, John Elliott					X	X					
JONES, C. H.									X		
JONES, Esther A.									X	X	X
JONES, Mable		X									
KLEPPER, Frank X. E. L.			X			X	X	X	X		X
KNOTT, John F.	X			X	X		X				
KUNZ-MEYER	X										
LANE, Lilly			X								

Artist's Name	1910	1911	1912	1913	1914	1915	1916	1917	1918	1919	1920
LAUDERDALE, Ursula								X	X		X
LEDGERWOOD, Ella Ray	X	X	X	X	X	X		X	X	X	X
LINGAN, Penelope						X					
LITTLEJOHN, Margaret	X	X	X	X	X		X	X		X	
MacDONALD, Mrs. R. H.									X		
MacKENZIE, M.									X		
MacLEAN, Christina	X	X	X		X	X	X	X	X	X	
McCAN, J. Ferdinand						X					
McDERMOTT, Cecilia							X				X
McGEE, W. T.					X			X			
McGILL, E. P.			X								
McLELLAN, Ralph				X							
McLENDON, Louise								X			
McMILLAN, Mary Jane	X	X	X								
MELTON, Mrs. Jesse J.	X										
MENDENHALL, Emma											X
MILAM, Anne Nelson			X	X			X	X	X	X	
MILAM, Mrs. R. L.		X									
MOODY, Henry			X		X	X					
MUMMERT, Sallie B.			X	X	X	X	X	X	X	X	X
NAUGLE, Lela									X		
NAVE, Royston	X		X	X	X	X	X				X
ONDERDONK, Julian		X	X	X	X	X		X			
ONDERDONK, Robert Jenkins		X	X	X	X		X				
RAGLAND, Portia Juanita								X	X		
RANDALL, La Baume Elliott											X
REAGAN, Ronna					X						
REAUGH, F.	X	X		X	X			X	X		X
ROGERS, Aileen Spencer						X					
ROSS, Sue Robertson										X	
SELLORS, Evaline Clark											X
SHARON, Jessie M.		X									
SIMKINS, Martha					X	X	X				
SLOAN, Jas. Blanding					X	X	X	X			
SLOAT, Blanche A.									X		
SPEER, Anniola											X
STRONG, Grace	X										
TARVER, Nell											X
TAYLOR, Harry										X	
TRAVIS, Olin H.					X	X	X	X	X		X
VAUGHAN, Ernest											X
VINSON (MITCHELL), Gladys M.						X	X	X	X	X	X
WATKINS, Mrs. W. J.			X								
WEEKLEY, Mary											X
WILLCOX, Rayte			X								
WRAGG, Eleanor		X									
WRIGHT, Gladys Yoakum										X	
YATES, Winifred					X				X		
ZIEGLER, Samuel P.									X	X	X

Texas Artists Exhibition at Fort Worth Index, 1922-30

Artist's Name	1922	1923	1924	1925	1926	1927	1928	1929	1930
ALLEN, Dan Elbert				X					
ALLEN, Mrs. F. W.					X			X	X
ALLEN, Mrs. George							X		X
ANDERSON, Margaret									X
ANDERSON, Mrs. M. C.		X		X					
ANDRESS, Annie Lee									X
ARMSTRONG, Voyle Naville					X	X			
ARPA, Jose				X	X	X	X		X
BAILEY, Beatrice S.									X
BAILEY, Russell					X	X			
BAKER, Ora Phelps									X
BAKER, William Henry									X
BASSETT, Reveau Mott		X	X	X	X	X			
BEHREND, Ella Beall					X	X	X	X	X
BEWLEY, Murray		X	X	X		X	X	X	X
BIGGERS, Mrs. N. L.			X			X			
BILLINGSLEY, Alys					X	X	X		
BLACKSHEAR, Kathleen									X
BOLDING, Nola				X					
BOLTON, Hale William	X								
BONNER, M.							X	X	
BOREN, Esther A. Jones	X	X							
BRISBINE, Margaret					X		X		
BROOKS, Mabel H.	X	X							
BROWN, Tom Linn	X	X							
BRUNET, Adele Laure							X	X	X
BRYAN, W. E.	X					X			
BUCHANAN, Laura			X	X	X	X		X	
BUCK, William Quinn							X	X	
BUIE, Helen Spencer									X
BULLOCK, Mary J. McLean						X	X	X	X
BYWATERS, Llewellyn		X							
CALDER, Frank Hill	X	X							
CAMMOCK (CAMMACK?), John F.				X	X				
CAMPBELL, Earl							X		
CANTEY, Maurine M. (Mrs. Craig C.)						X	X		X
CARD, Lottie Holman				X					X
CARSON, Lissa Bell	X								
CHERRY, E. R.	X	X	X	X		X	X	X	X
CHILLMAN, James, Jr.				X	X				
CHRISTIANSON, Carl					X	X	X	X	
COCKRELL, Dura B.	X	X	X						
COLEMAN, Harvey B.					X	X	X		
COLEMAN, Mary Darter		X		X	X	X	X		
COLEMAN, Mrs. W. P.						X			
COLLIER, Jack Atherton					X	X	X	X	X
COLLINS, Edna Gertrude				X	X	X	X	X	X
COMBE, Mary Postell	X								X

Artist's Name	1922	1923	1924	1925	1926	1927	1928	1929	1930
COOK, Paul Rodda						X	X	X	X
COSGROVE, Suzanna (Mrs. Jas. A.)								X	
COTTON, Leo	X	X							
CREWS, Seth Floyd						X		X	X
CRONIN, Marie							X	X	X
CROSS, Verna M.		X	X		X	X			
CROWTHER, Mollie L.		X	X						
CUSACK, Charles				X	X				
DAGGETT, Vivian S.			X	X	X	X			
DARTER, Dick			X						
DAVIDSON, Ola McNeill			X	X	X	X	X	X	X
DAWSON-WATSON, Dawson	X							X	X
DE YOUNG, Harry Anthony									X
DICKSON, Lillian R. (Mrs. Henry)						X	X	X	X
DILLARD, Emma D.									X
DOKE, George (Mrs. Fred)	X	X	X	X		X	X	X	
DOUGLASS, John E.						X			
DOW, Nell Pierce			X		X		X		
DOWNIE, Janet				X	X	X	X	X	X
DOZIER, Otis						X			
DRIVER, Beulah			X						
DUER, Clare Mae							X	X	
DURRETT, Nell M.									X
DuVALL, Jo						X			
EAST, Pattie R.			X	X	X	X	X	X	X
EBERHARDT, Eugenia McCorkle		X				X	X	X	X
ECKFORD, Jessiejo	X	X	X	X	X	X	X	X	X
EDWARDS, Emily	X								
EISENLOHR, E. G.	X	X?	X	X	X	X	X	X	X
ELMENDORF (TYLOR), Stella	X								
EMEREE, Berla Iyone							X	X	X
EMERY, Nellie Augusta	X	X	X	X	X	X	X		
ENSER, John F.						X	X	X	X
EVANS, Margaret					X				
EVERETT, Raymond	X			X	X	X	X	X	X
FALL, Willie Kay							X	X	X
FARMER, Evangeline				X					
FISH, Margaret							X	X	X
FLETCHER, Vallie					X		X	X	
FOSTER, Grace					X				X
FOWLER, Eva (Evangeline)				X	X		X	X	X
FRANKLIN, Geraldine					X	X	X	X	
FRITZ, Eleanor V. (Mrs. E. B.)						X	X	X	X
GARRETT, Mrs. M. K.							X		
GIDEON, Samuel E.	X			X	X	X	X		X
GILLESPIE, Sallie Meredith					X		X		X
GJURANOVIC, Mato		X		X					
GLASS, Frances W.					X				

Artist's Name	1922	1923	1924	1925	1926	1927	1928	1929	1930
GOFF, Lloyd L.				X	X	X	X	X	X
GOLDSTEIN, Louise Marks							X		
GONZALES, Boyer	X	X	X	X		X		X	
GONZALES, Xavier									X
GRAY, Margaret					X				X
GREATHOUSE, Carrie (Mrs. G. W	X	X	X	X	X		X		X
GRIGGS, Kate Brown					X		X		
GRUBBS, Kathleen								X	
GUILLOT, Ann	X	X			X	X	X		X
GUTHRIE, Emily								X	
HAINES, Marie Bruner						X	X	X	X
HALTOM, Minnie Hollis	X	X	X	X	X	X		X	X
HANSEN, Douglas Reid					X		X		
HARDIN, Ernest R.						X	X	X	X
HARPHAM, Caroline Rose						X			
HARWELL, Jerry, Jr.								X	X
HAWKINS, Elva Jane									X
HAZLEWOOD, Dollie									X
HELLMAN, Bertha Louise					X		X	X	X
HENDRICKS, Emma (Mrs. H. G.)						X	X	X	
HENRY, Rebecca Harriett						X	X	X	
HILL, Robert Jerome	X	X	X	X	X	X	X	X	
HOGUE, Alexandre				X	X	X	X	X	X
HOHNSTEDT, P. L.									X
HOLMES, Dwight Clay				X	X	X	X	X	X
HOLT, P. William		X	X	X					
HORN, Joe Roscoe						X	X	X	
HUDDLE, Nannie Z. (Mrs. W. H.)					X	X	X	X	X
HUDSON, Edith F. (Mrs. C. E.)							X		
HUGHES, Bess					X	X	X		
JACKSON, Everett Gee						X	X		
JARVIS, W. Frederick			X						
JEZ, Louise							X	X	X
JOHN, Grace S.				X	X				X
JOHNSON, Minnie W.							X		
JOHNSTON, Jessie Margaret									X
JONES, Laura	X	X							
JONES, Ruth M.					X	X	X		
KARL, Mabel Fairfax							X	X	
KEATING, Mary Aubrey									X
KEENER, Anna E.						X			
KING, Clinton Blair			X	X	X	X	X	X	X
KING, Walter Gillis						X			
KIRKLAND, Forrest	X								
KLEPPER, F. X. E. L.	X	X	X	X	X	X	X	X	
KRAFT, Emma Belle						X			
LAUDERDALE, Ursula	X	X			X		X		
LEBERMAN, Virginia					X	X	X	X	X

Artist's Name	1922	1923	1924	1925	1926	1927	1928	1929	1930
LEDGERWOOD, Ella Ray		X		X	X	X	X	X	X
LINQUIST, Margaret (Mrs. John)			X				X	X	X
LITTLEJOHN, Margaret			X	X	X	X	X	X	X	X
LONG, Eulah Biggers			X	X					
LOPEZ, Pedro	X								
MacDONNELL, Angela (M. A.)					X				
MacFADDEN, N.					X				
MacLEAN, Christina		X	X	X	X	X	X	X	X
MARTIN, J. B.			X	X	X	X	X	X	X
MARTIN, Trix					X				
MASTIN, Mignon			X						
MAVERICK, Lucy Madison	X								
McCARTHY, Mrs. Victor						X	X	X	X
McDERMOTT, Cecelia	X	X							
McFADDEN, Florence N.								X	
McGEE, Will T.			X	X					
McGILL, Eloise Polk	X	X	X	X		X	X	X	X
McGILL, Leona Leti						X			
McIVER, Portia Ragland	X	X					X		
McLAUGHLIN, Katherine									X
McLELLAN, Henry H.							X	X	X
McVEIGH, Blanche							X		X
MEWHINNEY, Ella K.				X	X	X			X	X
MITCHELL, Gladys Vinson	X	X	X	X					
MOORE, Percy Caruthers				X	X				
MORRIS, Lena					X				
MOSELEY, Nell			X	X	X	X	X	X	X	X
MUENCH, Julian Rhodes					X				
MUMMERT, Sallie B.	X	X	X	X	X	X	X	X	X
NASH, Nancy Kate				X					
NAVE, Royston	X	X			X				
NICOLS, Audley Dean						X			
NILSON, Gurine				X	X				
NOBLE, Mamie (Mrs. J. V.)						X	X	X	X
O'DONOHOE, Margaret									X
ONDERDONK, Julian			X	X					
OVERTON, Nan	X	X	X	X	X	X	X		
OWEN, Mrs. W. B.				X					
OWENS, Annie Laura (Mrs. Harry)								X	X
PALMER, Hattie V. (Mrs. C. F.)			X			X			
PALMER, Jessie A.				X	X	X	X	X	X
PANCOAST, Clara Caffrey									X
PEARCE, Mary Blake						X			
PENROD, Viola D.		X							
PETTY, Mrs. Thos. K.							X	X	X
PITTMAN, Beryl					X				
POHL, Hugo D.				X	X	X	X	X	X
POOL, Eugenia Pope							X		X

Artist's Name	1922	1923	1924	1925	1926	1927	1928	1929	1930
RANKIN, Margaret Fern							X		
RATLIFF, Mrs. Walter		X	X	X					
RAY, Alice		X							
REAUGH, Frank	X	X	X	X	X	X	X	X	
RICHART, Lucille									X
ROBINSON, F. Leroy									X
ROBINSON, Thelma V.					X		X	X	X
ROSE, Edwin Lawrence	X	X	X						
ROSS, Sue Robertson (Mrs. Zeno)									X
ROUNTREE, Ralph S.							X		
RUDMOSE, Zena L.			X	X					
RUHLIN, Helena Carlstad		X	X	X	X				
SALT, Anastasia							X	X	X
SANDERS, Mrs. A. H.						X	X	X	X
SCHUMANN, Paul R.		X	X	X	X	X	X	X	X
SEWALL, Blanche Harding			X	X					
SHOCKLEY, Pearle			X						
SIMKINS, Martha					X	X	X		X
SIMPSON, Wallace					X		X	X	X
SMITH, Gean				X	X	X	X		
SPEER, Anniola	X								
SPELLMAN, Coreen Mary							X	X	X
SPENCER, Henry Cecil							X		
SQUYRES, Willie			X						
STEVENS, Walter					X	X	X	X	
STRAHALM, Franz	X	X	X	X	X	X			X
STRONG, Grace				X					
SULLIVAN, Edna (Mrs. J. P.)								X	
TARVER, Nell H. (Mrs. Chas.)		X	X	X	X	X	X	X	X
TATE, Claire				X					
TAYLOR, Rolla S.	X	X		X	X	X		X	X
TEESDALE, Christopher H.	X	X	X	X	X	X	X	X	X
THOMAS, Frances E.			X	X	X		X	X	X
THOMPSON, Elaine Trulove						X			
THURSTON, Eugene						X	X		
TIDDEN, Agnes Lilienberg				X	X				
TIDDEN, John Clark				X					
TONKIN, Linley M.			X	X	X		X	X	
TRAVIS, Kathryne Hail		X	X	X	X	X	X		
TRAVIS, Olin H.		X	X	X	X	X	X		
TUPPER, Margaret Wright						X	X		X
TURNER, Ida L.						X			
TURNER, Miss Joe (Josephine?)									X
UHLER, Ruth P.			X	X	X	X			
VENNING, Mary Laura E.									X
WALKER, Hanna M. (Mrs. W. P.)						X			
WALLER, Mary (Mrs. Harold B.)	X	X	X	X	X	X	X	X	X
WANSLEY, Kate			X	X		X	X	X	X

Artist's Name	1922	1923	1924	1925	1926	1927	1928	1929	1930
WARD, Mrs. W. B.				X					
WEBB, Esther Elizabeth							X	X	X
WEISE, Paul R.		X	X						
WEISSER, Mrs. Fred W.						X	X	X	X
WELLS, Willie Sheets	X	X	X	X	X	X			
WHEATLEY, Helen Margaret							X	X	X
WILKINSON, Edward					X	X			
WILSON, Grace Louise			X	X	X				
WILSON, Robert, Jr.						X			
WINNER, Cecile Janin									X
WITHERSPOON, Mary Eleanor									X
YARBROUGH, Vivian Sloan								X	X
ZIEGLER, Sammuel P.	X		X	X	X	X	X	X	X

Texas Artists Exhibition at Fort Worth Index, 1931-37

Artist's Name	1931	1932	1933	1934	1935	1936	1937
ALBRIGHT, Lloyd L.						X	X
ALLEN, Mrs. F. W.		X	X	X	X		
ALLEN, Mrs. Geo.		X	X				
ANDERSON, Florence A. M. (Mrs. S. S.)				X	X	X	
ANKENEY, John S.	X		X	X			X
ASHMORE, Rose							X
ATKINSON, Marion				X	X		
AUSTIN, Belle				X	X	X	X
BAILEY, Beatrice							
BAKER, Ora Phelps	X	X	X	X	X	X	X
BAKER, William Henry	X	X	X	X	X	X	X
BALTZEL, Marjorie					X		
BEHREND, Ella Beall	X	X	X	X	X	X	X
BELL, Corinne Elizabeth						X	X
BLACKSHEAR, Kathleen	X	X	X	X	X	X	X
BOATRIGHT, Elizabeth Keefer					X		X
BONNER, Mary		X	X				
BOULTON, Joseph Lorkowski	X	X		X			
BOWLING, Charles T.				X			X
BRILES, Worthie Harwood						X	X
BRISAC, Edith Mae					X		X
BRISBINE, Margaret			X				
BROBECK, Irvin	X						
BROOKS, Helen				X			
BROWN, Don						X	
BROWN, Olivia		X	X				
BROWN, Rose							X
BRUNET, Adele Laure	X	X		X	X		X
BRYAN, W. E.		X			X		X
BUCHANAN, Laura	X	X	X	X	X	X	X
BUCHANAN, Louise			X	X			
BUCK, William Quinn	X	X	X	X	X	X	X
BUGBEE, Harold Dow					X		
BULLOCK, Mary J.	X	X	X	X	X	X	X

Artist's Name	1931	1932	1933	1934	1935	1936	1937
BUNTYN, Edrie			X				
BYWATERS, Jerry	X	X	X			X	X
CALLCOTT, Frank						X	X
CANADAY, John					X	X	
CANTEY, Maurine Martin	X						
CARD, Lottie Holman					X		
CARNOHAN, Harry							X
CARPENTER, A. M.				X	X		
CARR, Bess May				X	X	X	
CARRUTH, Margaret A.			X			X	X
CHERRY, E. R.	X	X	X	X	X	X	X
CHRISTENSEN, Andrew			X			X	X
CHRISTIANSON, Carl		X					
CLARKSON, Chas. W.			X				
CLAXTON, Virginia	X	X	X	X	X		X
COLEMAN, Mary Darter						X	X
COLLIER, Jack Atherton	X	X	X				X
COLLINS, Edna Gertrude	X	X	X				X
COLLINS, Hattie McGee	X						
CONNOR, Roma Reagan (Mrs. Edgar F.)					X	X	X
COOK, Paul Rodda			X			X	X
CRABB, Robert James						X	X
CREWS, Seth Floyd		X		X		X	
CRITTENDEN, Ethel Stuart					X	X	X
CRONIN, Marie						X	X
CULPS, Lucille P. (Mrs. A. C.)			X		X	X	
DARGE, Fred							X
DAVIDSON, Ola McNeill	X	X		X		X	
DAVIS, Helen Cruikshank			X		X		
DAVIS, Jessie	X	X	X	X	X	X	X
DAVITTE, Lola				X		X	
DAWSON-WATSON, Dawson	X	X	X	X	X	X	X
DEANE, Granville M.					X		
DELLENEY, Marie Isle				X			X

Texas Artists Exhibition at Fort Worth Index, 1931-37, Continued

Artist's Name	1931	1932	1933	1934	1935	1936	1937
DELSEMER, Rosalie	X						
DENTON, Lois	X	X					
DeYOUNG, Harry Anthony			X	X	X	X	X
DICKSON, Lillian	X	X	X	X	X	X	X
DOUGLASS, John E.			X				
DOW, Nell Pierce					X		
DOWNIE, Janet	X	X		X			
DRIVER, Rose Buford (Mrs. Sim)						X	
DROUGHT, Frederick Gerald				X			
DUER, Clare Mae (Clara?)			X				
DUGOSH, Ruby Evelyn					X		
EAST, Pattie R.	X	X	X	X	X	X	X
EBERHARDT, Eugenia McCorkle	X	X	X	X	X	X	X
ECKFORD, Jessiejo	X	X	X	X	X	X	X
EISENLOHR, E. G.	X	X	X	X	X	X	X
ELDER, Inez Staub			X	X	X	X	X
ELLIOTT, William C.			X				
EMEREE, Berla Iyone				X			X
ENSER, John F.	X	X	X				
ESTILL, Nell Gene				X		X	X
EVERETT, Raymond	X						
FALL, Willie Kay	X	X	X	X			
FILLIPPONE/FILIPPONE, John C.	X						
FISH, Margaret	X	X	X	X	X		
FISHER, Frank P., Jr.	X	X	X	X	X		
FLETCHER, Vallie			X				
FORD, Arva (Mrs. Vincent)	X	X	X	X	X		
FOSTER, May							X
FOWLER, Eva			X				
FRANCIS, Muriel Wilkins					X	X	X
FREEMAN, Leola			X		X		
FRITZ, Eleanor V. (Mrs. E. B.)	X	X	X	X	X	X	X
GANSER, Edna			X		X		
GARCIA, Antonio E.			X	X			

Artist's Name	1931	1932	1933	1934	1935	1936	1937
GHARIS, Charles					X		
GIDEON, Samuel E.			X	X			
GILCHRIST, Mrs. C. F.	X						
GILES, Fred P.	X	X	X	X	X	X	X
GILLESPIE, Sallie Meredith	X	X	X	X	X	X	X
GLASGOW, Ruth			X			X	
GOFF, Lloyd L.	X	X			X	X	
GONZALES, Boyer	X	X			X	X	X
GRAVES, Mattie Primrose	X	X	X		X		
GREATHOUSE, Carrie (Mrs. G. W.)				X			
GREEN, Katherine					X		
GREEN, Rena Maverick			X		X		
GREER, Jefferson Elliott					X		
GUERRA, Alfredo			X				
GUILLOT, Ann	X	X	X				
HALTOM, Minnie Hollis	X	X	X	X	X		X
HAMON, Viola				X	X		
HANSEN, Douglas Reid					X	X	X
HARDWICKE, Lindsay						X	X
HARRELL, Elizabeth			X	X	X		
HARRISON, Polly			X	X	X	X	
HARWELL, Jerry, III		X					
HARWELL, Jerry, Jr.	X		X				
HELLMAN, Bertha Louise				X	X		X
HENKEL, Estella M.					X		
HENRY, Rebecca Harriett	X	X		X	X	X	X
HIBINO, C. T.	X	X					
HILL, Robert Jerome	X		X	X	X	X	X
HOHNSTEDT, P. L.	X		X	X	X	X	X
HOLLINGSWORTH, Willie			X			X	
HOLMES, Dwight Clay	X			X	X	X	X
HOLT, Percy William	X				X	X	
HOLT, Rebecca				X			
HOTVEDT, Clarence A.			X	X	X		X

Texas Artists Exhibition at Fort Worth Index, 1931-37, Continued

Artist's Name	1931	1932	1933	1934	1935	1936	1937
HOUGHTON, Florence V.	X						
HOULISTON, William Jas.						X	X
HOWARD, Dorcas L. (Mrs. A. E.)		X	X	X	X	X	X
HOWELL, Florence					X		
HUNT, Eugenia Howard						X	
HUTCHINS, Roene							X
JARVIS, Mary					X	X	
JESTER, Kathrin							
JEZ, Louise	X	X	X	X	X	X	X
JOHN, Grace S.	X	X					
JOHNSON, Marjorie E.						X	X
JOHNSON, Mary Totten						X	X
JOHNSON, Minnie W.						X	X
JOLLY, Wade				X	X		
JONES, Mabel Thorpe	X	X			X	X	X
JONES, Mrs. Louis C.					X		
KARL, Mabel Fairfax					X	X	X
KEATING, Mary Aubrey					X	X	X
KIDD, Hari Matthew						X	X
KING, Clinton Blair	X	X	X			X	X
KITCHENS, Mrs. Clay				X			
KLEPPER, F. X. E. L.					X	X	
KOUBEK, Jerry							X
KRAFT, Emma-Belle			X				
KRAMER, Alice	X				X		X
LA MOND, Stella Lodge						X	X
LARSEN, Bessie Gage						X	
LAWRENCE, Harry Zachary				X	X	X	X
LAWRENCE, Kathleen G.			X		X	X	X
LAWRENCE, Kay	X			X			
LEBERMAN, Virginia	X	X					
LEDGERWOOD, Ella Ray	X	X	X	X	X	X	X
LEMMON, Thetis						X	X
LITTLEJOHN, Margaret	X	X	X	X	X	X	X

Artist's Name	1931	1932	1933	1934	1935	1936	1937
LOWDON, Elsie Motz					X		
LUCAS, Ann (Mrs. W. C.)		X	X				
MacDONNELL, Angela			X	X			X
MACK, Alexander Watson					X		
MacLEAN, Christina		X				X	
MAHAFFEY, Josephine							X
MARTIN, J. B.	X	X	X		X	X	X
MARTIN, Lottie E.				X	X	X	X
MASTIN, Mignon				X			
MATTHAEI, Beatrice		X		X	X	X	X
MATTHIES, Frances Glass		X					
MAVERICK, Lucy Madison					X		X
McCABE, J. Glenn	X						
McCANN, Charles L.	X						
McCARTHY, Lily (Mrs. Victor)	X		X	X	X	X	X
McCLAIN, George M.					X	X	
McCLUNG, Florence		X	X	X	X	X	X
McDADE, Ira					X	X	X
McDONALD, Sarah Inglish						X	X
McFADDEN, Florence N.		X				X	X
McFADDEN, Mrs. E. E.	X						
McGILL, E. P.		X	X	X	X	X	X
McGILL, Leona Leti						X	X
McINTOSH, Mrs. R. H.						X	
McVEIGH, Blanche	X	X	X	X	X	X	
MEDELLIN, Octavio					X		X
MELTON, Roxie			X			X	
MEWHINNEY, Ella K.		X	X	X	X	X	X
MEYSENBURG, Virginia C.				X		X	X
MILAM, Annie Nelson		X	X			X	
MONK, Mattie Lou (Mrs. B. D.)					X		X
MOORE, Gwendolyn		X	X			X	
MOORE, John M. ("Tex")						X	X
MORRIS, Elizabeth H.		X		X	X	X	X

Texas Artists Exhibition at Fort Worth Index, 1931-37, Continued

Artist's Name	1931	1932	1933	1934	1935	1936	1937
MORRISON, Olivia Brown					X	X	X
MOSELEY, Nell	X	X	X	X	X	X	X
MUENCH, Agnes Lilienberg							X
MUENCH, Julian Rhodes							X
MUMMERT, Sallie B.	X	X	X	X	X	X	X
MURPHEY, Mimi			X	X			
NEUHEISEL, Cecelia						X	X
NEUMANN, Gilbert F.				X			
NEYLAND, Watson			X				
NOBLE, Mamie (Mrs. J. V.)			X			X	X
NOWLIN, Eugenia Campbell					X		
OWENS, Annie Laura	X	X					
PALMER, Jessie		X	X	X	X	X	X
PANCOAST, Clara Caffrey			X	X			
PATTERSON, J. J.	X	X					
PENROD, Viola							X
PLOGER, Benjamin John						X	
POHL, Hugo D.			X	X	X		
PRITCHETT, Gloria J.						X	X
REAUGH, F.	X	X	X	X	X	X	X
REEDER, Dickson				X	X	X	
RICE, Lucy W. (Mrs. C. D.)	X	X		X	X	X	X
RICHHART, Lucille	X	X		X	X	X	
RIVERA, Rafaela	X		X		X	X	
ROBERTSON, H. O.	X	X	X				X
ROBINSON, Thelma Victoria						X	X
ROBINSON, Virginia Isabel					X	X	X
ROGERMAN, Gertrude	X						
RONEY, Harold A.	X	X	X				
RUDMOSE, Zena L.				X			
RUSS, Virginia Doures						X	
SALT, Anastasia (Mrs. W. F.)	X	X	X	X	X	X	X
SANDERS, Hedwyn (Mrs. A. H.)	X	X		X	X	X	X
SARGENT, Betty				X			

Artist's Name	1931	1932	1933	1934	1935	1936	1937
SARGENT, Lloyd L.		X					
SCHOW, May						X	X
SCHUMANN, Paul R.	X	X	X	X	X		X
SEARCY, Creola				X			
SELLORS, Evaline C.	X	X	X	X	X	X	X
SIMKINS, Martha						X	
SIMPSON, Wallace	X	X	X				
SKINNER, Frances Johnson							X
SMITH, Alexa (Mrs. J. T.)	X	X	X	X	X	X	X
SMITH, Emily Guthrie					X	X	X
SMITH, Jessie Stubblefield				X	X		
SMITH, Mary Loving		X					
SMITH, Sarah M.		X	X	X	X	X	X
SOCORRO, Sister Maria del							X
SPEED, Rosalie							X
SPELLMAN, Coreen Mary						X	X
SPRAGUE, Harold C.			X	X	X	X	
SPRUCE, Everett			X	X	X		
STAFFEL, Rudolf						X	X
STELL, Thomas, Jr.					X	X	X
STEVENS, Kelly Haygood							X
STONE, Ruby		X		X	X	X	
STRAHALM, Franz	X	X	X	X	X	X	
SWANN, James		X	X	X	X	X	
TARVER, Nell H. (Mrs. Chas.)	X	X	X	X	X	X	
TAYLOR, Rolla S.	X	X	X	X	X	X	X
TEEL, Lewis Woods		X	X	X	X	X	X
TEESDALE, Christopher H.							X
THOMAS, Frances E.	X	X	X	X	X	X	X
TRAMMELL, Mildred		X					X
TRAVIS, Kathryne Hail			X				
TRAVIS, Olin H.		X	X	X	X	X	X
TROTTER, Lilian							X
TUPPER, Margaret Wright	X			X		X	

Texas Artists Exhibition at Fort Worth Index, 1931-37, Continued

Artist's Name	1931	1932	1933	1934	1935	1936	1937
TURNER, Grace			X				
TURNER, Ida L.						X	
TURNER, Josephine (Miss Joe?)	X	X					
UHLER, Ruth P.	X	X					
VANCE, Helen Blesi						X	X
VAUGHAN, Ernest W.	X	X					
VENNING, M. Lauryl						X	
VINCENT, Jay J.				X		X	X
WALKER, Lonnie French (Mrs. Rich.)			X	X			
WANSLEY, Kate	X	X		X			
WARNER, William Riddle	X	X		X			
WARREN, Mallory Page						X	
WATSON, Maggie Joe					X		
WEBB, Esther Elizabeth	X	X					

Artist's Name	1931	1932	1933	1934	1935	1937
WEBER, Mrs. John E.						X
WEISBERG, Marie L.						X
WEISSER, Mrs. Fred W.			X	X		
WEST, Maud S.					X	
WHITE, Jessie Aline					X	X
WILLIAMS, Helen P. Carnell		X	X			
WILLIAMS, Ronald					X	
WILLIS, William Stephen, Jr.						X
WINANS, Mrs. Judith H.						X
WITHERSPOON, Mary Eleanor	X	X	X	X	X	X
WOLFFGRAM, Hertha					X	
WORK, Maud E.	X	X	X	X	X	X
YARBROUGH, Vivian Sloan	X	X	X	X	X	
ZIEGLER, Sammuel P.	X	X	X	X	X	X

Texas Centennial Exposition Index, 1936

ABRAMS, Lucian
ALBRIGHT, Lloyd L.
AYARS, Beulah
BALTZELL, Marjorie
BELL, Corinne
BERKOWITZ, Rosalie
BESSELL, Evelyn Byers
BLACKSHEAR, Kathleen
BLUMBERG, Ron
BOATRIGHT, Elizabeth Keefer
BOWLING, Charles T.
BRISAC, Edith M.
BRISBINE, Margaret
BROOKS, Helen
BROOKS, James
BROOKS, Mary Nell
BROWN, Don
BROWNE, Frederick
BUCHANAN, Laura
BYWATERS, Jerry
CALLCOTT, Frank
CANADAY, John
CANTEY, Maurine
CARNOHAN, Harry
CARR, Bess
CHERRY, Emma Richardson
COOK, Paul Rodda
COOKE, Regina Tatum
CRABB, Bob
CRITTENDEN, Ethel Stuart
CRONIN, Marie
CROWELL, Reid
DARGE, Fred
DAVIS, Helen Cruikshank

DAVIS, Velma
DELLENEY, Marie
DOUGLASS, John
DOZIER, Otis
DRIVER, Rose
DUGOSH, Ruby Evelyn
ECKFORD, Jessiejo
EISENLOHR, E. G.
ELDER, Inez Staub
EMEREE, Berla Iyone
FILIPPONE, John C.
FILSON, Genevieve
FISHER, Frank
FORD, Arva
FREDERICK, George
FREEMAN, Leola
FRITZ, Eleanor B.
GANSER, Edna
GARCIA, Antonio E.
GHARIS, Charles
GOFF, Lloyd
GOLDSTEIN, Louise Marks
GONZALES, Boyer, Jr.
GREEN, Katherine
GREEN, Rena Maverick
GREER, Jefferson Elliott
GUERRA, Alfredo
GUIDROZ, Emile
GUILBEAU, Honore
GUILLOT, Ann
HARDIN, Ernest R.
HARPER, Roberta Blewett
HELLMAN, Bertha Louise
HENKEL, Estelia M.

HOFFMAN, Polly
HOGUE, Alexandre
HOLMES, Calvin Joseph
HOOPER, Floy
HOULISTON, William J.
HOUSE, Dorothy Denslow
HUNT, Eugenia Howard
HURD, Peter
JACKSON, Everett Gee
JESTER, Kathrin
JOHNSON, Mary Totten
JOHNSON, Minnie W.
JOLLY, Wade
KEATING, Mary Aubrey
KIDD, Hari
KING, Clinton
KINZINGER, Edmund
KIRKLAND, Forrest
KLEPPER, Frank
KRAMER, Alice
LALLIER, Victor
LAMOND, Stella Lodge
LANDERS, Bertha M.
LANGHAM, Emily
LARSEN, Bessie
LAWRENCE, Harry
LEMMON, Thetis
LESTER, William
LIGHTFOOT, Mary
LIGON, Verda
LOCKARD, Robert Ivan
LOWDON, Elsie Motz
MACK, Alexander Watson
MAHONEY, James Owen

MATTHEWS, Harold J.
McCLAIN, George M.
McClung, Florence
McDADE, Ira
McDONALD, Sarah Inglish
McGILL, Leona
McNAUGHTON, Elizabeth Baskervil
McVEIGH, Blanche
MEDELLIN, Octavio
MEDRANO, Joaquin
MEWHINNEY, Ella K.
MEYSENBURG, Virginia C.
MITCHELL, Margaret
MORRIS, Elizebeth H.
MUENCH, Agnes Lilienberg
MUENCH, Julian Rhodes
MUMMERT, Sallie Blyth
NEUHEISEL, Cecelia
NICHOLS, Perry
NIENDORFF, Arthur Starr
NOBLE, Mamie
NOBLES, Kathryn
NORTHINGTON, Clara Beard
NOWLIN, Eugenie C.
OWEN, Michael
PAGAN, Jack
PEARCE, Mary Blake
PLOGER, Benjamin John
PRITCHETT, Gloria
REDLINGER, Frank
REEDER, Dickson
ROBINSON, Isabel
ROBINSON, Thelma Victoria
ROGERS, Florence E.

RUTLAND, Emily
SANDERS, Mrs. A. H.
SCHWETZ, E. M.
SCHOW, May
SCHUMANN, Paul R.
SELLORS, Evaline
SIMKINS, Martha
SKINNER, Frances
SPEED, Rosalie
SPELLMAN, Coreen Mary
SPRUCE, Everett
STAFFEL, Rudolf
STELL, Thomas M., Jr.
STEVENS, Kelly H.
STONE, Ruby
SWANN, James
TAYLOR, Lura Ann
TENNANT, Allie V.
THOMAS, Marian
TILSON, Beryl
TRAVIS, Kathryne Hail
TRAVIS, Olin H.
URBACH, Amelia
VANCE, Helen
WARREN, Mallory Page
WATSON, Maggie Joe
WEISBERG, Marie
WHITE, Jessie Aline
WILLIAMS, Ronald
WITHERSPOON, M. Eleanor
WORK, Maud Estelle
ZIEGLER, Samuel P.

ANDERSON, Mrs.

BAGBY, Miss

BARTELS, Miss

BEADLES, Mrs. W. S.

BLOYS, J. D.

BLUM, Andre

BROUSSARD, Laura

CHANDLER, Helen

CHERRY, E. R.

CLEVELAND, Mrs. Mary

COX, C. N.

CROCKER, J. C.

CURTIN, Alice M.

DOUGLASS, Miss

FISHER, Ella

GILBERT, Carrie

GONZALES, Boyer

GRESHAM, Walter

GRIBBLE, Miss

HANNA, Mrs.

HERTFORD, Mrs.

HOUSE, Edith

HUME, Kate

HUNTER, Miss

JOHNSON, Mrs. F. F.

JONES, Miss

KIMBALL, Mrs.

LAFARTHE, Miss

LIEB, Emanuel

LINDSAY, Miss

LOBIT, Bertha

MacGREGOR, Mrs. H. F.

MARCOS, Mrs.

McARDLE, H. A.

McATEE, Mrs.

McGILL Eloise Polk

MILLER, Mrs. Henry

MILLER, Zella

MOORE, C. M.

MORGAN, Mrs.

OVENDORF, M.

PUDOR, Mrs.

SHEAN, Annie

SMITH, Mrs. Louise

SOUTHWICK, Miss

STEPHENS, Mrs. M. A.

STOCKFLETH, Julius

UNDERWOOD, Laura

VAN DEMARK, Mrs.

WHEELER, Florence

WHITE, Mrs.

ZIEGLER, Mrs.

ADAMS, Della B.
AHRENBECK, Amelia
ALBRIGHT, Lloyd L.
ALLEN, Alice
ARPA, Jose
BACKLOUPE, Emma (Mrs. O. L.)
BAILEY, Beatrice S.
BARKER, Mrs. E. J.
BASSETT, Reveau
BEARD, Evelyn
BELL, Blanche B.
BENSON, J. F.
BILLINGTON, Mrs. J. T.
BLACK, Alma (Mrs. J. H.)
BLACKSHEAR, Kathleen
BLANTON, Hart B.
BLENNER, Carl
BLUDWORTH, Mrs. G. T.
BONNER, Mary
BOSSY, Mrs. H. G.
BOYD, Lydie Karbach
BRADFORD, Dewey
BREWER, Mrs. B.
BREWSTER, H. L.
BROCK, Gene H.
BROTCHER, Mrs. A. G.
BROWN, Mrs. C. A.
BROWN, Mrs. Genevieve S.
BROWN, Olivia
BRUCE, Mrs. Florence
BRUNET, Adele Laure
BUCHANAN, Laura
BUGBEE, H. D.
BURKS, Mrs. Ida Mae
BUSKS, Mrs. A. H.
BUTLER, Mrs. L.
CAMP, Fannie Taber
CARPENTER, A. M.
CARTER, Mrs. J. Oran
CARTWRIGHT, Isabel Branson
CASTLE, Mrs. A. M.
CAYLOR, H. W.
CHAFFIN, Margaret
CHAFFIN, Mary Rebecca
CHAFFIN, Mrs. Lina Evetts
CHAFFIN, Sudie
CHERRY, E. Richardson
CLAUSEN, A. B. L.
CLAXTON, Virgie

CLAY, Sybil
CLEVELAND, Sarah D.
COLEMAN, Mrs. Florence
CONN, Mrs. Leonard
CONNOR, Roma Reagan
COOK, Mary
COOK, Paul Rodda
COOKE, Regina Tatum
COONEY, Mary Wheeler
CORLEY, Mrs. Viola
COSGROVE, Susanna
COX, Miss Carroll
CRABTREE, Mary
CREWS, Floyd
CRONIN, Marie
CRUM, Dorothy
DAVIDSON, McNeill
DAVIS, Jessie
DAWSON, Mrs. J. T.
De LANEY, Mrs. Ellen Nora
DENTON, Lois C.
DICKARD, Bess Gray
DOOLEY, Maxine
DOOLEY, Mrs. C. C.
DRIVER, Rose
DUNN, Bert
EAST, Pattie R.
EISENLOHR, E.G.
ELKINS, Mrs. G. R.
ELLIOTT, Mrs. Minnie C.
EMEREE, Berla Iyone
EVERETT, Raymond
FAULKNER, Mrs. Margaret Y.
FILIPPONE, John C.
FISHER, Mrs. E. D.
FISHER, Oriole
FLANARY, Suzanne
FLECK, Joseph A.
FLEMING, Sallie K.
FLETCHER, Vallie
FORD, Mrs. Gus
FOSTER, Grace
FUTCH, Bessie Gunter
GARRISON, Elizabeth Howard
GARRISON, Minta H.
GIDEON, Samuel E.
GILLUM, Mrs. Don M.
GOETZ, Mrs. Gertrude
GOFF, Lloyd L.

GONZALES, Boyer
GONZALES, Cavier
GONZALES, Xavier
GRACE, Katherine
GRAVES, E. W.
GRAY, Daisy Gidney
GRAY, M.
GREEN, Mrs. Martha Wood
GRIMES, Mrs. E. E.
GROOMS, Mrs. M. O.
HALEY, Mrs. R.
HALTOM, M. Hollis
HAMILTON, J. L.
HAMILTON, Willie
HARDIN, Ernest R.
HARDWICKE, Lindsay
HART, Mrs. Alyce M.
HARWELL, Jerry, III
HENDRICKS, Mrs. H. G.
HILL, Mrs. Ben A.
HILL, Mrs. Guy P.
HINYARD, Mrs. Vera Wilson
HOFFMAN, Polly
HOGUE, Alexandre
HOLINSTEDT, P. L.
HOLLOMAN, G. W.
HOLMAN, Golda K.
HOPPE, Carl
HORNE, Eugenie Ligon
HUBBARD, Bess Bigham
HULL, Marie A.
HUNTER, R. Vernon
HUTCHISON, Frank Ray
IRELAND, Irma Thompson
JACKSON, Amy
JENKINS, John Eliot
JENNINGS, Jewell
JOHNSON, J. C.
JOHNSON, Minnie W.
JOHNSON, Miss Alice
KIESLING, Ninon
KING, J. A.
KING, Minnie Clark
KLEPPER, Frank
KRITSER, Harriet W.
KRUEGER, Alba
LACY, Suella
LAMOND, Allie Douglas
LAND, Marguerite

LARIMORE, Mrs. W. M.
LAUDERDALE, Ursula
LINCOLN, A.
LINN, Mrs. Lora
LOGGINS, Mrs. R. B.
LUCAS, Ann
LUDEMAN, Henrietta
MACK, A. W.
MACUNE, Katherine
MADDREY, Kate
MAPLES, Barbara
MARIETTA, Sister M.
MARTIN, Mrs. C. C.
MAST, Clara B.
McBRIDE, Mrs. E. R.
McCLINTOCK, Mrs. V. H.
McCLUNG, Florence
McELRATH, Eva
McKAY, Miss Adelle
McLEE, Mrs. Ella Frances
MEDLIN, Mrs. A. M.
MEWHINNEY, Ella K.
MILAM, Mrs. Lillian
MILLER, Sallie W.
MOORE, Mrs. W. L.
MORGAN, Mrs. R. D.
MORGAN, Portia L.
MORRIS, Mrs. Martha Wilson
NAUGHTON, Mary Mac
NEUMANN, Gilbert F.
NEWLIN, Mrs. Ora
NEWTON, J. H.
NICHOLS, Perry
NORMANN, C. S.
NORMANN, Fanny V.
NYSTEL, Mrs. N. P.
ONEAL, Mrs. E. U.
OWENS, Mrs. W. B.
PAIGE, Winnie O.
PALMER, Hattie Virginia
PANCOAST, Clara Caffery
PARK, Mrs. C. R.
PARKER, Essa Chauslor
PARSLEY, Mrs. Howard

PHILLIPS, Kenneth G.
POYNOR, Mrs. V. E.
PRESSON, Mrs. W. F.
PRIDEAUX, Mrs. T. R.
PRYOR, Nelle E.
RANDOLPH, Glenna
RATHBURN, Perry
REAVIS, Esma Jacobs
REDIN, Carl
RICE, Lucy W.
RILEY, Roy
RIPPETEAU, Hallie Crane
RISCICA, Vincent
RIVERA, Rafaela
ROBBINS, Mrs. W. B.
ROBERTS, Erie Young
ROBERTS, Mrs. W. J., Jr.
ROBINSON, Isabel
RONEY, Harold A.
RUTLAND, Mrs. Emily
SAEGERT, Mrs. J. F.
SANFORD, M. Thomas
SCHIWETZ, Edward M.
SCHMITT, Harold W.
SCHWEERS, Mrs. A. H.
SHARPE, J. H.
SHAW, Lois Hogue
SHAW, Nell
SHELTON, G. Harris
SHEPLER, I. D.
SHERWOOD, Wayman Adams
SIMMONS, Dr. L. E.
SLIMP, Mrs. Helen
SMITH, Alexa
SMITH, Alice Akin
SMITH, Amanda Fern
SMITH, Mrs. A. B.
SNEED, Mary C.
SPIGENER, H. Walton
STALLINGS, Mrs. Henry
STEVENS, Kelly H.
STOLLEIS, Miss L.
STOVALL, Ida Harrington
STRANGE, Olive B.

STUART, Carrie M.
SWIFT, Mrs. Chas.
TAGGART, George Henri
TAYLOR, Rolla
TEEL, Lewis Woods
TEESDALE, Christopheer H.
THEBO, Mrs. (A. V.) Anne Noble
THOMAS, Knox T.
THOMSON, Mrs. H. H.
TOBERMAN, Mrs. M. S.
TREUTHARDT, L.
TRIPLET, Gertrude Myrick
TRUITT, Mrs. J. J.
TUPPER, Margaret Wright
TURNLEY, Lucille
TUTT, Mrs. May
UFER, Walter
UHLER, Ruth Pershing
UNDERWOOD, Mrs. W. L.
VANTINE, Mrs. Emma Hawkins
WAHL, Nina E.
WALKER, Mrs. Phil
WATKINS, Mrs. Sue
WATSON, May M. Green
WATTS, Mrs. Beulah
WEISSER, Mrs. Fred W.
WELMAKER, Ethel
WEST, Maud S.
WHEELER, Mrs. A. C.
WHITE, Jessie Aline
WICKES, M. J.
WILDER, Mildred Morrill
WILDMAN, Louis
WILLIAMS, Elinor (Mrs. J. H. Thompson)
WILLIAMS, Mrs. Ben
WINFIELD, James H.
WINGO, Mrs. Ross
WINGO, Ross
WOOD, Mrs. William
WOODS, Nora
WRAY, Pearl
WRIGHT, Vela
YARBROUGH, Vivian Sloan
YOUNG, Mrs. R. L.

Texas Fine Arts Association Circuits, 1928-43

Artist's Name	1928	1929	1932	1933	1943
ANKENEY, John S.			X		
ATKINSON, Marion			X		
AXLEY, Martha					X
BAILEY, Ben P.			X		
BAILEY, Carden				X	
BEARD, Evelyn					X
BENSON, J. F.					X
BESSELL, Evelyne B.	X	X			
BEWLEY, Murray		X			
BLACKSHEAR, Kathleen		X			
BONNER, Mary	X		X		
BOSSY, Mrs. H. C.					X
BOWLING, Chas. T.		X	X		
BRENT, Adalie Margules					X
BRISAC, Edith M.					X
BRISBINE, Margaret	X	X			
BROWN, Olivia			X		
BROWNE, Frederic		X			
BRUNET, Adele			X		
BUCHANAN, Laura			X	X	
BUENZ, J. Fred				X	
BYWATERS, Jerry		X	X		
CALDWELL, Julia E.		X	X		
CAMP, Mrs. D. S.					X
CARR, Georgie					X
CHERRY, E. R.	X	X	X	X	
CHILLMAN, Jas.	X	X		X	
CLARKE, Lorena					X
CLAXTON, Virgie				X	
COLLINS, Edna				X	
CONNOR, Roma R.					X
COOK, Mary		X			
COOK, Sterling					X
CRISLER, Richard	X	X			

Artist's Name	1928	1929	1932	1933	1943
CRONIN, Marie		X			
DAVID, Lorene					X
DAVIDSON, McNeill	X	X	X		
DAVIS, Jessie		X	X	X	
DAWSON-WATSON, Daws	X	X			
De YOUNG, Harry A.				X	
DELAFIELD, Marjorie					X
DOZIER, Otis			X		
EAST, Pattie R.					X
ECKFORD, Jessiejo		X		X	
EDWARDS, Mrs. F. Z.	X		X		X
EISENLOHR, E. G.	X	X	X	X	
ELDER, Inez Staub			X	X	
EVERETT, Raymond	X	X		X	
FORSYTH, Constance					X
FOSTER, Cecile					X
GARRETT, Mildred Burrows			X		
GARRISON, Minta H.			X		
GIDEON, Sadie C.		X			
GIDEON, Samuel E.	X	X			
GOFF, Lloyd		X			
GONZALES, Boyer	X				
GONZALEZ, Xavier		X			
GRANBERRY, Read				X	
GREEN, Rena M.		X	X		
GUERRA, Alfredo			X		
GUILBEAU, Honore			X		
GUILLOT, Anne	X				
HANSEN, Douglas R.	X				
HARDIN, Ernest R.		X			
HELFENSTELLAR, Veronica					X
HELLMAN, Bertha L.	X	X		X	
HENRY, Rebecca		X	X		
HOFFMAN, Polly			X		

Texas Fine Arts Association Circuits, 1928-43, Continued

Artist's Name	1928	1929	1932	1933	1943
HOGUE, Alexandre	X	X	X		
HOUGHTON, Edna		X	X	X	
HOUSE, Dorothy D.		X			
HUHFER, Olive			X		
JACKSON, Amy				X	
JACKSON, Everett Gee	X				
JACKSON, Freida					X
JANE, Gwendolyn			X	X	
JESTER, Kathrin			X	X	
JOHN, Grace S.	X	X	X	X	
KEATING, Mary A.			X	X	
KEEFER, Elizabeth		X			
KELLY, Loucile					X
KEMP, Mrs. Anderson				X	
KING, Gillis	X	X			
KINZINGER, Edmund					X
KIRBY, Earleen				X	
KIRKLAND, Forrest			X		
KLEPPER, Frank		X	X	X	
LANDERS, Bertha					X
LANGHAM, Emily	X	X			
LAUDERDALE, Ursula	X				
LEADER, M. W.				X	
LEBERMAN, Virginia		X			
LEMMON, Thetis					X
LESTER, William					X
LOCKE, Lucie R.				X	
LUMPKINS, Chester					X
MacDONNELL, M. Angela	X				
MATHIS, Arthur, Jr.				X	
MATLOCK, Ruth Blanks				X	
MAUZEY, Merritt					X
MAYES, Isabelle			X		
McCLUNG, Florence				X	

Artist's Name	1928	1929	1932	1933	1943
McDADE, Helen					X
McGILL, Eloise P.				X	
McLELLAN, Ralph	X				
McVEIGH, Blanche				X	
MEAD, Ben Carlton			X		
MEDELLIN, Octavio			X		X
MEWHINNEY, Ella K.		X	X	X	
MEYERS, Jacqueline					X
MORA, Joaquin				X	
MORRIS, Elizabeth				X	
MUELLER, Lola					X
MUENCH, Agnes Lilienberg	X				
MUENCH, Julian R.		X			
MUMMERT, Sallie B.	X	X			
NAVE, Royston	X				
NAYLOR, Alice					X
NEUHEISEL, Cecilia					X
NEYLAND, Watson	X	X		X	
NICHOLS, Perry			X		
ORTH-WEISNER, Steffi				X	
PACKER, C. L.					
PALMER, Hattie V.		X			
PALMER, Jessie	X	X			
PANCOAST, Clara			X		
PEEPLES, Nina			X		
POHL, Hugo D.			X	X	
RANDALL, Annie Claire					X
RICE, Lucy W.	X	X			
ROGERS, Anne B.					X
RONEY, Harold A.					
ROWE, Richard				X	
RUTLAND, Emily					X
SCHIWETZ, E. M.			X	X	X
SCHUMANN, Paul R.	X	X	X		

Texas Fine Arts Association Circuits, 1928-43, Continued

Artist's Name	1928	1929	1932	1933	1943
SCHWARTZ, Mrs. Morris				X	
SCRUGGS, Margaret Ann			X	X	
SHAW, Nell				X	
SIMPSON, Dow					X
SKINNER, Frances					X
SMITH, Emily Guthrie					X
SMITH, Leora McNess					X
SNEED, Mary C.				X	
SPELLMAN, Coreen Mary			X	X	X
SPRUCE, Everett			X		X
STEVENS, Kelly H.		X	X		
STREET, Lois		X			
STUBBS, Ann				X	
TAYLOR, Edgar D.					X
TAYLOR, Rolla	X		X		

Artist's Name	1928	1929	1932	1933	1943
TRANTHAM, Harrelle					X
TRAVIS, Kathryne H.	X				
TRAVIS, Olin H.	X				X
TUPPER, Margaret W.					
UHLER, Ruth P.	X	X		X	
URBACH, Amelia					X
WALKER, Mrs. Phil			X		
WATSON, Margaret T.					X
WEISSER, Mrs. F. W.				X	
WHEELER, Ellie			X		
WISE, Vera					X
WOELTZ, Julius			X		
YARBROUGH, Vivian S.				X	
ZIEGLER, Samuel P.	X	X		X	

Texas General Exhibition Index, 1940-44

Artist's Name	1940	1941F	1942	1943	1944
ACHNING, Estellyn		X			X
ADAIR, Lucile					X
ADAMSON, Alma Calista	X	X			
ALDEN, Lowell				X	
ALLEN, Charles	X				X
ANTON, F.					X
AUSTIN, Dorothy	X				
AXLEY, Martha		X		X	
BAILEY, Ben P., Jr.	X	X			
BAILEY, Carden	X			X	
BAKER, Estes				X	X
BALTZEL, Marjorie					X
BARTON, Martha		X			
BEARD, Evelyn					X
BEARDEN, Ed				X	X
BENNETT, Bertha				X	
BERGQUIST, Carl O.	X				
BERKOWITZ, Rosalie	X	X	X	X	X
BESS, Forest	X				
BESSELL, Evelyne Byers	X				
BILLFALDT, Jeanne					X
BLACK, Harding	X		X		
BLACKMON, Lawson	X				
BLANC, Flora		X			X
BOMAR, Bill	X	X	X	X	X
BOWLING, Charles T.	X	X	X	X	X
BRENNAN, Joe, Jr.		X			
BRENT, Adalie Margules	X		X		
BRISAC, Edith M.	X				
BRODNAX, Ethel May			X		
BROWN, G. Turner		X			
BRYANT, William H.					X
BUCHANAN, Laura	X				
BURNETT, Elinor			X		
BURRIS, Burman	X				
BYWATERS, Jerry	X	X	X	X	X
CALDWELL, Marjorie		X	X		
CANTEY, Maurine	X	X		X	

Artist's Name	1940	1941F	1942	1943	1944
CARR, Georgie	X	X	X	X	X
CARRON, Maudee Lilyan					X
CARTTER, M. Gillette	X	X			
CASKEY, Lucile Orr	X				
CHARLTON, Gene	X			X	
CHENEY, F. Michael		X			
CLACK, Clyde C.		X	X		
CLARK, Lorena	X				
CLARK, Mary Lee	X				
CLAXTON, Virgie	X				
COLEMAN, Florence			X		
COMPTON, Carl Benton					X
COMPTON, Mildred		X	X		
CONNOR, Roma R.		X			
COOK, Paul Rodda	X				
COOK, Sterling	X				
CORBETT, Nancy D.	X				
CRABB, Bob	X				
CROCKETT, Grace				X	X
CROWELL, Reid	X				
CUILTY, Lia					X
DARGE, Fred		X			X
DAVID, Lorene	X				
DAVIS, Helen Cruikshank				X	
DAVIS, Jessie					X
DAVIS, Velma	X	X			
DeBORD, Marjorie		X			
DELLENEY, Marie		X			X
DENE, Pierre					X
DOLEJSKA, Frank	X				
DOZIER, Otis	X				
DREYER, Margaret Webb				X	X
DRIVER, Rose		X		X	X
DREYER, Martin				X	
DuBOIS, Donald E.					X
DUGOSH, Ruby Evelyn	X	X	X		
DUNNAHOO, Mildred F.		X			
EAST, Pattie R.	X		X	X	X

Artist					
EISENLOHR, E. G.	X	X			X
EMIG, Adolph P.	X	X			X
ENGELKING, Robert Sigismur	X	X			
ERWIN, J. B.				X	
EUBANK, Lydia		X			
FALL, Frieda Kay			X		
FARNSWORTH, Otis	X	X	X		
FEARING, Kelly				X	
FLANAGAN, Jack Key	X	X			
FORSYTH, Constance	X	X	X		
FRANKLIN, Ione Ruth	X	X	X		
FRAZER, James		X	X		
GARZA, Delio Flores	X				
GENIESSE, Stephen	X	X			
GENIN, Dan	X	X			
GILES, Lorita	X	X			
GONZALES, Boyer, Jr.	X	X	X		
GORDON, Allyn	X				
GORDON, Louise		X		X	
GRANVILLE, Robert	X	X			
GRUBER, Ruth	X	X	X		
GUERRA, Alfredo	X				
HAGNER, Lillie May	X				
HAMMARGREN, Frederick	X				
HARRIS, Georgia M.		X			
HARRIS, Kenneth	X		X		
HARWELL, Jerry, Jr.	X	X	X		
HELFENSTELLER, Veronica	X	X	X		
HOGUE, Alexandre	X				
HOOTON, Claude E.	X				
HOULISTON, William, Jr.	X	X			
HOWARD, Dorcas	X	X			
HUBBARD, Bess Bigham				X	
HUDGINS, Anne G.			X		
HUGHES, Mildred	X	X			
HUNTER, George L. C.	X	X			
HUNTER, Warren	X	X			
INGRAM, Sam	X				

Artist					
JEFFRIES, Lucile	X	X		X	X
JOHN, Grace Spaulding	X				
JOHNSON, Marjorie	X		X		X
JOYNER, Arista		X			
JOYNER, Howard Warren		X			
KAHLDEN, Sarah	X				
KEATING, Mary Aubrey	X	X	X	X	X
KELLY, Loucile	X				
KIDD, Hari	X				
KIEFNER, C. H.	X				
KINCHELOE, Marilyn M.	X			X	
KING, J. J.		X			
KINNEY, Cle		X			
KINZINGER, Edmund	X	X	X	X	
KRAMER, Alice	X				
LACY, Lucile Land				X	X
LALLIER, Victor	X				X
LaMOND, Stella	X				X
LANDERS, Bertha		X	X		X
LANDRUM, Mary Talbot	X				
LANGFORD, Ruth					X
LAYBURN, Grace E.			X		
LAZENBY, Georgia	X				
LEA, Mary Hornby	X				
LEA, Tom	X				
LEMMON, Thetis					X
LESTER, William	X	X	X	X	X
LEWIS, Laura B.	X				
LIGHTFOOT, Mary	X				X
LOCKWOOD, Ward	X	X	X		
LOVELADY, Ruth Philpott	X	X			X
MAPLES, Barbara	X	X		X	X
MASLEY, Alexander				X	X
MAUZEY, Merritt	X	X	X		X
McCLAIN, George M.	X	X			
McCLUNG, Florence	X	X			
McDADE, Helen					X
McFEE, Henry Lee	X				

Texas General Exhibition Index, 1940-44, Continued

Artist's Name	1940	1941F	1942	1943	1944
McGRAW, Hazel Fulton	X		X	X	X
McVEIGH, Blanche	X	X	X	X	X
McVEY, Leza S.				X	X
McVEY, William M.	X	X		X	
MEDELLIN, Octavio	X	X			X
MEUSEBACH, Iago		X			
MEYERS, Jacqueline				X	
MIMS, Louise Holden	X				
MONTMINY, Pierre					X
MOSKOWITZ, Shirley E.				X	X
MOZLEY, Loren	X	X	X	X	X
MUELLER, Lola	X	X	X	X	X
MUENCH, Agnes Lilienberg	X	X	X	X	X
NAYLOR, Alice					X
NEUHEISEL, Cecilia	X		X	X	X
NICE, Blanch Heim	X	X		X	X
NORMANN, Charles Berkeley	X				
NOWLIN, Eugenia C.	X				
PACHL, Delmar		X			
PENDERGRASS, Roger		X			
PREUSSER, Robert O.	X		X	X	X
RANDALL, Arne			X		
REEDER, Dickson		X	X	X	X
REES, Lonnie	X			X	X
REIL, Gaston		X			
ROBERTSON, H. O.					X
ROGERS, Ann B.			X	X	
ROSEN, Charles			X		
RUTLAND, Emily		X		X	X
SAMUELS, Joyce		X			
SCHIWETZ, Edward M.	X		X	X	X
SCHMALZ, J. P.		X			
SCHOENBERGER, Edward T.					X
SCHOENFELDT, Henry H.					X
SCOTT, Robert Gillam				X	X
SEARS, Mary Eula	X				
SELLORS, Evaline C.	X			X	
SHAND, Terry, Jr.				X	
SHANNON, Sara					X

Artist's Name	1940	1941F	1942	1943	1944
SIMPSON, Dow		X		X	X
SKINNER, Frances	X	X		X	X
SMITH, Artine					X
SMITH, Emily Guthrie		X		X	X
SNOWDEN, Chester				X	
SPEED, Rosalie		X			
SPELLMAN, Coreen Mary	X		X	X	X
SPRUCE, Everett	X	X	X	X	
STANLEY, Madeline		X			X
STEWART, William P.		X			
STREETMAN, Christine				X	
TAYLOR, A. Hinkle		X			
TAYLOR, Edgar		X	X	X	X
THURMOND, Ethel D.	X				X
TRACY, Elizabeth					X
TRANTHAM, Harrelle		X	X	X	X
TRAVIS, Olin H.				X	X
TRENTHAM, Eugene		X	X		X
TRIMBLE, A. M.	X				
TSANOFF, Katherine				X	
UHLER, Ruth Pershing	X			X	X
UMLAUF, Charles				X	X
UNDERWOOD, Maude R.			X	X	X
URBACH, Amelia	X		X	X	X
UTTER, Bror		X		X	X
VOGEL, Donald S.		X	X	X	X
VOGT, Augusta				X	X
WALKER, Dickman				X	X
WARLICK, Mildred				X	X
WEBB, Frank S.		X			
WHITE, Jessie Aline	X				
WILLIAMS, Ramond Hendrey	X		X		
WILLSON, Robert		X			
WILSON, Douthitt			X		
WILSON, Gary		X			
WILSON, Loma		X			
WOELTZ, Julius			X		X
WORTHINGTON, Virginia Lew	X				

ACHNING, Estellyn	DAY, Agnes Nelson	KINZINGER, Edmund	ROBERTSON, H. O.
AINSWORTH, Ford	DELLENEY, Marie	LACY, Lucile Land	ROOTS, Tom Smith
ALLEN, Charles	DOZIER, Otis	LaMOND, Stella	ROSENBAUM, Caroline
BABCOCK, Gertrude	EISENLOHR, E. G.	LANDERS, Bertha	ROSENFIELD, John, III
BERGQUIST, Carl	ELDER, Inez Staub	LEMMON, Thetis	RUTLAND, Emily
BLANC, Flora	EUBANK, Lydia	LESTER, William	SELLORS, Evaline
BOMAR, Bill, Jr.	FALL, Frieda Kay	LIGHTFOOT, Mary	SIMKINS, Martha
BOWLING, Charles T.	FISHER, Frank	LIGON, Verda	SKINNER, Frances
BRAND, Frances	FOXALL, Horace	LOCKE, Lucie H.	SNOWDEN, Chester
BRISAC, Edith M.	GENIN, Don	MARGULES, Adalie	SPEED, Rosalie
BUCHANAN, Laura	GLASSCOCK, Margaret	MAUZEY, Merritt	SPELLMAN, Coreen
BYWATERS, Jerry	GONZALES, Boyer Jr.	McCLUNG, Florence	TAYLOR, Lura Ann
CARR, Bess	GRANVILLE, Robert	McGRAW, Hazel	TENNANT, Allie
CARTTER, M. Gillette	GURLEY, Loulie	McVEIGH, Blanche	THURMOND, Ethel
CASKEY, Lucile	HARDIN, Ernest R.	McVEY, William	TRANTHAM, Harrelle
CHARLTON, Gene	HOGUE, Alexandre	MEDELLIN, Octavio	URBACH, Amelia
CHILDRESS, Doris	HOULISTON, William Jame	MEDRANO, Joaquin	UTTER, Bror
COMPTON, Carl Benton	HUNTER, Warren	NICE, Blanche Heim	VOGEL, Donald
COMPTON, Mildred	INGRAM, Sam	NICHOLS, Perry	WALMSLEY, Elizabeth
COOK, Paul Rodda	JEFFRIES, Lucile	PREUSSER, Robert	WILLIAMS, Ronald
DARGE, Fred	JOY, Robert	REEDER, Dickson	WILSON, Douthitt
DAVIDSON, Ola McNeill	KIDD, Hari	REES, Lonnie	

Texas Panorama

BOWLING, Charles T.	HOGUE, Alexandre	McCLUNG, Florence	SPRUCE, Everett
BYWATERS, Jerry	HUNTER, R. Vernon	MOZLEY, Loren	TRAVIS, Olin
DOZIER, Otis	KINZINGER, Edmund	NICHOLS, Perry	TRENTHAM, Eugene
EISENLOHR, E. G.	LANDERS, Bertha	REEDER, Dickson	URBACH, Amelia
GOFF, Lloyd	LESTER, William	ROBERTSON, H. O.	VOGEL, Donald
GONZALES, Boyer	LOCKWOOD, Ward	SKINNER, Frances	WOELTZ, Julius
HELFENSTELLER, Veronica	MAUZEY, Merritt	SPELLMAN, Coreen Mary	

Artist's Name	1941	1942	1944	1945	Artist's Name	1941	1942	1944	1945
ALLEN, Charles				X	LaSELLE, Dorothy ("Toni")			X	X
BACHMAN, Ruth				X	LESTER, William	X	X		
BEARDEN, Ed		X	X	X	LIGHTFOOT, Mary		X	X	X
BENNETT, Bertha				X	LIGON, Verda		X	X	X
BERKOWITZ, Rosalie		X	X		LOCKWOOD, Ward	X			
BOWLING, Chas. T.	X	X	X	X	MAHER, Cpl. Wm. H.				X
BOWLING, Jack		X			MAPLES, Barbara				X
BRISAC, Edith M.	X	X		X	MARTIN, Lottie E.		X		
BROCK, Gene H.				X	MASSEY, Robert		X		
BROUGH, Sgt. Richard				X	MAUZEY, Merritt		X	X	X
BYWATERS, Jerry	X	X	X		McCLUNG, Florence		X	X	X
CIAMPA, Sgt. Antonio				X	McGRAW, Hazel				X
CLARK, Clyde S.				X	McVEIGH, Blanche	X	X	X	X
COMITO, Cpl. Nicholas U.			X	X	MILLER, Florence Oom				X
COMPTON, Carl Benton				X	MORRISON, Cpl. Karl R.			X	X
CONNER, Roma Reagan		X			MOZLEY, Loren	X	X	X	
CROCKETT, Grace				X	MUELLER, Lola			X	X
DAVID, Lorene	X	X	X	X	MURRAY, Eileen		X		
DEEGAN, Cadet Jim			X		NAYLOR, Alice			X	X
DELLENEY, Marie		X		X	NICHOLS, Perry		X		
DESHA			X		NIES, William A.				X
DOUGLASS, John			X		PACHL, Delmar		X	X	
DUER, Clara Mae		X			PHILLIPS, Carolyn				X
EISENLOHR, Edward G.				X	REEDER, Dickson				X
FALL, Frieda Kay		X			ROBERTSON, H. O.		X	X	X
FORSYTH, CONSTANCE		X	X	X	ROBINSON, Isabel		X		
GENTLE, Robt. ("Mac")		X			ROTH, Eleanor				X
GILES, Lorita				X	RUTLAND, Emily			X	X
GRAZIANA, Sante				X	SCHOENBERGER, Sgt. Edward T.			X	X
GREBENAK, Cpl. Louis				X	SPELLMAN, Coreen M.		X	X	X
HELFENSTELLER, Veronica	X		X		SPRUCE, Everett	X		X	
HOGUE, Alexandre	X		X	X	STELL, Thos. M., Jr.		X		
HUBBARD, Bess Bigham		X		X	STOREY, Evelyn				X
ISAAC, Dell				X	TAYLOR, Lura Ann		X	X	
JEFFRIES, Lucille		X		X	TRANTHAM, Harelle		X		
JONES, Paul			X		TRAVIS, Olin			X	X
JOYNER, Arista A.				X	TSANOFF, Katherine		X	X	
KARPER, Mary Nelson		X			UTTER, Bror	X			
KELLY, Dee		X			VOGEL, Donald S.		X	X	X
KINZINGER, Alice		X			WADE, Ted W.		X		
KINZINGER, Edmund		X	X	X	WALMSLEY, Elizabeth		X	X	X
LACY, Lucile Land		X	X		WEBB, Frank Sexton		X		
LaGOW, Kate Elmore			X		WISE, Vera				X
LaMOND, Stella L.		X	X	X	WONNER, Paul				X
LANDERS, Bertha	X	X	X	X					

University Centennial Exposition 1, 1936

ALBRIGHT, Lloyd L.
BOATRIGHT, Elizabeth Keefer
BRUNET, Adele
BUGBEE, Harold D.
CHERRY, E. R.
COLLINS, Edna
COONEY, Mary W.
DeYOUNG, Harry Anthony
ENSER, John F.
EVERETT, Raymond
FLETCHER, Vallie
GARRISON, Minta H.
HARDIN, Ernest R.
HOHNSTEDT, P. L.

HUDDLE, Nannie
JEFFRIES, Lucile
KLEPPER, Frank
LACY, Lucile Land
LEADER, Walton
McCLUNG, Florence
MEWHINNEY, Ella K.
NAGLE, Mrs. E. T.
NEWMAN, George W.
REAVIS, E. J.
REEDER, Dickson
STEVENS, Kelly H.
TUPPER, Margaret Wright
WARREN, Mallory Page

University Centennial Exposition 2, 1936

BUCHANAN, Laura
CAMPBELL, Dorothy J.
CONNOR, Roma Reagan
DAVIS, Jessie
DeGRUMMOND, Mary Louise
DOWNIE, Janet
EAST, Pattie R.
EBERHARDT, Eugenia
ELDER, Inez Staub
FLETCHER, Vallie
HAINES, Marie

HOFFMAN, Polly
HUBBARD, Bess Bigham
JEFFREYS, A. B.
JOHNSON, Minnie W.
KLEPPER, Frank
LEADER, Walton
LEBERMAN, Virginia
LITTLEJOHN, Margaret
LOCKE, Lucie H.
MAST, Clara Glenn
McGILL, Eloise Polk

McLEAN, Mary J. (Bullock)
NAGLE, Mrs. E. T.
PRIDEAUX, Mado M.
REEDER, Dickson
RIPPETEAU, Hallie Crane
SCHULTZ, M. Frances
SCHWARTZ, Sandra
SMITH, Alexa
WALKER, Mrs. Phil
WEISSER, Mrs. Fred
WHEELER, E.

West Texas Art Exhibition, 1939-45

Artist's Name	1939	1940	1942	1943	1944	1945
ALLEN, Troy		X				
ANDERSON, Mrs. H. C.			X		X	X
BAUGH, Worth			X			X
BEADEL, Rosalie Muse	X					
BOATRIGHT, Elizabeth K.	X	X				
BRISAC, Edith M.	X	X	X	X	X	X
BROWNING, John G.		X	X			X
BUGBEE, H. D.	X	X				X
BUSH, Maurine	X	X	X			X
CAMP, Fannie Taber		X				X
COLLIER, M. Frances	X				X	
COLLINS, Pearle D.		X			X	
CONNOR, Roma Reagan (Mrs. E. F.)	X		X		X	X
CORLEY, Viola			X			X
DAUGHERTY, Louise	X	X			X	
DAVIDSON, Nathalee			X		X	
DELLENEY, Marie	X	X				
DOYLE, Mary	X	X				X
EDGE, Altha	X	X	X			X
EDWARDS, Ethel	X				X	X
FOSTER, Cecile	X	X	X		X	X
FREEMAN, Leola	X	X	X		X	X
GEESLIN, Lee Gaddis		X			X	
GIRAUD, Elizabeth M.			X		X	
GOATZ, Mary Ruth		X	X		X	
GONZALEZ, Xavier	X				X	
HAYNES, Cade	X	X			X	
HENAGAN, Beth Coombes	X	X	X		X	
HOFFMAN, Polly		X				X
HUBBARD, Bess Bigham		X	X		X	X
HUGHS, Tincie		X			X	X
JACKSON, Amy	X				X	X
KELLY, Lois Neville		X			X	X
KELLY, Loucile	X	X	X		X	X
KINZINGER, Alice Fish		X			X	
KINZINGER, Edmund Daniel			X		X	X
KOENIG, Mrs. Roy			X			
KOKERNOT, Golda			X			
LA VELLE, Edith	X					
LACY, Suella			X			
LANHAM, Alpha	X				X	X
LEAVITT, Clara Waide	X					X
LEE, Myrtle	X					X
LEMMON, Thetis	X				X	X
LEWIS, Laura Blocker					X	
LOCKARD, Robert I.	X				X	
LUDEMAN, Henriette		X			X	X
LUMPKINS, Chester L.		X				X
LYONS, J. R.	X				X	
LYONS, Jane Kirk		X			X	
MARTIN, Mrs. Howard	X				X	
MAST, Clara Glenn	X					X
MATLOCK, Ruth Blanks	X	X			X	X
McDONALD, Sarah Inglish	X				X	X
McELROY, Michael	X	X			X	X
McGRAW, Hazel Fulton	X	X			X	
McINTOSH, Mrs. R. H.		X			X	
MEYER, Grace Manton		X			X	
MOSELEY, Alice T.	X				X	
NICHOLS, Alice Welty	X	X				
O'BRIEN, Esse Forrester	X	X				
ORREN, Raymond	X	X				
REIL, W. Gaston		X			X	X
ROBINSON, Isabel	X	X				
SEARS, Mary Eula	X				X	X
SHAPARD, Mary		X			X	X
SHAW, Lois Hogue	X	X				X
SHELTON, G. Harris	X	X				X

West Texas Art Exhibition, 1939-45, Continued

Artist's Name	1939	1940	1942	1943	1944	1945
SMITH, Frances M.			X			
SPELLMAN, Coreen M.	X	X				
STALLINGS, Pearl S.		X				
STOVALL, Winona Young	X	X				
SUMMERHILL, Marinel		X				
SWINDELL, Jessie Volah	X					
TATE, Claire	X					
TEEL, Lewis W.	X	X	X			
TITTLE, Juanita	X		X			
TRANTHAM, Harrelle E.				X	X	X
TRANTHAM, Ruth Newberry				X		X
WHITE, Ila Mae				X		
WILLIAMS, Ramond H.					X	
WILLS, Le Becca					X	
WILSON, Loma						X
WISE, Vera						X
WOOD, Mrs. Guy N.						X

REFERENCES

ARCHIVES

All in Texas unless otherwise noted.

Archives of American Art, Smithsonian Institution, Washington, D.C.

Art Museum of Southeast Texas, Beaumont.

Austin History Center.

Jerry Bywaters Collection on Art of the Southwest, Hamon Arts Library, Southern Methodist University, Dallas.

Dallas Historical Society.

Dallas Museum of Art.

Dallas Public Library.

El Paso Museum of Art.

El Paso Public Library.

Fort Worth Public Library.

Harris County Heritage Society, Houston.

Harrison County Museum, Marshall.

Modern Art Museum of Fort Worth.

Museum of Fine Arts, Houston.

Panhandle-Plains Historical Museum, Canyon.

Rosenberg Library, Galveston.

Torch Energy, Houston.

Witte Memorial Museum, San Antonio.

PUBLISHED SOURCES

Abernethy, Francis Edward, ed. *The Bounty of Texas.* Texas Folklore Society Publication 49. Denton: University of North Texas Press, 1990.

Acheson, Sam H., et al., eds. *Texian Who's Who.* Dallas: Texian Company, 1937.

Amarillo City Directories. Panhandle-Plains Historical Museum, Canyon.

Annual Catalog: The West Texas State Teachers College. Canyon: West Texas State Teachers College, 1938.

Armstrong, Mary K. "East Texas Girl Wins Success as Sculptor." *Holland's, The Magazine of the South* (April 1928).

Art Directory: Houston, Texas. Houston: Bowman and Ross, 1931.

Benezit, Emmanuel. *Dictionnaire Critique et Documentaire des Peintres, Sculpteurs, Dessinateurs et Graveurs.* 8 vols. Paris: Librairie Grund, 1966.

Biddle, George. *An American Artist's Story.* Boston: Little, Brown and Company, 1939.

Borska, Ivan. "Wilson K. Nixon and His Work." *San Antonio Home and Club.* n.d.

Carraro, Francine. *Jerry Bywaters: A Life in Art.* Austin: University of Texas Press, 1995.

Church, Diana. "Edward G. Eisenlohr: The Education of an Artist." *Heritage News* (Summer 1984): 4–6; 10.

———. *Guide to Early Dallas Artists, 1890–1917.* Dallas: Diana Church, 1987.

Clark, Garth. *American Potters: The Work of Twenty Modern Masters.* New York: Watson-Guptil Publications, 1981.

Clarke, Mary W. "Jose Aceves: Mexican Artist of El Paso Excels in Landscapes and Westerns." *Cattleman* (November 1956): 43–45.

Clement, Clara Erskine, and Laurence Hutton. *Artists of the Nineteenth Century and Their Works.* Rev. ed. St. Louis: North Point, 1969.

Coleman, Arthur. "Can Marriage and a Career Be Combined? Ella K. Mewhinney Proves It Possible." *Holland's, The Magazine of the South.* (August 1929): 13, 61.

Coppini, Pompeo. *From Dawn to Sunset.* San Antonio: Naylor Company, 1949.

Davis, Walt. "Granville Bruce: The Creative Partnership Between Science and Art." *Southwest Art* (1982): 118–29.

Dawdy, Doris Ostrander. *Artists of the American West: A Biographical Dictionary.* 3 vols. Chicago: Swallow Press, 1974–81.

Earle, Helen L. *Biographical Sketches of American Artists.* 5th ed. Collingswood: Anthony C. Schmidt Fine Arts, 1972.

Eldredge, Charles C. *Ward Lockwood, 1894–1963.* Lawrence: University of Kansas Museum of Art, 1974.

Ennis, Michael. "His Name Was Forrest Bess." *Texas Monthly* (June 1987): 141–43; 240–47.

Falk, Peter Hastings, ed. *The Annual Exhibition Record of the Art Institute of Chicago, 1888–1950.* Madison: Sound View Press, 1990.

———. *The Annual Exhibition Record of the National Academy of Design, 1901–1950.* Madison: Sound View Press, 1990.

———. *The Annual Exhibition Record of the Pennsylvania Academy of the Fine Arts, 1807–1965.* 3 vols. Madison: Sound View Press, 1988.

———. *Who Was Who in American Art.* Madison: Sound View Press, 1985.

Farmer, David. "Constance Forsyth: Printmaker." *Tamarind Papers* 12 (1989): 46–54.

Farmer, David, and Paul Rogers Harris. *The Texas Printmakers.* Dallas: Meadows Museum, 1990.

Fisk, Frances Battaile. *A History of Texas Artists and Sculptors.* Abilene: Frances Battaile Fisk, 1928.

Flury, Dorothy Agnes. *Our Father, Godfrey: A Biography.* Austin: Hart Graphics and Office Centers, 1976.

Forrester-O'Brien, Esse. *Art and Artists of Texas.* Dallas: Tardy Publishing Company, 1935.

Frary, Michael. *Impressions of the Texas Panhandle.* College Station: Texas A&M University Press, 1977.

Galveston City Directories. Rosenberg Library, Galveston.

George, Mary Carolyn Hollers. *Mary Bonner: Impressions of a Printmaker.* San Antonio: Trinity University Press, 1982.

Goddard, Ruth. *Porfirio Salinas.* Austin: Rock House Press, 1975.

Grauer, Michael R. "Dusting Off the Roster: Women Artists of Texas, 1850–1950." part 1. *Southwest Art* (July 1993): 59–63.

———. "Dusting Off the Roster: Women Artists of Texas, 1850–1950," part 2. *Southwest Art* (August 1993): 89–93.

———. "Frank Reaugh: The Dean of Texas Artists." *Persimmon Hill* (Autumn 1994): 50–55.

———. "Lloyd L. Albright: Texas–New Mexico Connection." *Southwest Art* (April 1995): 70–74.

———. "The Artistic Legacy." *Panhandle-Plains Historical Review* 57 (1994): 15–41.

Groce, George C., and David H. Wallace. *The New York Historical Society's Dictionary of Artists in America, 1564–1860.* New Haven: Yale University Press, 1957.

Haley, J. Evetts. *F. Reaugh: Man and Artist.* El Paso: Carl Hertzog, 1960.

Hale, Leon, and Robert Calvert. *Buck Schiwetz Memories.* College Station: Texas A&M University Press, 1978.

Harwood, Buie. *Decorating Texas: Decorative Painting in the Lone Star State from the 1850s to the 1950s.* Fort Worth: Texas Christian University Press, 1993.

Havlice, Patricia Pate. *Index to Artistic Biography.* Metuchen: Scarecrow Press, 1973.

Hjerter, Kathleen G., comp. *The Art of Tom Lea.* College Station: Texas A&M University Press, 1989.

Houston Artists' Gallery. Houston, 1930.

Houston City Directories. Rosenberg Library, Galveston.

"Hugo David Pohl 1878–1960." *Southwest Art* (February 1975): 50–53.

Kendall, Dorothy Steinbomer. *Gentilz: Artist of the Old Southwest.* Austin and London: University of Texas Press, 1974.

Key, Hobart, Jr. *By My Strong Hand: The Key Family of Texas and Prince George County, Maryland.* Marshall: Port Caddo Press, 1965.

King, C. Richard, ed. *Marion T. Brown: Letters from Fort Sill, 1886–1887.* Austin: Encino Press, 1970.

King, Frank M. *Longhorn Trail Drivers.* Frank M. King, 1940.

Maddox, Cynthia. "Buck Winn: 'The Fires the Genius Kindles.'" *Texas Life* (Jan.–Feb. 1991): 26–31; 53–54.

Maguire, Jack. *Fredericksburg, Texas: 150 Years of Paintings and Drawings.* Fredericksburg: Fredericksburg 150th Anniversary, Inc., 1995.

Marlor, Clark S. *The Society of Independent Artists: The Exhibition Record, 1917–1944.* Park Ridge: Noyes Press, 1984.

McAdams, Ina May Ogletree. *Texas Women of Distinction.* Austin: McAdams Publishers, 1962.

McClure, C. Boone. "Harold Dow Bugbee: A Biographical Sketch." *Panhandle-Plains Historical Review* 30 (1957): 55–66.

———. "The Art of Harold Dow Bugbee in the Panhandle-Plains Museum." *Panhandle-Plains Historical Review* 30 (1957): 67–78.

McGuire, James Patrick. *Hermann Lungkwitz, Romantic Landscapist on the Texas Frontier.* San Antonio: University of Texas Institute of Texan Cultures at San Antonio, 1983.

———. *Iwonski: Painter and Citizen.* San Antonio: San Antonio Museum Association, 1976.

———. *Julius Stockfleth: Gulf Coast Marine and Landscape Painter.* San Antonio: Trinity University Press, 1976.

McKee Collection of Paintings, The. El Paso: El Paso Museum of Art, 1968.

Mears, Michell M., and Virginia Feaster. "Wax Medical Moulages: The Scott and White Collection, 1932–1955." *Texas Medicine* 89 (March 1993): 13–15.

Miller, Carol Price. "Eugene Thurston, Cartoonist: Portrait of an Artist Getting Started." *Password* 37 (Winter 1992): 159–70.

Moore, John M. "Tex." *The West.* Wichita Falls, 1935.

Moynihan, Odilia Jacques. "Porfirio Salinas." *Texas Parade* (September 1967): 42–45.

"Nationally Known Artist Selects San Antonio as Her Home [Ursula Lauderdale]." *San Antonio Home and Club.* Date unknown. Original in Witte Museum files.

Newcomb, William W., Jr. *German Artist on the Texas Frontier: Friedrich Richard Petri.* Austin: University of Texas Press, 1978.

———. *The Rock Art of Texas Indians.* Austin: University of Texas Press, 1967.

New Handbook of Texas, The. Austin: Texas State Historical Association, 1996.

Nicodemi, Giorgio. *Rodolfo Guzzardi.* Milan, Italy: Ariel Publishing House, 1952.

Northington, Clarissa B. *The Long White Road.* San Antonio: Munguia Printers, 1978.

"Oils and Watercolors by Gregorio Prestopino." *Art Alliance Bulletin* 36 (December 1957) 7, 14.

Opitz, Glen B., ed. *Dictionary of American Sculptors: 18th Century to Present.* Poughkeepsie: Apollo Books, 1984.

———. *Mantle Fielding's Dictionary of American Painters, Sculptors and Engravers.* Poughkeepsie, N.Y.: Apollo Books, 1987.

Pickle, Joe, ed. *H. W. Caylor: Frontier Artist.* College Station: Texas A&M University Press, 1981.

Pinckney, Pauline A. *Painting in Texas: The Nineteenth Century.* Austin: University of Texas Press for the Amon Carter Museum, 1967.

Porter, Dean A. *Victor Higgins: An American Master.* Salt Lake City: Peregrine Smith Books, 1991.

Price, Carol Ann. *Early El Paso Artists.* El Paso: Texas Western Press, 1983; *Index to Early El Paso Artists,* 1997.

Rabynor, Jozie. "The Paintings of Olin Travis." *Southwest Art* (January 1975): 34–37.

Ratcliffe, Sam DeShong. *Painting Texas History to 1900.* Austin: University of Texas Press, 1992.

Reaves, William E., Jr. *Texas Art and a Wildcatter's Dream: Edgar B. Davis and the San Antonio Art League.* College Station: Texas A&M University Press, 1998.

Rose, Barbara, and Susie Kalil. *Fresh Paint: The Houston School.* Austin: Texas Monthly Press for the Museum of Fine Arts, Houston, 1985.

Samuels, Peggy, and Harold Samuels. *Samuels' Encyclopedia of Artists of the American West.* Rev. ed. Secaucus, N.J.: Book Sales, 1985.

San Antonio City Directory. N.p., 1895–96; 1889–90.

Saxon, Gerald D. "Dallas Cartoonist John Knott Looks at World War I." *Legacies: A History Journal for Dallas and North Central Texas* (Spring 1992): 20–28.

Shuffler, R. Henderson, and John Edward Weems. *The Schiwetz Legacy: An Artist's Tribute to Texas.* Austin: University of Texas Press, 1972.

Smith, Goldie Capers. *The Creative Arts in Texas: A Handbook of Biography.* Dallas: Cokesbury Press, 1926.

Steinfeldt, Cecilia. *Art for History's Sake: The Texas Collection of the Witte Museum.* Austin: Texas State Historical Association, 1993.

———. *The Onderdonks: A Family of Texas Painters.* San Antonio: Trinity University Press for the San Antonio Museum Association, 1976.

———. *Texas Folk Art: One Hundred Fifty Years of the South-western Tradition.* Austin: Texas Monthly Press for the San Antonio Museum Association, 1981.

Stroud, Alice Bab, and Modena Stroud Dailey. *F. Reaugh: Texas Longhorn Painter.* Dallas: Royal Publishing Co., 1962.

Taft, Robert. *Artists and Illustrators of the Old West: 1850–1900.* New York: Charles Scribner's Sons, 1953.

Thompson, Eloise Reid, and Edna Wolf Miner. *Wildflower Portraits.* Norman: University of Oklahoma Press, 1964.

Tyler, Ron. *Pecos to the Rio Grande: Interpretations of Far West Texas by Eighteen Artists.* College Station: Texas A&M University Press, 1983.

———, ed. *The New Handbook of Texas.* Austin: Texas State Historical Association, 1996.

Utterback, Martha. *Early Texas Art in the Witte Museum.* San Antonio: Witte Memorial Museum, 1968.

Von Rosenberg, Marjorie. *German Artists of Early Texas.* Austin: Eakin Press, 1982.

Warwick, Mrs. Clyde W. *The Randall County Story, from 1541 to 1910.* Hereford, Tex.: Pioneer Publishers, 1969.

Weaver, Gordon, ed. *An Artist's Notebook: The Life and Art of Merritt Mauzey.* Memphis: Memphis State University Press, 1979.

Webb, Walter Prescott, H. Bailey Carroll, and Eldon Stephen Branda, eds. *The Handbook of Texas.* 3 vols. Austin: Texas State Historical Association, 1952, 1976.

Weismann, Donald L., intro. *Frank Reaugh: Painter to the Longhorns.* College Station: Texas A&M University Press, 1985.

West John O. *Jose Cisneros: An Artist's Journey.* El Paso: Texas Western Press, 1993.

West, Nancy Glass. "An Artist Who Molds Majesty from Opposites [A. D. Greer]." *Southwest Art* (June 1977): 52–57.

Wilbanks, Elsie Montgomery. *Art on the Texas Plains.* Lubbock: South Plains Art Guild, 1959.

"Young Artists Back [Eva and Imelda Schubart]." *Texas Week* (16 November 1946): 18.

Newspaper Articles

"Abilene Artist's Work Hung in Chicago Exhibit." Unknown newspaper, Nov. 26, 1940.

"Abstract Expressionist James Brooks Dies." *Dallas Morning News,* Mar. 12, 1992.

"Active Art Guild to Retain El Paso Artists Is Formed." *El Paso Herald,* Sept. 22, 1927.

"All Outdoors Is Subject and Her Automobile Is Studio for This El Paso Artist Who Has Painted Picture of Southwestern Landmark." *El Paso Herald-Post,* May 19, 1934.

Alpine (Tex.) Avalanche, Dec. 29, 1988. (George M. Livingston.)

Amarillo News-Globe, Jan. 18 and 25, 1931.

"Architect Opens Art Exhibition [Bubi Jessen]." *San Antonio Express,* Nov. 20, 1932.

"Arpa Students Exhibit Work." *San Antonio Express,* Mar. 4, 1928.

"Art Exhibit to Feature Work of Mother, Daughter [Frances Camp; Frances Bell]." N.p.

"Art Exhibits Awards Include Home People; Students Win Ribbons." *El Paso Herald,* Sept. 19, 1924.

"Artist Depicts How Dreams of Pioneers Here Realized [Seth Floyd Crews]." *El Paso Times,* Nov. 21, 1937.

"Artist Exhibits Paintings [Jack Redic]." *El Paso Times,* June 8, 1942.

"Artist Found Beaten to Death [Manuel Acosta]." *Amarillo Daily News,* Oct. 27, 1989.

"Artist Modena Stroud Dailey Dies at 93." *Dallas Morning News,* Jan. 12, 1990.

"Artist, Teacher Prefers Landscapes [Ethel Thurmond]." Unknown newspaper, n.d.

"Artist to Exhibit at Tourist Club [F. C. Schuchard]." Unknown newspaper, May 16, 1934.

"Artist Who Had Home Here Dies in New Haven, Conn. [Lucien Abrams]." *San Antonio Express,* Apr. 15, 1941.

"Atmosphere Brings Artist Back to E. P. [Robert Genung]." *El Paso Herald-Post,* Nov. 18, 1939.

"Audley Dean Nicols Dies at 66." *El Paso Herald-Post.* Nov. 13, 1941.

Beaumont Enterprise, Nov. 20, 1987.

"Beautiful Bit of Sculpture by El Paso Boy [Enrique Alfarez]." Unknown newspaper, n.d., El Paso Public Library.

"[Rosalie] Berkowitz's Art Known at Witte." *San Antonio Express-News,* May 23, 1990.

Brownwood Bulletin, Mar. 28, 1986.

Bywaters, Jerry. "Vernon Hunter, Painter of Panhandle." *Dallas Morning News,* July 18, 1937.

Carroll, Bess. "Water Color Exhibit at Museum [Ralph McClellan]." *San Antonio Light,* June 9, 1930.

"Cartoons, Illustrating New Class at Museum [John B. Wilson]." *San Antonio Express,* Apr. 16, 1935.

Cheney, Karen. "Ruth Conerly's Santas Even Appeared in C. R." *Tico Times* (San José, Costa Rica), Dec. 21, 1990.

"Civic Leader's Funeral Rites Slated Monday [Mary Aubrey Keating]." *San Antonio Express,* Dec. 13, 1953.

"Conerly Noted Alamo Artist." Unknown newspaper, May 28, 1994.

"Continue Art Show at Club [Eloise Hobble]." *El Paso Herald-Post,* Feb. 29, 1940.

Cooke, Regina Tatum. "Art Exhibit of First Rank, Writer Avers." *Amarillo Sunday News and Globe,* Sept. 27, 1931.

"County Names, Service Award for [Maxine] Perini." *Abilene Reporter-News,* Oct. 14, 1994.

"[Lessi Ellen Wooldridge] Culmer worked for Frost Bros." *San Antonio Express-News,* Feb. 28, 1989.

"Dawson-Watson Painter, Dead." *San Antonio Express,* Sept. 5, 1939.

"Denies He Is Red [Xavier Gonzalez]." *El Paso Times,* Aug. 27, 1935.

Denison Herald, Sept. 21, 1978.

"Desert Paintings on Exhibit at Las Cruces [Berla Emeree]." *El Paso Times,* July 27, 1929.

"[Ruby] Dugosh." *San Antonio Express,* Mar. 21, 1997.

"E. A. Means, Artist, Dies in New York." *El Paso Times,* July 30, 1962.

Edens, Ann. "Fussy, but Unafraid, Says Lady of Herself [Mary Cooney]." *San Antonio Light,* Sept. 2, 1955.

Eggerman, Don. "Death Stills Brush Of Artist Emil Hermann." *Wichita Falls Times,* May 1, 1966.

"El Paso Artist Features Scenes of Southwest in His Paintings [Ricardo Diaz]." Unknown newspaper, n.d.

El Paso Herald, Sept. 22, 1927.

El Paso Herald-Post. Aug. 22, 1935; Feb. 8 and Sept. 10, 1936; Feb. 11, 1938; July 10, 1940; Nov. 13, 1941; Sept. 29, 1944.

"El Paso Museum's First Resident Artist Arrives." *El Paso Times,* Apr. 7, 1965.

"El Paso Sculptor Offers Bust of JFK to Library [Bartolo Aceves]." *El Paso Times,* May 23, 1964.

El Paso Times. Feb. 13, 1922; Nov. 28, 1935; Nov. 25, 1937; July 10, 1941; July 19, 1942; Oct. 26, 1952; June 17, 1953; June 20, 1972; Sept. 29, 1974; Oct. 4, 1975; May 19, 1976; Jan. 20, 1977; Aug. 6, 1982.

"Emily Edwards Succumbs at 91." *San Antonio Express,* Feb. 17, 1980.

"Estelle Walker Gray." *San Antonio Express,* Sept. 15, 1950.

"Exhibit Teas Planned for Mr. [Xavier] Gonzales [sic]." *El Paso Post,* Aug. 15, 1930.

"F. M. Edwards 101-Year-Old Texan, Dies." *Dallas Morning News,* Dec. 18, 1946.

"FW Native, Artist, 80, Dies in France [Murray Bewley]." *Fort Worth Press,* Sept. 4, 1964.

"Famed Architect O'Neil Ford Dies." *San Antonio Express,* July 21, 1982.

"Final Plans Being Made for Texas Fine Arts Exhibit Here." *Amarillo Daily News,* Jan. 22, 1931.

"Five El Paso Artists Have Works Eligible for Final Showing at San Antonio." *El Paso Herald,* Feb. 7, 1928.

"Floyd Crews Dies at Age of 84." *El Paso Herald-Post.* Feb. 7, 1958.

"Former Abilenian's Miniatures on Display [Elsie Motz Lowdon]." Unknown newspaper, Nov. 18, 1985.

"Former Chairman of UT Art Department Dies [William Lester]." *Austin American-Statesman,* Nov. 28, 1991.

"Former E. P. Artist Dies at 66 [Hari Kidd]." *El Paso Herald-Post,* Nov. 30, 1964.

"Former El Pasoan Paints Huge Murals at Enid, Okla. [Ruth Augur]." *El Paso Times,* June 28, 1937.

"Former El Pasoan Returns as Sculptor; Work to Be Exhibited at Museum of Art [Enrique Alfarez]." *El Paso Herald-Post.* Nov. 11, 1961.

"Former Sun Carnival Artist Harris Shelton Dies in EP." *El Paso Times,* Apr. 11, 1976.

"Gallery Shows Nude Painting [Pedro Sanders]." *San Antonio Express,* Dec. 6, 1936.

"Gallery to Show Work of Woman Artist, Teacher [Belle Austin]." *Fort Worth Telegram,* Apr. 14, 1939.

Galveston Daily News. Oct. 6, 1901; Sept. 21, 1946; Mar. 10, 1970.

"Gilard Kargl, 84, Dies." *North San Antonio Times,* Feb. 17, 1983.

Goddard, Dan. "Culwell's War Art Is Vivid, Haunting." *San Antonio Sunday Express-News,* May 14, 1989.

"Goliad Mural Up in Capitol Lobby; Bubi Jessen's Work Being

Shown for Week." *Austin American,* Nov. 3, 1934.

Gossett, Louise. "Art and Artists: Brunet's Work to Be Shown." Unknown newspaper, n.d.

Grauer, Michael R. "Former Painter, Printmaker Known as 'Gracious, Dynamic.' [Florence McClung]" *Amarillo Daily News,* May 13, 1992.

"[Alfredo Guerra] Designed First Christmas Seal Stamp." *San Antonio Express-News,* Feb. 1, 1987.

"Harlingen Artist Exhibits at Museum." *San Antonio Express,* Sept. 25, 1938.

"Harriet Kritser, Panhandle Artist Rapidly Winning Recognition; Has Public Exhibition Ending Tonight." *Amarillo Daily News,* Nov. 30, 1929.

"Harry Carnohan Will Teach Painting at Fine Arts School." *Fort Worth Star-Telegram,* Oct. 29, 1938.

Heilman, Mollie. "Centennial Pictures at Witte Museum [Frank Callcott]." *San Antonio Light,* Oct. 23, 1938.

"Herring Coe: The Artist at 90." *Beaumont Enterprise,* July 27, 1997.

Hicks, Ida Belle. "Mrs. Amy Lynn Exhibits Mill Iron Portraits in Museum at Austin during February; Exhibit Will Be Shown at Ft. Worth Fat Stock Show in March." *Fort Worth Star-Telegram,* n.d.

————. "West Texas History on Canvas Aim of Artist." *Fort Worth Star-Telegram,* Feb. 11, 1945.

"Honor-Winning Art Teacher Taken by Death [Nell Scott]." Unknown newspaper, June 9, 1936.

Houston Post, Apr. 19, 1908. (Thurston J. Donnellen.)

"[Warren] Hunter Loved Teaching Art." *San Antonio Express-News,* May 10, 1993.

"Indian Sculptor Abandons Studio for Sun God's Shrine [Enrique Alfarez]." *El Paso Times,* June 14, 1926.

"Irving Schwartz's Etchings to Be Exhibited in Deming." *El Paso Times,* July 14, 1963.

"J. Ferdinand M'Can [sic], Renowned as Artist, Dies in San Antonio." Unknown Victoria, Tex., newspaper, n.d.

"J. Fred Buenz." *North San Antonio Times,* Mar. 14, 1991.

"James Brooks, an Artist, Is Dead; Abstract Expressionist Was 85." *New York Times,* Mar. 12, 1992.

"Josephine [Oliver] Travis, Former Dallas Symphony Violinist, Dies." *Dallas Morning News,* Sept. 7, 1991.

Kerrville Daily Times, Feb. 28, 1994. (Ike Koenig.)

Kilstofte, June. "Pots, Pans and Painting [Lola Mueller]." *San Antonio Express Magazine,* June 27, 1948.

Kutner, Janet. "Temple Artist Ben Culwell Drew on WWII Experiences." *Dallas Morning News,* Apr. 18, 1992.

Lansden, Ollie P. "Robert Genung, in Studio Here, Plans for New York Exhibition." Unknown newspaper, El Paso Public Library, n.d.

————. "Seen and Heard Around El Paso [Camille Craig]." *El Paso Times.* 7 June 1940.

Lapham, Bob. "MOA Plans Pollard tribute." *Abilene Reporter-News,* Sept. 25, 1994.

————. "Noted Local Artist Dies at 85 [Juanita Pollard]." *Abilene Reporter-News,* Sept. 16, 1994.

————. "Pollard Art Exhibit Closes ALOT's Year." *Abilene Reporter-News,* Dec. 1, 1989.

"Last Day of the Fair." *San Antonio Daily Express,* Dec. 1, 1888.

"Last Rites Set Friday for Frank E. Klepper." *Dallas Times-Herald,* June 5, 1952.

"League Orders Chosen Canvas from Exhibit [Pedro Sanders]." *San Antonio Express,* Nov. 7, 1936.

Leibson, Art. "It Took a While but He Finally Captured the Padre in Clay [Urbici Soler]." *El Paso Times,* Feb. 24, 1980.

"Lille Mae Hagner." *North San Antonio Times,* n.d.

"Local Artist [Amy Lynn] Wins in District Art Contest." Unknown newspaper, Apr. 26, 1934.

Luther, Betty. "Artists Do More Than Paint What They See." *El Paso Herald-Post,* Nov. 12, 1934.

————. "Tamakichi [Carl] Hibino Prefers American Art to Japanese." *El Paso Herald-Post,* Nov. 2, 1932.

Lynn, Rene. "Reading, Writing Came First for John Canaday." *North San Antonio Times,* July 25, 1985.

"M. McElroy, Exporer, Artist Dies." *El Paso Times,* Dec. 12, 1953.

"Mallory Page Warren Displays Canvases Painted during Her Studies in Europe." Unknown San Antonio newspaper, n.d.

McCarthy, Dennis. "Vallie Fletcher, Born on Valentine [sic] Day and Named for It, Earns Title of Beaumont's First Lady of Art." *Beaumont Sunday Enterprise,* n.d.

McNeil, Judy. "Art Career Embraced Worldwide Recognition and National Prestige [Ruth Conerly]." *Marshall News Messenger,* n.d.(1994).

Meyers, Jack. "[Ralph] Rowntree [sic] Exhibit of Pastels and Oils at Witte Museum Is Attracting Unusual Attention." *San Antonio Evening News,* May 23, 1929.

"Michael McElroy Taken by Death. " *El Paso Herald-Post,* Dec. 11, 1953.

"Miss Eloise Hobble's Paintings Will Be Shown at Woman's Club." *El Paso Times,* Feb. 25, 1940.

"Modernistic Mural Symbolizes History of Panhandle Plains [Margaret Seewald]." *Amarillo Sunday News and Globe,* July 2, 1933.

"Mrs. Berla Emeree Taken by Death." *El Paso Herald-Post,* Jan. 8, 1948.

"Mrs. Camille Kibler Craig Assists with the 'Mikad.'" *El Paso Times,* Mar. 19, 1939.

"Mrs. [Camille] Craig Paints Mural." *El Paso Times,* Oct. 30, 1936.

"Mrs. Darrell [Amy] Jackson." Unknown Galveston newspaper, Jan. 14, 1970.

"Mrs. Emeree, Well Known Artist, Dies." *El Paso Times,* Jan. 9, 1948.

"Mrs. [Kate] Ball's Scrolls to Be Shown in Library of Congress Exhibit." *El Paso Times,* June 29, 1952.

"Mrs. Kate Ball to Be Honored in Washington." *El Paso Times,* Sept. 7, 1952.

"Mrs. Kate Ball to Exhibit Paintings in Woman's Club." *El Paso Times.* Dec. 6, 1951.

"Mrs. [Helen King] Kendall, Noted Artist, Succumbs Here." *San Angelo Standard Times,* May 16, 1946.

"Mrs. [Lucy W.] Rice Last Rites Set Friday." Unknown Austin newspaper, Mar. 14, 1963.

"Mrs. W. H. Lynn Receives State-Wide Honor Last Week in Fine Arts Field." *Collingsworth Standard*, Nov. 22, 1934.

"Museum to Exhibit [Edward] Valentine Pictures." *San Antonio Express*, Oct. 6, 1933.

"National Honors Achieved by Helen Cruikshank Davis with Lifelike Miniatures." *Houston Chronicle*, Feb. 25, 1940.

"Native Artists to Have Exhibit for Month in Museum." Unknown newspaper, May 18, 1933.

"Noted Artist Succumbs at Age of 73 [Jessie Palmer]." *Dallas Morning News*, Feb. 4, 1956.

"Noted Painter in Retirement Here Is Dead; Gean Smith Nationally Known for Equestrian Pictures." *Galveston Tribune*, Dec. 8, 1928.

"Of Death of Hari Kidd." *El Paso Times*, Nov. 29, 1964.

"One of Most Famous Animal Painters of America Is in Galveston Doing Some Work [Gean Smith]." *Galveston Daily News*, July 24, 1924.

"Painter Finds It Hard to Quit at 81 [F. A. Cloonan]." Unknown newspaper, Aug. 19, 1946.

"Paintings of [Charles] Brobeck on Display." *San Antonio Light*, Nov. 8, 1931.

"Paintings Exhibited at College of Mines [Jack Redic]." *El Paso Herald-Post*. June 13, 1942.

"Paintings of Texas Artists Admirable." Unknown Galveston newspaper, July 14, 1916.

"Paintings on Display Here." *Amarillo News-Globe*, Apr. 16, 1933.

"Panhandle Artists Will Display Work in New Museum." Unknown newspaper, Apr. 13, 1933.

"Panhandle Paintings on Display Here [Amy Lynn]." Austin *Sunday American-Statesman*. Feb. 11, 1945.

Pisano, Marina. "Artist Remembers Century Spent Following Her Muse [Helen Ferne Slimp]." *San Antonio Express-News*, June 15, 1990.

"Plains Artist Gains Recognition in East; Panhandle Landscape Favorite [R. Vernon Hunter]." *Amarillo Sunday News and Globe*, Nov. 8, 1931.

Poff, Claudia. "She's Painted Many a Canvas [Bessie Cocke]." *San Antonio Light*, Jan. 15, 1956.

"Preusser." *Houston Post*, Nov. 22, 1992.

"Retired Painter Prepares Huge Cast of Soldier for City in Commemoration of El Paso Veterans [Bartolo Aceves]." *El Paso Herald-Post*, Sept. 19, 1961.

"Rites Set in France for Noted Artist [Murray Bewley]." *Fort Worth Star-Telegram*. Sept. 4, 1964.

"S. A. Artist Dies at Concert [Mary Aubrey Keating]" Unknown newspaper, Dec. 13, 1953.

"S. A. Artist Dies in Waco [Harry Anthony De Young]." *San Antonio Express*, Jan. 18, 1956.

"S. A. Artist Paints 3rd Generation of Students [Sr. Maria del Socorro]." *San Antonio Express*, Aug. 30, 1953.

"San Antonian Shows Paintings [A. W. Mack]." *San Antonio Express*, Nov. 4, 1934.

Sanders, Jean. "Canadian Woman's Home Art Treasury." *Amarillo Sunday News-Globe*, Jan. 18, 1931

"Sartor's to Have One-Man Show [Dr. Clifford Mott]." *Dallas Morning News*, Oct. 19, 1945.

"Seen and Heard Around El Paso." *El Paso Times*, Sept. 30, 1936.

"Service Saturday Here for Dr. Mott." *Denison Herald*, Feb. 11, 1977.

"Services Scheduled for El Paso Artist [G. Harris Shelton]." *El Paso Times*, Apr. 13, 1976.

"[Lonnie Rees] Shand Artist, Multi-Talented." *San Antonio Express-News*, June 12, 1990.

"Soldier Artist's Work Displayed in Special Exhibit at Museum." *San Antonio Express*, Aug. 22, 1943.

"Soldier's Art on Display." *San Antonio Light*, Aug. 22, 1943.

"Southern Artists Will Exhibit in Canyon." *Amarillo Sunday News and Globe*, Jan. 31, 1932.

"Spanish Painter, Well Known in S.A. Reported Dead in Seville at 94 [Jose Arpa]." *San Antonio Express*, Oct. 17, 1952.

"Susanna Taylor Shields." *North San Antonio Times*, May 21, 1992.

"Texas Artist's Work Given to Museum [Virginia Prather]." *San Antonio Express*, Aug. 8, 1943.

"Texas Exhibit of Art Coming to Amarillo." *Amarillo Daily News*. Jan. 15, 1931.

"To Show Paintings; Texas Artists [Amy Lynn and Jessie Palmer] Open Exhibit in Museum; Book Trailers Tea Hosts for Artists." *Austin Sunday American-Statesman*, Apr. 26, 1936.

"Tri-State Fair Art Department Is Given Praise." *Amarillo Sunday News and Globe*, Oct. 11, 1931.

"Two Brownwood Artists' Work in State Exhibit." Unknown newspaper, ca. 1930.

"Two Exhibits Are Opened at Witte Museum [Mary Aubrey Keating]." *San Antonio Express*, Oct. 18, 1943.

"Two Exhibits Open at Witte Museum [Mary Aubrey Keating]." *San Antonio Evening News*, Oct. 18, 1943.

"Vivid Scenes Displayed by Local Artist [J. V. Ford]." *Amarillo News Globe*, Dec. 18, 1932.

"W.T.S.T.C. to Sponsor Exhibit." *Amarillo News-Globe*, Nov. 5, 1933.

"[Lonnie French] Walker Exhibit Opens at Museum." *San Antonio Express*, Sept. 5, 1937.

"What Makes a Painter [Lucy Maverick]?" *San Antonio Express Magazine*, Mar. 9, 1952.

"William Ed Bryan, Texas Portrait Painter Passes Away Here." *Dublin Progress*, Mar. 2, 1951.

"Xavier Gonzales [sic] Heads Art Colony." *El Paso Times*, July 23, 1934.

"Xavier Gonzales's [sic] Pictures on Display." *El Paso Post*, Aug. 31, 1927.

Young, Melanie. "Marion Koogler McNay's Masterpiece." *San Antonio Express-News*, Oct. 25, 1994.

UNPUBLISHED SOURCES

Interview
Bruce, Granville, interview by Walter R. Davis II. February 2, 1982.

Scrapbooks
El Paso Woman's Club Scrapbook, El Paso Public Library.
Emma Hendricks Scrapbook, Collection of Susan Nelson, Houston.
Ruth Simon Bode Scrapbook, Collection of Edward C. Bode, Dallas.
San Antonio Art League Scrapbook, San Antonio.

Theses and Papers
Copies of unpublished papers are in possession of the authors.
Baker, James G. "Edwin Hampton Glaeser." 1997.
Baltsukonis, Dennis. "John Herbert Barnard." 1998.
Blain, Samuel Shannon, Jr. "Olin Herman Travis." 1995.
Bode, Edward C. "Ruth Simon Bode (Mrs. Ed. A.) 1901–1979." 1996.
Branigan, Michelle. "Frances Christian Brand." 1997.
Carraro, Francine. "Painters of the Southwest Landscape: Otis Dozier, William Lester, Everett Spruce." M.A. thesis, Southern Methodist University, Dallas, 1976.
Chatham, Patricia. "Lucretia Donnell Coke." 1997.
Claycomb, William B. "Raymond Everett." N.d.
Davis, Walter R., II. "Granville Bruce." 1982.
Duncan, Robert J. "Ben Carlton Mead: Painting the Southwest." M.A. thesis, University of North Texas, Denton, 1997.
Eiken, Sister Francisca. "Sister Maria del Socorro Lazo." 1997.
Goode, Margaret Bell. "Frances Taber Camp Bell." 1996.
Goode, Margaret Bell. "Sarah Frances Taber Camp." 1996.
Grauer, Michael R. "The Early Career of Frank Reaugh, 1860–1889." M.A. thesis, Southern Methodist University, Dallas, 1989.
Halinksi, Jolynda Hammock. "Adrian Louis Brewer (1891–1956): Visions of an Arkansas Painter." M.A. thesis, University of Arkansas at Little Rock, 1997.
Harris, Paul Rogers. "The Women Who Challenged: Interviews with Nine Artists and the Artists' Resumes." Dallas, 1990.
"John Francis Knott, 1878–1963." N.d.
Kuhn, Sister M. Campion. "Sister Marietta (Mary Esabelle Egerton) 1871–1949." 1997.
Lee, Amy Freeman. "Robert K. Reed." Transcript of radio address, Oct. 12, 1949.
"Lessi Ellen Wooldridge." N.d. Original in Witte Memorial Museum, San Antonio.
McDonald, J. P. "Beulah Watts (1873–1941)." 1997.
"Notes Concerning Mrs. Charles [Eugenie] Lavender." La Retama Public Library, Corpus Christi, Tex.
Palmer, Rebecca Gouldy. "Lina Evetts Chaffin." "Margaret Ann Chaffin." "Sudie Puett Chaffin." "Mary Rebecca Chaffin." 1996.

Patout, R. A., Jr. "In Memory of Eugenia C. Massenburg." N.d.
Plumly, Richard. "Santa Maria de Los Reyes Gina Mombelli Duran." 1998.
Prohaska, Edward E. "Advocating Art: The Texas Fine Arts Association, 1911–1943." M.A. thesis, University of Texas at Austin, 1993.
Quinn, Sister Anne. "A Monograph on Sister Maria del Socorro Lazo, C.C.V.I." Paper prepared for the Centennial of the Sisters of Charity of the Incarnate Word. 1969.
Rowe, Mrs. Willie Reed. "The Works of James Ferdinand McCan." 1963.
Shand, Mrs. Terry, Jr. "Lonnie Rees." N.d. Original in Witte Memorial Museum, San Antonio.
Smither, Murray. "Olin Herman Travis (1888–1976)." 1995.
Stellmacher, Willetta. "Alice Melinda Cobb." June 10, 1997.
Tichich, Richard. "Ernst Raba: San Antonio Artist and Photographer, 1874–1951." M.F.A. thesis, 1979.
Travis, Olin H. "Notes for Talk to Museum Personnel [Dallas Museum of Natural History]." Lecture, n.d.
Wagner, Mrs. E. S. "John Beckmann." N.d. Original in Witte Memorial Museum, San Antonio.
Ward, James, and P. G. Navarro. "Dellshau: The Enigmatic Man." N.d.

LETTERS

All correspondence with Michael R. Grauer, Panhandle-Plains Historical Museum, Canyon, Tex., unless otherwise indicated.
Alvarez, Alicia E., Dallas Museum of Art, Oct. 15, 1997.
Baker, James (College Station), Nov. 14, 1995.
Bandy, Jonelle Foster (Sudan, Tex.), Feb. 16, 1995.
Blakeley, Bill, (Round Rock, Tex.), July 10 and 21, 1997.
Bundy, Gene, Eastern New Mexico University (Portales, N.M.) Feb. 25, 1993.
Caldwell, Lou, Houston Public Library, to William Elton Green, May 27, 1993.
Chatham, Patricia, July 25, 1997.
Cheek, Bill, (Dallas), Nov. 25, 1996; Apr. 9, 1997; July 14, 1997.
Claycomb, William B. (Sedalia, Mo.) Nov. 30, 1996.
Coe, Herring (Beaumont), Oct. 20, 1997.
Coffee, Mrs. James L. (Baton Rouge, La.), to Bill Blakeley, July 16, 1997.
Compton, Stephany R. (Denton), Oct. 8, 1997.
Connor, Seymour V. (Lubbock), to Walter R. Davis, May 3, 1997.
Cox, Holly (El Paso), Mar. 20, 1996; Apr. 12 and 25, 1996; May 6, 1996; July 9, 1996; Jan. 9, 1997; Mar. 12, 1997; Apr. 27, 1997; June 23, 1997.
Dear, Elizabeth A., C. M. Russell Museum (Great Falls, Mont.), July 23, 1993.
Eiken, Sister Francisca, Incarnate Word Archives (San Antonio), Sept. 10, 1997.
Elliott, William (Dallas), Sept. 24, 1991.
Ellison, Barton (Bellevue, Wash.), to Rebecca Huffstutler (Witte Museum), July 17, 1997.

Erwin, J. B. (Dallas), Aug. 1, 1996.

Evans, Douglas W., Westmoreland Museum of Art (Greensburg, Pa.) June 3, 1996.

Ewing, Virginia M. (Santa Fe), to Panhandle-Plains Historical Society Museum, May 26, 1977.

Fuchs, Sister M. Tharsilla (San Antonio), Dec. 1 and 15, 1997.

Gibson, Ochsner, Adkins, Harlan & Hankins (attorneys) to County Clerk, Bexar County, Texas, Feb. 23, 1971. (Olive Haley Smith).

Gibson, Mary Rhodes (Navasota, Tex.), Apr. 24, 1997.

Greene, Alison de Lima, Museum of Fine Arts, Houston, Mar. 4, 1997.

Halff, Harry (San Antonio), Nov. 12, 1997.

Harris, Paul Rogers (Dallas), Apr. 10, 1997.

Hastedt, Catherine A., Office of University Art Collections and Exhibitions, Texas A&M University, May 23, 1997.

Haynsworth, Stuart (Houston), to Paula L. Grauer, June 2, 1997.

Holden, Carolyn, Dublin (Tex.) Public Library, n.d.

Holden, Carolyn, Dublin (Tex.) Public Library, to Vic Roper, Jan. 30, 1992.

Hooper, Mildred, Harrison County (Tex.) Historical Museum, Oct. 15, 1997.

Huffstutler, Rebecca, Witte Museum, Aug. 19, 1997.

Hunt, David C., Stark Museum of Art (Orange, Tex.), Jan. 7, 1998.

Jamison, Celia, to Sallie Gillespie, n.d., original in Modern Art Museum of Fort Worth Archives.

Jimenez, Alejandra, Museum of Fine Arts, Houston, June 13, 1995.

Kelly, Amy, Old Jail Art Center (Albany, Tex.) Oct. 14, 1997.

Kovinick, Phil (Los Angeles, Calif.) June 29 and Aug. 4, 1992.

Lackey, David L. (Houston), to Dictionary of Texas Artists Project, Apr. 29, 1997.

Lasley, Joyce Ann Billington (Stratford, Tex.), Dec. 1996.

Lea, Tom (El Paso), Aug. 19, 1993.

Lee, Marjorie Johnson (Fort Worth), Dec. 10, 1991.

Lunsford, John, Meadows Museum (Dallas), Oct. 13, 1997.

McCann, Melissa (Victoria [Tex.] Regional Museum Association) Feb. 20, 1997.

McQuiddy, W. A. (Austin, Tex.), to Paula Grauer, Feb. 11, 1998.

Medellin, Octavio (Bandera, Tex.) Sept. 10, 1991.

Montgomery, Robert (Museum of Fine Arts, Houston), Mar. 19 and 25, 1997.

O'Dowd, Mary Alice (Waco), Apr. 29, 1997.

Onderdonk, Eleanor (Witte Museum), to Mrs. Willie B. Rutland (Elisabet Ney Museum), Dec. 31, 1949. Original in Witte Museum.

Parkerson, John E. (Houston), Aug. 6, 1996.

Parnell, Shirley, (Lexington, S.C.), to Kevin Vogel, n.d.

Plumly, Richard (San Antonio), Apr. 25, 1997; Dec. 5, 1997; Jan. 27 and Mar. 16, 1998.

Rainone, Pete (Arlington), July 22, 1998.

Rebori, Lisa, Houston Museum of Natural Science, May 5, 1997.

Roos, Marlys Moxley (Atlanta, Ga.), May 29, 1997.

Roos, Marlys Moxley (Atlanta, Ga.) to Conny Martin, May 12, 1997.

Rork, Robert T. (San Antonio), Oct. 9, 1997.

Saunders, Roger E. (New York, N.Y.) Oct. 9, 1997.

Smaistria, Jerry, Wharton (Tex.) County Library, July 25, 1997.

Smither, Murray (Dallas), Mar. 18 and Apr. 8, 1997.

Starkey, Dr. Taylor (Victoria, Tex.), Aug. 10, 1997.

Talbott, Page (Bala Cynwyd, Pa.), Nov. 6, Oct. 9 and 15, 1996.

Thierman, Sue M. (Brownwood, Tex.), Dec. 22, 1996.

Valley House Gallery (Dallas), Jan. 15, 1997. (Donald S. Vogel).

Wackym, Paul (Dallas), Dec. 3, 1997.

Wells, Garland, Modern Art Museum of Fort Worth, to Walter R. Davis II, Apr. 2, 1997.

Witt, David, Harwood Museum (Taos, N.M.), Apr. 9, 1997.

EXHIBITION CATALOGUES

Annual Exhibitions

COTTON CARNIVAL, GALVESTON

Originals in a private collection.

Catalogue, Art Exhibit, Second Annual Cotton Carnival and Exposition. 1910.

Catalogue of the Art Exhibit, Third Annual Cotton Carnival and Exhibition. 1911.

Catalogue of the Art Exhibit, Fourth Annual Cotton Carnival and Exhibition. 1912.

DALLAS MUSEUM OF ART

Annual Allied Arts Exhibition of Dallas County, 1928–45. Originals in Dallas Museum of Art unless otherwise noted.

Catalog, Allied Arts Exhibition of Dallas County. Fair Park Gallery, 1928.

Second Annual Allied Arts Exhibition of Dallas County. Fair Park Gallery, 1929.

The Third Annual Exhibition of Allied Arts of Dallas County. Fair Park Gallery, 1930.

Catalog of the Fourth Annual Allied Arts Exhibition of Dallas County. Fair Park Art Gallery, 1931.

Fifth Annual Allied Arts Exhibition of Dallas County. Fair Park Art Gallery, 1932.

Sixth Annual Allied Arts Exhibition of Dallas County. Dallas Museum of Fine Arts, 1933.

Seventh Annual Dallas Allied Arts Exhibition. Dallas Museum of Fine Arts, 1935. Original in Frank Reaugh Papers, Research Center, Panhandle-Plains Historical Museum, Canyon, Tex.

Eighth Annual Allied Arts Exhibition. Dallas Museum of Fine Arts, 1937.

Ninth Annual Dallas Allied Arts Exhibition. Dallas Museum of Fine Arts, 1938.

Tenth Annual Dallas Allied Arts Exhibition. Dallas Museum of Fine Arts, 1939.

Eleventh Annual Dallas Allied Arts Exhibition. Dallas Museum of Fine Arts, 1940.

Twelfth Annual Dallas Allied Arts Exhibition. Dallas Museum of Fine Arts, 1941.

Thirteenth Annual Dallas Allied Arts Exhibition. Dallas Museum of Fine Arts, 1942.

Fourteenth Annual Dallas Allied Arts Exhibition. Dallas Museum of Fine Arts, 1943.

Fifteenth Annual Dallas Allied Arts Exhibition. Dallas Museum of Fine Arts, 1944.

Sixteenth Annual Dallas Allied Arts Exhibition. Dallas Museum of Fine Arts, 1945.

FORT WORTH MUSEUM OF ART

Annual Exhibitions of Work by Texas Artists, 1910–37. Originals in Fort Worth Public Library.

Exhibition by Dallas and Ft. Worth Artists. 1910.

Second Annual Exhibition of Selected Paintings by Texas Artists. 1911.

Third Annual Exhibition of Selected Paintings by Texas Artists. 1912.

Fourth Annual Exhibition of Selected Paintings by Texas Artists. 1913.

Fifth Annual Exhibition of Selected Paintings by Texas Artists. 1914.

Sixth Annual Exhibition of Selected Paintings by Texas Artists. 1915.

Seventh Annual Exhibition of Selected Paintings by Texas Artists. 1916.

Eighth Annual Exhibition of Selected Paintings by Texas Artists. 1917.

Ninth Annual Exhibition of Selected Paintings by Texas Artists. 1918.

Tenth Annual Exhibition of Selected Paintings by Texas Artists. 1919.

Eleventh Annual Exhibition of Selected Paintings by Texas Artists. 1920.

Twelfth Annual Exhibition of Selected Paintings by Texas Artists. 1922.

Thirteenth Annual Exhibition of Selected Paintings by Texas Artists. 1923.

Fourteenth Annual Exhibition of Selected Paintings by Texas Artists. 1924.

Fifteenth Annual Exhibition of Selected Paintings by Texas Artists. 1925.

Sixteenth Annual Exhibition of Selected Paintings by Texas Artists. 1926.

Seventeenth Annual Exhibition of Selected Paintings by Texas Artists. 1927.

Eighteenth Annual Exhibition of Selected Paintings by Texas Artists. 1928.

Nineteenth Annual Exhibition of Selected Paintings by Texas Artists. 1929.

Twentieth Annual Exhibition of Selected Paintings by Texas Artists. 1930.

Twenty-First Annual Exhibition of Selected Paintings by Texas Artists. 1931.

Twenty-Second Annual Exhibition by Texas Artists. 1932.

Twenty-Third Annual Exhibition by Texas Artists. 1933.

Twenty-Fourth Annual Exhibition by Texas Artists. 1934.

Twenty-Fifth Annual Exhibition by Texas Artists. 1935.

Twenty-Sixth Annual Exhibition by Texas Artists. 1936.

Twenty-Seventh Annual Exhibition by Texas Artists. 1937.

MUSEUM OF FINE ARTS, HOUSTON

Annual Exhibitions, 1925–45. Originals in the Archives of the Museum of Fine Arts, Houston.

First Annual Exhibition of Works by Houston Artists. 1925.

Second Annual Exhibition of Work by Houston Artists. 1926.

Third Annual Exhibition of Work by Houston Artists. 1927.

Fourth Annual Exhibition of Work by Houston Artists. 1928.

Fifth Annual Exhibition of Work by Houston Artists. 1929.

Sixth Annual Exhibition of Work by Houston Artists. 1930.

Seventh Annual Exhibition of Work by Houston Artists. 1931.

Ninth Annual Exhibition of Work by Houston Artists. 1933.

Tenth Annual Exhibition of Work by Houston Artists. 1934.

Eleventh Annual Exhibition of Work by Houston Artists. 1935.

Twelfth Annual Exhibition of Work by Houston Artists. 1936.

Thirteenth Annual Exhibition of Work by Houston Artists. 1937.

Fourteenth Annual Exhibition of Work by Houston Artists. 1938.

Fifteenth Annual Exhibition of Work by Houston Artists. 1939.

Sixteenth Annual Exhibition of Work by Houston Artists. 1940.

Seventeenth Annual Exhibition of Work by Houston Artists. 1942.

Eighteenth Annual Exhibition of Work by Houston Artists. 1943.

Nineteenth Annual Exhibition of Work by Houston Artists. 1944.

Twentieth Annual Exhibition of Work by Houston Artists. 1945.

PRINT EXHIBITIONS

Originals in Jerry Bywaters Collection on Art of the Southwest, Hamon Arts Library, Southern Methodist University, Dallas, unless otherwise indicated.

Second Annual Texas Print Exhibition. Dallas Museum of Fine Arts, 1942.

Third Annual Texas Print Exhibition. Dallas Museum of Fine Arts, 1943.

Fourth Annual Texas Print Exhibition. Dallas Museum of Fine Arts, 1944.

Lone Star Printmakers: First Circuit of Lithographs by Texas Artists. 1938–39.

Lone Star Printmakers: Second Circuit of Lithographs by Texas Artists. 1939–40.

Lone Star Printmakers: Third Circuit of Prints by Texas Artists. 1940–41.

Lone Star Printmakers: 4th Circuit of Prints by Texas Artists. 1941–42.

Lone Star Printmakers: List of Prints, 5th Circuit, 1942–43. Original in Witte Museum, San Antonio, Texas.

SOUTHERN STATES ART LEAGUE

Originals in Panhandle-Plains Historical Museum, Canyon, Tex., unless otherwise indicated.

Fourth Annual Exhibition of the Southern States Art League. Telfair Academy, Savannah, Ga., 1924.

Fifth Annual Exhibition of the Southern States Art League. Atlanta Biltmore Arcade, Atlanta, Ga., 1925.

Catalogue of the Ninth Annual Exhibition of the Southern States Art League. Witte Memorial Museum, San Antonio, Tex., 1929.

Catalogue, Thirteenth Annual Exhibition of the Southern States Art League. Birmingham Public Library, Birmingham, Ala., 1933.

Nineteenth Annual Exhibition of the Southern States Art League. Witte Memorial Museum, San Antonio, Tex., 1939. Original in Witte Museum.

Catalogue of the Twentieth Annual Exhibition of the Southern States Art League. Mint Museum of Art, Charlotte, N.C., 1940.

Catalogue of the Twenty-first Annual Exhibition of the Southern States Art League. Louisiana State Exhibit Building, Shreveport, La., 1941.

Twenty-third Annual Exhibition of the Southern States Art League. Brooks Memorial Art Gallery, Memphis, Tenn., 1943.

Catalogue of the Twenty-fourth Annual Exhibition of the Southern States Art League. Dallas Museum of Fine Arts, Dallas, Tex. 1944.

Twenty-fifth Annual Exhibition of the Southern States Art League. Birmingham Public Library, Birmingham, Ala., 1945.

STATE FAIR OF TEXAS

Annual Exhibitions, 1906–39. Originals in the Dallas Historical Society unless otherwise indicated.

Official Handbook, Art Department, State Fair of Texas. October 13–28, 1906.

Official Handbook, Art Department, State Fair of Texas. Oct. 19–Nov. 3, 1907.

Official Handbook, Art Department, State Fair of Texas. Oct. 17–Nov. 1, 1909.

Official Handbook, Art Department, State Fair of Texas. Oct. 16–31, 1909.

Official Handbook, Art Department, State Fair of Texas. Oct. 15–30, 1910.

Official Handbook, Art Department, State Fair of Texas 1913. Oct. 18–Nov. 2, 1913.

Official Catalogue, Art Department, State Fair of Texas and Mexican National Exhibition. Oct. 9–24, 1920.

Official Catalogue, Art Department, State Fair of Texas. Oct. 6–15, 1922.

Official Catalogue, Art Department, State Fair of Texas. Oct. 13–28, 1923.

Official Catalogue, Art Department, State Fair of Texas. Oct. 11–26, 1924.

Official Catalogue, Art Department, State Fair of Texas. Oct. 9–24, 1926.

Art Department, State Fair of Texas, Catalog of Paintings. 1927.

Official Catalog, Art Department, State Fair of Texas. 1928.

Art Department, State Fair of Texas, Official Catalog. 1930. Original in the Frank Reaugh Papers, Research Center, Panhandle-Plains Historical Museum, Canyon, Tex.

Art Department, State Fair of Texas, Official Catalogue, 1931. 1931.

Illustrated Catalog, Art Department, State Fair of Texas, 1933 Exhibition.

State Fair of Texas, Art Department 1934 Exhibition, Illustrated Catalogue. Original in the Frank Reaugh Papers, Research Center, Panhandle-Plains Historical Museum, Canyon, Tex.

Golden Jubilee Exhibition, State Fair of Texas, 1938. Dallas Museum of Fine Arts, 1938. Original in Frank Reaugh Papers, Panhandle-Plains Historical Museum, Canyon, Tex.

Exhibition of Spanish Art, Texas Paintings, Frank Reaugh, State Fair of Texas, 1939. Dallas Museum of Fine Arts, 1939.

TEXAS FINE ARTS ASSOCIATION

Exhibition of Paintings from Texas Fine Arts Association. June, 1929. Original in Witte Museum, San Antonio.

Exhibit of Texas Art, Assembled by the Texas Fine Arts Association for Circuit throughout Texas. Oct. 1929–June 1930. Original in Witte Museum, San Antonio.

Texas Fine Arts Exhibition. 1932–33. Originals in Texas Fine Arts Association.

Work of Texas Artists Sent in Circuit by the Texas Fine Arts Association. 1933–34.

Texas Fine Arts Association Annual Membership Show. Elizabet Ney Museum, Austin, Tex., 1943.

TEXAS GENERAL EXHIBITIONS, 1940–45

The Texas General Exhibit. Dallas Museum of Fine Arts; Museum of Fine Arts of Houston; Witte Memorial Museum, 1940.

Catalogue of the Second Texas-Oklahoma General Exhibition. Dallas Museum of Fine Arts; Museum of Fine Arts of Houston; Witte Memorial Museum; Philbrook Art Museum, Jan.–Apr. 1941.

Third Texas General Exhibition. Dallas Museum of Fine Arts; Museum of Fine Arts of Houston; Witte Memorial Museum, October 1941.

Fourth Texas General Exhibition. Dallas Museum of Fine Arts; Museum of Fine Arts of Houston; Witte Memorial Museum, Oct.–Dec., 1942.

Texas General Exhibition. Dallas Museum of Fine Arts; Museum of Fine Arts of Houston; Witte Memorial Museum, Oct. 1943–Jan. 1944.

Sixth Texas General Exhibition. Dallas Museum of Fine Arts; Museum of Fine Arts of Houston; Witte Memorial Museum; University of Texas, Austin; Oct. 1944–Feb. 1945.

Seventh Texas General Exhibition. Dallas Museum of Fine Arts; Museum of Fine Arts of Houston; Witte Memorial Museum; University of Texas, Austin, Oct. 7, 1945–Feb. 10, 1946.

WITTE MEMORIAL MUSEUM, SAN ANTONIO

Annual Exhibitions, 1928–45. Originals in Witte Museum.

The San Antonio Competitive Exhibition 1928. 1928.

The San Antonio Competitive Exhibition 1929. 1929.

San Antonio Local Artists Exhibition. 1930.

Fourth Annual Local Artists Exhibition. 1931.

Fifth Annual Local Artists Exhibition. 1934.

Sixth Annual Local Artists Exhibition. 1935.

Eighth Annual Local Artists Exhibition. 1937.